RENAISSANCE
AND
REFORMATION

RENAISSANCE
AND
REFORMATION

EDITOR

JAMES A. PATRICK

Chancellor, College of Saint Thomas More

ADVISERS

CHRISTOPHER FLETCHER

Queen Mary, University of London
Department of History

NATALIA NOWAKOWSKA

Oxford University
History Faculty

NORMAN TANNER, SJ

Pontificia Università Gregoriana
Faculty of Theology

RENAISSANCE
AND
REFORMATION

Editor
James A. Patrick

Chancellor, College of Saint Thomas More

5

Preaching – Wren, Christopher

mc Marshall Cavendish
Reference
New York

Marshall Cavendish
99 White Plains Road
Tarrytown, New York 10591-9001

www.marshallcavendish.us

© 2007 Marshall Cavendish Corporation

MARSHALL CAVENDISH
EDITOR: Thomas McCarthy
EDITORIAL DIRECTOR: Paul Bernabeo
PRODUCTION MANAGER: Michael Esposito

WHITE-THOMSON PUBLISHING
EDITORS: Steven Maddocks, Clare Hibbert, and
    Cath Senker
DESIGN: Derek Lee and Ross George
CARTOGRAPHER: Peter Bull Design
PICTURE RESEARCH: Amy Sparks
INDEXER: Cynthia Crippen, AEIOU, Inc.

Library of Congress Cataloging-in-Publication Data
Renaissance and Reformation / editor, James A. Patrick.
    p. cm.
    Includes bibliographical references.
    Contents: 1. Agincourt, Battle of–Dams and drainage -- 2. Descartes, René–
Households -- 3. Humanism and learning–Medicis, the -- 4. Michelangelo–
Portugal -- 5. Preaching–Wren, Christopher -- 6. Index.
    ISBN-13: 978-0-7614-7650-4 (set: alk. paper)
    ISBN-10: 0-7614-7650-4 (set: alk. paper)
    1. Renaissance--Encyclopedias. 2. Reformation--Encyclopedias. I. Patrick,
James, 1933-

    CB359.R455 2007
    940.2'1--dc22

                                                                    2006042600

ISBN-13: 978-0-7614-7650-4   (set)
ISBN-10: 0-7614-7650-4   (set)
ISBN-13: 978-0-7614-7655-9   (vol. 5)
ISBN-10: 0-7614-7655-5   (vol. 5)

Printed in Malaysia

10 09 08 07 06 5 4 3 2 1

ILLUSTRATION CREDITS
See page 1440.

COVER: A session toward the end of the Council of Trent, sixteenth century,
    widely attributed to Titian or his workshop (Art Archive/Musée du Louvre,
    Paris/Dagli Orti).
TITLE PAGE: Saint Helena, from the Altarpiece of the Holy Cross, from Blesa,
    Spain, 1485–1487 (Art Archive/Museo de Zaragoza, Spain).

Contents

Preaching

PREACHING HAS ALWAYS BEEN A BASIC MEANS OF TRANSMITTING THE CHRISTIAN MESSAGE. THROUGH PREACHING THE CHURCH GAINS CONVERTS AND INSTRUCTS BELIEVERS IN THE TENETS OF THE FAITH.

In the twelfth and thirteenth centuries the spiritual state of laypeople increasingly began to concern prelates and reformers. Preaching, always an essential element in Christian practice, thus assumed increasing importance. In 1214 the Fourth Lateran Council ordered the secular clergy, the bishops in particular, to meet basic requirements for preaching to the laity. At about the same time, Pope Innocent III (reigned 1198–1216) approved the establishment of two religious orders, the Friars Minor (the Franciscans) and the Order of Preachers (the Dominicans), each having specific tasks. From this time onward, preaching became an integral part of the religious experience of all European Christians. The fundamental purposes of preaching, however, remained what it was in classical times; as Saint Augustine of Hippo (354–430) had observed in the fifth century, the goal of preaching was to teach, to persuade, and to entertain (in that order), and thus it was in the Middle Ages.

The church's initial goal was modest: the Lateran Council wanted to ensure that every Christian heard at least four sermons each year. These quarterly sermons instructed the laity in the basic tenets of Christianity. Preachers explained the content and meaning of the creed (the formal statement of Christian beliefs), the Ten Commandments, the Gospel precepts (which include the injunctions "turn the other cheek," "love thy neighbor," and "resist not evil," among others), the seven vices and virtues, and the seven sacraments. This program of instruction was nonetheless ambitious at a time when most parish priests were ignorant of Latin and

▶ In this early-sixteenth-century draft for a tapestry destined for the Sistine Chapel, Raphael depicts Saint Paul preaching to an audience of disbelieving pagan philosophers in Athens.

A characteristic feature of medieval sermons was a short, didactic, illustrative story called an exemplum (plural, exempla). Preachers feared that common folk were unable to grasp the complex, abstract concepts of much of basic Christian theology and so tried to put them into concrete, familiar terms. As several medieval preaching manuals explain, just as infants are given milk before they are ready for solid food, so the laity should be offered truth in easily digestible forms. In the passage below, the author uses a lively ghost story to demonstrate the importance of good works, the reality of purgatory, and the dangers of failing to honor bequests. The tale is taken from a collection of sermons prepared around 1380 for the benefit of parish priests who might not have had access to a source of such stories owing to a lack of books, education, or broad experience.

A knight, as he rode toward battle, bade his cousin that should he die in battle he should sell his horse and use the money as alms for his soul. Then, when the knight was dead, the cousin well liked the horse and took it for his own use. Then, soon after, this knight appeared to his cousin and said: "For that you have not done by my horse as I bade you, you have made me be in purgatory for eight days. Wherefore God will take vengeance on thee, for thy soul shall go to hell, and my soul shall go to bliss." Then anon a horrible voice was heard in the air, as the roar of lions, and bears, and wolves, and they caught up the man bodily and bore him forth, and no one evermore heard of him again.

John Mirk, *Mirk's Festial*

lacked thorough grounding in theology. The burden of preaching thus fell squarely upon the bishops, most of whom promptly delegated this onerous chore to less important but nevertheless competent men who then toured the parishes in the bishops' stead. However, qualified men were in short supply, and therefore bishops turned to the appropriate preaching orders and to the universities for able personnel. In large part these efforts seem to have been successful, and although a weekly Sunday sermon was a rarity outside all but the wealthiest parishes, by the end of the Middle Ages, even rural priests felt obliged to preach regularly.

The Sunday sermon was just one of several important medieval preaching events. Sermons by itinerant friars—often held out of doors before large crowds—also became increasingly common, especially in towns during the seasons of Lent and Advent. Since the spiritual well-being of a community was an important civic responsibility, these itinerant preachers were usually employed by local magistrates and not by the bishops. They were either hired for a particular season or offered year-round employment. For example, in 1478 Johann Geiler von Kayserberg was recruited as the permanent preacher for the city of Strasbourg. He received four weeks of vacation each year but otherwise was forbidden to leave the city for even a single day; he was required to preach every Sunday and every feast day, as well as daily throughout Lent

◀ *Collections of sermons and preaching aids were among the most popular books of the Middle Ages. Many were simple, purely functional volumes, but some, including this fifteenth-century collection of Saint Augustine's sermons on the Gospel of John, were lavishly illustrated. The miniature depicts Augustine gazing upward, either toward heaven or toward the emblem of the Malatesta family immediately above his head.*

and on other occasions as deemed necessary (such as in the case of plague, war, or bad weather).

The Sermon

Since the early days of Christianity, the most important form of preaching was the sermon, a formal address that conformed to classical rhetorical principles; an *exordium* (introduction) preceded the *narratio* (narration) of relevant facts of the subject at issue, which was then followed by the *confirmatio* (argument), in which earlier claims were proved, and a *conclusio* (conclusion).

From the twelfth century onward, a sermon usually took as its subject a particular verse of the Bible. In the Middle Ages, the Bible, generally available only in Latin, was known well by Latin speakers alone—largely clerics. In a standard medieval sermon, the preacher translated a Bible verse into the vernacular and then gave a formal explanation of the text's various meanings. Among university-trained theologians, such sermons could become complicated scholarly treatises, but average parish sermons, primarily intended to impart basic moral teachings effectively, were relatively short—no more than an hour long—and often punctuated with colorful stories. On the feast day of a saint (usually the anniversary of the saint's death), the preacher might deliver a sermon on the life, merits, and miracles of the individual in question. To carry out these duties competently required considerable learning, but by the late Middle Ages there were numerous printed preaching aids for local priests. One collection of model sermons in outline form had the touching title *Dormi secure,* suggesting that the reader might sleep soundly on Saturday night, secure in the knowledge that he had a sermon ready to deliver the following morning.

Mass Appeal

The sermons of wandering preachers, usually friars, were a regular and highly anticipated event in late medieval and Renaissance urban life. When a well-known preacher came to town, almost the entire community came to see him—crowds of tens of thousands of people were not uncommon. With so many people in attendance,

▲ In medieval churches a rood screen separated the chancel and the altar, where the priest said Mass, from the nave, where the congregation gathered. Poorer churches had simple screens of thin wood, but some rood screens, such as this sixteenth-century stone version by the French sculptor Jean Gailde, were elaborate works of art.

THEOLOGY AND MEDIEVAL PREACHING

Since the days of the Reformation, some Protestants have charged that late medieval Catholicism promoted a cult of fear, guilt, and anxiety, in which people prayed to saints, the Virgin Mary, and other intercessors out of dread of an angry God rather than genuine spiritual devotion. This argument retains a certain force even in the modern world and is echoed in the work of prominent scholars such as Johan Huizinga (1872–1945) and the contemporary French historian Jean Delumeau, in part because of the evidence of medieval sermons. Well-known and influential late-medieval preachers, such as John of Capistrano (1386–1456), Bernardino of Siena (1380–1444), and Vincent Ferrer (1350–1419), wanted to inspire an immediate and dramatic reformation in the spiritual lives of their auditors. To this end they described the horrors of hell and the pains of purgatory in excruciating detail and emphasized repeatedly that the multitude would be damned while only a tiny number, perhaps one in a hundred, would be saved. In the context of these sermons, salvation appeared to be extremely difficult to attain and reserved for the select few. It required spectacular sacrifices, such as Girolamo Savonarola's bonfires of vanities (pyres of indiscriminately collected worldly and sinful goods; other, more selective preachers presided over bonfires made of offensive books, the trains of women's gowns, or playing cards). Reading these sermons and knowing the effect they could have on a medieval audience, one might readily believe that the fear of hell was paramount in medieval religion.

However, preachers with different pastoral concerns presented salvation in another light. In more typical medieval sermons, although the preacher emphasized that all were sinners, he also reassured his listeners that God was eager to meet them halfway—if they did their part and turned toward God, they could be sure of their own salvation. The motto of this pastorally oriented theology was that God would ask each person to do only "that which was in him" *(facere quod in se est).* The preacher reminded the flock that although Peter had denied Christ and Paul had persecuted him and although Mary Magdalene had been a common prostitute, all were now saints at God's right hand. This message of hope was tempered with responsibility; the outward signs that a person had indeed done what God asked were good works, charity toward one's fellow man in particular. Thus, medieval sermons presented two apparently incompatible paths to salvation—one fraught with dread and danger and one more optimistic and socially useful—and the path presented in a particular sermon depended above all on the pastoral goals of the preacher.

these sermons were necessarily given out of doors; favorite sites were the town or church square, the marketplace, an open field outside town, or the graveyard. The last venue was especially popular with preachers, since the sight of recent graves and the stench of putrefying corpses helped turn the minds of the audience to thoughts of death and the life beyond. Vincent Ferrer (later canonized) occasionally even decorated the foot of his pulpit with a pile of skulls.

The audiences for these sermons were varied, and social classes mingled fairly freely. Only the richest and most powerful had seats at the front; everyone else had to stand. Men and women, however, were kept separate (as they were in church) by rope barriers. In a typical audience women outnumbered men by a large margin—by four to one according to one medieval estimate—and men were regularly accused of shirking their obligation to attend. One medieval preacher noticed that none of the most important men in town attended his afternoon sermons, and he later discovered to his horror that they were all playing cards instead.

◀ A 1620 engraving, by J. Stow, of the churchyard of London's Saint Paul's Cathedral, where a priest is delivering a sermon from the pulpit beneath Paul's Cross. As the courtyard was the most prestigious preaching venue in Renaissance England (despite the occasional whiff of corpses), a typical congregation might include King James I and members of his court.

Bernardino of Siena 1380–1444

Bernardino of Siena was born into a wealthy and aristocratic Sienese family, but his initial good fortune did not last; his mother died when he was three years old, and his father followed her three years later. The young orphan was placed in the care of his aunt, until in 1391 she too died, and then went to live with an uncle in the city. Bernardino began formal schooling at twelve and studied for a doctorate in canon law until 1400, when an outbreak of plague placed him on a new path. While the plague raged in Siena, Bernardino was one of the few brave enough to care for the sick and bury the dead; eventually he contracted an illness that almost killed him. When at length he recovered, he was determined to enter religious life, and after a brief and unsuccessful sojourn as a lay hermit, he entered the Observant branch of the Franciscans (so called because this branch had returned to the austerity of Saint Francis's original rule). In 1404, at age twenty-four, Bernardino began his life's work as a wandering preacher; by the time he was thirty-eight, he was famous for his passionate sermons, his dedication to the Holy Name of Jesus (an important devotion among Catholics), and his forthright denunciations of sin. Bernardino saw preaching as vital both to individual salvation and to the collective spiritual welfare of Christian society. He once went so far as to declare that hearing a sermon was more important than hearing Mass.

Among the targets of Bernardino's preaching were those who charged exorbitant interest on loans. His sermons laid the groundwork for a chain of savings and loan societies, typically under Franciscan auspices, that spread throughout the Italian peninsula and endured for three centuries. The evidence suggests that Bernardino was a modest man as well as an inspiring one. His preaching won him great popularity, but it also brought the occasional jealous attack. In 1427, denounced to Pope Martin V (reigned 1417–1431) as a religious innovator, Bernardino submitted to a trial in the pope's presence. With the injustice of the charges exposed, Martin commended Bernardino and offered him the bishopric of Siena, which he declined.

Bernardino died in 1444 and was popularly acclaimed a saint immediately (people eager for a relic pulled every hair off his donkey's body). Bernardino was canonized just six years later, and 40,000 people from all over Europe attended the ceremony.

▶ *In this woodcut a Lutheran peasant may be seen preaching the Gospel to an assembly of his peers in 1524 or 1525, during the early stage of the Peasants' War. Lay preachers were far more common in the Reformed churches than in the Catholic Church.*

Preachers often complained that the men who did attend sermons appeared to be more interested in the women in the audience than in improving their souls. Preachers also had to contend with fights, hecklers, restless strollers, and large numbers of bored children, in addition to roaming dogs and other livestock—some nobles, eager to get a head start on the afternoon's hunting activities, brought their pet falcons.

To preach effectively under these conditions was difficult, and therefore the most popular preachers of the late Middle Ages were highly charismatic men, recognizable by the force of their personality, their personal sanctity, and their passionate spirituality. These men, exemplified by Bernardino of Siena and John of Capistrano among others, sought to transform the lives of their auditors. They called for immediate and dramatic reformation in the communities in which they preached, the rejection of sin, and an abiding reverence for Jesus. Their preaching was emotional, dramatic, and highly effective. As an example, Bernardino once preached about the martyrdom of Saint Paul, who was said to have cried out, "Jesus my love," both before and after the executioner cut off his head, "as if to say," Bernardino explained, "'I preached your name while alive, now I preach it dead.' Now, now, Jesus my love, Jesus my love!" In a frenzy of passion, Bernardino would then unveil a brightly painted sign bearing the Holy Name of Jesus (the monogram IHS—the first three letters of Jesus's name in Greek—over a golden sunburst on a blue background), at which point the crowd "began to cry aloud out of love for Jesus." This type of spectacle was not unusual; a mass outburst of weeping, shrieking, and fainting was a common conclusion to two or three hours of impassioned preaching.

Luther and the Reformation

Although preaching was an important part of the late medieval religious experience, it was also undeniably a subordinate part. The sacraments, through which God's saving grace was manifest, and the Eucharist above all—the miracle in which bread and wine became the flesh and blood of Jesus—were always at the center of medieval Christianity. Preaching was a necessary complement to this sacramental religion; preaching led people from the path of sin and urged them to penance and confession, but salvation ultimately was vested in the sacraments. For Martin Luther (1483–1546) and the Protestants, however, the roles of preaching and the sacraments were reversed, and as the job of the priest was transformed in Reformed thought from miracle-working intermediary between man and God to minister, preaching became correspondingly more important.

This change is perhaps most clearly observed in what was called preaching Christ (2 Corinthians 4:4–18). In medieval sermons preaching specifically about the life, ministry, and resurrection of Jesus was usually intended as a call to do penance and amend one's life. Luther,

▲ *This predella (a painting on the altar forming an appendage to the altarpiece), dating to around 1550, is located in Wittenberg, Germany, the town where Martin Luther posted the Ninety-five Theses. Lucas Cranach the Elder depicts the power of Luther's preaching: through his words, the Crucifixion becomes physically manifest to the congregation.*

however, focused more broadly on the life and especially the words of Jesus and used that focus as a critical part of his attack upon the traditional apparatus of medieval Christianity. For Luther preaching Christ involved both a reliance on scripture and a demonstration of justification by faith alone. According to Luther's program, the preacher had enormous responsibilities; he was required to explain scripture clearly and plainly and do so in a way that inspired his auditors to accept the word of God. Thus, Luther's sermons introduce and explicate passages of scripture to listeners, in Luther words, "as simply and as childishly and as popularly and as commonly as possible." To do so properly required more than just a clever mind and book learning—although these were usually necessary—it also required the Holy Spirit. For Luther, then, the clergy remained a necessary elite, whose words made the voice of God manifest on earth. As Luther

PREACHING AND THE SPREAD OF THE REFORMATION

Although printed texts were enormously influential in the spread of Luther's ideas throughout Europe, the role of preaching ought not to be underestimated; indeed, serious Reform movements in urban communities almost always tended to crystallize around persuasive preachers. As a typical example, in 1523 a former monk named Christian Ketelhodt arrived in the German town of Stralsund. He was obviously a Lutheran, and some of the people asked him to preach. Ketelhodt was at this time a hedge preacher (an unsanctioned, open-air, "street-corner" preacher), but soon he became so popular that a parish church was given over to his use, with the tacit agreement of the town council. The following year, the Catholic deputy mayor of the town tried to expel Ketelhodt, but he was met by a mob of citizens, evangelical town councilors among them, who defied his authority. For many years the people of the town also defied the efforts of their duke to expel the preacher.

This sort of popular preaching effectively spread Reforming ideas through receptive communities. In some places it led to conversions and the formal institution of a Protestant church, while in others it caused sectarian violence. In 1566 some fifty Calvinist preachers quietly entered the Netherlands to spread the Word. They came from varied backgrounds—some were from England, others from Germany, France, and Switzerland; a few were former laborers, five were artisans, sixteen were former Catholic clergymen, and sixteen others were upper-class laymen. They preached wherever they could find an audience: at informal dinners, in fields, on street corners, and—when permitted—in churches and from pulpits. They preached "hot Protestantism": they condemned the sacraments, saints, and idolatrous images and ceremonies and encouraged spiritual and social reform and the creation of godly communities. Their first supporters were lower-class laborers, but numbers grew until crowds estimated at between 7,000 and 15,000 attended their sermons. These crowds included members of the economic and political elite, who came to sermons well armed.

With rising support came increased confidence. The Englishman Richard Clough reported from Antwerp in 1566 that after a government proclamation forbade people to go to Reformed public sermons, "above sixteen thousand persons, all with their weapons in battle array," went out of town to hear a sermon and then returned to town and assaulted the house of the high bailiff, who had taken one preacher prisoner. They forced their way into the jail, freed the preacher, and departed. Tensions ran high, and iconoclastic rioting (with the intention to destroy sacred images) broke out despite the efforts of the government to reach an accommodation with the protesters. Ultimately, in 1567 Duke Álvarez de Toledo arrived from Spain to restore order, and those preachers who did not escape were burned alive.

himself once said, "To be sure, I do hear the sermon; however, I am wont to ask: 'Who is speaking?' The pastor? By no means! You do not hear the pastor. Of course, the voice is his, but the words he employs are really spoken by my God" (*Sermons on the Gospel of Saint John,* 1537). "In preaching," Luther wrote, "God becomes known"; preaching was thus the principal function of the church.

Protestant sermons were in other respects not very different from their medieval predecessors; this continuity is understandable since initially most Protestant preachers were themselves former members of the Catholic clergy. Their sermons were, however, self-consciously plain and straightforward, and this style accounted for some of their appeal. More important, Protestant preachers swayed their listeners through the content of their sermons: they claimed to speak the plain and unvarnished truth; they appealed constantly to the example of Jesus and the words of the Gospels; and they offered an easily comprehensible road to salvation—through faith alone. As Protestant preaching matured, these traditional themes competed with others more appropriate to an established Reformed community. Calvinist preaching, for example, placed an emphasis upon the construction and maintenance of the godly community. Calvin's sermons were thus filled with commands—moral and social imperatives that had to be acted on rather than merely believed. For John Calvin (1509–1564), "When the word of God is rightly expounded, the faithful are not only edified, but if an unbeliever comes into the church and hears the doctrine of God he is reproved and judged."

▼ *John Calvin condemned all artistic depictions of God, and acting upon this impulse, Calvinist preachers incited iconoclastic riots in the Netherlands. The "cleansing" of the churches of 1566, depicted here in a 1583 engraving by Franz Hogenberg, resulted in the destruction of countless works of medieval and Renaissance art and ultimately led to the intervention of the Spanish army.*

Nach wenigh Predication
Die Caluinsche Religion
Das bildens sturmen fiengen an
Das nicht ein bildt dauon bleib sfan
Anno Dñj. M. D. LXVI. XX Augusti
Kap Monstrantz, kilch, auch die altar
Vnd wes sonst dort vor handen war,
Zerbrochen all in kurtzer stundt
Glrich gar vil leuten das ist kundt.

John Donne   1572–1631

John Donne was born in London into a staunchly Catholic family, a distinct disadvantage in Protestant Elizabethan England. He attended both Oxford and Cambridge universities and studied law in London but became known as a poet, gambler, playboy, and soldier. Donne's ability and social connections opened the way to a promising civil service career. However, his secret marriage to Anne More, the daughter of an aristocratic family, angered her parents and destroyed Donne's opportunities for advancement. After many tribulations he gained the favor of King James I; as a condition of royal patronage, Donne renounced his Catholicism and took up a career in the Anglican Church. Ordained in 1615, he became first the king's chaplain and then the dean of Saint Paul's Cathedral. His public success, though, was tempered by private tragedy: his beloved wife died in childbirth in 1617. She had borne Donne twelve children, but only seven survived past infancy. These losses and his own ill health turned Donne's thoughts increasingly to death and the afterlife, themes that predominate in his later sermons. He even purchased his own coffin and installed it in his bedroom to remind him of his impending mortality. He died in 1631 after a prolonged illness.

Donne's sermons exhibit the same feel for the striking image that characterizes his poetry: "No man is an island, entire of itself; every man is a piece of the continent, a part of the main." *Devotions upon Emergent Occasions* (1624), a collection of sermons, contains a piece with the unassuming title Meditation XVII. Inspired by the tolling of church bells for the newly dead, Donne wrote what may be the best-known words from any sermon written in English (they are found in the same paragraph that contains the sentence quoted above): "Never send to know for whom the bell tolls; it tolls for thee." With words such as these, which appeal to the ear as well as the mind and the heart, the preacher sought to captivate and enlighten his hearers. Moving from the toils of life and the pains of death to the glories of paradise and eternal happiness, Donne's sermons bear a consistent message of hope.

◀ *In this anonymous portrait from around 1595, John Donne is depicted as a dashing young man. Although most people in modern times are familiar with John Donne through his poetry, he was best known during his life as a preacher of elegant, scholarly, witty, and emotionally powerful sermons.*

FURTHER READING

Mormondo, Franco. *The Preacher's Demons.* Chicago, 1999.

Owst, G. R. *Preaching in Medieval England.* New York, 1965.

Spencer, H. Leith. *English Preaching in the Late Middle Ages.* New York, 1993.

Taylor, Larissa. *Soldiers of Christ: Preaching in Late Medieval and Reformation France.* New York, 1992.

Wabuda, Susan. *Preaching during the English Reformation.* Cambridge, 2002.

Wilson, Paul Scott. *A Concise History of Preaching.* Nashville, TN, 1992.

Hans Peter Broedel

SEE ALSO

• Bibles • Calvinism • Church of England
• Elizabeth I • Established Churches • Heresy
• Lutheranism • Peasants' Revolts • Reformation
• Religious Orders

Printing

MECHANIZED PRINTING ENABLED THE MASS PRODUCTION OF BOOKS AND IS THUS CLOSELY ASSOCIATED WITH DEVELOPMENTS IN INTELLECTUAL AND SOCIAL HISTORY.

In mid-fifteenth-century Europe books were produced in manuscript—that is, they were handwritten by scribes. Laboring in workshops known as scriptoria, scribes, no matter how productive, were in their output no match even for early mechanical technologies. The introduction of printing in the second half of the fifteenth century therefore had an extraordinary impact on the capacity for book production; the quantity of books produced in Europe grew with remarkable rapidity in terms of both copies of individual publications and numbers of new titles. Printed books were cheaper to create and available in far greater numbers than their manuscript counterparts. They generated a marked increase in literacy rates, fostered the spread of the new ideas of the Renaissance and the Reformation, and quickly assumed an active role in shaping all the European societies of the sixteenth and seventeenth centuries.

Although print has been credited with revolutionizing the ways in which ideas were transmitted and distributed, the worlds of the manuscript book and of the illiterate or semiliterate many were not utterly lost. A print "culture" did not take over from that of the manuscript or the spoken word; rather, print became intertwined with these other media so that print, manuscript, and oral cultures developed reciprocal and interdependent relationships.

The Technology of Print

The printing of books with movable type required various materials and technologies, some newer than others. The first was paper, which was much cheaper than its alternative, parchment; the availability of paper was a precondition for mass-producing books and other textual materials. The introduction of paper

◀ An elaborately decorated late-fifteenth-century manuscript page from a French book of hours. Before the introduction of mechanized printing, an intricate handmade book might take months to complete.

▲ This 1628 engraving by J. van der Velde illustrates the bindery of Laurens Janszoon Koster (c.1370–c.1440). It is said that Koster, a rival of Gutenberg's, was printing with movable type as early as 1430, but there is no proof of this claim.

occurred long before the invention of the press. Paper initially reached Spain from the Far East and was first made in Europe in the twelfth century.

The circumstances of the invention of the press itself are not entirely clear. It seems most likely that the first press was built by a German, Johannes Gutenberg (1390/1400–1468), perhaps with some help or collaboration. The concept of a press was not new; it was often said that Gutenberg had been inspired by a wine press. The early printing presses are known as hand presses, as they were operated by a hand-pulled lever. Gutenberg put the press together with the other elements key to the efficient production of printed books. The first of these elements was movable type (which, like paper, had been known in China long before it was used in Europe). Before movable type was created, there had been some printing with carved blocks: movable type made the printing of text much more viable. Individual letters were cast as dies—devices with raised figures for stamping—in carefully composed metallic alloys. These letters were

then set into text using composing sticks, which held lines of text that were inserted into a galley, a tray that held a complete page. Because the pages were smaller than the sheets of paper to be printed on, each sheet was printed with a number of pages: the correct galleys were laid together on a form from which the sheet would be printed. The form was inserted into the press and inked with a special printing ink—another important contribution from Gutenberg. The ink was made from a pigment, lampblack, mixed with resin and linseed oil, a formula with some precedent in the Flemish development of oil painting. Sheets were printed from the inked form and dried before the other side was printed from another form. Printers had to be very careful to arrange the galleys correctly in the forms and to print both sides of the sheets with the proper pages.

Books were put together from one or more sheets, each printed on both sides with a number of pages, which were then folded and stitched or bound to create the finished product. Depending on the size of the book, the sheets could be printed with anywhere between two and sixty-four pages on each side. The biggest books, those in which the sheets of paper were folded only once, are known as folios; a book with two folds, in which the sheet is quartered, is called a quarto; one with three folds, an octavo; with four folds, a sextodecimo (or sixteenmo); and so on. Because the sheets had been folded and then stitched down the middle, the edges of the pages had to be cut before a book could be opened.

It was not just text that could be reproduced by printing. The possibilities for the transmission of images were also transformed by new technologies. Many books were illustrated and decorated with printed images. Some of the cheaper productions in particular had woodcut illustrations reused from earlier works, since it was easier for a printer to use a woodcut that he already possessed than to commission a new one.

The new technologies had important consequences. Their cultural and social impact is difficult to calculate with precision, although it was undoubtedly enormous. In physical terms the most obvious effect was a great increase in the number of books; the production of a title required far fewer hours of labor than before, and books became much cheaper to produce. There was a huge rise in the potential number of copies of any single text, although no one can judge the precise extent of this increase, not least because it is not possible to tell exactly how many copies were produced by the scriptoria or the stationers' shops. Another important consequence of the new technologies was the proliferation of near-identical copies. Although the limits to the capacity of early presses to produce multiple copies of a single book or pamphlet were greater than was once supposed, the press was clearly able to create a great many impressions from a single original. Essentially the same text or image could be produced in such quantities that it became possible for readers all over Europe to encounter a book at one and the same time.

The First Printed Books

From Gutenberg's press at Mainz, print technology quickly spread through Germany in the 1450s, to Italy in the 1460s, and then to France and the rest of Europe. The first European printed books, produced in the second half of the fifteenth century, are known as incunabula, from the Latin for "swaddling clothes" (taken to mean "beginnings" or "first stages"). Although they were produced in very different ways from medieval handwritten works, one of the most striking features of the incunabula is the similarity to their manuscript counterparts. The first printers tried hard to make their texts resemble manuscripts, and at the same time scribes attempted to make their script as uniform and

even as type. Like manuscripts, the first printed texts were often hand-decorated with elaborate and costly illustrations.

Early printed books were not perfect, fixed, or uniform. They were subject to error, and just as scribal production was characterized by a lack of uniformity, there were great variations in the quality of early print. However, despite the

▲ *Johannes Gutenberg is portrayed in this 1584 engraving by André Thevet.*

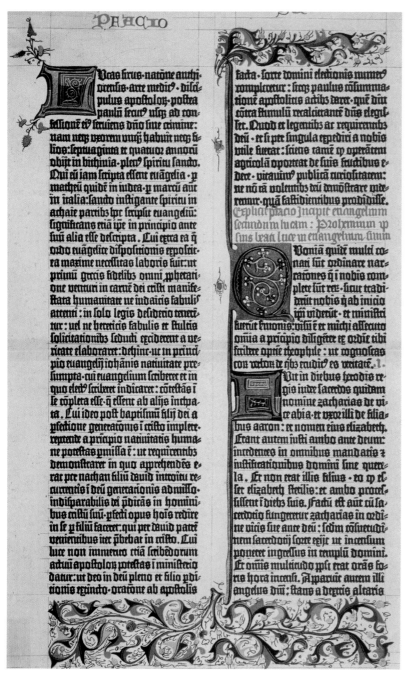

The Growth in Print Production

Gutenberg's first books illustrate the range and scope of the press. Printers produced cheap, single-sheet works alongside beautifully wrought bibles and other extremely expensive books; there were also various types of books in between those categories. From the beginning a varied market was envisioned for print. A great many of the earliest texts were religious in nature: catechisms, prayer books, sermons, theological treatises and commentaries on scripture, and scripture itself—from individual sections to full-length bibles.

The new technology altered the economic imperatives behind book production. There had been some important developments in book production and the financing of publishing before the fifteenth century. Printed block books (which used whole carved blocks for each page rather than movable type) existed before Gutenberg's printing press. Some manuscript book production had moved from monastic scriptoria to the shops of lay stationers, but the scriptoria continued to operate and underwent a revival in the fourteenth century. While the shift to print after Gutenberg's invention was also far from complete, the resulting change in the amount of investment required for the mass production of books—and the new possibilities for marketing and making profit from them—produced a radically different commercial environment for book production.

One of the most effective ways to control the presses was to harness these economic imperatives, as Queen Mary I did in England. In 1557 Mary granted a monopoly over printing to the newly incorporated Stationers' Company, which consequently ensured that its own regulatory procedures prevented the publication of inflammatory material. Perhaps owing to the fact that the investment required to produce printed books was so large and that the returns could be greater if a text proved popular, printers seem to have been more concerned to maximize the productivity of their presses and ensure the commercial success of their ventures than were the scribes and stationers involved in manuscript production. Small, cheap projects came to serve a special purpose for printing-press companies: they could

▲ *The Gutenberg Bible, also known as the Forty-two-Line Bible, produced in Germany between 1454 and 1455, was the earliest book printed in Europe using movable type. It is believed that 180 copies were produced over three years; it would have taken the same amount of time to produce one copy in a scriptorium. The page above shows the start of Luke's Gospel.*

similarities between the fluidity of manuscript transmission and that of print, there are significant differences. Print errors were engendered in the processes of copy reading, typesetting, and collation, rather than in individual scribal copying. Errors were reproduced over huge print runs, as in the notorious case of the 1631 "wicked Bible," which lost an essential word in the seventh of the Ten Commandments and thus instructed its readers "Thou shalt commit adultery." Owing to this fallibility, neither scribal nor print publications could be relied upon to be completely accurate.

mit d herberge. vñ ein yeqľlicher d erfchľaß fei   Sich. Ditz volcľ hat gefündt ein groffe fünd. vñ

PRINTED IMAGES

The invention of movable type was a key element in the mass production of printed books, but it was not just text that could be reproduced in print. Images of all kinds—pictures, illustrations, maps, diagrams, and symbols—were also suitable for mass production in the press. One of the most common types of images was the woodcut, frequently used to illustrate printed ballads (popular narrative poems, usually sung). This combination of image and text, with some text often incorporated into the picture itself, aided the development of literacy, since the image helped transmit the meaning of the words. In addition to the woodcut, the much more detailed copper engraving permitted the wide transmission of sophisticated works of art. Some of the most important artists of the northern Renaissance, including Albrecht Dürer (1471–1528) and Lucas Cranach the Elder (1472–1553), were important figures in the development of the printed image.

◄ *This page from the 1483 Bible printed by Anthony Koburger in Nuremberg depicts an Old Testament scene of Moses breaking the stone tablets. The use of woodcuts in this Bible— 109 were included—marked the start of a new epoch in printing.*

be used to produce a quick profit from a modest investment that itself might fund the publication of grander books. With small-scale projects ensuring that the presses were constantly at work, output and efficiency were maximized.

The great commercial potential of print led to rapid developments in the marketing of books. Booksellers began to advertise their wares, both in title pages in books and in separate printed sheets that could be displayed in public places— these sheets were sometimes copies of the title pages. In the competition for consumers, devices to attract and aid the reader were developed, including illustrations, contents pages, indexes, footnotes, cross-references, and the use of different typefaces for different purposes.

Reading Books

With the passage of time, it is very difficult to determine the audience for any one book or indeed for early print products in general. Reading leaves little evidence. It is clear, however, that the audience for books was substantially restricted at the inception of the printing process and that while the audience grew over subsequent centuries, by the 1700s significant obstacles remained. The first of these was cost. While the new technology could reduce printing costs, books were still essentially luxury items. With the vast majority of post-Renaissance Europeans living at subsistence level, they had little money to purchase anything but the necessities of life. On the other hand, there is good reason to

▶ This seventeenth-century engraving by Abraham van Weerdt depicts a printing shop with a lightly constructed wooden press. Pressure was exerted on the block to press the ink into the thick paper.

think books circulated beyond their initial buyers. The sheer numbers sold indicates that the cost of some books must have been within the reach of many besides the very rich.

Availability also restricted access to books. It is clear that books were most readily available in the towns where they were produced. Commercially astute booksellers also established businesses in smaller towns, however, and traveling salesmen were important distributors of printed materials, too. The other major factor that restricted access to books was literacy. Literacy varied enormously from place to place; it tended to be higher in towns than in the countryside and among men rather than women. The correlation between social standing and literacy is also clear. The relationship of literacy to print is complex. Print could help promote the need for literacy, as the proliferation of text made reading a more useful everyday skill. In addition, it could help improve literacy, as many aids to reading were increasingly available in print, including alphabet primers and schoolbooks.

Access to books was not limited to those who could afford them or those who could read. Written and oral interaction was an essential part of life all over Europe. Sermons and dramas were printed as well as voiced, and reading aloud was common. Printed materials were often displayed in public spaces—for example, ballads in the alehouse and proclamations in the marketplace—where the literate could read them to the illiterate.

Print and the Renaissance

The development of print greatly expanded the potential for the distribution of ideas. An important tool for education, printing became linked with the objectives of the humanist scholars of the Renaissance. The recovery of older texts was a central humanist project; many of the earliest printed works were not new texts but old ones, copies of which were thus increasingly widely available to a European community of scholars. Many Renaissance intellectuals, even those who expressed some unease about the new technology, quickly took advantage of the opportunities to bring their own works into the public domain. The diffusion of knowledge, whether from recovered ancient texts or world maps or the new sciences, was facilitated by print. It is likely, although impossible to quantify, that print was closely linked with the development of intellectual currents from the sixteenth century onward, as a more uniform and far more extensive corpus of knowledge became available. One consequence of this diffusion of information was the exposure of differences. Philosophical, theo-

Accurately assessing literacy rates is a difficult matter. The majority of people needed to write seldom, if ever, during their lifetime, and therefore left little evidence of whether they could write at all. The assessment of literacy is complicated because it was common to be able to read and not write or to be partially literate; there were many different types of literacy, and the ability to read leaves behind less evidence than the ability to write. One indication of literacy is book ownership, but the evidence of it is extremely patchy since many people did not leave wills or inventories of their goods; even when they did, small books might not have been valuable enough to be included. Another indication of literacy is the state of the educational system—both the Renaissance and the Reformation saw improvements in schooling. Nevertheless, it is difficult to assess levels of literacy from the history of education in general.

The most common and probably most reliable method of assessing literacy is to calculate how many people were able to sign their name. While ordinary people were not expected to write in the normal course of their lives, they would often be asked to sign their name when getting married, having their children baptized, or performing legal services. By examining the proportion of people able to sign their name, an estimate of the numbers who were literate can be reached.

Signature literacy, however, is not necessarily an accurate indication of the proportion of people who could write or who could read. Reading was often taught separately from writing and earlier, since writing was perceived as a much more vocational skill. It seems therefore that the elementary education received by many ordinary people extended as far as some reading but no writing. Thus, some people who could not sign their name might well have been able to read. Furthermore, for some people, signing their name was probably the limit of their ability to write and may not have accompanied proper reading literacy. Yet despite the drawbacks, signature literacy remains the best form of evidence for determining literacy rates in early modern Europe, and estimates based on signature rates demonstrate quite clearly that as print grew, so too did literacy.

TYPE-FOUNDING IN 1683 (FROM MOXON'S "MECHANICK EXERCISES").

▲ An illustrative plate from a 1683 book called Mechanick Exercises, the earliest full explanation of the process of mechanical printing and an example of the diffusion of knowledge permitted by print technology. Here, the caster pours metal into a mold to create a piece of type.

logical, scientific, and political clashes were laid open to scrutiny; the reader's task was to judge between competing accounts and opinions. Perhaps this process in itself contributed to the intellectual atmosphere that facilitated the scientific advances of the late Renaissance and the acceptance of a degree of religious tolerance by the end of the seventeenth century.

Many humanists thought that diversity of opinion was wasted or dangerous in the hands of the uneducated and were more interested in the growth of a community of scholars than in the diffusion of knowledge. The English scholar Thomas More (1478–1535), for example, was careful to have *Utopia* printed only in Latin and by European rather than English presses; he thereby limited access to the book to those whose learning resembled his own.

Print and the Reformation

Many people's fears about the divisive and dangerous potential of the press appeared to be realized in the sixteenth century. Protestantism has been particularly closely associated with print; one reason was the Protestant emphasis on scripture as the sole basis for doctrine. While Catholics were suspicious about lay use of the vernacular Bible, not least because it appeared to lead to schism, Protestant Reformers encouraged

RESTAVRATO SOTTO
BATISTA · SCHINELLA
DELL' ANNO 176.

This unattributed sixteenth-century painting depicts a craftsman binding a leather book. In order to hold in place the thick paper used by early presses, the binding ordinarily involved stitching leather covers on each side of the book.

Bible reading and thus may well have inspired much of the printing of vernacular scripture. Yet the attempts of the Reformers seem to have experienced limited success. Lay Bible reading remained relatively uncommon.

Religious printed matter was not limited to the Bible. A central tool of reform was the catechism, a summary of core doctrine in the form of simple questions and answers to be memorized. Luther produced the Shorter Catechism in 1529; John Calvin's catechism was published in 1541, and the new Calvinist Heidelberg Catechism followed in 1563. It was not just Protestants who catechized; the Jesuits in particular recognized the power of this tool, and their significant borrowings from Reformed catechisms indicates how much the different faiths had in common, both in terms of content and reforming strategy. The Council of Trent produced the definitive Catholic catechism in 1566. Countless variations of this printed adjunct of religious education existed, and it acted as an aid to literacy and encouraged the further spread of reading.

Printed Propaganda and News

Much religious print from the sixteenth century onward was propaganda in the confessional conflict that lasted into the seventeenth century and beyond. All of the sixteenth-century Reformers used print to disseminate their ideas. The potential for printed matter to gain converts to a religious or political cause was exemplified in the propaganda surrounding the Thirty Years War. Cheap, popular printed materials that appealed to national and religious sentiment were used by all sides to gain support. At the same time, widespread popular interest in the war helped generate a new genre of print: news. It was in the early

PRINT AND THE ENGLISH REFORMATION

The Tudor monarchs (reigned 1485–1603) were adept at employing the new technology of print to their own ends, perhaps most substantially in the realm of religion. From 1531 Henry VIII instructed scholars to defend in print his pursuit of a divorce and a reorganized church. Henry's consciousness of the power of print and its concomitant danger was revealed in 1543, when he attempted to limit the reading of the newly printed English Bible to an educated few. The government during the reign of Henry's son, Edward VI (1537–1553), was also conscious of the power of the printed word and used it extensively in the quest for a more thorough Reformation. While it has been assumed by many historians that Edward's regime in particular and Protestant rulers generally were more proficient in the use of printed propaganda than Catholic rulers, Edward's half sister Mary I (1553–1558) also used print in her attempts to restore the Catholic Church.

Showing more in common with her father (Henry) and half sister (Mary) than her half brother (Edward), Elizabeth I (1558–1603), who was conscious of print's capacity not just to persuade but also to challenge, continued to legislate against seditious printing—material inciting agitation against the authority of the state—and to keep tight control of the presses. This course of action could not, however, prevent the production in the late 1580s of a series of pamphlets, written under the pseudonym Martin Marprelate, that attacked the episcopal structure (government by bishops) of the Church of England and posed a huge challenge to Elizabeth's policies. One of the most dangerous aspects of these little books was their popular style: they introduced a topic hitherto limited to an exclusive audience to a much broader range of people. Elizabeth and members of her government believed that church reform was not an appropriate subject for discussion by ordinary people, but in order to counter the Marprelate pamphlets, they had to appeal to this same audience. Anti-Marprelate sermons and learned treatises were supplemented by government-sponsored pamphlets that were as popular and appealing as the originals had been. While they were eventually successful in their campaign against these illegal publications, the Elizabethan authorities had been forced to expand the forum of religious debate to include a more popular type of printed material.

▼ The author of the 1647 English pamphlet The World Turn'd Upside Down, *from which the title page is reproduced below, deplored the explosion of polemical print after the collapse of censorship in England in 1641.*

THE
World turn'd upfide down:
OR
A briefe defcription of the ridiculous Fafhions of thefe duttacted Times.

By T. J. a well-willer to King, Parliament and Kingdom.

seventeenth century that regular periodical news reports became common. With their arrival upon the scene, the origins of the modern printed newspaper are visible.

FURTHER READING

Boureau, Alain, et al. *The Culture of Print: Power and the Uses of Print in Early Modern Europe.* Cambridge, 1989.

Eisenstein, Elizabeth L. *The Printing Revolution in Early Modern Europe.* New York, 2005.

Febvre, Lucien, and Henri-Jean Martin. *The Coming of the Book: The Impact of Printing, 1450–1800.* New York, 1990.

Houston, Robert Allan. *Literacy in Early Modern Europe: Culture and Education, 1500–1800.* New York, 1988.

Johns, Adrian. *The Nature of the Book: Print and Knowledge in the Making.* Chicago, 1998.

Anna Bayman

SEE ALSO

• Bibles • Education • Humanism and Learning
• Languages, Classical • Languages, Vernacular
• Popular Culture • Science and Technology • Theater

Rabelais, François

ONE OF THE MOST INFLUENTIAL
LITERARY FIGURES IN EARLY-SIXTEENTH-
CENTURY FRANCE, FRANÇOIS RABELAIS
(1483–1553) IS BEST KNOWN FOR HIS
FIVE-BOOK COMIC MASTERPIECE,
GARGANTUA AND PANTAGRUEL.

Born in Touraine, a region of northwestern France, François Rabelais was the son of a lawyer. He joined the Franciscan order at an early age, but because the Franciscans lacked enthusiasm for humanism, he left and moved to the Benedictines instead. Following an education in Paris, Rabelais traveled south to Montpellier. He joined the local faculty of medicine and gained a

bachelor of medicine degree in December 1530, by which time he had abandoned monastic life entirely. During his formative years Rabelais also spent some time in Lyon, where he formed close links with prominent printers and was even employed as a corrector of humanist texts. He also earned a living by working as a doctor in the old hospital in Lyon.

Humanism and Religion

Rabelais's association with humanism was fundamental to his development as an author. He was deeply influenced by Desiderius Erasmus (c. 1466–1536), not merely because Erasmus called for the church to renew itself by returning afresh to the scriptures but also because of the Dutchman's repudiation of war and his belief that learning engendered virtue. Rabelais enthused about Francis I's patronage of the so-called New Learning and his foundation of the Royal College in 1530. Rabelais gradually associated himself with leading French humanists, including Guillaume Budé and Clément Marot, not to mention powerful patrons such as Jean du Bellay (c. 1492–1560) and Margaret of Angoulême (1492–1549), Francis I's sister. Rabelais's passion for humanist learning is unreservedly expounded in Gargantua's letter on education in *Gargantua* (1534). A hallmark of Rabelais's works is his syncretism—the fusion of classical and Christian elements that was so characteristic of the Christian Renaissance. It is manifest, for example, in the episode that describes the death of Pan, who is clearly identified with Christ.

French humanism cannot be disassociated from the broader religious context of early-sixteenth-century France. Yet the New Learning was not warmly received in all circles. Rabelais encountered serious opposition, particularly

◄ *Trained in theology, law, and medicine, François Rabelais, depicted here in an unattributed sixteenth-century portrait, was one of the leading scholars of his generation. In addition to being an influential member of French humanist circles, he was renowned for his literary classic* Gargantua and Pantagruel. *Although he certainly borrowed from a whole corpus of literary traditions, Rabelais's writing was remarkably innovative and original.*

Gargantua's letter to his son Pantagruel, which appears in chapter eight of Rabelais's second book, conveys the writer's own Christian form of humanism. The sentiments of the letter—which amounts to a humanist manifesto or a paean to the New Learning—were certainly also those of Rabelais's contemporaries Erasmus and Budé.

The times were still dark and feeling the effects of those miseries and calamities inflicted by the Goths, who had destroyed all good literature. But thanks to God's kindness, in my age enlightenment and dignity have once again been accorded to letters, and I see such an improvement that I would now hardly be accepted into the lowest class of little schoolboys, I who as a young man was reputed, and not without reason, to be the most learned man of the century. . . . Now all the learned disciplines have been restored, and the study of languages established: Greek, without which it is shameful that a man should proclaim himself to be learned, Hebrew, Chaldean, and Latin; the art of printing such elegant and accurate books, now in circulation, which was invented in my time by divine inspiration, just as, by contrast, artillery was inspired by diabolical suggestion. The whole world is full of learned men, very erudite teachers, and well-stocked libraries, and I am of the opinion that neither in the time of Plato, nor of Cicero, nor of Papinian were there ever such facilities for studying as one sees nowadays.

Pantagruel

▲ *The title page of a 1547 edition of* Gargantua. *This book, in common with everything else Rabelais wrote, was enormously popular in its own time. Fully thirty-six editions of Rabelais's books appeared in the first half of the sixteenth century.*

within the Sorbonne, the theological faculty at the University of Paris. The tensions within academic circles were fueled partly by the humanists' emphasis on individual study of the Bible (especially the original Greek and Hebrew texts), which threatened to undermine the church's authority. Rabelais was also treated with suspicion because he became associated with Clément Marot, Étienne Dolet, and Pierre Amy, all of whom had been accused of holding unorthodox beliefs. His early books were clearly indicative of an evangelistic critique of the Catholic Church; he was especially critical of monastic corruption in his portrayal of the abbey of Thélème. The attack on Rabelais was clearly reflected in the lengths to which the Sorbonne went to censure his books. In later works Rabelais toned down his evangelical criticisms and instead promoted Gallican views; Gallicanism represented the belief that the French church should seek to reform itself through a national council with little or no intervention from the Roman church.

The Importance of Patronage

Although Rabelais frequently criticized the church, he advanced in his career owing to support from powerful patrons. From the outset he was protected by his Benedictine abbot, Geoffroy d'Estissac, bishop of Maillezais. He subsequently met Jean du Bellay in 1533, bishop of

CHRONOLOGY

1483
François Rabelais is born in Touraine, France.

1510
After studying law, joins the Franciscans at La Baumette and later Fontenay-le-Comte.

1521
Transfers to the Benedictines at Saint-Pierre de Maillezais and takes holy orders.

1530
Leaves the Benedictines to study medicine in Montpellier.

1532
Edits Hippocrates' *Aphorisms* and Galen's *Art of Raising Children*, two key texts of Greek medicine. Is appointed physician to the hospital of Lyon. *Pantagruel* is published.

1534
Rabelais visits Rome. *Gargantua* is published just before the Affair of the Placards in Paris (a radical attack on the Catholic Mass).

1541
A new edition of *Gargantua and Pantagruel* is published (it is condemned by the Sorbonne two years later).

1546
Rabelais's third book, dedicated to Margaret of Angoulême, is published.

1553
Rabelais dies in Paris.

R abelais's five books are *Pantagruel* (1532); *Gargantua* (1534); *Tiers Livre* (1546); *Quart Livre* (1548, in full 1552); and *Cinquième Livre* (1564). (The last three titles are simply the French for third, fourth, and fifth book.) The books are linked by loose narratives and deal ostensibly with the deeds and adventures of two giants, Gargantua and his son Pantagruel. Although published second, *Gargantua* is reckoned to be the first book. In it Rabelais describes the genealogy, birth, and formative years of Gargantua. The work is striking for its marked emphasis on the carnivalesque elements of early modern society. Elsewhere, evangelical preachers are singled out for their wisdom and courage, while Sorbonne theologians are frequently treated as figures of fun.

The second book, *Pantagruel,* written in the comic tradition of the giant story, follows the birth, early life, travels, and exploits of Pantagruel. The book contains a considerable degree of parody and comic satire, normally at the expense of Sorbonne theologians, and also reflects the strong spirit of carnival. The book is best known for Gargantua's letter on education, which dwells on the intellectual golden age experienced by the French, represented principally by the foundation of the Royal College.

The third book, the first that was not written under the anagrammatic pseudonym Alcofribas Nasier, focuses principally on the matrimonial preoccupations of Panurge, a rather immoral and yet ingenious character (on one occasion he causes dogs to befoul a lady who rejects his advances). This book is not written in the giant story tradition as it is aimed at a more learned public. For example, antiwar sentiments are expressed in the prologue, and in a later part Gargantua condemns the church's official view on marriage, particularly the opinion that parental consent was not indispensable but merely desirable.

The fourth book, Rabelais's longest, was published in two installments, in 1548 and 1552. Rabelais reflects much French humanist opinion in his critique of the Council of Trent as a "national council of fools" and his description of the ignorance of the Papimaniac, who worshiped the pope as God on earth. Espousing greater independence for the French church, Rabelais displays his Gallican sympathies. The strength of the book lies in the way that Rabelais uses fantasy and satire both to veil and to reveal serious ideas.

The textual authenticity of the fifth book is questionable owing to its posthumous publication; it is thus harder to analyze. It certainly retains the features and characteristics of the earlier books, particularly the use of fantasy and satire. Moreover, it reflects the religious context of the 1560s, when evangelicals no longer played a prominent role.

Paris and later cardinal, whom he accompanied as a doctor. Bellay protected him in the critical decade of the 1530s, during which religious persecution intensified in the aftermath of the Affair of the Placards. Bellay's intervention ensured that Rabelais was absolved for having abandoned the Benedictine order without authorization. During the early 1540s Rabelais sought the protection of Francis I's sister, Margaret of Angoulême, to whom he dedicated the third book of the Gargantua-Pantagruel series. By the late 1540s and early 1550s, Rabelais had found a new protector, Cardinal Odet de Chastillon, who secured for him a royal privilege (such a privilege was necessary in order to print a book intended for the public domain). Despite this aristocratic support, many of Rabelais's books were censured by the Sorbonne and placed on the church's

◀ *A sixteenth-century portrait by an unknown artist of Francis I. As the founder of the Royal College, Francis became a bulwark of French humanism. Rabelais benefited immensely from the learned environment that developed around the king. Other clerics and aristocrats followed Francis's example, including Rabelais's last major patron, Cardinal Odet de Chastillon.*

Literary Contributions

Written in the French language, Rabelais's masterpiece proved a bestseller; in the sixteenth century alone, 100,000 copies of the five books were published. Rabelais did not invent French as a literary language, yet as the historian Paul Johnson states, he certainly demonstrated "its enormous potentialities and he made the French excited about their linguistic heritage for the first time." His works are characterized by their earthy language; the speech of the carnival and the marketplace are major cultural sources. His humor is coarse and grotesque; he uses obscene comedy not only to amuse but also to shock. In the words of Jean-Claude Margolin, "behind the fiction about giants, the excesses of languages, and the obscenities—and perhaps because of them—the gravest problems of the age and of the human condition are paraded before our eyes: the problems of war and peace, of marriage, education, and religion."

Despite his achievements, Rabelais's influence had become less pervasive by the mid-sixteenth century, when French humanism and evangelism were overshadowed by tensions between Calvinism and Catholicism.

FURTHER READING

Baumgartner, Frederic. *France in the Sixteenth Century.* New York, 1995.

Frame, Donald. *François Rabelais: A Study.* New York, 1977.

Hale, John. *The Civilization of Europe in the Renaissance.* New York, 1994.

Johnson, Paul. *The Renaissance: A Short History.* New York, 2000.

Margolin, Jean-Claude, "Humanism in France." In *The Impact of Humanism on Western Europe,* edited by Antony Goodman and Angus Mackay. New York, 1993.

Max von Habsburg

▲ *Margaret of Angoulême, the subject of this nineteenth-century painting by Atala Varcollier, played a formidable role as a patron of humanist scholars and wrote a number of works herself.*

Index of Forbidden Books. The writer was also criticized by John Calvin (1509–1564) and other Protestants. Like many Christian humanists of the time, including Erasmus, Rabelais found himself caught between the forces of reaction and innovation.

Raphael

ONE OF THE MASTER PAINTERS AND ARCHITECTS OF THE ITALIAN HIGH RENAISSANCE, RAPHAEL (1483–1520) IS WIDELY KNOWN FOR HIS MANY MADONNAS AND ALSO FOR LARGE GROUP COMPOSITIONS.

The date of Raphael's birth is uncertain. Sources indicate that he was born in Urbino, in central Italy, either on March 28 or April 6, 1483. His father, Giovanni Santi, was a painter.

His mother, Magia di Battista Ciarla, died when Raphael was only eight years old. His father remarried soon thereafter, but he died when Raphael (whose full name was Raffaello Sanzio) was eleven. As a young boy Raphael spent much of his time at his father's studio learning how to mix paints, prepare a wall for a fresco, and paint using various brush techniques. The first completed painting credited to Raphael is a fresco at his father's home depicting the Virgin Mary and Christ, although it is likely his father did much of the work.

▶ *This Madonna and Child, which was painted on a wall in the artist's birthplace in Urbino, is believed to be Raphael's first completed work.*

Duke Federigo II   1422–1482

On July 22, 1444, Lord Oddantonio of Urbino was assassinated by a group of his citizens. His twenty-one-year-old illegitimate half brother, Federigo, a well-trained soldier, quickly gathered an armed band of support and regained control of Urbino. He agreed that there would be no retaliation against the assassins and promised to rule justly; he subsequently won a popular election to succeed his brother. Duke Federigo governed Urbino for almost four decades and proved exemplary in his academic and military prowess. A portrait of him painted by Justus of Ghent (c. 1475) portrays the leader studying a manuscript while outfitted in nearly full armor.

Before rising to power, Federigo was a condottiere, or mercenary. It was common practice among Italian rulers from the Middle Ages until around the mid-fifteenth century to hire foreign soldiers. Federigo fought for cash under short-term agreements at different times for Venice, for the papacy, for the Aragonese in Naples, for Florence against the papacy, for the papacy against Florence, and for others. His loyalty lay not with any of these combatants but only to the contract at hand. His successes as a mercenary depended on the relations among Venice, Naples, Milan, Florence, and the papacy.

Federigo's territory after attaining power lay between Venice, Florence, and Rome. He extended his mountainous territories in the Apennines to include the fertile March of Ancona. His city, Urbino, enjoyed peace and benefited economically from the wars he waged in other city-states. The profits accrued from war enabled Federigo to keep taxes low and permitted him to build the ducal palace and acquire one of the largest library collections of the time (Federigo's library rivaled that of the Vatican).

Federigo was a passionate promoter of literature and art. Urbino experienced peace under his reign, and the highly cultured environment there was conducive to artistic endeavor. The duke hired great Italian artists from other city-states to complete commissioned works that would remain in the Umbrian region. It seems that Federigo also courted some of the finest Italian artisans of his time to work in Urbino. Records indicate that two chief architects, Luciano da Laurana and Francesco di Giorgio Martini, were probably responsible for the design of the magnificent ducal palace. Laurana left Urbino for Naples in 1472 with the palace far from complete; Federigo then hired Martini to continue the construction of the building and to strengthen many of the castles surrounding it. He employed renowned artists to decorate the interior of the palace, which remains one of the finest examples of Italian Renaissance architecture. Federigo died one year prior to Raphael's birth. Under Federigo's son, Duke Guidobaldo, Urbino retained its glory and reputation as a cultural haven.

CHRONOLOGY

1483
Raphael is born in Urbino, Italy.

1495
His father, Giovanni Santi, dies.

1495 or 1500
Raphael is apprenticed to Pietro Perugino in Perugia.

1503
One of Raphael's first major commissions, *The Crucifixion*, is completed. Perugino's commission, *Coronation of the Virgin*, is entrusted to Raphael.

1504
Raphael completes the small narrative paintings *The Knight's Dream* and *The Three Graces*.

1504 or 1505
Moves to Florence.

1508
Moves to Rome.

1511
Completes the Stanza della Segnatura.

1520
Dies on his thirty-seventh birthday.

Upon his father's death, Raphael inherited his art studio. At the time Urbino was a cultural center, and so Raphael was able to develop his artistic skills in a supportive environment. However, his relationship with his stepmother was not strong, and some time between 1495 and 1500, the young artist left Urbino to apprentice with Pietro Perugino (c. 1450–1523), known as the Master of the Umbrian School, in the town of Perugia in Umbria. Perugino had apprenticed under the guidance of Andrea del Verrocchio at about the same time as Leonardo da Vinci, with the result that Perugino and da Vinci have similar influences represented in their respective styles.

The exact date of Raphael's apprenticeship is not certain. It is generally believed that he arrived in Perugia in 1495, soon after his father's death. However, the earliest record of any activity by Raphael in Perugia dates to December 10, 1500. The document indicates that he had already

◄ *Piero della Francesca completed this oil-on-panel profile of Duke Federigo of Montefeltro around 1465 along with a portrait of the duke's wife, Batista Sforza.*

▲ Raphael's oil-on-wood self-portrait was completed in 1506 or 1509. The serene expression on the face of the youthful artist reveals no sign of inner tension.

behind Jesus on the cross. Saint Jerome and Mary Magdalene kneel as they gaze up at him, while Saint John and the Virgin Mary stand looking out at the worshipers.

Around 1502 to 1503, Perugino was commissioned to produce a painting for the Church of San Francesco in Perugia. He entrusted its completion to his young pupil Raphael; the completed work is the *Coronation of the Virgin*. The altarpiece combines two scenes: the crowning of Mary in the upper portion and the presentation of the girdle to Saint Thomas in the lower portion. There is a clear division of composition; some experts contend that this division indicates the artist was uncertain of his abilities. Regardless, the human forms and perspective are advanced for such a young artist, and Raphael's drawings reveal the amount of attention he devoted to the work's realization. While his overall composition may seem uncertain, authorities agree that details such as individual faces and the background landscape exemplify masterful skill.

Early Works

In 1504 Raphael completed one of the first major works credited entirely to him. This painting, *Spozalizio* (a depiction of the engagement of the Virgin Mary) demonstrates the influence that Perugino had on Raphael's style. Treatment of perspective, the relationships between the people and the architecture, the gentleness of the figures, and other characteristics of Perugino's work are all evident. However, the differences in the two men's styles are also apparent. The relationships between the people and the architectural background are less strict in the former student's work than in Perugino's. Also, the spatial relationships among Raphael's figures are less formal. He paints with brighter animation, and so his figures have an almost exaggerated gentleness. Art historians and scholars believe that Perugino's *Christ Delivering the Keys to Saint Peter*, from the fresco cycle of the Sistine Chapel, inspired this work by Raphael.

Following the completion of *Spozalizio,* Raphael developed two small works—each is approximately seven square inches (45 cm²)— that became masterful examples of narrative

achieved the title of master at age seventeen and, along with another artist, received a commission to paint an altarpiece that was delivered on September 13, 1501. This altarpiece was damaged in an earthquake in the late eighteenth century and then cut into several pieces. In the present day three of those pieces are located in museums in Brescia, Naples, and Paris.

Raphael in Perugia

In Perugia, Raphael received a commission from Domenico Gavari for the chapel in Città di Castello. The work, *Crucifixion with Saints Mary the Virgin, Mary Magdalene, John, and Jerome,* was dedicated in 1503. In this oil on panel, two angels tiptoe on clouds positioned slightly

painting. The first, *The Knight's Dream* (also known as the *Allegory*), is an oil-on-wood image of a young knight asleep in front of a laurel tree that divides the picture in two symmetrically. Each half of the painting contains a depiction of a beautiful young woman. The figure on the left holding a book and a sword is said to be Minerva, the goddess of virtue. The figure on the right, who presents the young knight with a flower, is said to represent Venus, the goddess of pleasure. The most likely meaning of the allegory is that the young man's task is to find harmony among these opposing influences.

The second of these small paintings is *The Three Graces,* an oil-on-panel depiction of the classical figures who symbolized grace and beauty. The central figure has her back turned; her arms, which are raised upward and outward, conceal the bosoms of the other two figures, who face forward on either side of the central figure. Each of the women is holding an apple in her outstretched hand, said to be a reward for the young knight, who chose virtue over pleasure. *The Three Graces* is Raphael's first study of female nudes in both front and back views.

Raphael Moves to Florence

Giorgio Vasari, Raphael's first biographer, indicates that Raphael followed a Perugian painter named Pinturicchio to Siena and then moved to Florence. Raphael may have been drawn to that city by reports of the works of Leonardo da Vinci and Michelangelo. Raphael probably arrived in Florence soon after October 1, 1504, the date of his recommendation letter to the Florentine republic. It is unknown if this was his first visit to the city. Raphael intended to study in Florence, but there is little indication that he became a permanent resident of the city. In fact, between the years 1504 and 1507 it is recorded that Raphael resided in Perugia, Urbino, and Rome, as well as Florence. Vasari indicates that Raphael studied the works of Leonardo da Vinci, Michelangelo,

▲ The Three Graces, *an oil on panel completed by Raphael in 1503 or 1504, is a typical Renaissance treatment of the female nude. The painting was probably based on the classical sculpture of the Three Graces in Siena rather than on living models.*

One of the greatest contributions to the preservation of the Italian Renaissance came not from paintings or sculptures but from the biographical accounts produced by the Italian painter and historian Giorgio Vasari (1511–1574). He discusses Raphael in the following passage:

[The] liberality with which Heaven now and again unites in one person the inexhaustible riches of its treasures and all those graces and rare gifts which are usually shared among many over a long period is seen in Raphael Sanzio of Urbino, who was as excellent as gracious, and endowed with a natural modesty and goodness sometimes seen in those who possess to an unusual degree a humane and gentle nature adorned with affability and good fellowship, and he always showed himself sweet and pleasant with persons of every degree and all circumstances. Thus Nature created Michelangelo Buonarroti to excel and conquer in art, but Raphael to excel in art and in manners also.

Giorgio Vasari, *Lives of the Most Eminent Painters, Sculptors, and Architects*

▶ *The* Madonna of the Meadow *is an oil on wood completed by Raphael in 1505. The influence of both Michelangelo and Leonardo is apparent in the style and composition of this work.*

and Fra Bartolomeo to gain an appreciation of the style of the masters of the High Renaissance and that he also studied works of the masters of the early Renaissance who first departed from the Gothic styles. Still, Leonardo da Vinci and Michelangelo would have the greatest influence on works completed by Raphael between 1504 and 1507. Most noteworthy of Raphael's paintings during this period is a series of Madonnas.

Madonna del Prato (Madonna of the Meadow), an oil on wood completed in 1506, is the first of a series of full-length figure composi-

tions. Raphael portrays the biblical supposition that John the Baptist recognized and worshiped Christ as the Redeemer even when they were both in infancy. He depicts the young John handing a cross to the young Christ. This painting illustrates the influence that Leonardo and Michelangelo had on Raphael's style: the figures are arranged in a pyramidal structure, after Leonardo's manner, that is dominated by the Virgin Mary. The spatial relationship between the two children, who do not face each other along a straight line, requires the kind of skillful depiction of anatomy that is one of Michelangelo's hallmarks.

Madonna del Cardellino (Madonna of the Goldfinch) was painted by Raphael for the marriage of his friend Lorenzo Nasi to Sandra di Matteo di Giovanni Canigiani. This oil on wood was completed in 1507; Vasari records that it was damaged when the Nasi house collapsed in 1547 and was subsequently restored by Ridolfo Ghirlandaio. In this painting the Christ child is gently stroking a goldfinch presented to him by the boy Baptist. Because a goldfinch feeds among thorns, the bird has come to symbolize the Passion. The figure composition is quite similar to that of the *Madonna of the Meadow*, with the exception that the children are more closely in touch with the central figure. The color foreshadows a style that is indicative of many of Raphael's works, and the landscape and background architecture reflect Flemish and Umbrian influences.

While Raphael was influenced by both Leonardo and Michelangelo during his time in Florence, Michelangelo's influence is more prevalent in Raphael's later works. In 1507 Raphael was commissioned to paint the *Deposition of Christ*. The *Deposition* (the word refers to Christ's entombment) was painted as a memorial to Grifoneto Baglioni, who was killed in a piazza in Perugia because of a family feud. Raphael breaks from tradition and does not depict the deposition itself. Rather, he shows the dead Christ being carried to the tomb. The sorrow of the figures, who are not openly weeping, is demonstrated subtly by their facial expressions. The open space in the background is certainly reflective of Michelangelo, as is the anatomical detail given to the central figure.

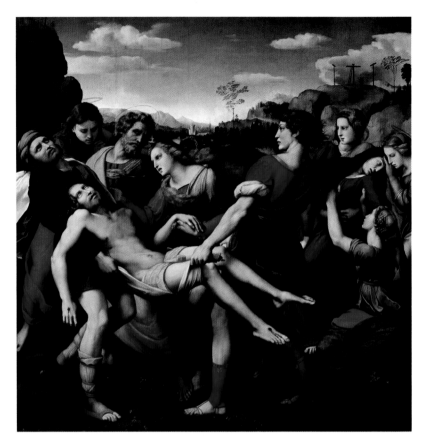

▲ Raphael's oil on panel the Deposition of Christ *was completed in 1507.*

STYLISTIC INFLUENCES

Raphael's introduction to art came from his father, Giovanni Santi, who, according to Vasari, was "a painter of no great merit." However, Giovanni was generous and intelligent, and he wanted his son to have the opportunities that he himself had been afforded as a child. With this motivation Giovanni introduced his son to painting at an early age. The young boy demonstrated such talent that Giovanni allowed Raphael to work in his studio. Once Giovanni had nothing left to teach his son, he sought to send him elsewhere so that he could learn from a master. Giovanni arranged for Raphael to work with Pietro Perugino, one of the finest Umbrian painters of the time. Vasari documents that as Raphael was studying Perugino's style, he was soon able to copy the teacher so closely that many could not distinguish who had completed some of the paintings.

When Raphael moved to Florence, he carefully studied the works and styles of Leonardo and Michelangelo, who were the greatest artists of the High Renaissance period. Additionally, he studied early Renaissance artists, such as Masaccio, whom Vasari called "a pioneer of the naturalism that marked the departure of the early Renaissance from the Gothic." By the time Raphael moved to Rome, his style was distinctly his own, but it continued to demonstrate the influence of the masters from whom he learned. In his later years Raphael departed from the serene gentleness exhibited in his Florentine Madonnas to focus on qualities of energetic movement, as can be seen in his *Alba Madonna* (1508). In the early part of the sixteenth century, Raphael became the most important portraitist in Rome. Most experts agree that his finest work in this genre is the portrait entitled *Leo X with Two Cardinals* (1517–1519).

Raphael's Years in Rome

In 1508 Raphael was called to Rome by Pope Julius II, and he spent the final twelve years of his life there. Although he was little known in the city, it did not take Raphael long to make an impression. His first project was to paint a cycle of frescoes in the Vatican apartments where Julius II lived. These rooms are known simply as the *stanze* (Italian for "rooms").

There are four main fresco walls in the Stanza della Segnatura, which was completed in 1509. The two most important frescoes on the larger walls are the *School of Athens* and *La Disputa. School of Athens,* a depiction of classical philosophy, includes figures from a variety of disciplines, with Plato and Aristotle at the center. *La Disputa,* also known as the *Disputation on the Holy Sacrament,* has clearly distinguished upper and lower portions. The upper portion is the Church Triumphant, while the lower portion depicts the Church Militant. In each the figures are arranged in a semicircular pattern. On the smaller walls are the *Parnassus* and the *Cardinal Virtues.* In classical myth, Mount Parnassus is the dwelling place of Apollo and the Muses and the home of poetry; Raphael's fresco includes eminent contemporary as well as classical poets. The *Cardinal Virtues,* painted in a lunette (an arching aperture in the wall), depicts three allegorical figures: Fortitude, Prudence, and Temperance. Prudence is placed in the center sitting atop a pedestal with Fortitude and Temperance below and to either side. In addition to these frescoes, Raphael painted a series of frescoes on the ceiling of the Segnatura. The figures represent Philosophy, Poetry, Theology, and Justice. The design of the ceiling is credited to Sodoma, who also painted the central octagonal section.

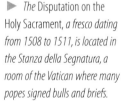

► *The* Disputation on the Holy Sacrament, *a fresco dating from 1508 to 1511, is located in the Stanza della Segnatura, a room of the Vatican where many popes signed bulls and briefs.*

Upon completion of the Segnatura, Raphael began work on the adjacent room, the Stanza di Eliodoro. Pope Julius II died during the execution of this room, but his successor, Pope Leo X, ensured its completion. The general theme of the room, God's intervention in human destiny, is portrayed through frescoes that illustrate four stories; the design was specifically chosen for Julius II. The four stories concern the expulsion of Heliodorus from the temple, the liberation of Saint Peter, the meeting between Leo the Great and Attila, and the mass at Bolsena. They are taken from the Acts of the Apostles, the Apocrypha, and church history. The ceiling vaults represent such episodes as the Burning Bush, the announcement of the Flood to Noah, and the Sacrifice of Isaac—stories of divine intervention in the history of Israel.

The Stanza dell'Incendio di Borgo became Raphael's workshop from 1514 to 1518. The narrative painting therein illustrates historical events in which popes named Leo become the main characters. One of the frescoes, *Fire in the Borgo,* concerns a fire in Rome in 847 that Pope Leo IV had extinguished. Another is the *Battle of Ostia,* in which the presence of Leo IV caused the Saracens to be lost at sea. The coronation of Charlemagne by Pope Leo III on Christmas Day of the year 800 is also portrayed. While this room was primarily designed by Raphael, his pupils and assistants were mostly responsible for the execution of the frescoes.

Raphael's final masterpiece is the *Transfiguration,* which is painted in two parts. The lower level depicts the miracle of a possessed boy, while the background portrays the transfiguration of Christ. Christ floats in the clouds and light above the hill with Moses and Elijah at either side. The boy is surrounded by a crowd of onlookers who are amazed by the miracle and whose arms are outstretched toward Christ. Raphael died on April 6, 1520, with the painting unfinished. Giulio Romano, one of Raphael's assistants, completed the work.

Although Raphael lived a relatively short life, he joins Leonardo and Michelangelo as one of the three greatest artists of the High Renaissance. His skill and talent, Vasari contends, were so exceptional that they must have been passed to him

from divinity. For the twenty years of his life that Raphael was considered a master, he lived up to the title and perhaps even exceeded it.

FURTHER READING

Jones, Roger, and Nicholas Penny. *Raphael.* New Haven, CT, 1983.

Pope-Hennessy, John. *Raphael.* New York, 1970.

Vasari, Giorgio. *Lives of the Most Eminent Painters, Sculptors, and Architects.* New York, 1979.

Brian A. Carriere

SEE ALSO

• Architecture • Bramante, Donato
• Florence • Leonardo da Vinci • Michelangelo
• Painting and Sculpture • Renaissance
• Urbino

▲ *This oil on wood, titled* Transfiguration, *was completed by Raphael in 1519. A mosaic replica was created in the eighteenth century for the altarpiece of Saint Peter's Basilica in Rome.*

Reformation

THE PROTESTANT REFORMATION BEGAN AS A MOVEMENT OF MORAL AND DOCTRINAL REFORM. BY ITS END THE POLITICAL AND RELIGIOUS STRUCTURES OF WESTERN CHRISTIANITY WERE IN FRAGMENTS.

To Protestant scholars the Reformation was a movement of genuine Christian renewal. Catholic scholars consider it a revolt, a deviation from religious truth into secularist tendencies. Both sides acknowledge, although it took Catholics longer to admit it, that Western Christianity was in a state of crisis at the time the Reformation began. Whatever the specifics of the crisis, Catholics contend, both church and society were still quite stable. For centuries clergymen had been more concerned with the political aspects of their positions of authority than with the religious or spiritual aspects. The church in general had acquired great landholdings since

▶ This oil on wood was painted by artists from the studio of Lucas Cranach the Elder around 1532. The central figure is John Frederick the Magnanimous, elector of Saxony. Martin Luther stands to the elector's left.

the early Middle Ages and had become quite influential in the realm of European political affairs. Bishops and other high-ranking clergy were often appointed to important positions as political favors, although some were not educated in the basics of Latin, literature, or theology.

In the early sixteenth century the Holy Roman Empire, a loose confederation of German states, was in disorder owing to uncertainties about political boundaries. The various imperial states relied heavily on the towns for financial resources but simultaneously suppressed the political aspirations of the townspeople. The Catholic Church held a very influential position within the empire because of the deficiencies of imperial government. Yet the hierarchy of the church was greatly removed from the everyday life of parishioners and local clergy. Since the eighth century most bishops and cardinals had been drawn from the ranks of the wealthy and powerful; their superior position left them largely out of touch with the needs of the common parishioner. Meanwhile, many parish priests, who were in daily contact with their parishioners, were poorly educated and often confused about the specifics of orthodox belief.

By the late fifteenth century, humanists began calling for the church to alleviate such problems. Desiderius Erasmus and other humanists consid-ered the papacy too far disengaged and the clergy too ignorant or too greedy. Erasmus urged a return to the outlook and practice of the early church. By the early 1500s the religious affairs of the church had become so entangled with political structures that it was difficult to tell whether the church was a religious or a political entity.

Nevertheless, despite abundant criticism the church seemed stable and demands for reform seemed realistic. There was little to indicate that an unprecedented upheaval was in the offing.

◀ Originally built around 1500, the church door at Wittenberg, in Germany, to which Martin Luther attached the Ninety-five Theses, was destroyed by a fire in 1760. The north portal replica door built in 1858 is pictured here.

MARTIN LUTHER'S BACKGROUND

The movement for reform began with a German monk named Martin Luther. Born in 1483 in Eisleben, Germany, Luther earned a master's degree by 1505 and entered law school at the University of Erfurt. His life changed when he was nearly struck by lightning; he subsequently devoted himself to God as a means of demonstrating his graciousness. Luther performed selfless deeds to help others but had trouble finding peace with God. In 1507 he was ordained a priest and soon began teaching theology at the University of Wittenberg, where he was awarded a doctorate in theology in 1512.

Luther's close study of theology focused on the scriptures. His reading of Romans 1:17 ("The just shall live by faith") led him to conclude that the church had lost sight of the fundamental nature of salvation. He began teaching that God grants salvation to all who believe in the divinity of Christ. The church, however, taught that salvation required, besides faith, repentance for sins and the doing of good works. This doctrinal disagreement did not of itself provoke the Reformation; the controversy over indulgences tipped the scales. An indulgence exempted its receiver from part or all of the punishment owed in the afterlife for confessed and repented sins. Despite numerous papal denunciations of abuse of indulgences, by Luther's time their nature was widely mis-understood. Many Christians believed wrongly that they forgave sins and could be had for a price. Corrupt cler-gymen—bishops, cardinals, even a few popes—cynically exploited the laity's ignorance for their own enrichment. The practice infuriated Luther. When a bishop named Johann Tetzel arrived in Wittenberg to sell indulgences, Luther wrote out ninety-five theses (points of debate) detailing ecclesiastical corruption and abuse and nailed them to the church door. This simple gesture of conviction began the Reformation.

The Controversy over Indulgences

It has been long and widely held that the origins of the Reformation lie in the reaction to the sale of indulgences. An indulgence is a formal ecclesiatical remission of part or all of the punishment owed for confessed sins; any Catholic can gain an indulgence by simply saying the prayers or performing the pious acts that the church specifies for it. It does not substitute for remorse for sin, confession to a priest, an act of contrition, and performance of a penance (basic requirements of the Catholic faith); that is, it does not forgive sins, either past or future ones. By the Renaissance, however, lay ignorance and clerical venality had combined to create the widespread belief that indulgences could absolve sins and be gotten for cash. Many people came to believe that they could buy their way into God's favor, and some churchmen were glad to exploit this error to their profit.

In 1517 construction of Saint Peter's Basilica in Rome, which had been ongoing for years, was still incomplete. The pope at the time, Leo X,

▼ This unattributed oil on canvas of Saint Peter's Square in Rome dates from around 1665. Construction of the basilica, portrayed in the background, was loosely linked to the sale of indulgences.

encouraged his bishops to sell indulgences within their dioceses to raise funds. Albert of Brandenburg wanted to be appointed archbishop of Mainz; to win papal favor, he promised to pay Leo part of the proceeds gained by selling special indulgences and thus help the pope continue work on the basilica. Albert left the task of selling indulgences to a bishop named Johann Tetzel, who was scheduled to arrive in Wittenberg, where Martin Luther worked as a preacher and district vicar, on All Saints' Day in 1517. Although Frederick the Wise, duke of Saxony, had prohibited the sale of indulgences in his lands, many of Luther's parishioners traveled to Tetzel to purchase them anyway. When they returned to Wittenberg, they believed they no longer needed to repent their sins because the indulgence had secured forgiveness for them.

Luther had prepared a challenge to the church hierarchy in the form of the Ninety-five Theses. Whether Luther actually nailed the theses to the church door, as has long been believed, or merely sent a copy of them to the

In 1541 Martin Luther wrote about Johann Tetzel and the practice of selling indulgences as absolution for sins:

It happened in 1517 that a Dominican monk named Johann Tetzel, a braggart, caused a great stir. Maximilian once sentenced him to drowning in the River Inn—presumably because of his great virtue—but Duke Frederick rescued him in Innsbruck from the punishment of being drowned. Duke Frederick reminded him of this incident when he began to denounce us Wittenbergers. Actually, he admitted it quite openly. This same Tetzel now began to peddle indulgences. With might and main he sold grace for money as dearly or as cheaply as he could. At the time I was preacher here in the cloister and was filled as a new doctor with an ardent love for the scriptures.

When many people from Wittenberg ran after indulgences to Jüterborg and Zerbst [two neighboring towns that people went to because selling indulgences was prohibited in Wittenberg], I did not know—as surely as my Lord Christ has redeemed me—what [these] indulgences were, but no one else knew either. I carefully began to preach that one could do something better and more certain than to purchase indulgences. On an earlier occasion I had already preached here in the castle against indulgences, but was not very graciously received by Duke Frederick, who was fond of his collegiate church. Now, to speak about the real cause for the "Lutheran scandal," at first I let everything continue its course. Then it was reported to me, however, that Tetzel was preaching some cruel and terrible propositions, such as the following: if anyone put money into the coffer for a soul in purgatory, the soul would leave purgatory for heaven in the moment one could hear the penny hit the bottom. Also the grace of indulgences is the grace by which man is reconciled with God. Furthermore, it is not necessary to show remorse or sorrow or do penance for sins when purchasing indulgences or a letter of indulgence. He even sold indulgences for future sins. Such abominable things he did abundantly. He was merely interested in money. At the time I did not yet know who was to get the money. Then there appeared a booklet with the illustrious coat of arms of the Bishop of Magdeburg. In it the commissioners of indulgences were ordered to preach some of the propositions. Thus it came to light that Bishop Albert had employed Tetzel, because he was such a braggart.

Wider Hans Wurst

archbishop is not entirely clear. Luther probably did nail them to the door, albeit not in a defiant manner. Because the church was centrally located and many people passed it daily, the door had become a common place to post public notices.

Luther's challenges were revolutionary because of their questioning of doctrine in addition to their attack on corruption. Luther criticized not only the practice of selling indulgences but also the doctrinal contention of the church that one achieved redemption and gained God's grace and deliverance from sin and damnation through performance of good works. Luther advocated that God's grace is gained by faith alone. This attack on a central doctrine of the Roman Catholic Church set Luther apart from prior critics and reformers, who had simply tried to draw attention to corruption in practice or belief by clerics or members of the laity.

CHRONOLOGY

1518
Frederick the Wise grants Martin Luther his protection.

1521
Pope Leo X declares Henry VIII Defender of the Faith.

1522
The Anabaptist movement begins in Germany.

1526
The Reformation spreads to Sweden and Denmark.

1529
Henry VIII begins to cut ties with Rome.

1530
The Schmalkaldic League is formed.

1532
John Calvin brings the Reformation to France.

1534
Pope Paul III is crowned.

1535
Charles V forms the Catholic Defense League.

1540
The newly formed Society of Jesus, which will become the chief agent of the Counter-Reformation, receives papal approval.

1546
Martin Luther dies.

1618
A rebellion in Bohemia starts the Thirty Years War.

1648
The Treaty of Westphalia officially brings the Thirty Years War to an end.

Johannes Tetzel von Leipzig
S.S. Theol. Doctor und Profesor der ...

◀ *This eighteenth-century copper engraving by Nikolaus Bruhl depicts Bishop Johann Tetzel, the man whose actions led Martin Luther to openly question church doctrine in the Ninety-five Theses.*

The Spread of the Reformation

Luther's ideas and critique of church doctrine quickly found an attentive public. They were published in pamphlets and distributed in French, German, English, and later other languages. People converged on Wittenberg to hear Luther preach. Although church leaders had initially discounted Luther as a disgruntled German monk, they began to heed his message when his popularity grew. In 1520 Luther attacked the sacraments in a pamphlet called *Prelude on the Babylonian Captivity of the Church;* Leo X immediately issued an edict that ordered Luther to recant—that is, withdraw and renounce—specific items from his writings. When Luther refused, the pope excommunicated him on January 3, 1521.

Memories of the Hussite troubles of the previous century were aroused, and the church set out to quell this disruption as quickly as possible. (Jan Hus, a Bohemian religious reformer, was burned at the stake in 1415. His death sparked a conflict that was not completely put to rest until the Battle of White Mountain in 1620.) In May 1521 the Edict of Worms officially declared Luther a political outlaw and confirmed his excommunication. Luther was thereby temporarily removed from the scene, but the message of religious reform he preached was spread by his supporters. At this point the Reformation may truly be said to have begun.

Using the relatively new invention of the movable-metal-type printing press, numerous Reformist pamphlets were published between 1517 and 1525; they carried themes simple enough for those with minimal literacy skills to follow. For example, a pamphlet entitled *Totenfreser* (Corpse Eater) likened the sale of indulgences to feeding on the dead. By the end of the 1520s, over one million copies of Reformation literature had been distributed in Germany alone, and the Reformation was firmly planted in the southern and central parts of the region. Although the publications lacked a properly defined theological focus, they displayed a common theme: reform.

▶ *This 1523 woodcut appears on the front of an anonymous pamphlet entitled* Ein schöner Dialogus von Martino Luther und der geschickten Botschaft aus der Hölle *(A Dialogue between Martin Luther and the Messenger Sent from Hell). The woodcut depicts Luther (left) joined by some devilishly masked clergymen.*

THE PRINTING PRESS AND THE REFORMATION

The earliest method of printing was known as block printing, a process that involves pressing sheets of paper over carved wooden blocks that have been daubed with ink. Each block, carved with tiny letters, produces a single page of text. A book might require numerous such blocks, and so block printing was a laborious and expensive process that was rarely used until the mid-fifteenth century.

Movable type was first developed in China in 1041. In this printing process individual type letters can be rearranged and revised. Although it is not clear whether knowledge of movable type had reached Europe by the mid-fifteenth century, in the 1440s a German inventor, Johannes Gutenberg, produced a movable-type printing press made of metal. Metal-type presses were more durable than earlier clay-type presses. Gutenberg is also credited with being the first to use an oil-based ink in the printing process.

Books were a rare commodity in Europe prior to mechanized printing; because they were hand-copied by scribes or monks, only wealthy nobles could afford books. Even after printed books became widespread, many nobles considered their "copied" versions to have a greater value, both financial and literary. The nobility's misgivings notwithstanding, thanks to the printing press, books were less expensive and more readily available to a wider audience. Before the printing press most people had no opportunity to read the Bible because they could not afford to buy a copy. They simply had to rely upon the information provided by their priest. Once literate members of the population could read the Bible and other texts for themselves, dependence on priestly interpretation waned. As illuminated manuscripts emphasized pictures, books became a resource attractive to the illiterate majority as well.

Few inventions in human history have matched in significance the movable-type printing press, a development that changed the way Europeans thought. The printing press facilitated the spread of the Protestant Reformation by bringing reading matter to the literate. After Martin Luther translated the Bible from Latin to German in the 1520s and 1530s, Gutenberg's press allowed copies of that Bible to be produced so that people could read it for themselves.

The Diet (conference) of Speyer in 1526 resolved that the Reformation was so firmly rooted that the Edict of Worms had become impossible to enforce. From that point until the Peace of Augsburg (1555), Reformed Christianity continued to expand but simultaneously sought to coexist with Catholicism. Much of the support for the movement came from the cities, which were centers of economic power and literacy. As the inhabitants of rural areas were mostly illiterate, they tended to be little concerned with doctrinal debate.

Reformist Divisions

The Reform movement experienced widespread growth throughout the 1520s. While its followers held a common opposition to aspects of the Catholic Church, they did not forge a unified doctrinal message. The first division in Reformist ranks occurred in 1522, when one of Luther's colleagues, Andreas Karlstadt, publicly disagreed with Luther. Thomas Münzer soon published pamphlets that charged Luther with failure to go far enough. Münzer preached strong opposition to those he called godless rulers.

▶ *This illuminated French miniature printed on vellum, dating from around 1537, depicts the interior of an early printing works. Printing technology spread rapidly throughout Europe.*

▲ *A portrait of the Swiss Reformer Huldrych Zwingli, leader of the Swiss Protestant movement, by an unknown artist. Like Luther, Zwingli insisted that the Bible was the only source of religious authority—with himself as its sole legitimate interpreter.*

Another major division was introduced by the Swiss Reformer Huldrych Zwingli of Zurich. In 1519 he was appointed people's priest, the most important clerical position in the city, by Pope Leo X, but he had already accepted Luther's arguments for reform. Zwingli helped the Protestant movement spread throughout Switzerland. Unlike other Reformers, who wrote extensively on a variety of topics, Zwingli focused on a single theme in all of his writings. His simple theology was based on a literal interpretation of the Old and New Testaments. He argued that if the Bible did not say something explicitly, then it should not be believed or practiced; literal meanings of the Old and New Testaments were to be uncritically accepted.

The single most divisive issue in the Reformist movement concerned the doctrine and signification of the Eucharist, or the Lord's Supper. The Roman Catholic doctrine, called transubstantia-

tion, asserted that during the sacramental Eucharist the substance of the bread and wine becomes the body and blood of Christ. Luther rejected this doctrine. He argued that Christ is actually present in the Eucharist only because of his omnipresence (presence in all places at all times). Zwingli favored what came to be called consubstantiation—a doctrine that contended that during the consecration of the Eucharist, the body and blood of Christ become present alongside the bread and wine. The controversy between Luther and Zwingli became public in 1525, and the position of each side stiffened as the years passed. In 1529 a meeting took place in Marburg in an attempt to unite the Reformed congregation. Luther and Zwingli, although still in disagreement over the issue of the Eucharist, agreed to meet with each other. The discussions failed to prevent a continued division of the movement, and Zwingli's strong influence in Zurich crossed into southwestern Germany. Zwingli died on the battlefield of Kappel in 1531 in the second of two wars between Catholics and Protestants in Switzerland.

In the mid-1520s some of Zwingli's followers broke ranks and formed yet another confession within Protestantism, the Anabaptists. The Anabaptists contended that Zwingli and other major Reformers were not serious enough in their efforts to restore true Christianity. They argued that these Reformers and others had failed to go far enough to promote a personal commitment to follow Christ, which for the Anabaptists was made manifest in the act of adult baptism. Anabaptists opposed the Catholic Church's practice of infant baptism, a practice few other Reformers quarreled with. Anabaptists believed that church membership should be entirely voluntary and that only in adulthood could one come to the knowledge and experience to make the choice to be baptized into Christ.

John Calvin

A third major division of Protestantism was developed by a French lawyer named John Calvin. In 1536 Calvin published his creed of Reformation in the Institutes of the Christian Religion, a work that he revised and expanded a number of times over the years. As he began

ANABAPTISTS

The Anabaptists formed a major division within the Reformation movement. Their name, derived from a Greek word meaning "rebaptizer," indicates the fundamental assertion of the Anabaptists: that baptism should not be performed in infancy but rather in adulthood, as a symbol of the individual's decision to devote him or herself to Christianity. Anabaptists emphasized a personal commitment to follow Christ. They also viewed the church as a voluntary group of believers and wanted it to be separate from the political realm.

It is difficult to trace the exact origin of Anabaptism, but it appears that in the mid-1520s some Reformers, of diverse views, felt that the pace of religious reform was not fast enough. The Anabaptist movement spread through central Europe primarily via lay preachers who developed small congregations. The Anabaptists were considered by many religious and secular groups to be dangerously revolutionary. As a result, there grew up a a pattern of persecution that forced the Anabaptists underground; nevertheless, the Anabaptists experienced a widespread expansion, albeit a clandestine one.

A more open Anabaptist movement arose in the German town of Münster in the early 1530s. In 1534 Jan van Leyden, an Anabaptist leader, declared himself king of Münster and dubbed the town the New Jerusalem. His requirement that men practice polygamy (the taking of multiple wives simultaneously) quickly prompted both Catholics and Protestants to besiege the city until its fall in the spring of 1535. Given that fears that religious dissent might escalate into political revolution seemed to have been justified, attempts to completely suppress the Anabaptists increased.

A Dutch priest named Menno Simons became the leader of the Anabaptist movement around 1536, at its lowest point. Concluding that the existing structures of the church were sound, Simons urged the Anabaptists to adapt to the unfavorable political situation. He encouraged his followers to practice a quiet Christianity that was divorced from active political involvement. Simons emphasized earlier teachings of Anabaptism such as nonviolence and withdrawal from society. His homeland, the Netherlands, became the center of the Anabaptist movement, along with Switzerland.

disseminating his ideas for reform throughout Paris, his life was threatened. His French followers (known as Huguenots) experienced repression at the hands of the Catholic majority, and Calvin fled France. He eventually settled in Geneva, Switzerland, but was expelled from the city in 1538 because of a conflict with civic authorities. He was allowed to return three years later and spent the remainder of his life there.

In 1536 Calvin established a school dedicated to religious reform called the Academy of Geneva. Like many other Reformers, he heeded Luther's advice to study the Bible. Calvin's interpretation of the Bible led him to adopt the notion that God is omnipotent (all-powerful), omniscient (all-knowing), and omnipresent. He concluded that because of these characteristics, God not only knows the past and the present but also the future. Calvin believed fundamentally that a man does not possess free will and that his destiny—salvation or damnation—is predetermined by God; this belief is known as predestination. Calvin's view was the antithesis of the Catholic doctrine that salvation is available to all;

◀ This woodcut, titled Executed Anabaptists, was published in 1536 to commemorate the end of the fifteen-month reign of the Anabaptists in Münster. Three key leaders of the movement are suspended in cages in the tower of Münster's Lamberti Church.

one need only live by God's law and seek his grace for it to be granted.

Calvin set out to reform not just the church but all of society. Other Reformers came to Geneva to study at his academy and returned home to spread the movement. Calvinist doctrine took root throughout Europe. Switzerland remained its stronghold, but it also spread to France, the German Rhineland, the Netherlands, Scotland, and even England (in the form of Puritanism).

The English Reformation

King Henry VIII of England spoke out in defense of the Catholic Church at the start of the Reformation, and Pope Leo X declared Henry Defender of the Faith for his efforts. However, the king's orthodoxy soon succumbed to dynastic needs. Henry sought from the church an annulment of his marriage to Catherine of Aragon, who had failed to produce a male heir to inherit his kingdom. In 1533, after Pope Clement VII definitively declined Henry's petitions, the king

▶ This unattributed painting depicting John Calvin at age twenty-seven was completed in 1536, the year that Calvin arrived in Geneva after fleeing persecution in France.

◀ *This unattributed fresco, painted around 1580 on a wall in the Oratorio San Rocco in Seregno, near Milan, depicts Carlo Borromeo, who helped his uncle, Pope Pius IV, plan and oversee the Council of Trent. Borromeo, a key figure in the Counter-Reformation, was canonized in 1610.*

THE CATHOLIC COUNTER-REFORMATION

The Catholic response to the Reformation, commonly referred to as the Counter-Reformation, was instituted by the Roman Catholic Church as a reaction to the Protestant Reformation and culminated with the Council of Trent. In 1534 Pope Paul III appointed a commission of cardinals to examine the need for institutional but not doctrinal reforms. The Council of Trent subsequently met in three sessions between 1545 and 1563. It upheld the basic structure of the church, especially its sacramental system and doctrine, both of which had been so strongly criticized by the Protestant Reformers. The council also responded to two key challenges made by Reformers. First, it reaffirmed the creed of salvation by faith and good deeds. (Luther argued that salvation was not attained by redemption and grace but by faith alone.) Second, the council upheld the transubstantiation of the Holy Eucharist. The Roman Catholic Church contended that during the celebration of the Holy Eucharist, the bread and wine "substantially" became the body and blood of Christ. Luther believed that the body of Christ was physically present in the elements because he is omnipresent.

The Catholic Counter-Reformation was both retaliatory and reformist. The council retaliated against Protestantism by defending the fundamental doctrines of the church that had been attacked by Luther and other Reformers. It also set out to reform the administrative system of the church—even Pope Leo X recognized that the church suffered from corruption and organizational deficiencies. Many parish priests, especially in rural areas, were not well educated; few could speak Latin, and they had little opportunity for theological education. The council took steps to remedy this situation. It also introduced measures to improve the discipline of church officials and the bureaucratic system of administration. The appointment of bishops as a political favor was no longer tolerated. For centuries the church had garnered wide landholdings throughout Europe, and many bishops functioned more as land regulators than as clerics serving their parish. This problem of absenteeism was now addressed. In Italy, Carlo Borromeo (1538–1584), the archbishop of Milan, set the standard by visiting even the most remote parishes in his archdiocese.

In 1542 Pope Paul IV instituted the Inquisition, which included the censorship of prohibited books, and commissioned the first publication of an Index of Forbidden Books in 1559. Heretics were burned at the stake, and a stricter emphasis was placed on canon law. The Counter-Reformation's stress on devotion to Christ led to an individualistic approach to religious experience, as exemplified by the Catholic recitation of the rosary, which is intended to bring the individual closer to the Holy Trinity. This movement did strengthen the faith of Roman Catholics, but it came almost thirty years after the posting of the Ninety-five Theses, too late to prevent a breakup of the Western church.

A portrait of King Henry VIII by Hans Holbein the Younger (c. 1497–1543). Once Henry declared himself the head of the church in England, pro-Reformation forces soon gained the upper hand.

the age of sixteen. Initially the new Anglican Church did not differ greatly from the Catholic Church in liturgical and doctrinal matters. One key liturgical change came in 1549, when under Cranmer's leadership, the Book of Common Prayer was issued.

Henry's second daughter, Elizabeth, came to the throne in 1558. Her half sister, Mary (reigned 1553–1558), had worked tirelessly to restore Catholicism in England, but by the time of Elizabeth's accession, the Protestant movement had gained significant support. Elizabeth managed to achieve an uneasy settlement between Catholics and Protestants that would allow the two sides to coexist, although the country leaned toward Protestantism; this settlement is known as the Elizabethan Compromise.

Within just one year of the Elizabethan Compromise, strong opposition to the settlement emerged from a group that believed it did not lean far enough toward Protestantism. The critics argued that the Anglican Church retained too many remnants of the Catholic Church, especially the use of images in worship, which they considered idolatrous. They wanted the new church to be "purified" of all Catholic tendencies and hence soon became known as Puritans. On the mainland of Europe, the religious situation had stablized by the end of the sixteenth century. In England, however, the Puritan movement remained a powerful, separate Protestant force whose members believed that the Anglican Church had not effectively reformed itself. Thus, there were two forms of Protestantism in England: Anglicanism and Puritanism.

Final Stages of the Reformation

By the mid-sixteenth century Lutheranism dominated northern Europe. In eastern Europe weak kings ruled disconnected territories and were unable to control Reformist tendencies; in this region some very radical Protestant sects developed. Calvinism had taken root in Switzerland, as well as in France, Scotland, the German Rhineland, and other areas, although it typically existed under a different name in each place. The English Reformation was more political than religious in origin, but Anglicanism had spawned Puritanism, a true Protestant sect. Spain and Italy

got Parliament to pass the Act in Restraint of Appeals to Rome, which effectively separated England from the Catholic Church. The Anglican Church was established as the official church, with the English monarch as its head. Henry then ordered the archbishop of Canterbury, Thomas Cranmer, to annul the marriage to Catherine.

Henry married six times and eventually did produce a male heir. Upon the king's death in 1547, Henry's son by his third wife, Jane Seymour, took the throne as Edward VI. Only ten years old at his coronation, Edward died at

Ignatius of Loyola   1491–1556

The Counter-Reformation rejuvenated the Catholic Church. One of the greatest leaders of this effort of renewal and reform was Ignatius of Loyola, who founded the Society of Jesus. Ignatius was born in Guipúzcoa, Spain, in 1491. His mother died when he was seven years old. At age sixteen he was sent to serve as page to Juan Velázquez of Castile. In 1521 he became a soldier in the Spanish army and fought against the French in defense of the city of Pamplona. During the conflict Ignatius was injured in the leg by a cannonball; rather than take him prisoner, French soldiers carried him to his home in Loyola to recuperate. His fractured leg was reset at least twice but never healed properly, and Ignatius walked with a limp for the remainder of his days.

During his convalescence, Ignatius requested reading materials and was provided with books that discussed the lives of Jesus and the saints. Ignatius had been a free-living man but now was induced to contemplate the importance of imitating the lives of the saints. He decided that his mission was the conversion of non-Christians in the Holy Land. This task would prove difficult, however, because of renewed conflict between the Christians and Muslims in Jerusalem.

Ignatius visited the Dominican monastery at Montserrat in 1522 and soon after decided to devote his life to the service of God. He entered the University of Paris in 1528, where he studied literature and theology for over seven years. In that city, on August 15, 1534, Ignatius and his six key followers founded the Society of Jesus, commonly known as the Jesuits, "to enter upon hospital and missionary work in Jerusalem, or to go without questioning wherever the pope might direct." They were admitted to the priesthood in 1537 by Pope Paul III, and the seven men set out to preach and perform charitable work throughout Italy. (The state of war between the Ottoman Empire and Western Christian forces made journeying to Jerusalem impossible.) Paul III gave official approval to the Society of Jesus in 1540 but limited its membership to sixty; this restriction was lifted three years later by a new papal bull.

Ignatius became the first superior general of the Jesuits, and his missionaries traveled around Europe to establish schools, colleges, and seminaries—training colleges for Jesuit priests. His book, *Spiritual Exercises*, printed in 1548, acknowledges that intellect and emotions work together to aid understanding of the action of the Holy Spirit in people's daily lives. The fundamental teaching of Ignatius centered on the principle that all actions should be performed for the greater glory of God.

The Jesuits contributed significantly to the success of the Catholic Counter-Reformation. Ignatius died in Rome on March 12, 1556, and was canonized in 1622.

▲ *This painting of Saint Ignatius of Loyola was created by the Mexican artist Juan Correa in the seventeenth century. The words displayed on the book he is holding are the motto of the Jesuit order and translate as "to the greater glory of God."*

remained the last bastions of Catholic orthodoxy in Europe and became the centers of the Counter-Reformation.

As was stated earlier, Protestants view the Reformation as a return to biblical Christianity, while Catholics see it as a revolt against truth, motivated by secularism. The two primary doctrinal differences concerned the principles of authority and salvation. Catholics contend that authority comes from the Bible and the church, while Protestants contend that the Bible alone is authoritative. Catholics believe that salvation is attained through God's grace and the performance of good deeds, while Protestants claim that grace alone is necessary for salvation. These differences, along with Rome's failure to respond promptly to Luther's challenge, brought about the continuing fragmentation of the Western church.

FURTHER READING

Elton, G. R. *Reformation Europe, 1517–1559.* Cleveland, 1963.

Hillerbrand, Hans J. *The World of the Reformation.* New York, 1973.

Lindsay, Thomas M. *A History of the Reformation.* 2 vols. New York, 1906–1907.

Lortz, Joseph. *The Reformation in Germany.* New York, 1968.

MacCulloch, Diarmaid. *The Reformation: A History.* New York, 2003.

New, John F. H. *The Renaissance and Reformation: A Short History.* New York, 1977.

Brian A. Carriere

SEE ALSO

• Augsburg, Peace of • Calvinism • Charles V
• Church of England • Clement VII • Elizabeth I
• Erasmus, Desiderius • Established Churches
• Henry VIII • Humanism and Learning
• Leo X • Lutheranism • Printing • Thirty Years War
• Trent, Council of

THE PEACE OF AUGSBURG, 1555

Lutheranism was officially outlawed by the Diet of Worms in 1521. By the end of the decade, the Holy Roman emperor Charles V sent official word to all German cities that Roman Catholicism would be restored. Many cities and princes protested this mandate, which conversely had the effect of strengthening the Protestant Reformation. A military alliance of Lutherans known as the Schmalkaldic League came into existence. In response the Catholic League was formed to defend the church from Protestantism. The Lutherans went to war with the emperor's Catholic forces for more than two decades, and eventually Charles was forced to negotiate. He agreed to hold a diet to settle the controversial issue of the coexistence of two separate churches. The diet, which was not convened until 1555, was held in the city of Augsburg, in southern Germany. On September 25, 1555, Charles signed a peace agreement with the Schmalkaldic League and officially acknowledged the tolerance of Lutheranism in the Holy Roman Empire. The Augsburg settlement contained some provisos, however. First, Anabaptists and Calvinists were not given the same freedoms within the Holy Roman Empire as Lutherans. Calvinists were not granted equality until almost a century later, upon the adoption of the Treaty of Westphalia. Second, although Lutheranism was tolerated, the settlement embodied the policy called *cuius regio, eius religio:* the religion of the local prince would determine the religion of the province. Those in a given locale who practiced a different religion were allowed a grace period to organize their affairs and relocate without penalty. Whatever the other ramifications of this religious settlement, it virtually guaranteed that the German-speaking lands would continue long to exist as a great mass of tiny states. The nationalism strongly evident elsewhere in western Europe became a force in Germany only in the nineteenth century. Nevertheless, the Peace of Augsburg, marking as it does the legal acceptance of Protestantism, can be credited with bringing stability at a time of tumult.

Religious Orders

WITHIN CHRISTIANITY, A RELIGIOUS
ORDER IS A COMMUNITY OF MEN OR
WOMEN DEVOTED TO THE SERVICE OF
GOD AND OF THE FAITH.

Commitment to a full and intense religious life has featured in all major religions. The founder and inspiration of Christianity, Jesus Christ, urged upon his followers a complete conversion to the lifestyle and values of the gospel. When the Roman emperor Constantine converted to Christianity in the fourth century, he brought peace to the church and an end to the persecution of Christians. In this new era martrydom—hitherto the most heroic act for Christians—was no longer a frequent occurrence, and so other forms of dedication were sought. Around that time, Paul of Thebes, Anthony, and Pachomius became well known as hermits, and the latter two also as founders of monasteries in Egypt. In Asia Minor, Basil of Caesarea (c. 329–379) wrote a rule for the monasteries he founded that has remained the basic code of conduct for monasticism in the Orthodox Church ever since. In the West, Saint Benedict (c. 480–540) was the father figure. The rule he wrote for monks living in community, or "religious life" as it came to be called, exercised great and lasting influence and inspired a range of religious commitments. Further developments occurred in the thirteenth century with the establishment of religious orders of friars. The best known were the Franciscans and Dominicans, founded by Saint Francis of Assisi and Saint Dominic, respectively; important too were the Augustinians and Carmelites. Friars led an active life, in contrast to the more contemplative lifestyle of monks, and were directly concerned with the salvation of their neighbors.

By 1300, therefore, Europe contained a wide range of male religious orders, each with its own lifestyle and mission. There were similar developments for women, although on a smaller scale. The Benedictine nuns, inspired by Saint Scholastica, sister of Saint Benedict, and the Poor Clares, founded by Clare of Assisi, friend of Saint Francis, were two major orders of women. Clergy and laity often criticized members of religious orders, both male and female, for failing to live up to their high ideals. In the fourteenth and fifteenth centuries these complaints became increasingly vocal.

Impact of the Reformation

Religious orders were a prime target of attack during the Reformation. Martin Luther, the first and most important architect of the movement, launched a sweeping rejection of them. He denounced the orders as human inventions, without foundation in the Bible, and as glaring examples of the way the Catholic Church had departed from God's will. There was a personal dimension to Luther's opposition. Having himself been an Augustinian friar, he had left his monastery and quite soon afterward married a former nun, Katharina von Bora.

▼ In this painting by Benedetto Veli (1564–1639), Saint Francis of Assisi eats a meal with Saint Clare, while cherubs hover above the diners.

▲ *This illustration, from a manuscript known as the Ellesmere Chaucer, dating from the early 1400s, depicts the prioress in Chaucer's* Canterbury Tales. *A polite and sprightly lady, she is one of the main characters in the book and the teller of a story.*

In all the countries where the Reformation took root, religious orders were suppressed, and their properties confiscated and sold. Along with the religious implications of this change, massive social upheaval followed because the members of religious orders were numerous—probably between a quarter and a half million people out of a total population in western and central Europe of around 60 million in 1500. In addition, the orders owned much property—the fine buildings of their own monasteries and friaries and, according to estimates, up to a third of the land in some countries—and they were engaged in many social and educational enterprises. In England the dissolution of religious houses was carried out on the orders of King Henry VIII (reigned 1509–1547) with remarkable speed and surprisingly little resistance.

Attitudes Underlying Suppression

In the years before the Reformation, monks, friars, and nuns sometimes served as figures of fun for Geoffrey Chaucer and other writers. Frequently caricatured were those who departed

---

CHAUCER'S MONK, FRIAR, AND TWO NUNS

Geoffrey Chaucer wrote *The Canterbury Tales* in stages between 1387 and his death in 1400. In the prologue his biting portraits of the monk and the friar are among the best-known critiques of the alleged decline of religious orders before the Reformation. The monk was "a leader of the fashions; inspecting farms and hunting were his passions." The rule of Benedict, which he was meant to follow, "as old and strict he tended to ignore … and followed the new world's more spacious way." He despised the saying "that a monk out of his cloister is like a fish out of water, flapping on the pier." A worldly man and a glutton, "he enjoyed a fat swan best and roasted whole."

The friar was "a wanton one and merry … a very festive fellow." In all the orders of friars, "there was none so mellow as he in flattery and dalliant speech.… He knew the taverns well in every town and every innkeeper and barmaid too." Though vowed to a poor life, he had nothing to do with "slum and gutter dwellers, but mixed only with the rich and merchants." A crafty and devious man, "he lisped a little out of wantonness to make his English sweet upon his tongue."

In the stories told by the pilgrims, the friar fares badly in "The Summoner's Tale" and in "The Friar's Tale" (which he narrates himself), and the monk little better in "The Monk's Tale." Chaucer had traveled and read widely: he spent time in France and Italy and knew well the literature of both countries. His portrayals of the monk and the friar in *The Canterbury Tales* may be regarded as criticisms of religious orders throughout Europe, not just in England. His remarks are similar in tone to comments in other popular works of the thirteenth and fourteenth centuries, including Giovanni Boccaccio's *Decameron* (c. 1350) and the *Roman de la rose* (between c. 1237 and 1280), written by the Frenchmen Guillaume de Lorris and Jean de Meun.

Chaucer seems less critical of the two nuns. The prioress—the title given to a nun in authority within her convent—is polite and sprightly. The favorable portrait of her, however, is marred by the character of the tale she tells: that of Jews killing a Christian boy and of savage punishments meted out to the perpetrators. The other nun's personality is not developed, and her tale of the "chaste marriage" between Saint Cecilia and a pagan knight is typical of Chaucer's refined ambiguity.

from the high ideals of their religious orders. Writers tended to mix criticism and drama to enliven their stories. The general public had a robust sense of humor; so the caricatures may appear harsher to modern observers than they would have to contemporaries. Many young men and women continued to join religious orders, and there was widespread support for their doing so.

The Reformation brought a more sustained and principled attack on the ideals and motivation of religious orders—but again, it is important to see how principle and personality are intertwined. Many of the leaders of the Reformation, not Luther alone, had been priests or members of religious orders. Coming from within the clerical establishment, as it were, their rejection of the world to which they had once belonged was often particularly sharp. No interpretation of events should overlook this highly charged personal and psychological context.

In countries where the Reformation took root, there were people who profited from the suppression of religious orders, principally those who acquired the lands and houses that had once belonged to the orders. Beneficiaries of suppression clearly did not want the religious orders to be restored. They had an interest in accepting and promoting a negative image of religious orders that antedated the Reformation in order to justify the suppression of the institutions and their own acquisition of the orders' properties. A clear example of this situation may be seen in England after Henry VIII's dissolution of the monasteries (between 1536 and 1540).

An additional force was in play. Even among Catholics, especially after about 1550, there was some readiness to portray religious orders in existence before the Reformation in a poor light. Catholics had to attempt to explain the remarkable success of the Reformation without providing justifications for it.

▲ *The remains of Rievaulx Abbey in Yorkshire, northern England. This Cistercian monastery was dissolved by Henry VIII in 1538; the buildings were pulled down, and the stone plundered for other construction projects.*

In this painting by Carlo Maratti (1625–1713), the Virgin Mary and the child Jesus, accompanied by Saints Peter and Paul, appear to Saint Philip Neri in prayer. Philip's humble familiarity with Jesus and the three saints is highlighted. The content and exuberant style of the painting are representative of Counter-Reformation art.

One argument was that, though church doctrine and teaching remained untainted during the Middle Ages, the constantly growing failure of clergy and laity alike to practice what the church preached explained why many people welcomed the Reformation. The decadent state of religious orders was regarded as one of the prime examples of moral slippage. Such a line of argument, moreover, was attractive to those who championed the new religious orders of the Counter-Reformation, especially the Society of Jesus (the Jesuits). A settled body of belief and interpretation concerning the Reformation and the Counter-Reformation came to characterize Catholic thought for four centuries. Still, the new orders, however justified their creation, encountered some hostility within the church. Some came to believe, rightly or wrongly, that the older orders —Benedictines, Franciscans, Dominicans, and others—had performed inadequately in the late Middle Ages and let down the church. Hence, the foundation of new orders, to address new problems, was necessary.

Religious Orders in the Counter-Reformation

After the initial sweeping advances of the Reformation, the Catholic Church slowly began to regain confidence. The resulting movement—traditionally called the Counter-Reformation—gathered momentum; it lasted from around 1530 to 1650. Religious orders played a central role in the movement. In most male religious orders during this period, the majority of members were priests or young men preparing for the priesthood, and much of the work, accordingly, was of a priestly nature.

Two of the earliest new religious orders for men were the Theatines and Barnabites, founded in 1524 and 1530, respectively. The former order took its name from one of its four founders, Gian Pietro Carafa, who was bishop of Chieti (Theate, in Latin), an Italian town; he later became Pope Paul IV. The latter took its name from the Church of Saint Barnabas in Milan, which was the first church run by the order (it remained the order's mother house). Both orders emphasized austerity of life and the importance of work—in education, parochial care, and missionary activity. Both spread beyond Italy to various countries of Catholic Europe; the Theatines also established communities in India and other countries of Asia.

The Oratorians emerged from the group of priests gathered around Philip Neri (1515–1595), an energetic and charismatic Roman priest. The name derives from the oratory (a place of prayer) next to the church in Rome where the group assembled for prayer and other spiritual activities. With Philip Neri as its founder and guiding figure, the order received papal approval in 1575. The houses of the order, called oratories, were established mainly in the larger

Francis Xavier   1506–1552

Like Ignatius, Francis Xavier also came from Loyola, in the Basque region of Spain. He attended the University of Paris, where he was known as a popular student and an athlete. Xavier came under the influence of Ignatius—a fellow student though considerably older—and was eventually led by him to a more committed and religious way of life. Xavier was one of the seven founder members of the Society of Jesus, and he became Ignatius's closest friend. In 1541 he left Europe, initially at the invitation of the king of Portugal, and embarked upon missionary journeys to various places in modern-day India, Sri Lanka, Malaysia, Indonesia, and Japan. He died on his way to mainland China. Remarkable are both the extent of his journeys and the number of people who converted to Christianity through his efforts—an estimated 700,000. Xavier was a vigorous preacher, inventive in his methods of evangelization, and his organization of new converts into Christian communities produced lasting results. After his death he was soon recognized as one of the most outstanding Christian missionaries of all time.

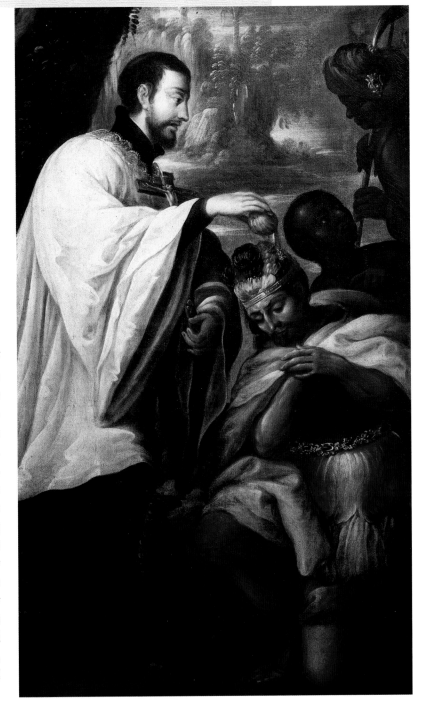

▼ *This painting by the Mexican artist Juan Rodriguez Juarez (1657–1728) portrays Saint Francis Xavier baptizing an Indian man. No other missionary ever had Xavier's success at converting non-Western peoples.*

cities of Europe and in a few cities in the Americas. A principal aim was to offer an intelligent and attractive type of Christianity to the citizens that incorporated engaging church services, with special attention to preaching and music; hearing of confessions; and group meetings for prayer, talks, and discussion. Some Oratorians became important scholars, notably Cardinal Cesare Baronio (1538–1607), the church historian. Pierre de Bérulle (1575–1629), founder and head of the influential oratory in Paris, became well known as a preacher, spiritual writer, and counselor. The order played a notable and distinctive role in the renewal of Catholic life in the Counter-Reformation.

The Jesuits

The best known and largest of the new orders of men was the Society of Jesus, whose members were called Jesuits. Ignatius of Loyola was the founder of the order, and Francis Xavier its best-known early member. Both were declared saints of the Catholic Church by Pope Gregory XV in 1622. Ignatius, the son of the lord of Loyola in the Basque region of Spain, became a soldier in 1521. After being seriously wounded during a siege, he underwent a conversion during his long convalescence. As his faith deepened, Ignatius subsequently undertook a series of religiously inspired wanderings, including a pilgrimage to Jerusalem, followed by several years of study for the priesthood at Paris University. In Paris a group of like-minded men gathered round him, and together they formed the order, which was officially approved by Pope Paul III in 1540.

This painting by Matteo Loves (flourished 1615–1633) portrays Alfonso III, who abdicated as duke of Modena to become a Capuchin friar.

thing depended on God and work as if everything depended on us." Therefore work became an important focus for Jesuits, notably in the field of education, and they established a network of schools and universities throughout Catholic Europe and beyond. Their pupils came largely from the middle and upper classes and subsequently exercised great influence in many walks of life. The philosopher René Descartes (1596–1650) was a pupil at La Flèche, the prestigious Jesuit school near Angers, in western France.

Jesuits worked as preachers, counselors, writers, and scholars and were active as missionaries both in Catholic and Protestant Europe and in the parts of America, Africa, and Asia recently discovered by Europeans. Roberto de Nobili (1577–1656) in India and Matteo Ricci (1552–1610) in China were persistent and inventive in their efforts at enculturation—their goal was to enable people of these countries and cultures to feel at home in the way they lived as Christians and expressed their Christianity. Martyrs such as Edmund Campion (1540–1581) and some thirty others in Britain and the six French Jesuits and their two lay assistants who were put to death in North America between 1642 and 1649—and many more elsewhere—proved the dedication of members of the order. Opponents accused the Jesuits of being too close to the wealthy and powerful. The Jesuits responded that all their work was done in accord with the motto of their order, *Ad maiorem Dei gloriam* (AMDG), "to God's greater glory."

Ignatius was elected head of the Jesuits by the other members, and he spent the last sixteen years of his life in Rome guiding and governing the order. He wrote and revised *Constitutions*—a rule for the new order—as well as *Spiritual Exercises,* a guide to living a good life in harmony with God's will that was based on his own experiences of religious conversion; the guide had great influence within and beyond the Jesuit order.

The Jesuit order expanded rapidly in numbers and influence, growing to some 8,500 members in 1600 and nearly 20,000 in 1700. Ignatius's principle was that "we should pray as if every-

Capuchins and Carmelites

Most of the older religious orders underwent varying degrees of reform during the Counter-Reformation. The most dramatic were the reforms among Franciscans and Carmelites. The Capuchin order—the name comes from the *capuche* (pointed hood) that forms part of the Capuchin habit—was founded by Matteo da Bascio (c. 1495–1552), an Italian Franciscan friar who sought to return to the primitive simplicity of Saint Francis of Assisi. Failing to achieve the desired reform among the Franciscans, he established the Capuchins as a separate religious order in 1528. The Capuchins were enthusiastic in preaching and missionary work and gained much popular support; they became a potent force in the Counter-Reformation.

Two remarkable Spaniards, Teresa of Ávila (1515–1582) and her disciple, John of the Cross, initiated reform of the Carmelites, the religious orders for men and women that had been founded in the thirteenth century. Teresa became a Carmelite nun at the age of twenty, but after some years she felt the call to adopt a stricter way of life and to found a house where the original rule of the order would be better observed. As a result, despite strong opposition, she founded a reformed convent in the town of Ávila in 1562. Much of the rest of her life was devoted to establishing other convents for a new and reformed order of Carmelite nuns. At the same time Teresa devoted herself to long hours of prayer, during which she experienced the closeness and friendship of God in an exceptional way. She wrote down her experiences in a series of works that continue to be widely read and have made her one of the most important mystics and authorities on prayer in the Christian tradition. The works include her autobiography, *The Way of*

John of the Cross   1542–1591

John of the Cross was born of a noble yet impoverished family of Toledo, in central Spain. Brought up by his widowed mother, he went to a school for the poor and was apprenticed to a silk weaver. John was unsuccessful at his trade and left to study at a Jesuit college. He became a Carmelite friar in 1563, studied at Salamanca University, and was ordained as a priest in 1567. He came to know Teresa of Ávila and, dissatisfied with the laxity of his order, tried to introduce her reforms to the Carmelite friars. He met with much opposition and was imprisoned for almost a year in a monastery, from which he managed to escape. Soon afterward the reformed Carmelite friars were established as a separate religious order. John's sufferings continued. He had disagreements with some members of the new order, who deprived him of his posts of responsibility and banished him to Ubeda, in the province of Andalusia, where he died after a severe illness, virtually in exile from the order. John wrote some beautiful and very influential works on prayer, many of them in the form of poetry, which, like the works of Teresa, were published as books only after his death. John's writings include *Ascent of Mount Carmel,* in which he describes the "dark night of the soul" through which a person intent on God must normally pass; other works are *Spiritual Canticle* and *Living Flame of Love.*

Perfection (written for her nuns), *Foundations,* and perhaps most popular, *The Interior Castle.* All of these works were written in stages and published as books after her death.

◀ This oil on canvas of Teresa of Ávila was executed in 1576 at the insistence of her religious superiors, who wished to preserve a likeness of her. Teresa, then sixty-one, is reported to have wryly told the painter, a friar known as Juan de la Miseria (c. 1526–1616), "May God forgive you, Brother Juan, you've made me a bleary-eyed old hag." The Latin words on the banner above Teresa's head mean "I shall sing the Lord's mercies forever."

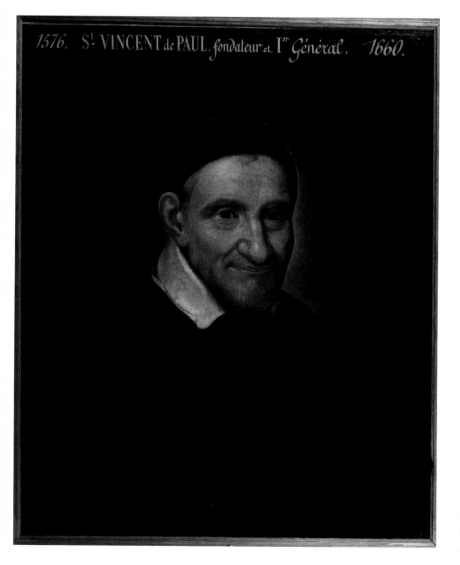

▼ A seventeenth-century oil-on-canvas portrait by Simon François depicting Vincent de Paul; notable for his extensive charity work, Vincent was canonized in 1737.

1576. St. VINCENT de PAUL, fondateur et 1er Général. 1660.

The two orders of reformed Carmelites, for men and for women, spread to most countries of Catholic Europe. Missionary activity was important to the movement, and a number of houses, or carmels as they were called, were founded outside Europe. Individual and contemplative prayer lay at the heart of the daily life of the reformed Carmelites. Indeed, the order may be said to have added a new dimension to prayer and spiritual life within the Catholic Church.

Seventeenth Century

Throughout the seventeenth century religious orders continued to play an important role in the Catholic Church. There was growth in the orders founded in the sixteenth century, the further reform of some medieval orders, and the foundation of new ones. Two of the new orders were founded by Vincent de Paul (1581–1660). Ordained a priest as a young man, he was captured soon afterward by pirates and spent two years as a slave in Tunisia. He managed to escape and return to France, where he came under the influence of the Oratorian priest Pierre de Bérulle. Vincent de Paul resolved to devote his life to works of charity. Among his many activities, he founded the Congregation of the Mission, sometimes called the Vincentians, to provide preachers who would give missions—involving sermons, the sacraments of confession and the Eucharist, and material help—in parishes, especially in country districts, and to help with the education of the clergy. Later, together with Louise de Marillac, he founded the Sisters of Charity, whose main work was to care for the sick and the poor. Their way of life proved attractive to young women who desired to serve God and their neighbors.

Third Orders

In addition to their two main branches—monks and friars for men, and nuns for women—most religious orders in the Middle Ages had an additional branch, a third order (a term still in use). This third order was established for lay men and women who wanted to share in the life and ideals of the order while maintaining a family and pursuing a normal secular occupation. Those who committed themselves to this way of life were called tertiaries of the order.

Most of these third orders survived in Catholic countries throughout the Counter-Reformation, and some of the best-known saints belonged to them. Isabel de Flores (1586–1617), called Rose, lived all her life in Lima, Peru, and became a member of the third order of Dominicans. She was specially noted for her austere way of life and her acceptance of sufferings, which resulted from illness, alienation from her family and friends, inner desolation, and various other trials. Pope Clement XI declared Rose of Lima a saint in 1671. Many religious orders founded during the Counter-Reformation followed a similar pattern and established either a third order or some other form of association with the primary order.

Conclusions

All the religious orders, whether new or old, experienced difficulties during the Renaissance and Reformation. For example, Bernardino Ochino, the head of the Capuchins, abandoned his religious order in 1541 and became a Lutheran. Many lesser-known individuals and institutions had similar stories. Hostility toward the Jesuits on the part of Catholic rulers and some politicians led to the suppression of the order by Pope Clement XIV in 1773 (the order was revived in 1814). In general, however, religious orders were remarkable for their energy and creativity and for their faithfulness to the Catholic Church. Their influence extended to most areas of Catholic Europe through their religious activities and their work in communities. Although religious orders were a feature of the Catholic Church alone, their role was paralleled by the commitment of many individuals and groups in the churches of the Reformation.

▲ In this painting by Carlo Cignani (1628–1724), Rose of Lima, who is receiving the crown of sainthood from the Blessed Virgin Mary, is permitted to hold the infant Jesus as a heavenly reward for her sufferings and penitential life.

FURTHER READING
Bangert, William. *A History of the Society of Jesus.* Saint Louis, 1972.
Farmer, David, ed. *The Oxford Dictionary of Saints.* 5th ed. Oxford, 2004.
Littlehales, Margaret. *Mary Ward: Pilgrim and Mystic 1585–1645.* London, 1998.
Mullett, Michael. *The Catholic Reformation.* New York, 1999.
New Catholic Encyclopedia. 2nd ed. Various articles on religious orders. Detroit, MI, 2003.

Norman Tanner

SEE ALSO

• Boccaccio, Giovanni • Descartes, René
• Education • Henry VIII • Trent, Council of
• Universities

Rembrandt

A MASTER OF PORTRAITURE, HISTORY PAINTING, AND ETCHING, THE DUTCH ARTIST REMBRANDT VAN RIJN (1606–1669) STROVE ABOVE ALL TO CAPTURE THE INNER EMOTIONAL LIFE OF HIS SUBJECTS.

Rembrandt Harmenszoon van Rijn was born on July 15, 1606, in the city of Leiden, in the south-western Netherlands. His father was a miller, and his mother came from a family of bakers. The family lived comfortably, but the choice to remain Catholic in the Protestant city of Leiden was nevertheless a brave one. Rembrandt must have exhibited an intellectual bent from an early age, for he was sent to the nearby Latin school and then attended the University of Leiden. His scholarly career was short lived; by 1619 he was studying with the Catholic painter Jacob Isaacszoon van Swanenburg (1571–1638). From van Swanenburg, Rembrandt probably absorbed the basic technical skills required of a painter (including draftsmanship and the handling of pigments), but he appears to have borrowed little from his teacher's personal style. More influential on the young artist's development was the Amsterdam painter Pieter Lastman (1538–1633), with whom Rembrandt studied for six months from late 1623. An extremely successful artist, Lastman specialized in history paintings. Lastman was heavily influenced by contemporary Italian painting, both in his choice of subjects and in his use of chiaroscuro (strong contrasts between light and dark) to heighten the dramatic effect of his compositions. Rembrandt's

▶ In this early example from his many painted self-portraits, Rembrandt already displays the innovative brushwork and use of dramatic lighting that will become the hallmarks of his work.

Young Man Playing the Lute *(c. 1630), an oil on panel, is typical of Jan Lievens work, whose hallmarks are strong, light, nearly life-size figures and obvious gestures. In contrast, Rembrandt's shadowy works have a distinctive air of mystery.*

brief time with Lastman had a significant impact on the young artist. Upon Rembrandt's return to Leiden in 1624, Lastman's influence was strengthened by the friendship between Rembrandt and Lastman's student Jan Lievens (1607–1674).

The Leiden Period

By choosing to study with Pieter Lastman, Rembrandt displayed from his youth a desire to achieve fame and financial success as an artist; history painters were far more highly respected and better paid than those who painted the numerous genre scenes, still lifes, and landscapes that adorned the walls of Dutch townhouses. In his earliest known works, Rembrandt borrowed frequently from the works of other artists. From Lastman, Rembrandt obtained a sense of monumentality (even when painting on a small scale) and a careful attention to historical details of costume and setting. The German Italianate painter Adam Elsheimer (1578–1610), etchings of whose works Rembrandt undoubtedly knew, stimulated Rembrandt's interest in dramatic lighting and emotive gestures and facial expressions. Finally, the Dutch Caravaggisti, a group of painters from Utrecht who specialized in the dramatic lighting popularized by the Italian painter Caravaggio (Michelangelo Merisi; 1573–1610), provided further impetus for Rembrandt's fascination with the endless visual possibilities of subtle contrasts between light and shadow.

Similar influences surfaced in the work of Jan Lievens; indeed, by 1628 the two painters appear to have shared a studio. The careers of Jan Lievens and Rembrandt were extremely closely intertwined in the late 1620s; in fact, the precise attribution of certain works of the period has proved extremely difficult. Both painters seemed destined for great things, according to the Dutch humanist Constantijn Huygens (1596–1687), who praised their skills in his autobiography of around 1630 and singled out Rembrandt for the emotion and mystery conveyed even within the smallest of his works.

Jan Lievens 1607–1674

Jan Lievens was born in the Dutch city of Leiden, where he studied with the painter Joris van Schooten from 1616 to 1618. In the next two years he trained in Amsterdam with Pieter Lastman before returning to Leiden, where he shared a studio with Rembrandt. (Some scholars believe that Rembrandt went to Amsterdam to study with Lastman because Lastman had taught Lievens, alongside whom Rembrandt was working in Leiden.) Lievens may well have introduced Rembrandt to the work of the Utrecht Caravaggisti. Lievens worked in Leiden in close connection with Rembrandt until the former left to work in England (1632–1634) and Antwerp (1635–1644). When he returned to the Netherlands, he settled in Amsterdam; his painting style was greatly affected by the Flemish baroque works of Peter Paul Rubens (1577–1640) and Anthony Van Dyck (1599–1641). Though his finances and personal life were often precarious as he grew older, he continued to receive important artistic commissions. His best-known works, often portraits, date from his time in Leiden with Rembrandt.

Rembrandt's ability to capture the complex inner workings of the human psyche—its emotions, motivations, and uncertainties—separates Rembrandt from Lievens, from his contemporary fellow Dutch painters, and from virtually all painters since. This psychological component of Rembrandt's work is found not only in his early history paintings, such as the *Stoning of Saint Stephen* (1625) and *Judas Returning the Thirty Pieces of Silver* (1629), but also in the many studies of heads—often referred to as portraits of Rembrandt's family members—drawn or painted throughout his career.

Early Success in Amsterdam

In 1632 Lievens left Leiden for England, after which he settled in Antwerp. By July, Rembrandt had moved to Amsterdam, where he resided in the house of Hendrick van Uylenburgh, a successful art dealer. Over the next few years Rembrandt received numerous commissions for group and individual portraits, and there is little doubt that the painter relished his status as a highly sought after artist. The earliest major commission he received was for a group portrait, known as the *Anatomy Lesson of Doctor Tulp*.

Dated 1632, the portrait is revolutionary in its ingenious composition; Rembrandt has carefully portrayed the features of each figure while at the same time subordinating each within a composition centered on the activity that provided the initial impetus for the portrait's commission. The concentration and interior thought processes displayed by each of the figures listening to Doctor Tulp can also be seen in Rembrandt's individual portraits. Rembrandt does not need to rely on a specific activity to achieve the naturalistic depiction of an animated, intelligent subject; he can achieve this end through lighting, careful brushwork, and subtle facial expressions and gestures.

Around this time Rembrandt met his first wife, Saskia, an orphaned cousin of Hendrick van Uylenburgh. They married in 1634, and despite the early death of three of their four children, Rembrandt and Saskia were happy in their life together. With Rembrandt's work in great demand by the major artistic patrons of the day, the family's financial and social standing steadily improved throughout the late 1630s. Rembrandt's perception of himself as a painter on a par with internationally acclaimed artists, such as the Fleming Peter Paul Rubens, is best

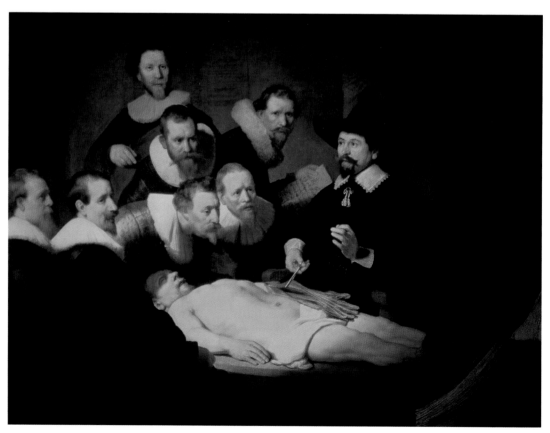

▶ This group portrait, The Anatomy Lesson of Doctor Tulp, depicts Dr. Nicolaes Tulp demonstrating the anatomy of the left arm and hand of a cadaver. Tulp stands alone on the right side of the composition, his hat the only obvious demarcation of his importance. Two figures, those at the far left and the top, appear to have been added later.

During Saskia's final illness and death, Rembrandt was at work on one of his best-known paintings, a group portrait commissioned to hang in the militia headquarters in Amsterdam. Now measuring 11.8 by 14.4 feet (3.6 by 4.4 meters)—it was cropped in 1715—this vast canvas originally adorned a large hall along with a number of life-size group portraits by several of Rembrandt's contemporaries. The painting has been known as *The Night Watch* since before 1800, despite the fact that it is daylight that illuminates the scene. The central figure is Captain Frans Banning Cocq, and his importance is underscored by his position at the central crossing of two compositional diagonals: the first begins at the upper left with the flag and continues through Cocq's red sash and the shadow of his outstretched left hand; the second follows the line of heads to the right of Cocq (echoed by a raised spear) and terminates in the leg to Cocq's right. The glowing ocher of the costume worn by Cocq's lieutenant is echoed by the luminous girl in the left background, a device that adds depth to the painting; Cocq's strongly foreshortened left hand and the halberd (a weapon used by foot soldiers) held in his right hand act as similar *repoussoirs*—items that emphasize the projected space between the painted scene and the viewer. The spatial depth, variety of activity, and unified composition are all remarkable within a work of this size and complexity. Full of carefully portrayed individual figures, the painting is essentially conceived not as a group portrait but as a history painting. The narrative portrayed, however, appears to be Rembrandt's creation; the contents of the conversation between Captain Banning Cocq and his lieutenant, as well as the identity and actions of the highlighted girl to their left, are left to the imagination of the viewer.

◄ The Night Watch, *painted by Rembrandt in 1642. The popular name of this celebrated painting, which hangs in Amsterdam's Rijksmuseum, stems from the coat of dark varnish that covered it until the 1940s. An apter title might be "The Company of Captain Frans Banning Cocq."*

exhibited in his works of this period; he frequently reproduced subjects and compositions made popular by Italian masters, including Raphael and Titian, and painted works on a large scale, as did other (Catholic) baroque painters. The five paintings of the Passion of Christ that he completed for the Dutch stadtholder (province governor) Frederick Hendrick by 1639 are among his best-known works from this period. Although Rembrandt was certainly influenced by the large, bold canvases of the Italianate baroque style, his essential artistic genius remained purely his own. His personal style was always at odds with the tastes of the typical Dutch patron, and his limited palette and insistence on the minute exploration of the huge range of human emotions always present in his works could render them at times unpalatable even to the most dedicated patron of the high baroque style. By 1640 Rembrandt's popularity was waning.

Personal Tragedy and Artistic Maturity

In 1640 Rembrandt's mother, Neeltje, died. The birth in the following year of Rembrandt's son Titus was largely overshadowed by Saskia's death, probably from tuberculosis, in June 1642. For the following decade financial difficulties and complex personal entanglements plagued the bereaved Rembrandt. He also had to care for his young son. Shortly after the 1640s, Rembrandt exhibited a growing fascination with the inner life of his subjects. Gradually abandoning the obvious trappings of wealth and status—and thus going against the tide of Dutch artistic taste of the period—he forsook a broad palette of colors for muted browns, golds, and neutral tints. His handling of pigments was increasingly bold; he often applied them with his palette knife in a technique known as impasto, which adds texture to the surface of a painting and a sense of movement to its composition.

By this point Rembrandt had radically reduced the dramatic effects of chiaroscuro and developed instead a technique that emphasized the subtle and ever-changing shifts between light and shadow, in effect, depicting the world as the eye sees it; he created volume and set moods not with line or color or bold shading, but by the subtlest modulation of tones in shifting light. This optical realism is a key element of Rembrandt's style and can be seen as the external equivalent of Rembrandt's relentless efforts to reveal the complex interior lives of his figures. Rembrandt continued to draw a wide variety of subjects; he

▲ In Self-Portrait Leaning on a Sill, *an oil on canvas from 1640, Rembrandt's costume and stance display his familiarity with portraiture of the Italian Renaissance.*

REMBRANDT'S SELF-PORTRAITS

Rembrandt painted his own image many times. Some self-portraits are quick sketches, others are large paintings, but all display a similar approach to Rembrandt's physical features and his state of mind. Rembrandt, always seeking to portray the truth as he experienced it, used himself as a representative of humanity. He emerged from the in-depth study a wiser and more compassionate man. His self-portraits often have a touch of irony about them, as if Rembrandt never lost sight of the transitory nature of life; he learned that youth, happiness, and security are more often a temporary gift of circumstance than a lasting state of being, as *Self-Portrait, Leaning on a Sill* of 1640 demonstrates. Based on portraits by the Renaissance masters Raphael and Titian, Rembrandt's image shows the artist dressed as a wealthy man of some standing, but his somewhat tentative facial expression (highlighted to give it prominence) belies the self-assuredness that his pose and costume imply. Nearly twenty years later, in Rembrandt's *Self-Portrait at the Age of Fifty-Two*, the contrast between his mastery of technique and his beleaguered expression is even more pronounced; here the artist exhibits unease with the external trappings of success, a subtle acknowledgment of the reality of his life at this time.

now treated those subjects, however, with such individualism as to deny them an obvious place within the established categories of Dutch painting. His *Holy Family with Curtain* (1646), for example, is much closer in essence to a contemporary genre scene than to the biblical history paintings that might be suggested by its subject. Although he is now acclaimed for his artistic genius, at the time, his works appealed to only a few dedicated collectors. Important commissions—both public and private—became increasingly rare.

While Rembrandt's idiosyncratic style certainly affected the marketability of his paintings, his drawings and etchings remained extremely popular. His etching *Christ Healing the Sick* (known as the *Hundred Guilder Print*) was completed at the end of the 1640s and, as its later name implies, was intended to improve Rembrandt's disastrous financial situation. In this scene, which is drawn from Saint Matthew's

Gospel, Rembrandt has achieved a superb unity of composition, technique, and content. The standing figure of Christ, dramatically lit and with rays of light emanating from his head, forms a central anchor for the whole composition. The sick—crawling and bent double—hobble in from the murky gloom to Christ's left, while the healed, fully upright, can be seen at his right hand. Rembrandt has used light and shadow to great effect here: as the sick creep closer to their healer, they emerge from the gloom and are seen in greatest detail at the moment they are healed. They subsequently become so filled with the divine spirit—represented here as light—that they, like the enlightened Pharisees who accompany them, lose much of their corporeality and appear as lacking in detail and substance as those shadowy figures awaiting the healing touch of the Christ figure. God's healing love has brought these people from physical, spiritual, and literal darkness into the light.

▲ *This etching,* Christ Healing the Sick, *displays Rembrandt's mastery of technique. Note in particular the effective use of shading and the careful attention to detail.*

Toward the end of his life, Rembrandt presented a refined version of the composition he used in 1632 in his group portrait with Dr. Tulp. In this later work, called The Syndics of the Clothmakers' Guild, Rembrandt paints the figures as if seen from slightly below (perhaps to underscore the notion that one should look up to these men), and he uses the covered table in the foreground to exclude the viewer from the space occupied by the painted figures.

Bowed but never broken by the tribulations of his middle years, Rembrandt retained his fertile artistic imagination and painted prolifically until his death in 1669. By the 1650s Rembrandt had a new, common-law wife, Hendrickje Stoffels (c. 1625–1663), who bore him a daughter, Cornelia, in 1654. His reputation was more secure than his finances. A number of patrons still avidly collected his works, but Rembrandt received few commissions, and so in 1656 he was forced to declare bankruptcy and sell many of his works at auction. Perhaps the vicissitudes of life added to his creativity; Rembrandt certainly remained undaunted by personal tragedy, and his artistic abilities appear to have been greatly enriched by his struggles.

Although the essential elements of Rembrandt's style were in place from very early in his career, they were refined immeasurably as he reached old age; his later works are far more rarefied than the works of his youth. Instead of vivid emotions and high drama, he examined moments of introspection and subtly conflicting feelings. He found grandeur in the mundane. With a stroke of his brush, he reduced a grand biblical hero to an everyday human struggling with complex emotions or invested a young girl leaning on a window sill with the quiet dignity of a refined gentlewoman. His style grew less detailed, more impressionistic, and yet better able to convey the world both as it is seen through the eyes and lived within the heart and mind. His palette was reduced even further—often to the darker earth tones alone—for Rembrandt could see such a wealth of variation within a single color that he had little need of the full spectrum so crucial to the works of other painters. (It is important to note, however, that the "muddy" browns often seen in his works—particularly in the backgrounds—have darkened with age and

▼ *The original title of this work, now called* The Jewish Bride, *is unknown, and scholars have long debated the identities of the two figures. Whether they are a contemporary Jewish couple—perhaps Rembrandt's friends or neighbors—or Old Testament figures, such as Isaac and Rebecca, the couple's deep love is apparent in every aspect of Rembrandt's composition.*

would originally have been treated with the same delicate modulation that is evident in the foregrounds.)

Some of Rembrandt's best-known works were painted during his final years, among them *The Jewish Bride* (c. 1662) and the *Return of the Prodigal Son* (1668–1669). Rembrandt's lifelong obsession with portraiture remained; *Titus at His Desk* (1655) and *Hendrickje at a Window* (1656–1657) are familiar to all admirers of Rembrandt's work. The group portrait, to which Rembrandt had brought such originality earlier in his career, continued to interest him; in the *Syndics of the Clothmakers' Guild (De Staalmeesters)*, painted in 1662, Rembrandt refined the composition he had used for *The Anatomy Lesson of Doctor Tulp* thirty years earlier. In the later work each of the figures is fully integrated into the composition, and the slightly labored use of a corpse to draw the attention of Doctor Tulp's students is replaced by the clever suggestion of a focus outside the painting and within the real world of the viewer.

A year after this painting was completed, Hendrickje died, followed in 1668 by Rembrandt's son, Titus. Rembrandt himself died on October 4, 1669. His final self-portrait, from the last year of his life, is painted with the masterful economy of color and brushwork always present in his work. The artist one sees in this portrait is humble and careworn but with an animated presence and a brutal honesty that makes his an unforgettable face.

FURTHER READING

Blankert, Albert. *Rembrandt: A Genius and His Impact.* Zwolle, Netherlands, 1997.

Schwartz, Gary. *Rembrandt: His Life, His Paintings.* New York, 1991.

Wetering, Ernst van de. *Rembrandt: The Painter at Work.* Berkeley, CA, 2000.

Caroline S. Hull

SEE ALSO

• Caravaggio • Painting and Sculpture • Raphael
• Rubens, Peter Paul

Renaissance

THE RENAISSANCE WAS THE CENTRAL EVENT OF EUROPEAN HISTORY FROM ROUGHLY 1400 TO 1620. TRULY A CULTURAL REBIRTH, IT PRODUCED AN UNPRECEDENTED FLOWERING OF ART, LEARNING, AND LITERATURE.

Renaissance means "rebirth," and a rebirth is what some Italians saw happening in their own time in the late fourteenth and early fifteenth centuries. A series of events marked the beginning of the Renaissance. Around 1350 the writer and humanist Petrarch (1304–1374) strongly criticized medieval learning and habits of mind. As a better alternative, he urged his readers to adopt the ideals and literature of ancient Greece and Rome as models to emulate. By 1450 numerous Italian intellectuals had come to agree with Petrarch's criticism of medieval learning and supported a classical revival. The result of this revival was an intellectual movement called humanism, which dominated the education, scholarship, ethical ideas, and public discourse of the Renaissance. Italian humanism spread to the rest of Europe in the late fifteenth and early sixteenth centuries. The invention of movable type in the 1450s by Johannes Gutenberg (1390/1400–1468) helped spread new ideas and made the break with the Middle Ages sharper. The availability of large numbers of printed books had a huge impact on practically every area of life, especially intellectual and religious life.

Next, a series of major developments in northern Europe between 1450 and 1500 changed the continent's politics. Spain, France, and England emerged as powerful monarchies in the late fifteenth century. Their wars with each other and interventions in the affairs of smaller states dominated the European scene for the following century and a half. These intellectual, social, and political changes combined to produce the Renaissance and make it a period markedly different from the Middle Ages.

Humanism

Humanism, the defining intellectual movement of the Renaissance, was based on the belief that the literary, scientific, and philosophical works of ancient Greece and Rome provided the best guides for learning and living. Humanists also looked to the New Testament and early Christian authors, rather than to medieval theologians, for spiritual advice. The study of grammar, rhetoric, poetry, history, and

► In 1468 the sculptor Antonio Rossellino (1427–1479) created this marble bust of the Florentine officeholder and scholar Matteo Palmieri, who believed that a new age was beginning.

The three magi (wise men) adore the infant Jesus in this painting, the Adoration of the Magi (c. 1482) by the Italian Sandro Botticelli. Note the many figures in contemporary Renaissance clothes.

moral philosophy, all derived from or based on the reading of the standard authors of classical Rome and, to a lesser extent, Greece, became the foundation of humanist scholarship. These humanistic studies were soon adopted as the preferred curriculum in schools across Europe. Indeed, education founded on the classics lasted far beyond the Renaissance and still shapes liberal arts education in modern times.

However, Renaissance humanism involved more than skill in Latin and the reading of Cicero and Virgil, the two favorite ancient authors of the Renaissance. Humanists tried to teach the principles of living a moral, responsible, and successful life on this earth. The movement was not antireligious; rather, ancient secular learning was meant to supplement, not supplant, Christian beliefs and morality.

Humanism embodied a sharply critical attitude toward received values and institutions, especially those that failed to live up to humanist principles. Renaissance men and women studied ancient Rome and Greece to acquire the chronological perspective and intellectual tools to analyze, criticize, and change their own world. Once the humanist habit of critical appraisal was well developed, the focus shifted to the present. Humanists found fault with contemporary art, government, philosophy, and approaches to religion inherited from the Middle Ages. Bolstered

Europeans were well aware that they were embarking on a new era and witnessing a cultural rebirth. In the 1430s Matteo Palmieri (1406–1475), a Florentine public office holder and scholar, wrote about the new age of the Renaissance. He lamented the cultural barrenness of the Middle Ages and praised the dawn of a new age in his own time:

[As for the Middle Ages] of letters and liberal studies at large it were best to be silent altogether. For these … have been lost to mankind for 800 years and more. It is only in our own day that men dare to boast that they see the dawn of better things. … Now, indeed, may every thoughtful spirit thank God that it has been permitted to him to be born in this new age, so full of hope and promise.

Quoted in William Harrison Woodward, *Studies in Education during the Age of the Renaissance, 1400–1600*

Jacob Burckhardt   1818–1897

The modern historian who did the most to focus attention on the Renaissance, Jacob Burckhardt was born in Basel, Switzerland, and studied at the University of Berlin, in Germany, with some of the most illustrious historians of his day; he later returned home to teach history and art history at the University of Basel for the rest of his life. A man of great curiosity and learning, Burckhardt studied and lectured on topics ranging from the ancient world to his own time. In 1860 he published (in German) *The Civilization of the Renaissance in Italy: An Essay*, the most influential book on the Italian Renaissance ever written.

Burckhardt wrote not narrative history but what he called cultural history, which involved identifying the "spirit of the age," the fundamental character of a period of history. Burckhardt concluded that a whole nation in a particular age possessed a distinctive spirit. The task of the historian is to identify this spirit and to describe how it was manifested in the people and actions of the era. For Burckhardt the spirit of the Italian Renaissance from 1300 to about 1530 was individualism, and the purpose of his book was to describe how the essence of individualism manifested itself in all areas of life.

The book achieved immediate acclaim that continues to this day. However, no contemporary historian agrees with everything that Burckhardt wrote. He made the division between the Middle Ages and the Italian Renaissance too sharp, and he overemphasized the individualism, worldliness, and immorality of the Renaissance. Despite its faults, *The Civilization of the Renaissance in Italy* remains a provocative synthesis and a masterpiece of historical scholarship.

► *In this 1519 painting of Mary, the Christ child, and Saint Anne, by the German artist Albrecht Dürer, the faces are human and loving.*

by the learning and critical perspective that humanism fostered, the people of the Renaissance became original and creative.

Art and Literature

Art is undoubtedly the best-known and best-loved aspect of the Renaissance. There is almost universal admiration for the masterpieces of such painters as the German Albrecht Dürer (1471–1528) and the Italians Raphael (1483–1520) and Michelangelo (1475–1564). Their works show a restrained, classical style that combines serene beauty, bright colors, idyllic settings, and appealing human figures, including representations of Jesus, Mary, and the saints.

The people of the Renaissance had a passion for art. Kings, popes, princes, cardinals, nobles, abbots, merchants, lowborn mercenary captains, and many others commissioned works of art. Members of the middle classes and probably the

CHRONOLOGY

1511
Erasmus's *The Praise of Folly* is published.

1513
Niccolò Machiavelli writes *The Prince*.

1517
Martin Luther posts his Ninety-five Theses.

1522
Luther's German translation of the New Testament is published.

1528
Baldassare Castiglione's *The Courtier* is published.

1543
Nicolaus Copernicus publishes *On the Revolutions of the Heavenly Spheres*.

1555
The Peace of Augsburg imposes peace between Protestants and Catholics in Germany.

1558
Elizabeth I becomes queen of England.

1559
The Peace of Cateau-Cambrésis ends the Italian wars.

1606
Part 1 of Cervantes's *Don Quixote* is issued.

1611
The King James Bible appears.

◄ *This 1512 painting by Raphael portrays Mary and the Christ child with Saint Sixtus II and Saint Barbara, both of whom were martyred in the third century.*

▲ In this oil-on-canvas painting from around 1515, the great Venetian artist Titian (c. 1488–1576) depicts sacred, or divine, love (the woman clothed) and profane, or human, love—two aspects of human existence.

working classes desired small devotional images of Mary, the crucified Jesus, and patron saints. Civic leaders wanted their council halls decorated with huge murals, frescoes, and tapestries depicting great moments in the history of the city. Artists were commissioned to paint frescoes in the cells and refectories of monasteries that would inspire the inhabitants to greater devotion. Civic, dynastic, and religious leaders hired architects to erect buildings at enormous expense to beautify their city or to serve as semipublic residences. Artists, architects, and artisans met the demand by producing a great many works of art—not only paintings, sculptures, and buildings but also elegant furniture, silver and gold objects, small pieces of metalwork, table decorations, household objects, colorful ceramics, candlesticks, and priestly vestments.

The social and intellectual position of artists changed. At the beginning of the Renaissance, the artist was an anonymous craftsman who occupied a relatively low social position. He was tied to his guild, followed local artistic traditions, and produced paintings for local patrons, probably for low fees. In the course of the Renaissance, artists became self-conscious creators of original and complex works of art. They conversed with humanists and negotiated with kings and popes, who valued their services. Successful artists became wealthy and had honors heaped upon them. For example, in 1533 Emperor Charles V conferred a knighthood on the Venetian artist Titian (1488/90–1576).

The Renaissance also saw the development of vernacular languages. In 1400 the modern forms of English, French, German, Portuguese, Spanish, and other languages did not exist. People spoke and wrote a variety of what would now be called regional dialects; spelling was haphazard, and vocabularies varied from place to place. By the end of the Renaissance, most of these languages had made significant progress toward standardization. The actions of governments, the printing press, and the creation of literary masterpieces combined to produce this result.

The development of the German language was typical. German-speaking lands inherited many forms of German from the medieval period. In the fifteenth century some state governments began to use German instead of Latin for their documents and pronouncements. Hence, versions of German used by the governments of the most important states, including the East Middle Saxon dialect used by the government of the electorate of Saxony, became more influential. Next, printing encouraged writers and editors to standardize spelling and usage in order to reach a wider readership and sell more books. Most significant, Martin Luther (1483–1546) published his German translation of the Bible (New Testament in 1522; complete Bible in 1534), which had enormous diffusion. Many Germans began to imitate Luther's style, usage, and vocabulary. Since he wrote in East Middle Saxon, this version of German eventually became standard modern German. A similar

RENAISSANCE DIPLOMACY

An ambassador is an honest man sent to lie abroad for the good of his country." Thus wrote Henry Wotton (1568–1639), who served as the English ambassador to several foreign governments in 1604. While Wotton intended to be witty, his comment had some truth to it and highlighted the importance of diplomacy in the Renaissance.

The use of resident ambassadors began in the Renaissance. In the Middle Ages a king or government sent a personal representative to another ruler or government only when a specific message had to be delivered. The diplomat went to the foreign court, stayed a few days or weeks, and then returned with the response of the foreign government. Because Renaissance governments had many disputes to resolve, they needed to remain in continuous contact; so they employed resident ambassadors who lived in a foreign capital for two to three years at a time. The resident ambassador was empowered by his government to speak and negotiate on its behalf. He was always available to smooth over differences or negotiate treaties. Naturally, the ambassador tried to portray his home government in the best possible light—and therefore, he did not always tell the truth.

The resident ambassador was almost always a nobleman who had the confidence of his ruler. He usually spoke the language of his host country and tried to be on friendly terms with members of the government. Because governments recognized that resident ambassadors served useful functions, ambassadors had diplomatic immunity—they could not be arrested for minor crimes. In rare circumstances the host government might refuse to speak to the ambassador; he then had to leave and was replaced.

Resident ambassadors were expected to gather intelligence for their home government. They paid informants and spies to obtain information, such as the size of an army or the true intentions of a ruler. The resident ambassador sent one or two letters a week to his home government by diplomatic pouch, that is, mail that the officials of the host government agreed not to open. Because officials did not always keep their word, ambassadors wrote the most sensitive and important information in code. Diplomatic communication was surprisingly fast; a courier could travel between Rome and Vienna in twelve to fifteen days and from Rome to Venice in two.

Even though resident ambassadors vastly improved communications between governments in the Renaissance and played a key role in resolving disputes, they could not prevent conflict if two states were determined to go to war.

▲ *Two French ambassadors are pictured in this painting by the German artist Hans Holbein (c. 1497–1543). Richly and soberly dressed as befits their importance, they are surrounded by objects that symbolize their responsibilities, including a globe.*

process occurred elsewhere. For example, the combination of Shakespeare's genius, a series of eloquent English translations of the Bible, and the printing press created modern English.

Politics

The Renaissance presented a complex and constantly shifting political scene. There were three basic forms of government: princedoms, monarchies, and oligarchies, which were called republics during the Renaissance. Many small states were princedoms. Whether called duke, count, marquis, or signore (lord), the prince was an individual who ruled a state, usually with the support of his family. He (and occasionally she—there were some female rulers) had the authority to make decisions concerning all inhabitants of the princedom without check by representative body, constitution, or court. Nevertheless, princely power was seldom absolute. Most princes depended on some accommodation with powerful forces within the state, typically the nobility or the merchant community. A prince's power was often insecure and short lived. Many princes owed their position to the use of force, and so their heirs often found force used against them.

VS
NICOL MACCHIAVELLI

▲ *This oil-on-wood portrait of the Florentine civil servant and political writer Niccolò Machiavelli (1469–1527) was painted by an unknown artist at the end of the sixteenth century.*

political office. The members of government were always drawn from the leading merchants, manufacturers, bankers, and lawyers, some of whom claimed noble status. Italy and Germany had many republican city-states, most of them small.

Two political trends were dominant in the Renaissance. More powerful states, especially monarchies, absorbed smaller states, often through war. For example, Spain took control of the kingdom of Naples in 1504 by military force and the duchy of Milan in 1535 by treaty when the reigning duke died without an heir. In addition, some republican city-state oligarchies became princedoms when a powerful individual or family within the city took control while maintaining a facade of republican institutions and councils. The gradual transformation of the republic of Florence into a princedom ruled by members of the Medici family is the classic example. By 1600 Europe had fewer states, and the monarchies of France, Spain, and England dominated European politics, diplomacy, and war. Many writers drafted treatises explaining the intricacies of Renaissance politics. The Florentine civil servant Niccolò Machiavelli (1469–1527) wrote political masterpieces that are still read in modern times.

The End of the Renaissance

The artistic, intellectual, literary, and political Renaissance had run its course by the early seventeenth century, by which time patterns of thought, styles of art, and political policies had changed. The new patterns were not necessarily worse or better; they were merely different. The changes were the natural consequence of the continuous, restless, and natural flow of human history. The great revival of the learning of ancient Greece and Rome through humanism had been integrated into the curricula of European schools and universities. Scholars took humanism for granted and moved into new speculations. The serene, classicizing Renaissance painting of Leonardo da Vinci (1452–1519) and Raphael gave way to the dramatic and flamboyant baroque painting of the early seventeenth century—an approach that was equally fascinating but quite different.

A monarchy was a princedom sanctioned by a much longer tradition, stronger institutions, and greater claims of legitimacy for its rulers. England, France, Portugal, Scotland, and Spain were well-established monarchies. They developed laws and rules that determined the succession in advance, and the rules of succession normally prevailed. Occasionally the succession was broken through the lack of a legitimate heir, a bitter dispute within the ruling family, or foreign conquest.

A republic was a small political unit, usually a city-state, which consisted of a major city and its surrounding territory of farms and villages. Most often, a combination of a legislative body and executive committees governed a republic. Only a small number of men, typically 5 to 20 percent of the adult males in the city, could vote and hold

Although the Renaissance was a period of remarkable human achievement and great works of art, literature, political thought, and philosophy, the benefits were neither uniform nor enjoyed by all. Life was hard for the vast majority of the population, whose lives were restricted by poverty, disease, war, and a lack of political rights. The Renaissance was not a democratic age, and the improvement of living standards and the elimination of deadly diseases were far in the future. In addition, certain scholars contend that for women there was no Renaissance. They argue that women enjoyed no greater rights and freedoms than their predecessors in the Middle Ages. Although women ruled some kingdoms (Mary I and Elizabeth I of England and Isabella of Spain are examples) and more women writers achieved fame in the Renaissance than ever before, the lives of the majority of women, like those of the majority of men, were limited by laws, customs, poverty, and legal barriers.

Nevertheless, for those whose social status enabled them to take advantage of opportunities, the Renaissance was an age of remarkable personal achievement. The extraordinary number of writers, painters, scholars, philosophers, scientists, theologians, kings, queens, princes, and princesses of the Renaissance whose words and deeds remain influential in the twenty-first century testifies to the dynamism and importance of the Renaissance.

▶ This statue of a woman, who represents the art of sculpture, now sleeping because Michelangelo (1475–1564) has died, forms part of the monument to Michelangelo erected by Giorgio Vasari (1511–1574) in the Church of Santa Croce in Florence.

Art lovers may debate whether the baroque sculptor and architect Gian Lorenzo Bernini (1598–1680) was superior or inferior to the Renaissance genius Michelangelo, but for a historian the point lies elsewhere. The great age of English Renaissance literature ended with the death of William Shakespeare in 1616. Others continued to write good drama and poetry but in different styles. In politics and statecraft the beginning of the Thirty Years War (1618–1648) and the transformations of various monarchies in the first quarter of the seventeenth century

A minority of scholars argue that the Renaissance did not die a natural death but was murdered. Anticlerical scholars in Italy and some Protestant scholars elsewhere have argued that the Counter-Reformation suppressed freedom of thought and creativity in the middle of the sixteenth century. According to this view, the Catholic Church, in its fight against Protestantism, went too far and killed the Renaissance. It established the Roman Inquisition in 1542 in order to root out and convert or punish Protestants. In 1564 it issued the Tridentine Index of Forbidden Books, a list of works by Protestants and other titles judged immoral and seditious. Forbidden books could not be printed, possessed, or read. These measures, according to some scholars, suppressed innovation and created an atmosphere of fear. The trial and conviction of Galileo Galilei (1564–1642) by the Roman Inquisition in 1633 for willfully disobeying a previous command not to hold and teach the Copernican doctrine that the earth revolves around the sun is sometimes described as the climax of a campaign of repression of free thought by clerical authorities.

The condemnation of Galileo, for which the late Pope John Paul II apologized centuries later, was undoubtedly harmful to science, and the battles between Catholics and Protestants in the late Renaissance produced some suppression of freedom of inquiry on both sides of the religious divide. Nevertheless, it is an exaggeration to say that the Counter-Reformation "killed" the Renaissance. A broad Europe-wide movement and period of history involving politics, art, and learning, the Renaissance eventually ran its course.

◄ *The Porta Pia, one of the monumental gates in the old walls of the city of Rome, is named for Pope Pius IV, who commissioned it. This final architectual work by Michelangelo, erected between 1561 and 1564, is more decorative and flamboyant than most of his other creations.*

ushered in a new period in European political history. Yet despite the changes, much of the legacy of the Renaissance remains evident in the modern world.

FURTHER READING

Ferguson, Wallace K. *The Renaissance in Historical Thought: Five Centuries of Interpretation.* Boston, 1948.

Grendler, Paul F. *Schooling in Renaissance Italy: Literacy and Learning, 1300–1600.* Baltimore, 1989.

Grendler, Paul F., et al., eds. *Encyclopedia of the Renaissance.* 6 vols. New York, 1999.

Paoletti, John, and Gary Radke. *Art in Renaissance Italy.* 2nd ed. New York, 2002.

Rabil, Albert, Jr., ed. *Renaissance Humanism: Foundations, Forms, and Legacy.* 3 vols. Philadelphia, 1988.

Paul F. Grendler

SEE ALSO

• Bernini, Gian Lorenzo • England • Florence
• France • Galilei, Galileo • Humanism and Learning
• Italian City-States • Leonardo da Vinci
• Michelangelo • Petrarch • Reformation • Spain

Rome

IN 1500 RENAISSANCE ROME WAS A CENTER OF ART, ARCHITECTURE, AND LEARNING, BUT BY 1650 THE CITY'S IMPORTANCE IN EUROPEAN CULTURE AND POLITICS HAD DIMINISHED.

The landscape of Rome in 1300 was dominated by the ruins of the classical city, which literally overshadowed the agricultural town. Most of the territory within the Aurelian Walls, built in antiquity to enclose a metropolis of over a million people, was either uninhabited or used for orchards and vineyards. Of the eleven aqueducts that had carried water to the hills of ancient Rome, only one was functional, and therefore most of the city's meager population of perhaps 35,000 lived in the lowlands near the bend of the Tiber River. Along with the ruins of antiquity, the vista was punctuated by a few basilicas and by brick towers belonging to powerful noble families—private fortifications into which they and their supporters could withdraw in times of political unrest.

At the first papal jubilee, in 1300, Pope Boniface VIII (reigned 1294–1303) claimed to be emperor as well as pope, but his triumph was illusory. In 1303 a representative of the French king, Philip IV, whom Boniface was about to excommunicate, besieged the pope at his family's palace in the countryside. Supported by the troops of a Roman noble, the marquis Sciarra Colonna, Philip coerced Boniface into submission. Later that decade, under Pope Clement V (reigned 1305–1314), elected with Philip IV's strong support, the papacy moved to Avignon.

The immediate consequence for Rome was a return to unrivaled domination by local families. In 1307 the Holy Roman emperor, Henry VII, announced that he would go to Italy to restore peace and to be crowned in Rome. The coronation took place in 1312 amid warfare and chaos, and the banquet afterward was disrupted by an angry mob that pelted rocks through the windows. In 1347 Cola di Rienzo (1313–1354), a tavern keeper's son who had risen to prominence in the civic government, sought to control the barons' power by reviving the political institutions of classical Rome. Declaring himself tribune of the Roman people—an ancient title—Rienzo inspired many followers, including the humanist Petrarch. Two years later, however, the Colonna and Orsini families joined together to force Rienzo from power.

Although Gregory XI returned the papacy to Rome in 1378, upon his death that year, a schism followed, in which two and at times three rivals, each supported by a contingent of cardinals, laid claim to the papacy. The schism was eventually resolved by a church council in Constance, in modern-day Germany (1414–1418), at which the assembled bishops chose a new pope to displace all current claimants. The election of the Roman baron Oddo Colonna as Pope Martin V (reigned 1417–1431) ended the Western Schism and was a major gain for Rome; at last, a pope could reside there with the security that a base of local familial power afforded.

Government in the Fifteenth Century

The Rome to which Martin V returned the papacy in 1420 had a population of around 20,000, perhaps a third less than it had a half century earlier. The small civic government, which grandly called itself the Senate and People of Rome in accordance with classical precedent,

Although massive aqueducts, including the Aqua Claudia pictured below, towered over medieval and Renaissance Rome, only one—the Aqua Virgo—functioned until the later sixteenth century, when the restoration of others made possible the construction of large-scale public fountains, many of which have survived down to modern times.

For medieval pilgrims and visitors to Rome, the ruins of ancient buildings were objects that inspired wonder. For Renaissance humanists, by contrast, the juxtaposition of classical and contemporary structures presented an occasion for reflection. In 1337 the humanist poet and scholar Petrarch (Francesco Petrarca, 1304–1374) visited Rome. In a letter to his friend Giovanni Colonna, Petrarch recalled their walks through the city, during which he had compared the physical ruins they had seen with the descriptions of the structures that he remembered reading in classical texts. The dissonance between the two helped trigger an important shift in Petrarch's thinking: by comparing the ruins with his readings and then viewing both in the context of the inferior buildings of his own age, Petrarch became acutely aware of the vast gulf that separated his own culture from that of antiquity. Ancient culture, also viewed as distinct from what had followed, provided an alternative to the present and a model for emulation. That culture also served as a point of reference from which to examine critically the culture of his own time.

▲ The Castel Sant'Angelo was built between 135 and 139 CE as a mausoleum for Emperor Hadrian (reigned 76–138). It stands on the banks of the Tiber River by the Ponte Sant'Angelo, one of ancient Rome's most important bridges. Throughout the Middle Ages and during the Renaissance, the castle served as a refuge; Pope Clement VII sheltered there during the sack of Rome by the troops of Charles V in 1527.

was subordinate to the papacy but had some judicial powers, and it provided a forum for the aristocracy to voice its interests. The top civic officials were a senator and three conservators. The senator, a non-Roman appointed by the pope, headed the Capitoline tribunal, the foremost nonecclesiastical law court. The conservators, chosen by lot from the city's fourteen districts to serve three-month terms, oversaw the trade guilds and presided over council meetings. Even these limited functions, however, would come to be dominated by the papacy.

The economy of the Roman countryside remained underdeveloped. Land that had been drained for farming in antiquity had since returned to marshland, and the papacy found renting land for pasturage a more reliable source of income than agricultural cultivation. Rome lacked strong industry, with the exception of the building trade, which was financed by the papacy and by high clerical officials. The church's banking needs were served overwhelmingly by merchant bankers from firms based elsewhere, notably in Augsburg, Genoa, and Florence, and so profits mostly left Rome. A vital if unreliable source of income for the work of rebuilding Rome was provided by the influx of visitors, who required a range of services: more than 100,000 pilgrims visited Rome each year, the number peaking during Holy Week.

The papacy drew in revenues from its lands and dioceses throughout Europe, augmented irregularly by proceeds from the sale of church offices. Although much of this income was needed to fund and maintain the Papal States in central Italy, enough remained to finance an expanding church bureaucracy and to provide the capital for a building boom. Pope Nicholas V (reigned 1447–1455) began the rebuilding of Rome. At his instigation two new palaces were constructed on the Capitoline Hill to house the communal government, one for the senator and one for the conservators. In addition to funding the renovation of Rome's ancient churches, Pope Nicholas began to reconstruct the area around the Vatican Palace to reflect classical ideals of symmetry and rational order. Encompassing Saint Peter's Basilica as well as the Castel Sant'Angelo, a fortress built on the base of the emperor Hadrian's tomb, this region across the Tiber from the heart of classical Rome became a focal point of Roman Renaissance culture in subsequent decades. In his urban renovation projects, Nicholas drew extensively upon the expertise of the multitalented Leon Battista Alberti (1404–1472), an outstanding humanist, artist, and architect who had been active already in Rome under Nicholas's predecessor, Pope Eugenius IV (reigned 1431–1447).

The Early Renaissance

Nicholas's ideal for rebuilding Rome required not only physical renovation but also a revival of learning. The pope himself had read widely in history, philosophy, and literature and had mastered both Greek and Latin writings by the church fathers, especially Saint Augustine. In addition, he was an avid book collector. For decades the popes had employed humanists as scribes, secretaries, and bureaucrats, but only now did a pope systematically nurture their scholarly pursuits with the goal of restoring Rome's cultural prestige. Nicholas commissioned esteemed intellectuals, including Poggio Bracciolini, Guarino Guarini, and Vespasiano da Bisticci, to translate Greek classics into Latin in order to make them accessible to educated men throughout western Christendom. He employed innovative artists from Tuscany, such as Andrea del Castagno and Fra Angelico, who decorated the Vatican Palace with frescoes that drew consciously upon classical Roman precedents.

Nicholas's grand designs for Rome did, however, encounter local resistance. Stefano Porcari, a noble with a gift for oratory, led a faction of Romans intent upon establishing a republican government. Nicholas had Porcari exiled, but Porcari managed to return to Rome and lead a conspiracy intended to oust the pope and cardinals from political power and institute a republic. Although the coup failed and Porcari was executed in 1453, the incident illustrates the vitality of the Roman aristocracy, which sporadically challenged papal secular and political authority well into the sixteenth century.

◀ Painted for the private chapel of Pope Nicholas V, this fresco by Fra Angelico (1447–1449) depicts Lawrence, an early Christian saint, distributing the treasures of the church to the needy. The sanctuary interior behind him, with its twin colonnades, evokes Nicholas's contemporary restoration of the old Saint Peter's Basilica.

Consolidation and Efflorescence

▼ *At the center of this marble relief on the tomb of Pope Pius II, produced by the workshop of Andrea Bregno around 1465, is a reliquary that once supposedly contained the head of Saint Andrew, the brother of Saint Peter. Pius used the relic's arrival in Rome in 1462 as an occasion to preach a crusade against the Turks, whose territorial expansion had threatened the shrine in Greece where the head had been displayed. Pope Paul VI returned the relic to the Greek Orthodox Church in 1964.*

In the decades after the mid-fifteenth century, Rome's urban and cultural development depended substantially upon who was pope. Pius II (reigned 1458–1464) focused his energies and the papal coffers on two foreign projects: he sought to organize a crusade against the Ottoman Turks, who had taken Constantinople in 1453 and were expanding into the northeastern Mediterranean, and to rebuild his hometown in central Italy in accordance with classical architectural models and principles. Yet he also furthered the cultural agenda for Rome that Nicholas had developed. He renewed building in the Vatican, sponsored humanists' study of the classics and the writings of the church fathers, and commissioned marble statues of Saints Peter and Paul, as well as a reliquary tabernacle to house the head of Saint Andrew. Meanwhile, prominent cardinals advanced both their own reputations and Rome's renewal by commissioning the reconstruction and decoration of churches with which they were associated.

The rebuilding was given added impetus by Pope Sixtus IV (reigned 1471–1484), whose public works projects included the Ponte Sisto, a new bridge across the Tiber that linked the city center with the district of Trastevere. Particularly crucial was his alteration of church law concerning the inheritance of property. Previously, if a high-ranking cleric had used church money to build houses in Rome, upon his death that property could be confiscated. Now, such property could safely be passed on to his heirs. This ruling made the construction of lavish palaces in Rome an attractive family investment for cardinals and other leading churchmen and so contributed to the building boom.

Beyond his interest in Rome's physical and cultural development, Pope Sixtus was intent upon promoting family members in the church hierarchy and commemorating his own accomplishments. Shortly after his election, he elevated to the cardinalate two of his nephews, Pietro Riario and Giuliano della Rovere (the future Pope Julius II), and entrusted them with important diplomatic responsibilities. Among the works of art that he commissioned was a series of frescoes of his own life, painted in the years 1476 to 1480, in the Ospedale di Santo Spirito in Rome. This series appropriated the imagery of saints to narrate Sixtus's achievements. Following five frames left blank for representations of subsequent achievements, the series ended with two finished paintings, the last of which showed Saint Peter ushering Sixtus into heaven.

Like his predecessors, Pope Sixtus commissioned translations of classical texts, but his most lasting act of literary patronage was the establishment of the Vatican Library in 1475 as the public library that Nicholas V had intended it to be. His patronage of artists, too, bore lasting results, notably a fresco cycle on the walls of the Sistine Chapel that includes paintings by Sandro Botticelli, Domenico Ghirlandaio, and Pietro Perugino.

Sixtus prosecuted expensive wars in central Italy to reduce the Papal States to obedience (and thus make them reliable sources of tax income), a move with long-term benefits but immediate costs. To finance the war effort, he first sold church offices, including cardinalates, and he even created entire new divisions in the curia (the papal court) for notaries and secretaries, who had to purchase their positions. Second, he strongly promoted the sale of indulgences, and in 1476 he issued a bull (official proclamation) establishing that the efficacy of indulgences could in some cases extend to those who had already died.

Pope Alexander VI (reigned 1492–1503), from the Spanish Borgia family, continued the renovation of Rome. Cardinals and foreign sovereigns played an increasingly prominent role as patrons of lavish new buildings. Thus, in 1502 Ferdinand of Aragon and Isabella of Castile hired the architect Donato Bramante to design the Tempietto (a small circular chapel on the supposed site of the martyrdom of Saint Peter) for the Church of San Pietro in Montorio. Alexander's pontificate also encompassed more ominous foreign interventions: a French army descended into Italy in 1494, and within a decade Spanish troops followed. Rome's High Renaissance in the early sixteenth century would take place against the backdrop of a struggle for political autonomy, as France and Spain fought over control of the peninsula.

The High Renaissance

Renaissance culture in Rome reached its apogee in the early sixteenth century. Pope Julius II (reigned 1503–1513), the nephew of Sixtus IV, was keenly aware of how Rome's physical

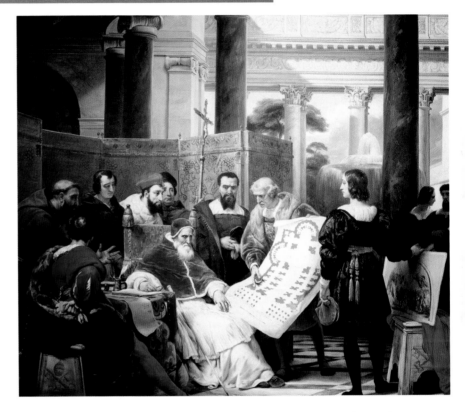

renewal would enhance his own reputation. Under Julius's patronage, Bramante began construction of the Belvedere and of the new Saint Peter's Basilica (1506), Michelangelo painted the Sistine Chapel ceiling, and the Via Giulia and the Via della Lungara were built—two roads running in parallel on either side of the Tiber River. The Via Giulia was intended to connect the Ponte Sisto to a new bridge near the Vatican, although the bridge was never built. The Via della Lungara connected the district of Trastevere with the environs of the Vatican to its north.

Together with the humanists and artists he employed, Julius envisioned Rome as the site of a new golden age. The pope, as rightful heir both to the imperial sway of classical Rome and to the ecclesiastical authority of the church, was ideally

▲ Julius II Ordering Work on the Vatican *(1827), painted on a ceiling in the Musée Charles X in the Louvre, by Émile-Jean-Horace Vernet. With the architect Bramante displaying his plan for the new Saint Peter's Basilica, the painting celebrates Pope Julius's contribution as a key patron of artistic endeavor in High Renaissance Rome.*

▲ *Pilgrims to Rome traditionally visited the seven major basilicas (Saint Paul outside the Walls, Saint Sebastian, Saint John Lateran, Santa Croce, Saint Lawrence outside the Walls, Saint Mary Major, and Saint Peter's) in a single procession that was completed in one day. Geography was thus integral to their experience of the Eternal City. This engraving of the pilgrims' tour by Bernard Picart dates to 1737.*

situated to bring Rome and Christendom into the new age. Imagery of classical and Christian precedents coalesced in a public spectacle—Julius's triumphal entry into Rome on Palm Sunday of 1507 linked him explicitly with Julius Caesar and Christ.

Both the imagery of the golden age and the rebuilding of Rome continued under Julius's successors, including Leo X (reigned 1513–1521), Clement VII (reigned 1523–1534), and Paul III (reigned 1534–1549). They sponsored substantial work on Saint Peter's Basilica and the continued rationalization of the city's street plan. Financial crises during Clement's pontificate, particularly after the sack of Rome (1527), caused delays in both projects, but they were restarted and advanced by his successor. Paul III significantly expanded the construction of urban thoroughfares; he had the fortifications of the Vatican strengthened, and the Campidoglio, the seat of the city government, was rebuilt in accordance with designs by Michelangelo. Thus, though the sack of Rome caused major short-term economic and political disruptions and undercut the optimism of the High Renaissance, the artistic, architectural, and urbanizing

program that Julius II and Leo X had fostered nonetheless continued into midcentury.

Erasmus and Luther Visit Rome

Two of the most important religious figures of the early years of the Reformation, the Dutch humanist Desiderius Erasmus (1466–1536) and the German monk Martin Luther (1483–1546), visited Rome in the High Renaissance but left with differing impressions. Erasmus, who spent much of 1509 and 1510 in Rome, remembered it fondly. Although he occasionally criticized the morals of the papal court as well as the intrusion of pagan elements into a sermon he heard there, he longed to return to the city. Three years after he left, he wrote, "Had I not torn myself from Rome, I could never have resolved to leave. There one enjoys sweet liberty, rich libraries, the charming friendship of writers and scholars, and the sight of antique monuments."

Soon after Erasmus's departure, Luther visited Rome (1510–1511). A receptive pilgrim, he marveled at the ruins, listened attentively to tour guides' stories, and on his knees he climbed the Scala Sancta ("holy steps"), a stairway said to have been brought to Rome from Pontius Pilate's court, where Jesus had ascended it; the indulgence Luther gained from this act was to obtain his grandfather's release from purgatory. At the top of the stairs, Luther expressed doubt: "Who knows if it is so?" Following his excommunication by Leo X in 1521, Luther recalled his trip in darker terms; he railed against the moral corruption of the city and the papal court and frequently cited the proverbial saying "If there is a hell, Rome is built over it."

The Ascendancy of Spain

The first half of the sixteenth century proved to be a critical time in Rome's history. Julius II and Leo X had long successfully played off the French and Spanish forces against each other and so prevented either from becoming dominant in the Italian peninsula. By the mid-1520s, however, the combined might of Spain and the Holy Roman Empire, united under Emperor Charles V, became decisive. The League of Cognac (1526), a final effort to unify various Italian polities and the French, was a failure.

Although the sack of Rome had only a limited impact on the city's economy and society, it initially gave rise to pessimism. One humanist in the service of Clement VII, who had found refuge in the Castel Sant'Angelo during the attack, wrote about Rome as follows in 1527:

That city which used to rejoice in the commerce of foreigners on account of the suitability of its location and the character and principles of its citizens, to boast of asylum for those who had suffered calamities, and to be richly ornamented with a concourse of pilgrims, and which was easily the first city over all others, now lacks its population, is afflicted with famine, and clings to no vestige of its former esteem and beauty.

Pietro Alcionio, *Oration on the Need to Restore the Republic*

The league's disorganized forces were unable to stop an imperial army from marching on Rome and sacking it on May 6, 1527.

Forced to face up to Spain's predominance, Clement VII made peace with Charles V. Thereafter, Spanish sovereigns often played a key role as defenders of Rome. Pope Paul IV (reigned 1555–1559) attempted to reverse this trend; he formed an alliance with France in the hope of driving the Spaniards from Italy. However, in 1557 an imperial army commanded by the duke of Alba encamped near Rome, and Paul had to make peace. French losses soon led to the Peace of Cateau-Cambrésis (1559). Thereafter, Spain enjoyed a unique symbiotic relationship with Rome. Spanish kings influenced the papal court and gained control over much of the church's revenue in Spain; in turn, the kings endowed religious institutions in Rome and supported the papacy militarily.

▼ *This copper engraving by Matthäus Merian (1593–1650) depicts a parody of a papal procession staged by the mercenary troops who sacked Rome in 1527. The occupying army desecrated relics, stripped gold from churches, and even imprisoned Andrea della Valle and other cardinals, freeing them only upon payment of a ransom.*

Although Spain retained influence over papal Rome well into the seventeenth century, in the 1620s the balance of power between Spain and France shifted temporarily toward the latter, and Urban VIII (reigned 1623–1644) was elevated to the papacy with the strong support of French cardinals. Following the Peace of Westphalia (1648), religion became a less significant factor in European politics, and Roman support less critical to the dynastic strategies of nation-states. Rome's civic government still retained some judicial powers, but by the late 1600s all major state officials were churchmen. Rome's noble families maintained prominence in ceremonial functions but influenced political decisions only insofar as family members held high offices in the curia.

Counter-Reformation and the Baroque Era

From the 1520s onward, despite the loss of many Western Christians to the new Protestant denominations, Rome remained the center of Catholicism. Paul III established the Roman Inquisition, and in 1545 he convened the Council of Trent (it met intermittently until 1563), which enacted doctrinal and institutional reforms. The Index of Forbidden Books, first issued in 1559, attempted to control unorthodox theological expression, but Rome remained a center of philosophical and literary creativity. Although the trial of Galileo Galilei (in 1632

▲ *Pope Urban VIII (reigned 1623–1644), depicted here in a painting by Gian Lorenzo Bernini (1598–1680), appointed members of his family (the Barberinis) to the cardinalate and other major church offices; the family used much of the wealth thus gained to patronize art and architecture. Urban's impressive achievements as patron have been overshadowed by the trial of Galileo by the Office of the Inquisition, a process that he allowed to take place.*

THE *CHINEA* AS SYMBOLIC GIFT

Following the Spanish defeat of Paul IV in 1557, Philip II designed a treaty stipulating that the pope was to recognize him as an "obedient son, and that he act toward him as an affectionate father, as he does for the other princes, and that he give to his majesty and to his subjects the same favors and gifts as to the other princes, kings, and nations." Thus, using the traditional language of feudal deference, Philip sought to secure for Spain papal recognition of its control over Naples. In exchange, he would pay the annual feudal dues of seven thousand ducats and would present as a gift a white Neapolitan horse, known as the *chinea*.

Since taking the dues and the gift horse would imply recognition of Spanish rule in Naples, Paul IV initially refused, but in time he resigned himself to accepting them. For nearly a century and a half, his successors continued the tradition. The ritual presentation would take place after the Spanish ambassador led an elaborate procession to Saint Peter's Basilica and thereby demonstrated publicly the vitality of Spain's special relationship with the papacy.

The waning of Spanish hegemony in seventeenth-century Rome would be evident, too, in this ritualized gift giving. In 1624 the Spanish ambassador anticipated presenting Pope Urban VIII with the annual tribute and the *chinea* on the feast of Saint Peter (June 29), as was the custom. The pontiff, whose sympathies lay with France, ordered that the gift be made a day earlier, to the papal treasurer rather than directly to the pope. This ceremonial affront evidently provoked a response in kind: the morning of the feast day, the *chinea*, now in papal possession, was found dead, presumably poisoned.

and 1633) sharply curtailed astronomical speculation, scholars at the Lincei and other scientific academies undertook a wide range of investigation. Meanwhile, the private collecting of manuscripts and antiquities grew ever more fashionable.

Around 1600 Rome was still attracting talented painters such as Annibale Carracci (1560–1609) and Caravaggio (1573–1610). Gian Lorenzo Bernini (1598–1680) sculpted enduring masterpieces, including the *Ecstasy of Saint Teresa* (completed in 1652) in the Church of Santa Maria della Vittoria and the *Fountain of the Four Rivers* (1651) in Piazza Navona. More critical for the topography of Rome were Bernini's architectural projects, which included the supervision of the completion of Saint Peter's Basilica and the design of the colonnade that surrounds its piazza. Another talented architect, Francesco Borromini (1599–1667), was commissioned in 1638 to build the Church of San Carlo alle Quattro Fontane, for which he later designed an imposing curved facade.

By the mid-seventeenth century Rome had been transformed from the rustic backwater in which Boniface VIII had held the first papal jubilee into a grand baroque city. The previously depopulated landscape now bustled with more than 100,000 people. Although many narrow streets survived, new thoroughfares made the city far easier to traverse. Rome was no longer as important to European culture as it had been, but the Renaissance and the Reformation had left a legacy that still retains much of its strength.

FURTHER READING

Dandelet, Thomas James. *Spanish Rome, 1500–1700.* New Haven, CT, 2001.

Hall, Marcia B., ed. *Rome.* New York, 2005.

Pastor, Ludwig. *The History of the Popes from the Close of the Middle Ages.* Vols. 1–30. St. Louis, 1923–1956.

Signorotto, Gianvittorio, and Maria Antonietta Visceglia, eds. *Court and Politics in Papal Rome, 1492–1700.* New York, 2002.

Stinger, Charles L. *The Renaissance in Rome.* Bloomington, IN, 1998.

Kenneth Gouwens

▲ The Fountain of the Four Rivers, in Piazza Navona in Rome. Anthropomorphic figures representing major rivers from four continents—the Danube, Ganges, Plate, and Nile—surround an Egyptian obelisk that Bernini incorporated into the design.

SEE ALSO

- Borgia, Lucrezia • Bramante, Donato • Caravaggio
- Christina • Clement VII • Galilei, Galileo
- Humanism and Learning • Italian Wars • Leo X
- Medicis, The • Michelangelo • Papacy • Paul V
- Petrarch • Pius II • Raphael • Reformation
- Renaissance

Rubens, Peter Paul

THE FLEMISH ARTIST PETER PAUL RUBENS (1577–1640) WAS THE MOST IMPORTANT PAINTER OF THE BAROQUE ERA. HIS LARGE, DRAMATIC CANVASES, WITH THEIR SENSUOUS FIGURES AND RICH PALETTES, BROUGHT RUBENS INTERNATIONAL FAME.

Peter Paul Rubens was the son of Jan Rubens (1530–1587), a prominent Antwerp lawyer, and his wife, Maria Pypelinckx (1537–1608). To avoid persecution for his firmly held Calvinist views, Jan fled with his family to Germany, where he became an adviser to the Protestant Princess Anna of Saxony (1544–1577). Owing to a romantic attachment between Jan and the princess (which resulted in the birth of a daughter), the Rubens family was exiled to Siegen in Westphalia (in modern-day western Germany), and it is here that the Rubens's son, Peter Paul, was born on June 28, 1577. On Jan's death in 1587, the four surviving Rubens offspring returned to Antwerp to be raised by their mother; they also returned to the Roman Catholic faith. After apprenticeships with two local painters,

Rubens's cousin Tobias Verhaecht (1561–1631) and Adam van Noort (1561–1641), Peter Paul Rubens entered the studio of Otto van Veen (1556–1629), the leading painter in Antwerp in the 1590s. Under van Veen's tutelage Rubens developed a deep appreciation of the works of the Italian Renaissance masters and their mannerist successors and a taste for the courtly lifestyle and impressive social status that the best Italian artists could now command. In May 1600 Rubens embarked on a lengthy sojourn to Italy to better his knowledge of Italian art, classical culture, and the lifestyle of the Italian painter.

Formative Years Abroad

The eight years that Rubens spent in Italy dramatically altered every aspect of his career. He traveled throughout the peninsula and copied the works of Italy's foremost artists. In Venice he became familiar with the Venetian taste for rich, expressive color, lyrical narrative, and free brushwork through seeing the works of Titian (Tiziano Vecelli; 1488/90–1576), Tintoretto (1518–1594), and their contemporaries. In Florence and Rome, Rubens encountered firsthand the ordered, geometric rationality and time-

▼ Saint George and the Dragon (1606–1607) displays all of the high drama, frenzied motion, and lavish color that are typically associated with Rubens's paintings. The free brushwork and the emphasis on a defining dramatic moment are also hallmarks of Rubens's style.

Otto van Veen ▌ 1556–1629

Though he was a native of the Dutch city of Leiden, Otto van Veen lived and worked in Flanders and is best described as a Flemish painter. The growing political tension between the Dutch and their Spanish overlords forced him to flee Leiden in 1572 for Liège in the southern Netherlands, where he studied with the Flemish painter Dominic Lampsonius (1532–1599). Van Veen's mannerist style is heavily influenced by the works of earlier Italian masters that he encountered in the late 1570s during his travels in Italy. He studied briefly with Federico Zuccari (c. 1542–1609), at that time one of Italy's best-known living painters, and returned to Antwerp in 1592 with a love of Italian culture and art that would remain with him throughout his life. Rubens entered van Veen's studio around 1595; van Veen may well have played a role in persuading Rubens to leave for Italy in 1600. Like Rubens, van Veen was fond of the courtly lifestyle and worked hard to achieve an esteemed position among noble patrons of the arts in Flanders, though his popularity waned slightly with the return of Rubens in 1608. Van Veen was also highly respected for his intellectual abilities, and toward the end of his career, he began to compile learned studies of signs and symbols, known as emblem books; the most important of these is his *Amorum emblemata (The Emblems of Love)* of 1608, which he published under the latinized version of his name, Otto Vaenius.

CHRONOLOGY

1577
Peter Paul Rubens is born on June 28 in Siegen, Westphalia.

1597
Paints his earliest surviving dated work, *Portrait of a Young Man*.

1603
Paints an equestrian portrait of the duke of Lerma at the Spanish court.

1616
Receives his first commission: a tapestry series depicting the life of Decius Mus, the legendary Roman consul.

1621
Is appointed by the infanta Isabella of Spain to help negotiate peace between Flanders and the Dutch Republic.

1628–1629
In Madrid studies the works of Titian and meets the young Diego Rodríguez de Silva Velázquez.

1631
Is knighted by Philip IV for diplomatic service to Spain.

1635
Purchases the Château Steen outside of Antwerp, where he spends most of his final years.

1640
Dies on May 30 at his house in Antwerp.

◄ The Last Supper *(1592), one of Otto van Veen's best-known works. Its classical details, circular composition, and dramatic contrasts of light and shadow all derive from Italian painting techniques of the sixteenth century.*

less classicism of the High Renaissance, as well as the refined compositions of the mannerists, with their emphasis on elegance and movement. Despite his fascination with the work of earlier Italian masters, Rubens was not uninterested in contemporary Italian painting; early baroque painters such as Annibale Carracci (1560–1609) and the revolutionary Caravaggio (1571–1610) provided tremendous stimulation for the young Fleming's developing penchant for dynamic nat-

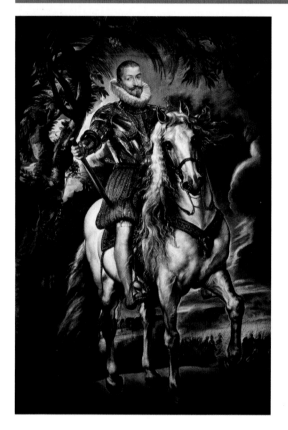

► *This portrait of Francisco Gomez de Sandoval y Rojas, entitled* The Duke of Lerma on Horseback, *was painted in 1603, just four years after Philip III of Spain gave the duke his title. This is one of a number of well-known portraits of aristocrats Rubens painted during this period.*

uralism and dramatic compositions executed on a large scale.

Once in Italy, Rubens was soon offered employment at the court of Vincenzo I Gonzaga (1562–1612), duke of Mantua. Hired to paint copies of famous Renaissance paintings and act as curator of the duke's extensive art collection, Rubens was able to experience at first hand the opulence of life at court and to benefit directly from the relatively recent elevation (in Italy, if less so in northern Europe) of the artist from skilled artisan to talented artiste. Rubens's natural affinity for his new lifestyle at court was quite exceptional. Within months he was accompanying Vincenzo on visits of state, and in 1603 Rubens undertook his first diplomatic assignment for the

duke: the delivery of a shipment of paintings to Philip III of Spain (1578–1621). Largely under the auspices of Vincenzo, Rubens traveled extensively throughout Italy and amassed an impressive collection of classical artifacts in addition to gaining a comprehensive overview of Italian painting. He traveled to Rome in 1601 to paint copies of earlier works for Vincenzo and visited for a second time in 1605, when he shared lodgings with his brother Philip Rubens, the librarian to Cardinal Ascanio Colonna (died 1608).

Around this time Rubens began to seek private commissions to supplement his irregular salary from Duke Vincenzo. His portraits of courtiers from Mantua and Genoa were highly successful, and Rubens soon gathered admirers for his own works as well as for his acclaimed copies of earlier Italian paintings. Among Rubens's best-known works from his time in Italy are the altarpiece for the newly rebuilt Roman Church of Santa Maria in Vallicella and the painting *Adoration of the Shepherds*, produced for the Oratory Church in the Marchian town of Fermo. Both works were completed by 1608.

Artistic Maturity

Rubens returned to Antwerp in 1608, shortly after the death of his mother. Determined to settle and work in his family's native city, he rapidly established himself as Antwerp's foremost painter. He met and married Isabella Brant (1591–1626), the daughter of a local merchant, in 1609. Rubens was soon overwhelmed with commissions from all over Flanders. Following the model adopted by busy Italian artists, he set up a workshop and employed a number of fully qualified artists as well as young assistants and apprentices. In 1611 he purchased an imposing

The central panel of an imposing altarpiece titled The Descent from the Cross, *this deposition scene is among Rubens's best-known works. The strong diagonal of Christ's body, his shroud, and the strongly lit women at his feet are counterbalanced by the diagonal created by the torso of the figure at the upper left and the figure clothed in red at the bottom right. Though the stark lighting and compositional devices derive from Italian painting, the attention to surfaces, notably Christ's naked body, is a feature that can be traced to Rubens's Flemish roots.*

residence on the Wapper, a street in Antwerp, which he rebuilt as a home for his family and which included a large workshop.

During the early years of his residence in Antwerp, Rubens received many commissions for religious paintings, but his output at this period was by no means confined to this genre; he produced numerous portraits and impressive scenes from ancient history and classical mythology as well. From this period date two of Rubens's best-known works: *The Raising of the Cross* (1610) and *The Descent from the Cross* (1611–1614). Rubens asserts his own strong artistic presence in both of these paintings; the complex yet subtle compositions, the lavish applications of rich color, and the sense of vitality in the numerous figures

hovering around the images of the dead Christ all betray the hand of a mature master.

Though his debt to his Italian forerunners must be acknowledged, Rubens should not be seen merely as the vehicle for the introduction of the baroque style to northern Europe. He was fully conversant with the Italian masters upon whose works the baroque style was founded, but to their legacy he brought a firm grounding in Flemish realism as well as a characteristic exuberance. His dynamism of composition, color sense, and brushwork ensure him a place among the greatest European artists.

In addition to his success at home, Rubens became increasingly popular outside Flanders. The grandeur of his Italianate style, his deeply held religious beliefs, and his sophisticated worldliness made him the darling of Catholic (and occasionally Protestant) courts throughout Europe. His monumental canvases at once embodied the religious fervor of the Counter-Reformation, the classical erudition of Italian humanism, and the opulence of the royal courts. His services, both as a painter and a diplomat, were required most by the rulers of his native

▲ This portrait of Marie de Médicis was painted by Rubens around 1622, shortly after he received the commission for a series of paintings depicting her life. Though she was known for her beauty, Marie was also a shrewd ruler, capable of manipulating even those she loved in order to retain her powerful position.

Marie de Médicis 1573–1642

Marie de Médicis was the daughter of Francesco de' Medici (1541–1587), grand duke of Tuscany. She became the second wife of Henry IV of France (Henry of Navarre; 1553–1610) in 1600 and regent for her son Louis XIII (1601–1643) after Henry's assassination in 1610. Always outspoken and willful, Marie made numerous enemies as she struggled to retain political control, among them her son Louis and her former ally and Louis's erstwhile chief adviser, Armand-Jean du Plessis, cardinal of Richelieu. After Marie's first exile from court, in 1617, she was (perhaps unwisely) readmitted to Paris, where she took up residence at the newly built Palais du Luxembourg. Early in 1622 Marie commissioned Rubens to paint two cycles of paintings to decorate her new home. One was to commemorate the life of Marie herself, the other that of her husband, Henry; in the end, only the one concerning Marie was executed. The cycle consists of twenty-four large-scale works (three portraits and twenty-one scenes from Marie's life), which Rubens and his assistants completed within three years of the commission.

Rubens had to be extremely diplomatic when designing the compositions. He needed to satisfy Marie, a very demanding patron, while not offending the king and his advisers; often locked in bitter conflict with Marie, they were themselves potentially important patrons for Rubens's work. A large number of mythological and allegorical figures populate the cycle, and though they are mostly in keeping with classical elements of baroque history painting, their use can be seen partly as a deft and ultimately successful attempt by Rubens to impress and placate Marie without angering Louis. The imposing figures of deities, the powerful messages of the allegories, and the sensual attraction of the frequently nude minor classical figures (including nymphs and muses) add a grandeur to the scenes that Marie must have appreciated, while avoiding any accurate historical observations that might have caused trouble between Rubens and the royal court. The fact that it is often these fictional characters and not Marie herself who occupy center stage in the compositions may suggest a certain distaste on Rubens's part for the whole project—or perhaps for the conceit of his patron.

Catholic Flanders, the infanta Isabella (1566–1633) and her husband, Archduke Albert (1559–1621)—the viceroys of the Spanish Netherlands—but he was also called upon by the secular and ecclesiastical rulers of France, Italy, Spain, the archduchy of Austria, Germany, and England. In Rubens's workshop, his assistants transformed his drawings and oil sketches into the vast canvasses that became his trademark. They produced literally thousands of commissioned works destined for churches, palaces, and civic buildings all over Europe. Among these works are the impressive cycle of the life of Marie de Médicis for the Palais du Luxembourg in Paris (1622–1625), the ceiling paintings for the

Banqueting Hall in London (completed in 1634), and his designs for scenes from the writings of classical authors for the Torre de la Parada, a royal hunting lodge near Madrid (this work was left unfinished at his death in 1640). Rubens's influence was felt everywhere through his own works, through the impact of his paintings on later artists, and through the works of artists such as Anthony Van Dyck (1599–1641) and Frans Snyders (1579–1657), who worked in close association with him.

Artist, Diplomat, Husband, and Father
In 1626 Isabella Brant Rubens died; the bereft Rubens was left with two young sons (the

◀ The Debarkation at Marseilles *(1622–1625), a depiction of Marie de Médicis's arrival in France, is crowded with mythological and allegorical figures, as are most of the paintings about Marie's life. While these figures add to the grandeur of the scene, Rubens may also have intended them to draw the viewer's attention away from his patroness or the French king.*

couple's only daughter had died in 1623) to care for and a large house to manage as well as a thriving career to maintain. A long-time favorite of the Spanish rulers of Flanders, Rubens had previously been entrusted with a number of diplomatic assignments, the most important of which involved an attempt to renegotiate the peace treaty between the Dutch Netherlands and the Spanish-controlled southern Netherlands in the early 1620s. After Isabella's death, perhaps in an attempt to stem his grief, Rubens undertook further diplomatic tasks, often on behalf of Philip IV of Spain (1605–1665). In 1630 he successfully concluded a treaty between Spain and England, for which he was knighted by the English king, Charles I (1600–1649).

Rubens returned to Antwerp in 1630 and married Helena Fourment (1614–1673), a girl of sixteen renowned for her beauty; Helena bore Rubens five children (the last one several months after his death) and modeled for a number of his later works. Having retired from his diplomatic duties, Rubens bought a large country house and devoted himself to his growing family. A highly organized and efficient man, he continued to paint throughout the last decade of his life. During this period he undertook a number of commissions for religious and historical works

and also painted his finest landscapes and peasant scenes, as well as a number of touching family portraits.

Rubens died on May 30, 1640, at his house in Antwerp. Toward the end of his life, his ability to work had been hampered by repeated attacks of arthritis and gout, but he appears to have remained a prolific artist despite these physical impairments. As an artist, statesman, father, and husband, he was highly respected; he exhibited a keen intelligence—one that encompassed an impressive knowledge of classical history and literature as well as fluency in five languages—and received numerous official accolades with grace and relative humility. He harnessed his huge creative energy into the establishment of an efficient business venture in a manner almost unheard of among artists of his caliber.

In purely artistic terms, Rubens was a painter's painter. His works and those in his style could be seen by young artists all over Europe and were extremely influential for the formation of many of Europe's great artists, among them his younger Spanish contemporaries Diego Rodríguez de Silva Velázquez (1599–1660) and Bartolomé Esteban Murillo (1617–1682) and such later artists as Joshua Reynolds (1723–1792) and Pierre-Auguste Renoir (1841–1919).

▶ When Rubens married his second wife, Helena Fourment, she was sixteen and already well known for her beauty. She appears in a number of Rubens's portraits, with and without their children, and also posed as a model for various figures from ancient history and mythology. This painting from around 1631 is entitled Rubens and Helena Fourment in the Garden.

Anthony Van Dyck 1599–1641

Anthony Van Dyck, a native of Antwerp, is perhaps best described as an assistant or affiliate of Rubens; he worked for some time in Rubens's workshop, but there is no evidence that he ever did so as a student. Though clearly influenced by Rubens's vivid, baroque style and the older artist's courtly aspirations, Anthony Van Dyck largely avoids the high drama and bold use of color that form the basis of Rubens's work. Instead, Van Dyck's strength lies in his ability to capture the essential character of his subject with an apparent spontaneity that is at once dignified and informal. This quality is characteristic of Van Dyck's works in general but is most obvious in the large number of portraits for which he is best known. Van Dyck's extremely free handling of paint, another departure from the slow layering of pigments and highly finished surfaces of Rubens's works, adds greatly to the animated presence of his figures. Van Dyck's portrait subjects are drawn from the nobility and intelligentsia all over Europe, though he is known in particular for his numerous images of the English royal family and courtiers from the reign of King Charles I, from whom he received a knighthood in 1632. Van Dyck's portraits had a telling influence on later portraiture in England; artists such as Peter Lely (1618–1680) and Thomas Gainsborough (1727–1788) were clearly influenced by the Flemish master.

▲ This full-length portrait by Anthony Van Dyck entitled Charles I, King of England, at the Hunt (1635) displays studied elegance combined with an informal pose, traits that characterize Van Dyck's portraiture.

In the debate over line versus color that raged in France following the foundation of the Royal Academy in 1648, Rubens's distinctive style was championed by those painters who saw the dramatic and emotive qualities of color as paramount; these painters became known as Rubenistes. (Those artists who placed the greatest emphasis on line and drawing were called Poussinistes, after the French classical painter Nicolas Poussin [1594–1665].) Rubens's immense success and sophisticated lifestyle were even envied by the Dutch master Rembrandt van Rijn (1606–1669); Rembrandt's subtly modulated palette and his endeavor to capture on canvas his subjects' inner life give his paintings a very different quality from those of Peter Paul Rubens, which are characterized by pageantry, vitality, and joyful exuberance.

FURTHER READING

Alpers, Svetlana. *The Making of Rubens.* New Haven, CT, 1995.

Feghelm, Dagmar, and Markus Kersting. *Rubens and His Women.* New York, 2005.

Held, Julius S. *Rubens and His Circle: Studies.* Princeton, NJ, 1982.

Kraftner, Johann. *Peter Paul Rubens: 1577–1640.* New York, 2005.

Caroline S. Hull

SEE ALSO

• Caravaggio • Eyck, Jan van • Jones, Inigo
• Painting and Sculpture • Rembrandt
• Velázquez, Diego Rodríguez de Silva

Schütz, Heinrich

THE WORK OF THE GERMAN COMPOSER HEINRICH SCHÜTZ (1585–1672) SPANNED THE DIVIDE BETWEEN THE RENAISSANCE AND BAROQUE MUSICAL STYLES AND MARKED A TRUE FUSION OF GERMAN AND ITALIAN INFLUENCES.

One of the most acclaimed composers of his day, Heinrich Schütz was largely forgotten until a nineteenth-century revival demonstrated that in his work the fundamental elements of German baroque style first became fully evident. A transitional figure, he played the role in Germany that Claudio Monteverdi (1567–1643) did in Italy: a bridge between old and new. Schütz was a prolific composer: more than five hundred of his compositions survive. Fourteen large collections of his music were published during his lifetime; many more works survive only in manuscript form. Schütz is known as the preeminent composer of Protestant church music of his time, partly because his music for the theater and his only opera are no longer extant.

Heinrich Schütz was born on October 8, 1585, in the small town of Köstritz, Saxony, where his father was an innkeeper. Young Heinrich became known as a singer; his reputation was so widespread that Landgrave Moritz of Hessen-Kassel came to hear Schütz perform, and in 1599 he took the boy to his court in Kassel to sing in the court choir. Schütz's parents were hesitant, fearing that music was an uncertain career choice, but their eldest son received a good classical education while in Kassel. He was undoubtedly well prepared when in 1608 he yielded to his parents' wishes and enrolled at the University of Marburg to study law.

However, Schütz did not proceed with his legal studies. He believed he had been preordained by God to be a musician, and his patron, Landgrave Moritz, agreed. Moritz offered his young protégé the exceptional opportunity of a trip to Venice to study with the renowned composer Giovanni Gabrieli. Schütz's parents reluctantly agreed, and the young musician went to Italy, where he remained from 1609 to 1612. He proved to be Gabrieli's most gifted disciple; the old master demonstrated his affection by leaving Schütz a favorite ring when he died.

Early Career and Family

While still in Venice, Schütz published a collection of five-part Italian madrigals (part-songs for several voices, typically without instrumental

◀ *This unattributed oil of Heinrich Schütz was painted when the composer was about seventy-five years old. Some of Schütz's finest music dates from this period.*

THE BAROQUE

Heinrich Schütz was one of the last important German composers to write music in the Renaissance style but also the first major figure to write in the new baroque style. One distinguishing characteristic among many of baroque choral music is that it largely abandoned the equality of voices characteristic of Renaissance music. It frequently emphasized solo lines, often highly florid, supported in counterpoint by other lines whose function was more harmonic than melodic. The baroque style was shaped by Italian musical influences; Schütz, with his Italian training, served as an ideal intermediary to spread the new style to northern Europe. Elements of the baroque are already clear in the *Psalms of David* of 1619, including the tendency toward theatricality. Schütz never completely abandoned the style of his youth, however. Even late in life he alternated freely between Renaissance and baroque forms and methods.

◀ *This 1621 copper engraving shows Elector John George I of Saxony, Schütz's employer for most of his career.*

accompaniment). Upon his return to Italy, however, the young composer did not produce any significant works for several years; it is possible that during this period he was searching for his own individual style. Schütz's time was spent productively nevertheless. In 1613 he was appointed as second organist at the Kassel court, a post Moritz created especially for him. Schütz was reputed to be one of the finest organists in Germany. Despite this honor, the period appears

to have been one of self-doubt and uncertainty, and Schütz's parents convinced their son to return to his legal studies.

If Schütz had felt unsure of his vocation, his doubts proved short lived. In 1614 the elector of Saxony, one of the great princes of Germany, "borrowed" the musician from Landgrave Moritz to help celebrate a family baptism. The elector was then reluctant to let Schütz return to his employer. Negotiations continued for some time, but early in 1617 Schütz was finally released. Back in Dresden he took a permanent position as director of music for Elector John George I (reigned 1611–1656). He held that position from 1617 until the end of his life.

Schütz's first fully mature music to receive publication was the *Psalmen Davids (Psalms of David),* a collection of twenty polyphonic settings of psalms and other biblical texts. The publication date was artificially set at June 1, 1619, at the composer's request. On that day he planned to marry Magdalena Wildeck, the eighteen-year-old daughter of a Dresden court official. Schütz sent copies of the newly published psalms out with the wedding invitations—and received a fine array of gifts in return. These short compositions established the composer's musical stature beyond question. Two of the works, settings of Psalms 98 and 100, had been performed for the centennial celebration of the Reformation on October 31, 1617. The entire collection was soon lauded throughout Protestant Germany.

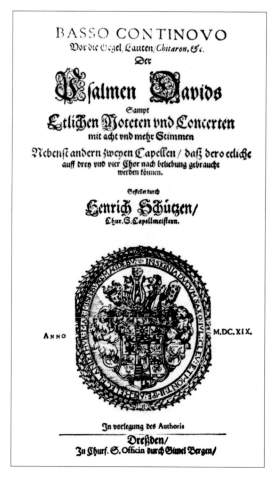

► *The title page of the* Psalms of David, *published in Dresden in 1619. Schütz composed the psalms over a period of several years.*

Schütz was less fortunate in his marriage, which lasted less than six years owing to his wife's death, probably from smallpox. Several compositions commemorate the loss, which he evidently felt deeply. Schütz never remarried, and his two daughters were raised by their maternal grandmother. Throughout his life the composer maintained close ties with his family; he demonstrated a sense of duty and integrity that won him many friends.

The Broadening of Style

Modern scholars trace Schütz's musical development by his collections of sacred music, from the *Psalms of David* to the Latin motets, collected as *Cantiones sacrae* in 1625, to the four-part harmonic settings of the German psalter in 1628. Being a court composer, however, Schütz did not have the luxury of confining himself to a single genre. He was expected to produce music for theater and court occasions. The most important of these works was his 1627 opera, the libretto of which was a German translation of Jacopo Peri's *Dafne.* The music was unfortunately destroyed in a fire in 1760.

During Schütz's second visit to Venice (1628–1629), he came under the influence of Alessandro Grandi (c. 1577–1630), who composed many works for solo voice and instrumental accompaniment. Schütz found this form very congenial.

In 1618 the Thirty Years War broke out; some of the privations extended even to court musicians. Schütz found his opportunities increasingly limited at the Dresden court; despite his pleas, his musicians' salaries were unpaid, and the grand court occasions where he could display his skills became infrequent. Consequently, in 1633 he took a post as conductor at the Danish royal court in Copenhagen, where he stayed two years (he returned for two more in 1642). Schütz's Copenhagen compositions were written for the reduced chapel of a country at war. Most notable are the *Kleine geistliche Konzerte* ("small sacred concerti"), published in 1636 and 1639. These pieces, motets for one to five solo voices and organ accompaniment, contrast with the splendor of his earlier Dresden works and the oratorios of his last years.

▲ *Heinrich Schütz's house in Weissenfels has been preserved as a historical monument.*

Final Years

In 1645 the sixty-year-old Schütz asked to retire. The Saxon elector refused (he did so again in 1651) but did permit the composer to make annual retreats to the quiet town of Weissenfels, where Schütz often spent several months at a time. Finally in 1657 the new elector, John George II, allowed Schütz to retire. The elector gave him a generous pension and the honorary title of music director of the court chapel.

Retirement did not slow Schütz's musical output. He still provided music for important occasions, although apparently he moved permanently to Weissenfels. Some of Schütz's greatest works date from his final years. These include the *Christmas Oratorio* (1664) and four passions. The latter are semidramatic polyphonic settings of the gospel accounts of Christ's suffering and death, a distinctly Lutheran musical genre normally performed during Holy Week. Schütz's *Matthew Passion* in particular is still frequently performed. It is a work of restrained intensity, filled with carefully wrought word painting to heighten the impact of the text. Especially noteworthy are the choral sections in which the crowd denies Jesus and calls for his death; they have a visceral force rare in baroque music before Bach.

The aged composer moved back to Dresden in 1670, his health already failing. He died on November 6, 1672.

FURTHER READING

Blume, Friedrich. *Protestant Church Music: A History.* New York, 1974.

Smallman, Basil. *Schütz.* New York, 2000.

Spagnoli, Gina, ed. and trans. *Letters and Documents of Heinrich Schütz, 1656–1672: An Annotated Translation.* Rochester, NY, 1992.

Phyllis G. Jestice

SEE ALSO

• Lutheranism • Monteverdi, Claudio • Music
• Thirty Years War

Science and Technology

SCIENCE AND TECHNOLOGY DEVELOPED SO SWIFTLY AND RADICALLY IN THE RENAISSANCE AND THE REFORMATION THAT THE EVENTS OF THE CENTURY AND A HALF FROM COPERNICUS TO NEWTON ARE CALLED THE SCIENTIFIC REVOLUTION.

Advances in scientific knowledge began with Renaissance scholars who radically rethought aspects of the role of human beings within nature. Scientists, theologians, philosophers, humanists, and mathematicians all participated in vigorous debates and discussions concerning the natural world. Indeed, many scholars worked in several fields of inquiry simultaneously. Later, religious discord, overseas exploration, and economic growth contributed to the ferment. Regardless of its roots, the scientific revolution marked an intellectual watershed in human history. By the late sixteenth and seventeenth centuries, scholars were applying recognizably modern scientific methods in their attempts to validate or negate the explanations of the natural world that had been proffered by their predecessors in the early Renaissance.

The Development of Scientific Inquiry

Renaissance thinkers did not generally use the term *science* (derived from the Latin word *scire*, "to know") to describe their work. Instead, they called it natural philosophy or the philosophy of nature. They defined nature as the natural world—all that was not made by human hands. With the greatly widened dissemination of ideas in printed form following the development of the printing press, some Renaissance thinkers began to call their pursuit science. Typically, the field of science was thought to include the study of astronomy and mathematics. In each of these fields of study, thinkers throughout Europe proposed, discussed, and tested theories and hypotheses. During the seventeenth century, basic scientific ideas came under constant scrutiny and revision as knowledge expanded.

Although this tradition of scientific inquiry was founded largely on the work of earlier

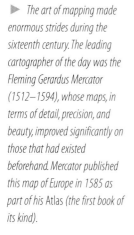

▶ The art of mapping made enormous strides during the sixteenth century. The leading cartographer of the day was the Fleming Gerardus Mercator (1512–1594), whose maps, in terms of detail, precision, and beauty, improved significantly on those that had existed beforehand. Mercator published this map of Europe in 1585 as part of his Atlas (the first book of its kind).

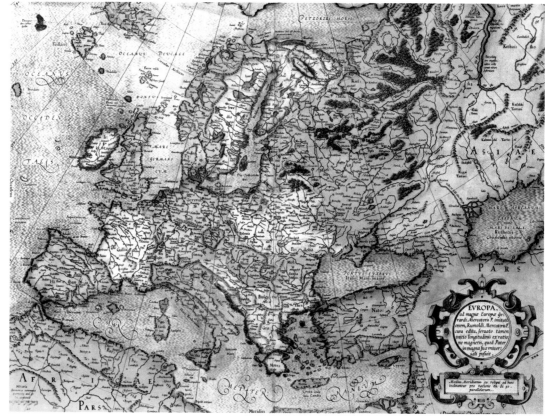

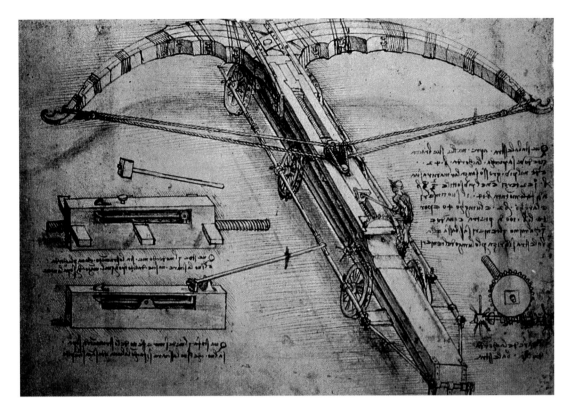

thinkers, including Aristotle, Saint Augustine, Thomas Aquinas, and Dante, Renaissance scholars attempted to break free from received wisdom. They did not just criticize the medieval worldview; they replaced it with their own. They sought to explain the world using theories based in observation, mathematics, and mechanics.

Astronomy and Cosmology

One of the earliest areas of inquiry was the grandest in its dimension: the universe and its components. Most medieval ideas grew from those of the Egyptian geographer and astronomer Claudius Ptolemy. The primary organizing principle of the Ptolemaic system placed the stars on a fixed sphere around Earth. At the center of the universe, Earth was orbited by the Moon, Sun, Mercury, Venus, Mars, and Jupiter, and then by the stars, each in its own fixed concentric sphere. It was accepted in medieval times that God organized the entire universe. In addition, Ptolemy's argument that planets moved in epicycles (uneven spheres) helped explain why planets appeared to move in one direction, stop, change directions, and then continue their journey in the original direction. The apparent phenomenon of backward, or retrograde, motion was accepted as part of Ptolemy's system.

THE CONTRIBUTION OF LEONARDO DA VINCI

Without scientific institutions, laboratories, or investigative tools, early scientists were merely individuals with inquiring minds, many of whom became skilled in the arts, writing, and science simultaneously. The best example of such a scholar was the Italian Leonardo da Vinci (1452–1519). Well known for his works of art, including the renowned *Mona Lisa,* Leonardo also personified the new era of scientific experimentation. His drawings and writings demonstrate that he pursued extensive research in human anatomy. He also sketched machines of his own devising, including a parachute, a military tank, and a flying machine. Implicit in Leonardo's work is a profound shift in the European view of the role of mankind in the world: he postulated that human experience was and should be the central concern of human beings. Through his actions and writing, Leonardo also stressed that human sensory experience, especially vision, could be trusted as a reliable tool for gathering knowledge and that by analyzing their experiences, people could begin to understand both the larger universe and the world immediately around them. Leonardo's ideas constitute a significant step forward on the road of human self-confidence.

1514
Nicolaus Copernicus first arrives at the theory of heliocentrism.

1518
The Royal College of Physicians is established.

1522
Ferdinand Magellan's voyage to circumnavigate the globe is completed.

1530–1536
Portraits of Living Plants, by the German botanist Otto Brunfels, is published.

1543
De humani corporis fabrica (On the Structure of the Human Body), by Andreas Vesalius, is published.

1551
The Collegio Romano is founded to educate Jesuits.

1569
The Flemish mapmaker Gerardus Mercator (1512–1594) publishes his cartographic projection system.

1585
The Flemish mathematician Simon Stevin proposes the use of decimals.

1604
Johannes Kepler argues that light rays diminish in intensity by the inverse square of their distance as they travel from the light source.

Few people argued with the Ptolemaic model. One significant reason was the lack of technological means to discover other models. Most observation of space had been performed with the use of an astrolabe. The principles of astrolabe projection had been known since before 150 BCE, and the instrument was introduced to Europe from Islamic Spain in the early twelfth century. Once the movable components were adjusted to a specific date and time, the entire sky, both visible and invisible, was represented on the face of the instrument. It could then be used to measure the altitude of celestial bodies. By the mid-seventeenth century other devices—the quadrant, the telescope, and finally the sextant—had begun to replace the astrolabe and with new skills of observation reinforced criticism of Ptolemy's ideas.

Copernicus and the Heliocentric Universe

Nicolaus Copernicus made a vital contribution to people's understanding of the organization of the universe. Born in Poland in 1473,

Copernicus studied mathematics at Kraków University and obtained a law degree from the University of Bologna. While in Rome in 1500, he witnessed a lunar eclipse. Through his observation of the eclipse, Copernicus determined that the sun was at the center of the cosmos and that the earth moved. He went on to challenge the geocentrism of Ptolemy's theories (the belief that the earth is the center of the universe) with his own heliocentric theory.

Primarily, the Copernican system offended the medieval sense of the order of the cosmos because it contradicted the belief that the earth was at the center of the universe. Copernicus therefore withheld his findings until 1543, the same year in which he died. Concerned that his observations and deductions should be properly understood, Copernicus made a specific appeal to mathematicians. Only they, he thought, could grasp and appreciate the simplicity and order of his system. The type of mathematical thinking that grew out of the discourse over Copernicus's ideas began the scientific revolution.

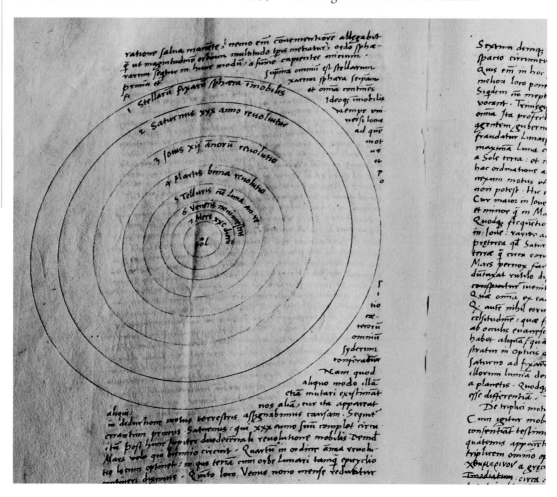

► In this drawing from De revolutionibus, *published in 1543, Nicolaus Copernicus depicts a heliocentric universe. Within a century his theories had shaken the foundations of scientific thought.*

TYCHO BRAHE'S OBSERVATORY

Tools and new instruments for research played an extremely important role in new scientific understanding. In the era prior to telescopes, one of the grandest of these innovations belonged to the astronomer Tycho Brahe (1546–1601). Uraniborg, built by Brahe between 1576 and 1580 on Ven, an island off Denmark, was the world's first astronomical and astrological observatory. Uraniborg became an early research institute that attracted students from many regions. The institute also housed equipment for alchemical research. Nearby was Brahe's subterranean Stjerneborg observatory, which he built when he found that Uraniborg was not stable enough for his precision instruments.

A contemporary of Copernicus, Brahe became convinced that Copernicus's theory of the universe was incorrect. If the earth was moving, one would expect that the alignment of the stars as viewed from the earth would vary according to the position of the planet at the time. With the equipment Brahe was using, he could not detect angular variation (the variation, known as parallax shift, can be observed with the aid of modern telescopes). In an attempt to prove that the earth was indeed the center of the universe, Brahe cataloged a vast number of astronomical observations and calculations. These tables of calculations formed the best astronomical observations produced anywhere in the world at this time. Ironically, Brahe's observations became the basis for proving that the Copernican system was accurate.

Even though it was impossible for Brahe to see a star's parallax shift with his unaided eye, he used rigorous methods to test his ideas, a crucial element in the development of science. Brahe had royal support for his endeavors. However, when he lost the support of King Christian IV of Denmark in the 1590s, he abandoned his work on Ven, and ultimately both Uraniborg and Stjerneborg were destroyed.

CHRONOLOGY

1616
An injunction is issued warning Galileo Galilei not to advance the heliocentric theory as fact.

1626
Francis Bacon publishes the *New Atlantis*, a utopian fantasy that envisions technologically advanced societies.

1628
William Harvey's *Exercitatio anatomica de motu cordis et sanguinis in animalibus (An Anatomical Exercise concerning the Motion of the Heart and Blood in Animals)* is published.

1633
Galileo is called before the Inquisition in Rome.

1662
René Descartes's *Treatise on Man*, wherein he argues that human anatomy and physiology follow mechanical principles, is published posthumously.

1687
Isaac Newton completes the *Principia mathematica*.

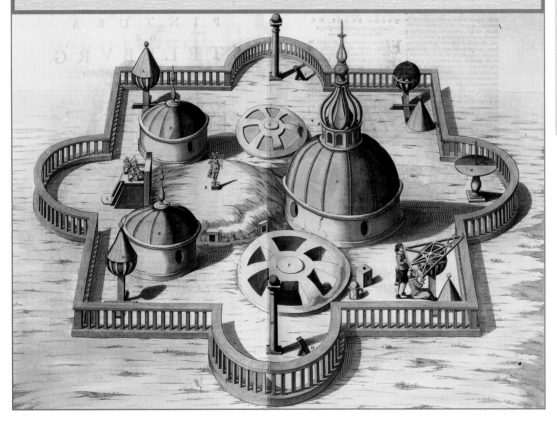

◀ *This painting from the seventeenth-century* Blaeu Atlas *depicts one of the world's first scientific installations, Tycho Brahe's Uraniborg. Ultimately, Uraniborg did not satisfy the technical needs of the Danish astronomer.*

The Development of Astronomy

The astronomer Tycho Brahe took part in the new discourse even though he opposed Copernicus's model of the universe. After Brahe, the German astronomer Johannes Kepler (1571–1630) was the next significant thinker to contribute to the debate. Brahe and Kepler, working with the naked eye alone, both observed one of the brightest occurrences in the sky: supernovas—the explosion of old stars. From Brahe, Kepler learned that it was necessary to take accurate measurements while observing the movement of the heavenly bodies. In doing so, Kepler determined three laws of planetary motion,

Between 1592 and 1610 his mathematics lectures at the University of Padua attracted students from across Europe.

The Telescope

Most of the great thinkers of the era, Galileo included, used the telescope to advance their understanding of the components of the universe. This instrument contributed to the scientific revolution more than any other. The first telescope was made in the Netherlands by a Dutch lens maker, Hans Lippershey, who realized that if he placed two lenses at each end of a tube and looked through it, the image viewed through the tube was magnified. Galileo read about this invention in a letter and built his own device. He ground the lenses, constructed a tube, and produced a telescope with a power of magnification approximately ten times that of the naked eye—more than twice as powerful as Lippershey's model.

Galileo built the telescope in 1610. Initially, he planned to make money from his invention. He demonstrated it to Venetian businessmen and showed them that with his device they would be able to see ships entering the port of Venice long before they were visible to the naked eye. By noting the colors and shapes of approaching ships, businessmen on shore could identify them and prepare for the approaching cargo. This innovation could provide them with crucial market knowledge hours ahead of their competitors. Galileo soon had orders to build large numbers of telescopes. Having achieved some financial security, he was able to pursue his real aim: to examine the heavens. He began to point his telescope toward the night sky.

Evidence for the Copernican Theory

More than any other scholar of the era, Galileo combined the roles of observer and theorist. He had always been an advocate of the Copernican model of the universe, and using telescopic observations of the planets, he was now able to prove that the planets orbited the sun. Galileo also identified mountains on the moon. Until this time the moon had been regarded as more or less gaseous; the presence of mountains implied that the moon was terrestrial and much more

▲ *This portrait of Hans Lippershey derives from a 1655 portrait by Hendrik Berkman. Lippershey applied for a patent for his telescope in 1608, and Galileo learned about the invention the following year.*

which he published between 1609 and 1619. These laws, which stipulate that planets move in elliptical orbits, explained their varying speeds and what seemed to be retrograde motion (that is, motion in reverse direction). With the discovery of Kepler's three laws, the paths of the planets were mapped forever. All that remained was to see these three laws as part of a single unity—a single law that explained the motion of each planet in its orbit about the sun.

The Italian astronomer and mathematician Galileo Galilei also explored the theory of the heliocentric universe. Born in Pisa in 1564, Galileo studied medicine and mathematics and became a professor at the University of Pisa in the late 1580s. However, the faculty was hostile to his views; so Galileo decided to move to Florence. He subsequently settled in Padua.

On April 12, 1615, Cardinal Robert Bellarmine wrote a letter to Paolo Antonio Foscarini to express his displeasure with Copernican theory. The following year, Galileo was summoned to Rome, where he agreed he would not persist in teaching the theory as if it were proven fact.

… It seems to me that your Reverence and Signor Galileo act prudently when you content yourselves with speaking hypothetically and not absolutely, as I have always understood that Copernicus spoke. To say that on the supposition of the Earth's movement and the Sun's quiescence all the celestial appearances are explained better than by the theory of eccentrics and epicycles is to speak with excellent good sense and to run no risk whatever. Such a manner of speaking is enough for a mathematician. But to want to affirm that the Sun, in very truth, is at the center of the universe and only rotates on its axis without going from east to west, is a very dangerous attitude and one calculated not only to arouse all Scholastic philosophers and theologians but also to injure our holy faith by contradicting the Scriptures.… The Council of Trent [1545–1563, intermittently] forbids the interpretation of the Scriptures in a way contrary to the common opinion of the holy Fathers. Now if your Reverence will read, not merely the Fathers, but modern commentators on Genesis, the Psalms, Ecclesiastes, and Joshua, you will discover that all agree in interpreting them literally as teaching that the Sun is in the heavens and revolves round the Earth with immense speed and that the Earth is very distant from the heavens, at the center of the universe, and motionless.…

From my house, April 12, 1615

Your very Reverend Paternity's brother.

R. Car. Bellarmino

Quoted in Solange Strong Hertz, "Galileo Recanted"

▼ *In order to defend the interests of the church, Cardinal Bellarmine, portrayed here in a seventeenth-century engraving by Johannes Valdor, first warned Galileo to regard Copernican theory as merely hypothesis but subsequently declared it "false and erroneous."*

like earth than had previously been imagined. Galileo subsequently observed four moonlike bodies orbiting the planet Jupiter.

In 1610 Galileo reported his findings in a book, *The Starry Messenger.* Criticism of his observations followed immediately. Italian scholars had absolute faith in Aristotle's geocentric theory. Additionally, there was no confidence in findings recorded using the telescope, a man-made device; most people trusted the naked eye alone. In 1611 Galileo moved to Rome, where, despite a warm welcome, his reputation won him no friends among his academic colleagues. According to his fellow professors, the Copernican theory was turning the world upside down. By 1615 church authorities had also begun to voice their concerns publicly.

In order to minimize controversy, Galileo agreed to write about Copernican theory only as a hypothesis. It was becoming increasingly clear that church leaders did not deem the new science appropriate for discussion in the vernacular. In Galileo's mind, however, the new science was a body of knowledge not intended only for the learned elite. Writing in Latin limited the range of public consumption. By switching to Italian, it was inevitable that Galileo's ideas would reach a large audience. When they did so in the 1630s, the Office of the Inquisition charged him with failing to keep his sworn word. He was also suspected of heresy, a charge he never assented to.

Despite his conviction his books and ideas spread across Europe even though the weight of church authority succeeded in temporarily slowing the advance of the new science in Italy. Elsewhere scientists used and built on Galileo's findings and strove to get a more accurate picture of how the universe functioned.

Human Anatomy

The evolution of medicine and the understanding of human anatomy developed rapidly during the sixteenth and seventeenth centuries. One subject of particular interest to researchers was the human body. Disease was no longer considered a punishment for misbehavior or the work of evil forces in the universe. When they began to investigate other sources of disease, the question of prevention came to light.

Many early assumptions about human anatomy proved incorrect. Pupils of Galileo, for instance, used the microscope to study the anatomy of animals and insects. Although they made valuable discoveries, the connections they tried to draw between animal and human anatomy were often erroneous. Nevertheless, their efforts resulted in the publication of the first comprehensive guide to human anatomy. This first attempt, however inadequate, initiated an ongoing discourse that allowed later scholars to revise incorrect assumptions.

After 1500, through the work of Andreas Vesalius and other scientific thinkers, a more proactive approach to disease developed. Scholars with an interest in the human body took advantage of public demonstrations and dissections, especially public anatomy lessons, at which scientists and laymen alike were invited to witness the dissection of a human cadaver, often, the body of a criminal. During the procedure the participating surgeon would announce and display each organ as it was removed from the body. Through the refinement of the knowledge gained from dissection, modern medicine began to take shape.

◄ *A sixteenth-century oil painting on brown paper by John Banister illustrating the findings of scientific dissection undertaken in London. This depiction of muscle tendon and skinned sinew and other anatomical diagrams like it imparted new revelations about the human body and provided material for other researchers.*

Newly acquired confidence in questioning existing knowledge helped contribute to many new insights into the human body. In this passage from his 1628 book, the English physician William Harvey deduces the role of the blood and heart in the human body:

The blood, therefore, [is] required to have motion, and indeed such a motion that it should return again to the heart; for sent to the external parts of the body far from its fountain, as Aristotle says, and without motion, it would become congealed. For we see motion generating and keeping up heat and spirits under all circumstances, and rest allowing them to escape and be dissipated. The blood, therefore, becoming thick or congealed by the cold of the extreme and outward parts, and robbed of its spirits, just as it is in the dead, it was imperative that from its fount and origin, it should again receive heat and spirits, and all else requisite to its preservation—that, by returning, it should be renovated and restored....

But how can parts attract in which the heat and life are almost extinct? Or how should they whose passages are filled with condensed and frigid blood, admit fresh aliment-renovated blood—unless they had first got rid of their old contents? Unless the heart were truly that fountain where life and heat are restored to the refrigerated fluid, and whence new blood, warm, imbued with spirits, being sent out by the arteries, that which has become cooled and effete is forced on, and all the particles recover their heat which was failing, and their vital stimulus well-nigh exhausted.

Hence it is that if the heart be unaffected, life and health may be restored to almost all the other parts of the body; but if the heart be chilled, or smitten with any serious disease, it seems matter of necessity that the whole animal fabric should suffer and fall into decay. When the source is corrupted, there is nothing, as Aristotle says, which can be of service either to it or aught that depends on it.

An Anatomical Exercise concerning the Motion of the Heart and Blood in Animals

▼ *William Harvey, depicted in this seventeenth-century portrait by John Riley (1646–1691), focused his anatomical inquiry on blood circulation.*

Schools of Thought and the New Science

The new era of scientific thought, often referred to as the New Science, spread rapidly through universities such as Oxford, Cambridge, Bologna, Padua, and Paris. These universities collected the new scientific treatises, which were bound into books. Each time a scholar published his findings, responses followed and were themselves answered; as comments and critiques went back and forth, a growing body of scientific literature developed. By the end of the seventeenth century, new societies and academies were established to maintain a supply of these publications and to offer scholars the opportunity to discuss novel ideas and participate in intellectual discourse. The patrons of the academies believed that information should be exchanged so that scientists could concentrate on specific areas of a project rather than waste time duplicating others' research. The academies enabled researchers to keep up to date with revolutionary changes in science and technology.

HON.
ROBERT BOYLE.

▲ *The anatomical scientist Robert Boyle, the subject of this 1690 copy of an original oil portrait by Johann Kerseboom, founded the Royal Society but in 1680 refused to become its first president because he was unwilling to take an oath of allegiance to the monarchy. The Irish-born chemist and physicist experimented with air, vacuums, combustion, and respiration and in 1661 published* The Sceptical Chymist, *in which he criticized current theories of matter, particularly those relating to alchemy.*

The Royal Society of England

Although it was not the first such academy in Europe, the Royal Society in England was perhaps the first permanent organization dedicated to scientific activity. It was founded at Oxford University during the English civil wars, when ousted scholars established an "invisible college" in order to elude discovery by the revolutionaries. The group included only one scientist, Robert Boyle. In 1660 twelve members, including Boyle and Christopher Wren, formed an official organization, the Royal Society of London for Improving Natural Knowledge. In 1662 the society was granted a royal charter by Charles II.

The purpose of the Royal Society originated with the philosophy of Francis Bacon (1561–

1626), who stressed the importance of gathering all knowledge about nature, particularly information that might be beneficial to the public good. Soon it became clear that the society's principal function was to serve as a clearing center for research; correspondence was maintained at the academy, and foreign scholars were encouraged to submit their discoveries. In 1665 the Royal Society launched *Philosophical Transactions,* the first professional scientific journal. The English example was followed on the European continent: in 1666 Louis XIV accepted the founding of the French Royal Academy of Sciences, and by 1700 similar organizations were established in Naples and Berlin. In addition to spreading knowledge, these societies also controlled participation in research by placing certain restrictions on their membership.

Isaac Newton

The new academies of science helped create a culture of learning, but there remained limits. The discourse over new knowledge was more intense in some countries than others. In addition, although some women were privy to the ideas of great scholars through social interaction, women as a group were excluded from participating in most academic societies.

With the Galileo affair slowing scientific speculation in Italy, innovation in the later seventeenth century came mostly from England, the Netherlands, and Germany—Protestant regions whose ecclesiastical authorities, whether sympathetic to the New Science or not, lacked Rome's impact. The leading scientist of this era was the English physicist and mathematician Isaac Newton (1642–1727).

Inspired by Galileo, Newton discovered a novel approach to unraveling the mysteries of the universe. He articulated laws that govern the movement of all objects, whatever their size. Between 1660 and 1690, Newton lived an academic life at Cambridge. As the chair of mathematics, he lectured weekly and gained a devoted following. Newton's mechanistic view of the universe was soon applied to other phenomena. If the universe was a machine and could be understood rationally, then perhaps economics, history, politics, and ethics (the study of human

The English academic societies served an important purpose and were widely admired, but they were not without their critics. Margaret Lucas, who had been maid of honor to Queen Henrietta Maria (the wife of Charles I) from 1643 to 1645, wrote philosophical treatises, science fiction, a biography, an autobiography, essays, letters, poetry, orations, and several plays. She also expressed some views that nowadays would be called feminist. The letter below, published in 1655, was directed at the members of the Royal Scientific Society, whom she felt did not believe women capable of scientific thought.

Most Famously Learned,

I here present to you this philosophical work, not that I can hope wise school-men and industrious laborious students should value it for any worth, but to receive it without scorn, for the good encouragement of our sex, lest in time we should grow irrational as idiots, by the dejectedness of our spirits, through the careless neglects and despisements of the masculine sex to the female, thinking it impossible we should have either learning or understanding, wit or judgment, as if we had not rational souls as well as men, and we out of a custom of dejectedness think so too, which makes us quit all industry toward profitable knowledge, being employed only in low and petty employments, which take away not only our abilities toward arts, but higher capacities in speculations, so as we are become like worms, that only live in the dull earth of ignorance, winding our selves sometimes out by the help of some refreshing rain of good education, which seldom is given us, for we are kept like birds in cages, to hop up and down in our houses, not suffered to fly abroad, to see the several changes of fortune, and the various humors, ordained and created by nature, and wanting the experience of nature, we must needs want the understanding and knowledge, and so consequently prudence, and invention of men.

Philosophical and Physical Opinions

character) could be comprehended in this way, too. Furthermore, if these fields were mechanical, they could be explained without recourse to religion. In addition, it might prove possible to manipulate them, as one would a machine, to make them function more effectively.

Newton had a great impact on English society, even among those people who could not understand Newtonian physics or mathematics. In 1727, the year of Newton's death, the English poet Alexander Pope composed the epitaph for Newton's grave at Westminster Abbey: "Nature and Nature's laws lay hid in night: God said, Let Newton be! and all was light." By 1700 science had become an issue of public discourse. The number of scholars involved in the pursuit of scientific understanding grew, and by the mid-eighteenth century even women had become significantly involved in science.

▶ *Queen Henrietta Maria, seen in this seventeenth-century portrait by Anthony Van Dyck, became involved in politics in support of her husband, Charles I. Both she and Margaret Lucas, her maid of honor, were determined to have a role in the public sphere.*

PHILOSOPHIÆ

NATURALIS

PRINCIPIA

MATHEMATICA.

AUCTORE
ISAACO NEWTONO, Eq. Aur.

Editio tertia aucta & emendata.

LONDINI:
Apud Guil. & Joh. Innys, Regiæ Societatis typographos.
MDCCXXVI.

ISAACUS NEWTON EQ. AUR. ÆT. 83.
I. Vanderbank pinxit 1725.   Geo. Vertue Sculpsit 1726.

▲ *The frontispiece and title page of Isaac Newton's revolutionary* Principia mathematica, *first published in 1687. Newton's work marked the culmination of a century's effort to found scientific ideas on experiment and observation rather than the received wisdom of the ancients.*

The Systematization of Knowledge

Using the ideas and methods of Renaissance thinkers, many later scientists sought to organize their understanding of the world by carrying out vast cataloging projects. The greatest strides in the systematization of science were made in biology.

Just as Galileo had utilized the telescope, researchers used the microscope to open up new realms. In the second half of the seventeenth century, the earliest scientists to study the natural world with a microscope, Robert Hooke, in England, and Jan Swammerdam and Antoni van Leeuwenhoek, in the Netherlands, discovered that plant and animal tissues were made out of cells. The Swedish botanist Carl von Linné, also known as Carolus Linnaeus, systematized the vast amount of new biological information in his *Systema naturae,* published in 1735. He cataloged all living creatures into a single system that defined their relationship to one another in what became known as the Linnaean classification system. Morphologically distinct living creatures (creatures with different forms) he called species, which means individuals. Morphologically related species were designated a genus—a kind. The scale continued to include more abstract morphological relationships: family, class, order, phylum, and kingdom. Each individual species was marked by both its species and its genus name; this classification system, with some modifications, still dominates scientists' understanding of the living world.

Linnaeus helped spread research into the natural world by arranging for his students to go on trade and exploration voyages to all parts of the globe; nineteen of Linnaeus's students went on these voyages of discovery. Perhaps his best-known student was Daniel Solander, who served as the naturalist on Captain James Cook's first scientific expedition to the Pacific Ocean (1768–1771). He returned to Europe with the first plant collections from Australia and the South Pacific. Another student, Anders Sparrman, was a botanist on Cook's second

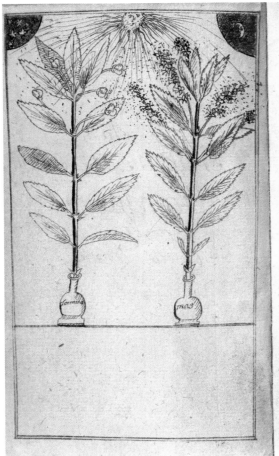

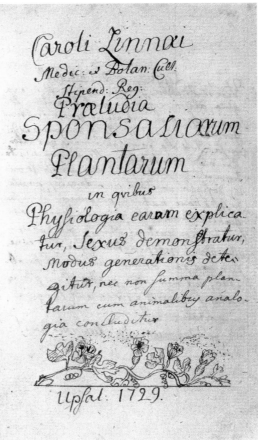

The frontispiece of an early manuscript by Carolus Linnaeus, the Swedish botanist, naturalist, and explorer, dating to 1729. In addition to classifying the plant and animal kingdoms, Linnaeus also systematized minerals and drew up a treatise on diseases.

voyage. Pehr Kalm traveled in the northeastern American colonies for three years and studied American plants, and Carl Peter Thunberg was the first Western naturalist to visit Japan in over a century. While these researchers demonstrated the unique features of different regions, their work also began to show the common elements of all life and ecosystems.

The Legacy of Renaissance Science

In addition to enabling a better understanding of the world, the ideas of Renaissance scientists liberated individuals to experiment and innovate in order to solve problems. Together with the practical knowledge gained by Newton and other thinkers, this spirit of innovation combined with economic philosophies to orient efforts toward the growth and development of European economies. Thus, new technologies became an important path to profit and wealth. During the eighteenth century, the steam engine radically altered life in England and in the following century became the backbone of the industrial revolution throughout Europe.

FURTHER READING

Blackwell, Richard J. A. *Science, Religion, and Authority: Lessons from the Galileo Affair.* Milwaukee, WI, 1998.

Jacob, James R. *The Scientific Revolution: Aspirations and Achievements, 1500–1700.* Atlantic Highlands, NJ, 1998.

Kaufmann, Thomas DaCosta. *The Mastery of Nature: Aspects of Art, Science, and Humanism in the Renaissance.* Princeton, NJ, 1993.

Kuhn, Thomas S. *The Essential Tension: Selected Studies in Scientific Tradition and Change.* Chicago, 1979.

Margolis, Howard. *It Started with Copernicus: How Turning the World Inside Out Led to the Scientific Revolution.* New York, 2002.

Brian Black

SEE ALSO
....
• Architecture • Copernicus, Nicolaus
• Dams and Drainage • Disease • Galilei, Galileo
• Leonardo da Vinci • Machines • Manufacturing
• Universities

Scotland

SCOTLAND, RULED BY THE HOUSE OF
STUART FROM 1371, WAS UNIFIED
WITH ENGLAND UNDER ONE CROWN BY
THE ACCESSION OF JAMES VI TO THE
ENGLISH THRONE IN 1603.

Early modern Scotland shared similar social hierarchies and economic conditions with its southern neighbor England. As elsewhere in Britain and Europe, urbanization was a feature of the period, and the population grew after the ravages of the Black Death. Agriculture was the dominant occupation and wool the principal export.

The vast majority of Scottish people were peasants. The localities were dominated by the lairds (lesser nobility), while central government was the preserve of the greatest of the Scottish nobles, the lords. Over the sixteenth century, however, lairds became more involved in national as well as local issues.

The government of Scotland had a correspondingly local focus. Central government was concentrated in the southeast of the country, and its extension into the north and west was limited, especially at the beginning of the period. In the north and west were the highlands, where Gaelic culture and language predominated, while in the

▶ *The medieval kingdom of Scotland between 1266 and 1542. Scotland fought several battles with its southern neighbor England before the two lands were united under a single monarch in 1603.*

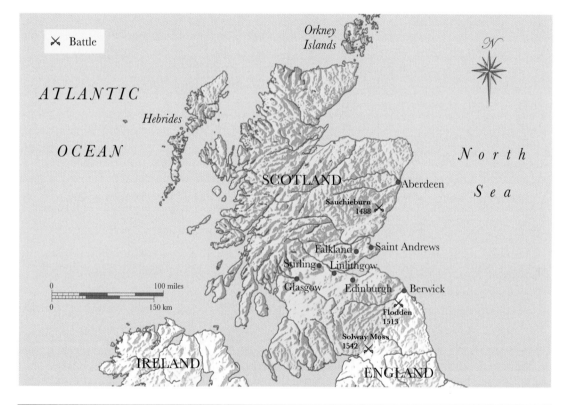

SCOTTISH NATIONAL IDENTITY

By the arrival of the early modern period, the development of a Scottish national identity had been in process for a long time; great pride in the successful resistance of centuries of English aggression was an important aspect of this identity. One manifestation of national consciousness was the emergence of a tradition of national histories. The earliest examples of these nationalist histories of Scotland include John of Fordun's *Chronica gentis scotorum* (c. 1365–1385), Andrew of Wyntoun's *Orygynale Cronykil* of Scotland (c. 1410–1420), and Walter Bower's *Scotichronicon* (completed 1447). This national consciousness should not, however, disguise the multiplicity of Scottish identities; as Fordun observed of the difference between Highlands and Lowlands, "The customs and habits of the Scots differ according to the difference of language." Loyalties and identities were complex and layered.

southern lowlands the people spoke Scots (a language close to English), and there was much greater cultural assimilation with western Europe.

Scottish government was far less laden with bureaucratic structure than its English counterpart and many other contemporary governments. Yet although the Scottish government may have appeared "backward" to certain contemporaries and some historians, it was not inefficient. In the absence of an elaborate institutional structure, the personal relationship that a monarch had with his nobles was essential: for this reason governance in Scotland tended to suffer when a king came to the throne before he was fully of age. Nevertheless, the Stuart monarchy retained and extended its authority throughout the Renaissance despite periods of disturbance—testimony to the essential strength of the system. Like the bouts of unrest among the nobility, the continuance of feuds in Scotland contributed to an image of the country as barbaric and bloodthirsty, although in fact evidence suggests that the effect of feuds was to stabilize social relations. Scotland's reputed backwardness and barbarism were to a large extent attributable to the perhaps misconceived views of others with fixed ideas about "correct" government.

The Political Background

While early modern Scottish society could operate with greater stability than has sometimes been supposed and the Stuart dynasty and system of kingship remained powerful, the fate of various individual Stuart monarchs reflected some of the more precarious aspects of Scottish government, in particular the potential power of the nobility and the importance of the relationship with England.

Noble rebellion remained a significant threat to rulers throughout the period. King James III died after a skirmish with noble rebels at Sauchieburn on June 11, 1488. Despite continuing noble disaffection, his son James IV extended royal authority farther into his kingdom, especially into the northern and western highlands. James managed successfully to control the domestic balance of power, but he could not achieve the same degree of success in his relations with England. Although he married Henry VII's daughter Margaret Tudor in 1503, James was eventually forced to choose the traditional alliance with France (the so-called Auld Alliance) over a treaty with England. He was killed at the Battle of Flodden, which was fought on September 9, 1513, against the army of his brother-in-law, Henry VIII.

James's son inherited the throne as James V at the age of just seventeen months. Friction and fighting between factions of the nobility was widespread during his minority. James may not ever have come of age in 1528 had he not escaped the control of the earl of Angus. In order to successfully challenge Angus, James made a deal with Henry VIII. James, like his father, was vigorous in his assertion of royal prerogatives throughout his realm. Unfortunately, in a further parallel with his father's reign, James's rule ended in ignominious defeat at the hands of the English. After the collapse of his invading army at Solway Moss in November 1542, James died in December—of a broken heart, according to romantic chroniclers, though the cause was probably disease.

¶ Hereafter ensue the trewe encountre or.. Bataple lately don betwene. Englade and: Scotlande. In whiche bataple the. Scottsshe. Kynge was slayne.

¶ The maner of th aduaueesynge of my lord of Surrey tresourier and. Marshall of. Englande and leuetenute generall of the noyth pties of the same with. rrvi. M. men to wardes the kynge of. Scott and his. Armye vewed and nombred to an i hundred thousande men at the leest.

The unattributed woodcut on this page from an account of the Battle of Flodden pictures Henry VIII of England with his knights after the English victory over the Scots in 1513. The Scottish army was annihilated during the battle; in addition to James IV, around ten thousand of his subjects were killed.

The next Stuart's reign illustrates both the Scottish nobility's capacity to deal with inadequate monarchs and the potential threat from the English. Mary Stuart succeeded her father, James V, in 1542, when she was less than a month old. Security was sought in foreign alliance, and a treaty with England was negotiated. However, the determination of Henry VIII to enforce his own unreasonable conditions upon the marriage proposed between his son, Edward, and the infant queen ensured the failure of the treaty. Henry then embarked on the so-called Rough Wooing of Scotland, in which the borders were ruthlessly and violently harried. The consequent war dragged on for many years and drained the resources of both countries. Instead of alliance with England, the minority

government turned to the Auld Alliance with France. Mary was engaged to Francis, the son of Henry II of France, and married him in April 1558. She lived at the French court from 1548 until her husband, by then Francis II, died in December 1560. When she returned to Scotland, Mary Stuart was old enough to rule in her own right, but failure to manage the government and some extraordinarily bad decisions regarding her marriages led to her forced abdication in 1567. She fled into exile in England in 1568, leaving her infant son, James, as king. Mary was executed by her cousin Elizabeth I on February 8, 1587. Her position as Elizabeth's immediate if unrecognized heir and the focus of Catholic attempts to depose the English queen had made Mary far too great a threat to tolerate.

James VI's minority provided further opportunities for ambitious magnates. Rivalry between different factions took its most dramatic turn in August 1582, when the teenage king was kidnapped by the Ruthven Raiders, the Protestant earls of Gowrie and Angus. James did not escape his captors until June of the following year.

Scotland's relationship with England changed radically upon Elizabeth's death in 1603. Mary's son, James VI of Scotland, inherited the English throne as James I. The accession brought great prestige to the Stuart dynasty, and nobody was more conscious of the possibilities presented by the union of the crowns of Scotland, England, and Ireland than James himself. However, it is arguable that James's subsequent absence from Scotland destabilized the system of personal relations on which the Scottish monarchy had rested. The potential power and threat of the Scottish nobility remained. James's son Charles I misunderstood his northern kingdom—perhaps willfuly—and the noble threat was eventually realized in the most dramatic way. A rebellion against the prescribed use of the Anglican Prayer Book began in Edinburgh in 1637 and paved the way for civil wars across the British Isles.

The Renaissance in Scotland

Although in Scotland the economy was not as strong as elsewhere in Europe and the Scottish crown in particular had fewer resources than many other monarchs, there was a notable flow-

▼ This nineteenth-century painting, by Calixte-Joseph Serrur, after a work by François Clouet, shows Mary Stuart in a white mourning veil, which she wore after the death of her first husband, Francis II.

James V initiated major building work at Stirling Castle in 1531; construction of a palace at the castle began in 1537. The palace was completed after James's death under the direction of his widow, Mary of Guise.

ering of learning and culture in Scotland that formed part of the wider European Renaissance. In part, this situation came about because Scotland's resources were not expended on expensive foreign wars. Scottish learning formed an integral part of the educated culture of northwestern Europe. Three Scottish universities were founded in the fifteenth century, in Saint Andrews, Glasgow, and Aberdeen. In 1511 and 1538 new colleges were established in Saint Andrews, and in 1593, after the Reformation had taken root, a new college was founded in Aberdeen. Many of Scotland's intellectuals, such as George Buchanan, achieved high standing in European institutions. Scottish historical writing took on especial prominence as the learned disciplines developed; the Roman historian Livy, rediscovered during the European Renaissance,

became a particularly important authority in Scotland. In society as a whole, literacy and education in general—promoted not least by the efforts at religious reform of Catholics prior to 1560 and of Protestants after 1560—gradually improved. The growth of print technology was also an important factor.

The great building projects of the Scottish monarchs constitute some of the finest examples of Renaissance culture in Scotland. James V in particular, like many Renaissance monarchs of continental Europe, took a systematic approach to his building program. His first project was the construction of a new tower at Holyrood (built betweeen 1528 and 1532; the west range followed in 1535 and 1536. The tower was in a high Gothic style, similar to his other early building work at Linlithgow and Falkland Palace. After

George Buchanan   1506–1582

The Scottish humanist, educator, and poet George Buchanan was born in Stirlingshire. His provocative early work led to imprisonment for heresy in 1539. He escaped to the Continent, where he achieved great distinction as a scholar and poet. However, he was also incarcerated for heresy in France and Portugal. Buchanan eventually returned to Scotland around 1560 and quickly found royal favor; in 1566 he became the principal of Saint Leonard's College in Saint Andrews. After Mary Stuart married for the third time, Buchanan became involved in the opposition movement against her. He remained a significant figure in national politics through the minority of Mary's son, most notoriously as tutor (with Peter Young) to the young king. James VI's later accounts describe a disciplinarian, even terrifying regime under Buchanan's tutelage. It was in these later stages of his career that Buchanan produced his most notable works of political theory, in which he stressed that the people were the source of power and that the monarchy could and should be constrained. James learned much from his tutor; the contrast between Buchanan's views and James's supposed emphasis on the divine right of kings may have been exaggerated, but there is no doubt that Buchanan's former pupil developed great resistance to the argument that tyranny should be resisted and monarchical power limited.

▲ A snipe (wading bird), from the Oxburghe Hangings, embroidered around 1570 by Mary, Queen of Scots, and Elizabeth Talbot, the countess of Shrewsbury, while Mary was in captivity in England.

Meanwhile, the lords and lairds had developed a far more obviously native architectural expression: the distinctively Scottish castellated baronial style, in which Renaissance influence was limited to decorative motifs and superficial references on solidly vernacular constructions. A spectacular bout of regional building projects continued in the later sixteenth century and early seventeenth century, throughout which the baronial style remained of central importance.

James V's court introduced other forms of Renaissance influence to the arts. The representations of James III on some coins brought a Renaissance style to a wide audience. James V was enthusiastic about music, and he imported the French chanson and the consort of viols to Scotland. He employed musicians from across Europe, who brought a diversity of continental influences to the court.

While her father had engaged in chivalric pursuits, Mary Stuart introduced the elaborate Renaissance courtly activities to which she had become accustomed in the court of her father-in-law, Henry II of France. Marian courtly decorative arts, such as jewelry, tapestry, and costume, also displayed Renaissance influences. Perhaps because of financial restrictions, there was greater investment in these arts under Mary than in the fields of architecture, painting, or sculpture.

James's 1537 marriage to Madeleine, daughter of the French king Francis I, a great champion of Renaissance culture, that program was particularly inspired by the Scottish monarch's experiences in France. The French influence was consolidated by James's subsequent marriage, to Mary of Guise, and is visible most strikingly in the later works at Falkland and Stirling. French masons used a classical Italianate style to build the courtyard facades of Falkland Palace and a new palace block at Stirling Castle.

During the minority of James VI, portrait painters developed a more European style by focusing on individual characteristics and naturalistic detail. The influence of the Netherlands was particularly strong, owing to the activity of the court painters Arnold Bronckorst (flourished 1565–1583) and Adrian Vanson (flourished 1581–c. 1602).

The Scottish Reformation

In Scotland, unlike many other European countries, a Reformed national church was instituted against the express wishes of the regime. The Scottish Reformation eventually resulted in one of the most thoroughly Reformed Calvinist churches in Europe, self-consciously and proudly ahead of its English equivalent, which many Scots saw as hopelessly riddled with Catholic error. The substantial differences between the Scottish Kirk and the churches in England and Ireland are seen by scholars as one of the most important causes of the civil wars in the mid-seventeenth century.

The early progress of Protestantism in Scotland did not, however, anticipate the later thoroughgoing reforms. In the first half of the sixteenth century, Protestantism was not completely absent from Scotland, but it was weak. Instead, the need for religious reform was met by Catholic revival, which has led to the facetious suggestion that the Counter-Reformation took place in Scotland before the Reformation. James V's marriage to Mary of Guise indicated Scottish commitment to the European Catholic alliance that stood in opposition to Henry VIII of England. Yet while James's international stance was Catholic and while he allowed some heresy persecutions, he also favored future Reformers as well as staunch Catholics at court. Persecution of Protestantism was limited after James V's death as well; Mary of Guise, who was regent for her daughter Mary Stuart, made assurances to the minority Protestant nobles that their faith would be tolerated.

In 1558 the situation changed dramatically for Scotland's Protestant minority. After the death of Mary Tudor, the Protestant Elizabeth I succeeded to the English throne. The potential for an international Protestant alliance now improved, and the lords of the congregation (as the faction of Protestant nobles called themselves) began to push their cause more aggressively. In the meantime French attention had turned to the struggle against heresy after the Peace of Cateau-

Cambrésis in 1559 removed the distraction of war with Spain. Henry II asked the pope to direct a campaign against heresy in Scotland.

In May of that year, the outspoken and vigorous Reformer John Knox returned from his exile in Geneva. Knox's *History of the Reformation* rather exaggerates his role in the process, and it is in part as a result of his own words that he has long been accorded great distinction as the central figure in the Scottish Reformation. Nevertheless, he was undoubtedly immensely important; he roused great enthusiasm for the

▲ *This 1571 oil-on-panel portrait, attributed to Arnold Bronckorst, pictures James VI, aged five, holding a hawk.*

► *This unsigned engraving after a contemporary portrait depicts the Scottish Reformer John Knox, who held the conviction that the Reformation was God's cause and must ultimately triumph. Knox had a significant influence on the development of the Reformed church in Scotland.*

Reformed cause through his preaching and played a pivotal if not exclusive role in the subsequent political turmoil. The Catholic cause was also weakened by unrest within France and the death of Mary of Guise in June 1560. In July, under the Treaty of Edinburgh, all foreign troops withdrew, and in August the Reformation Parliament met to institute the new religion.

One important reason for the success of the Reform movement was the failure of Mary Stuart to institute effective measures to resist the changes. She remained in France until August 1561 (despite the death of her husband the previous December), and her inability to assert her authority greatly weakened the Catholic cause with which she came to be so closely associated. When she did return, the restoration of Catholicism was apparently not a priority.

The Kirk and the People

As elsewhere in Europe, in Scotland the reform of religious practices was a far more gradual and uneven process than political reorganization. Nevertheless, by the end of the sixteenth century, proponents of Reform had been remarkably successful. One reason for their success might have been the appeal that lay in the close involvement of the Calvinist-style Kirk in lay discipline and morals. The Kirk (established church) provided the ordinary men and women of Scotland with the basic elements of welfare and social organization, from education to legal arbitration—services that generally had not existed previously. In addition, an effective and well-educated preaching ministry was gradually created for the Kirk, which slowly helped evangelize the population.

JOHN KNOX IN EXILE

John Knox's early Reforming ministry was conducted at Saint Andrews in 1546 after the castle was seized by rebel Reformers. In July 1547, however, the castle was recaptured by the French, and Knox was sent to the galleys (ships rowed by prisoners). He was released in February 1549 and sent to preach in Berwick, England, on the Scottish borders. There he used a more radically reformed liturgy than was prescribed by the English Book of Common Prayer. Under the patronage of the duke of Northumberland, the new leader of the English regency government, Knox came to London as royal chaplain to the young Edward VI in 1551. Among other religious criticisms, Knox, in the summer of 1552, as the new Book of Common Prayer was in production, made an outspoken attack on the practice of kneeling at communion. Archbishop Thomas Cranmer was angered, but he did add to the new prayer book the so-called black rubric, a statement explaining that kneeling before the bread and wine did not imply adoration of them, as it would have at the Catholic Mass (Catholics believed that when, during Mass, the priest consecrated the bread and wine, they were transformed in substance into the body of Christ; all Reformed denominations rejected this doctrine, called transubstantiation; some even regarded veneration of the sacramental elements as idolatrous).

After the Catholic Mary Tudor came to the English throne in 1553, Knox went into exile. He spent time with Swiss Reformers in Zurich and Geneva before he was invited by English Protestant exiles in Frankfurt, in the German state of Hesse, to be their minister. However, Knox was forced out following internal disagreements. He went to Geneva in March 1555, where, after a brief return to Scotland, he was invited by the radical group of English exiles from Frankfurt to lead their new congregation alongside Christopher Goodman. In Geneva, Knox achieved a close approximation to his ideal Reformed community.

In March 1557 Scottish Protestant nobles asked Knox to return to Scotland; although he eventually agreed, his homecoming was delayed by the Scottish lords. During this frustrating further exile, he wrote a furious attack on female rule, *The First Blast*, aimed specifically at Mary Tudor and intended as an address to what Knox saw as the deplorable situation in England. He also wrote a number of treatises about the need for reform in Scotland. He finally returned to his homeland in May 1559.

Another corollary of the drive to "purify" Scottish society, along with the attempts of local authorities to assert their interests, was the violent persecution of a significant number of witches, which peaked in the later sixteenth century and the seventeenth century.

One indication of the success of the Scottish Reformation is the extraordinarily high number of subscribers to the National Covenant in response to the clumsy reforms of Charles I and Archbishop William Laud. The National Covenant was a document drawn up in February 1638 as part of the protest against Charles I's attempts to reform the Kirk in Scotland. Huge numbers of Scots who subscribed to it thus declared their intention to defend the "true religion, liberties, and laws of the kingdom." The intent was to preserve the integrity and purity of the Kirk and was certainly not in itself thought by the Scots to constitute an act of rebellion. The practice of covenanting, or taking oaths, was a traditional Scottish device used to negotiate complaints. Charles failed to understand this custom, however, as he failed to comprehend so much about his northern kingdom. He saw the protests as a direct challenge to his authority and responded with force. In June 1639 he embarked on what became known as the Bishops' Wars against his Scottish subjects. This conflict led eventually to civil war in Scotland and subsequently across the British Isles.

FURTHER READING

Goodare, Julian. *State and Society in Early Modern Scotland.* New York, 1999.

MacQueen, John, ed. *Humanism in Renaissance Scotland.* Edinburgh, 1990.

Mason, Roger A. *Kingship and the Commonweal: Political Thought in Renaissance and Reformation Scotland.* East Lothian, Scotland, 1998.

Todd, Margo. *The Culture of Protestantism in Early Modern Scotland.* New Haven, CT, 2002.

Wormald, Jenny. *Scotland: A History.* Oxford, 2005.

Anna Bayman

SEE ALSO

• Calvinism • England • English Civil Wars
• Reformation • Stuarts, The

Shakespeare, William

THE GREATEST ENGLISH PLAYWRIGHT,
WILLIAM SHAKESPEARE (1564–1616),
IS ALSO ACCLAIMED AS A POET. HIS
WORK, IN ENGLISH OR TRANSLATION, IS
READ AND PERFORMED THROUGHOUT
THE WORLD.

William Shakespeare was born in Stratford-upon-Avon, in Warwickshire, England, in April 1564. Little is known of Shakespeare's early life (indeed, virtually every date given below is, strictly speaking, speculative). His father was a wealthy businessman and member of the town council. Although young William is believed to have attended Stratford grammar school, he did not proceed to university. Instead, at age eighteen he married Anne Hathaway, who was twenty-six at the time. Seven months later, the couple had the first of three children.

Early Career

Shakespeare may have become familiar with the great works of Roman and Greek literature while at grammar school and might also have been exposed to the intricacies of language and rhetoric. It is even possible that he and his schoolmates would have read aloud some of the ancient tragedies and comedies.

The first records that provide a picture of the playwright's life emerge in 1592. That year a theater group performed a short play that may have been an early version of *Henry IV*. References appear at the time to an "upstart" playwright, who most scholars believe was Shakespeare. In that year, too, Shakespeare may have met the prominent English playwright Christopher Marlowe and the noted actor Edward Alleyne. Shakespeare seems to have toured with various acting companies as he tried to perfect his thespian abilities. He may also have worked on his theatrical writing and poetry. Shakespeare's accomplishments and talents seem to have caught the attention of the earl of Southampton, who subsequently became the young playwright's patron and introduced him to prominent members of London society.

By 1593 Shakespeare had found success both as an actor and as a poet, with the publication of his long poem *Venus and Adonis*. The poem proved extremely popular, and nine editions were printed. A year later, Shakespeare repeated this success with *The Rape of Lucrece*, a poem that proved almost as popular as *Venus*. Scholars have speculated that he may have devoted more time to poetry because the London theaters had been ordered closed in 1593 in an effort to slow the spread of plague following an outbreak.

◀ *By the age of thirty, Shakespeare had gained a widespread reputation as an actor and poet. This 1588 miniature by Nicholas Hilliard is believed to be a young Shakespeare clasping a hand from the heavens in recognition of the divine inspiration of his talents.*

Anne Hathaway c. 1556–1623

Little is known about the early life of Shakespeare's wife, Anne Hathaway, other than that she lived in the small village of Shottery, close to Stratford-upon-Avon. The eldest of eight children, Anne stayed with her stepmother and siblings after the death of her father in 1581 and acted as a housekeeper. Since it was common for many young women of the day to be married by the age of twenty-one, it was likely that Anne, now in her mid-twenties, was considered a spinster. Apparently, Anne became pregnant before her marriage to William; the couple was betrothed on November 26, 1582, and their first child, Susanna, was born and baptized in May 1583. The pregnancy was the most probable reason for the marriage, which would otherwise have proved damaging to the reputation of the couple's families. William and Anne later had twins, a girl named Judith, and a boy, Hamnet. It was unusual during the Renaissance for a couple to have only three children; high infant mortality rates generally prompted parents to produce large families.

After the wedding Anne moved in with Shakespeare, who still lived with his parents. At some point between 1585 and 1592, Shakespeare moved to London in an effort to establish a career as an actor, leaving Anne and the three children in Stratford-upon-Avon. Even as Shakespeare grew more successful, Anne and the family remained in the country while he interacted with the elite of English society in London. Throughout his career Shakespeare spent the year in London and returned to Stratford-upon-Avon only for the forty-day period of Lent, when the theaters were closed. Nonetheless, Shakespeare's fame translated into social success and standing for Anne within the area of their hometown. His growing prestige also made the family relatively affluent. In 1597 Shakespeare purchased the second largest house in Stratford-upon-Avon and began investing in various businesses as well as in property. By 1602 the Shakespeare household included servants and attendants.

Anne oversaw her elder daughter's wedding in 1607 and Judith's in 1616. William lived to see only one of his grandchildren. After her husband's death in 1616, Anne lived a comfortable life until she died at the age of sixty-seven.

CHRONOLOGY

1564
William Shakespeare is born in Stratford-upon-Avon.

1592
Shakespeare's wife gives birth to twins.

1594
A Shakespeare play is performed before Queen Elizabeth I for the first time.

1596
Shakespeare's son, Hamnet, dies.

1603
Shakespeare is given the title groom of the chamber by James I.

1609
Moves back to Stratford-upon-Avon.

1613
The Globe Theatre burns to the ground during a performance of *Henry VIII*.

1616
Shakespeare dies on April 23 (May 3, New Style).

◀ *After her husband's death, Anne Hathaway Shakespeare lived a comfortable life. Pictured is the cottage in Shottery in which she spent her later years.*

Richard Burbage c. 1567–1619

Richard Burbage was one of the greatest actors of Shakespeare's day. He performed in many of Shakespeare's plays and became a member of both the Chamberlain's Men and the King's Men. Burbage was the son of one of England's early theatrical promoters, James Burbage, who built and managed a theater just outside London. By the age of twenty, Richard was regarded as one of the country's most capable actors, and he appeared in a variety of plays by Ben Jonson and other contemporary playwrights.

Burbage's acting skills kept him in demand as a performer. In 1594 he joined the Chamberlain's Men and became one of the star performers of Shakespeare's plays. His many roles included Othello, Hamlet, King Lear, and Richard III. It was as Richard III that Burbage received his greatest acclaim and popular fame. He continued to perform with Shakespeare's acting troupe when it became the King's Men; his last performance was in 1610.

After the death of his father in 1597, Burbage and his brother took over the management of the family's theater, but they decided to move the operation to London the following year. They were joined in their new venture by Shakespeare and his company, the Chamberlain's Men. The rebuilt theater was named the Globe, and the Burbages received half of the profits of the venue while Shakespeare and the Chamberlain's Men split the remainder. Burbage also joined with Shakespeare in the purchase of a second theater.

In addition to his acting talents, Burbage was known as a painter and also designed crests and shields for the nobility. Shakespeare left the actor money in his will to purchase a ring as a reminder of their close friendship of many years' standing.

▼ *Richard Burbage, Shakespeare's great friend and fellow actor, is portrayed in this anonymous oil painting from the seventeenth century.*

Shakespeare's Poetry

Shakespeare's poetic style evolved considerably over the course of his career. His early poems employed a direct, often blunt use of simile and metaphor. As time passed, the poet and playwright became more sophisticated in his use of imagery, which grew increasingly subtle and far more elaborate. By the time of his later works, Shakespeare was constructing complicated and intricate metaphors that often ran throughout a particular speech or sonnet.

Shakespeare made use of verse both in the sonnet—a popular form of the day—and in the plays. In all, Shakespeare wrote 154 sonnets, which were well received even by connoisseurs with little interest in theater. He used poetry—mostly blank verse, though the early plays employ rhyme, too—in all his plays. On the Elizabethan stage usually only servants and other "lowborn" characters spoke in prose.

Commercial Success

With the end of the plague and the reopening of the theaters in 1594, Shakespeare joined an acting troupe, the Chamberlain's Men, so called because it was the favored group of the royal chamberlain. The group performed in a theater in north London. After the death of Marlowe in 1593, Shakespeare became the most popular playwright in England. Over the next few years, the Chamberlain's Men performed a number of Shakespeare's plays, including *Richard III, Love's Labour's Lost, The Comedy of Errors,* and *The Taming of the Shrew.* The popularity of these plays brought Shakespeare commercial success and wide acclaim.

Shakespeare followed the public acclaim of his early plays with a series of even more popular works. Between 1594 and 1597 he wrote and produced *Richard II, A Midsummer Night's Dream,* and *The Merchant of Venice.* He also completed the first part of *Henry IV.* Owing to a dispute with the owner of the land on which their theater was built, the Chamberlain's Men decided to relocate to central London. With the financial backing of members of the troupe, including the actor Richard Burbage, Shakespeare and company disassembled their existing theater, moved it, and reassembled it as the Globe Theatre in 1598.

Following the relocation of the theater and company to London, Shakespeare established himself as the greatest playwright of the day. His plays were attended both by ordinary Londoners and by Queen Elizabeth I and members of the royal court, and his works met with critical and popular acclaim. A good indication of the success and popularity of Shakespeare's plays is that many were printed in pirated editions crammed with errors, and in some cases other acting companies performed illicit or unauthorized versions of the works in various places.

Shakespeare evidently made a considerable amount of money. Thanks to his growing fortune, he was able to purchase a large house and estate in Stratford-upon-Avon. He was also given the honor, rare for a commoner, of having a coat of arms registered for his family.

Royal Favor

Elizabeth I enjoyed Shakespeare's plays; he responded by writing a series of history plays, most of them on the Wars of the Roses, the civil wars that led to the establishment of her dynasty, the Tudors. The latest of the plays, *Henry VIII,* includes the birth of Elizabeth.

By 1600 Shakespeare's style had reached full maturity; most of his greatest comedies, tragedies,

▲ This drawing of the Globe Theatre, by James Stow, was first published in 1793. Stow copied a depiction of the Globe that appeared on a panoramic engraving of London made by Claes Jansz Visscher in 1616.

and romances are thought to date from this year or later. Among them are the comedies *As You Like It, The Merry Wives of Windsor,* and *Twelfth Night;* the tragedies *Hamlet, King Lear,* and *Macbeth;* and the romances *Cymbeline, The Winter's Tale,* and *The Tempest.*

ELISABETA REG DINGILTERA

In 1603 Elizabeth I died, and James VI of Scotland—the son of Elizabeth's bitter foe Mary, Queen of Scots—assumed the throne of England as James I. The new king, it turned out, was an even more enthusiastic supporter of the theater than his predecessor had been. James assumed the patronage of the Chamberlain's Men, and the troupe was subsequently renamed the King's Men. In addition to giving public performances, the King's Men frequently mounted productions of their plays at court, with the king often in attendance. Presumably in response to the royal favor, Shakespeare's output continued at a prodigious rate. In the first few years of James's reign, Shakespeare, in addition to the plays mentioned above, completed the comedies *All's Well That Ends Well* and *Measure for Measure,* the tragedies *Othello, Coriolanus,* and *Antony and Cleopatra,* and the romance *Pericles, Prince of Tyre.*

◀ *Elizabeth I, one of Shakespeare's early patrons, cultivated a regal and commanding image. This contemporary oil painting by John Bettes the Elder presents Elizabeth with the jewels and finery that marked her royal presence.*

Shakespeare is famous for his many soliloquies—a soliloquy is an interior monologue in which a character reveals his inmost feelings, aims, and desires—but he wrote scenes of a far more public nature, too, including several rousing battle speeches. What follows is the celebrated closing section of King Henry V's passionate address to the English troops as they prepare to clash with their French foes at the Battle of Agincourt (1415):

This day is call'd the Feast of Crispian:
He that outlives this day, and comes safe home,
Will stand a tip-toe when this day is named,
And rouse him at the name of Crispian.
He that shall live this day, and see old age,
Will yearly on the vigil feast his neighbours,
And say, "To-morrow is Saint Crispian."
Then will he strip his sleeve and show his scars;
And say, "These wounds I had on Crispin's day."
Old men forget; yet all shall be forgot:
But he'll remember, with advantages,
What feats he did that day. Then shall our names,
Familiar in his mouth as household words,
Harry the King, Bedford and Exeter,
Warwick and Talbot, Salisbury and Gloucester,

Be in their flowing cups freshly remember'd.
This story shall the good man teach his son:
And Crispin Crispian shall ne'er go by,
From this day to the ending of the world,
But we in it shall be remembered;
We few, we happy few, we band of brothers:
For he to-day that sheds his blood with me,
Shall be my brother: be he ne'er so vile,
This day shall gentle his condition.
And gentlemen in England, now a-bed,
Shall think themselves accurs'd they were not here;
And hold their manhoods cheap, whiles any speaks,
That fought with us upon Saint Crispin's day.

Henry V, act 4, scene 3

◀ One of the earliest surviving images of an actor in costume, this 1662 oil-on-canvas painting by John Greenhill portrays Henry Harris as Cardinal Wolsey in Shakespeare's Henry VIII. The costume, not necessarily historically accurate, was intended to make the character easily identifiable by the audience.

Theatrical Forms and Techniques

Shakespeare's plays are often divided into three broad categories by type: histories, comedies, and tragedies (in this categorization the late romances are classed as comedies). The techniques employed within the categories were not exclusive; the playwright frequently incorporated comedic elements into his tragedies and tragic and comedic elements into his historical works. Many of Shakespeare's plays were set in the past even though they often dealt with contemporary themes; the plays that are based on actual historical circumstances include *Henry IV, Henry V, Richard III,* and *Henry VIII.* By using a historical setting as a backdrop, Shakespeare could offer a critique of contemporary politics and mores with a much reduced fear of retribution. His works often concern the fall of a great noble whose demise occurs because of some character flaw or fatal mistake. These plays were especially poignant for the English people because the decades-long strife between the houses of York and Lancaster (1455–1487) had recently ended and along with it a period of conflict and bloodshed over the monarchy. Shakespeare's use of history also had a practical component; many of the stories, especially in the history plays, were familiar to audiences.

While Shakespeare's history plays dealt with serious themes and contained high drama, his comedies were designed to appeal to a wide audience, noblemen and commoners alike, seeking to escape from the drudgery and problems of everyday life. His comedies include *The Taming of the Shrew, A Midsummer's Night Dream, The Merchant of Venice,* and *As You Like It.* All of these plays have common structural elements, the romantic struggles of one or more couples and complicating factors that serve to keep the lovers apart. These comedies all end conventionally with the actual or looked-for marriage of the loving couples. Secondary characters also frequently find themselves paired up with mates, although the mates are not always those the characters would have preferred. The comedies also include plot twists and low humor, both popular devices during the era.

It is widely held that Shakespeare's tragedies are his greatest plays. As was customary, they typically ended with the death of at least the principal character (and usually many others). The focal element in each tragedy is generally a moral transgression or failing that brings about the hero's downfall. Good examples of such a "tragic flaw" are Macbeth's ambition and Othello's jealousy, which bring ruin and death not only to themselves but also to many around them. In the tragedies, the protagonist (principal character) may be good or evil; the point is that events and the actions of other characters combine with his tragic flaw to bring about his undoing. This pattern of misfortune is present in all of Shakespeare's tragedies.

The brilliance with which Shakespeare develops characters is often cited as one of the main reasons for the enduring success of his work. He constructed characters whose emotions, problems, and actions transcend time and place. Shakespeare's plays are not novels or poems; they were seen and heard by live audiences rather than read. Hence, the playwright used varied techniques to ensure that the members of the audience understood the background, personality, and situation of each individual character and—most important of all—experienced the character as a living human being.

While his central figures are highly complex, Shakespeare's minor characters are more broadly drawn, and their words and actions often act as a counterpoint to what the protagonists say and do. Characters are differentiated through their vocabulary and their manner of speaking, and linguistic style also sets the tone and tempo of a play. For instance, poetry (both rhymed and blank verse) alternates with prose and songs. The mature plays are mostly composed in blank verse, but even in them rhymed couplets bring a sense of closure to critical scenes and episodes. Songs act as a means to convey information about a character or scene, to provide an emotional context for subsequent action, or simply to reach across the footlights to the audience.

Later Life

Like his father, Shakespeare was evidently an astute businessman. In addition to adroitly managing the finances of his acting company, he invested his profits in commercial enterprises in and around Stratford-upon-Avon. In 1601 Shakespeare purchased just over one hundred

► This unattributed copper engraving from 1600 portrays Shakespeare at the height of his fame. An artist known only by the initials W. M. later added color to the engraving, which also contains a written homage to the poet and playwright.

This Shadowe is renowned Shakespear's? Soule of th'age
The applause? delight? the wonder of the Stage.
Nature her selfe, was proud of his defignes
And joy'd to weare the dreffing of his lines;
The learned will Confeff, his works are fuch,
As neither man, nor Mufe, can prayfe to much.
For ever live thy fame, the world to tell,
Thy like, no age, shall ever paralell.
W. M. fculpfit.

acres of farmland near his home. Over the next few years, he bought more land. By renting this property to farmers, he secured a steady income.

Shakespeare also expanded his influence on the London stage through the purchase in 1608 of a second theater, the Blackfriars, with other members of the King's Men. The new theater was private; it offered performances for courtiers and the well-to-do at a premium admission price. Most scholars assume that around this time Shakespeare retired from acting and confined his activities to directing plays. Soon after, he must have moved back to Stratford-upon-Avon. Although he continued to write (assuming that the standard dating of his plays is correct), he increasingly left the management of the acting troupes to others. His later plays, including *The Winter's Tale* and *The Tempest*, are usually called tragicomedies or romances. They have much in common with the comedies: the central characters endure problems that are resolved, and the plays end on a joyous note. Yet they deal acutely with separation and loss and are suffused with a bittersweet mood.

By 1611 Shakespeare was living in semiretirement; he did not write any further plays and produced only some minor works. He became preoccupied with the management of his estate and the oversight of his businesses in Stratford-

◀ *Built between 1616 and 1623, this stone and marble monument to Shakespeare in the Holy Trinity Church in Stratford-upon-Avon was carved by the Dutch artist Gheerart Janssen.*

upon-Avon. With his daughters married, Shakespeare also apparently became more involved in family life, especially after the birth of his grandchild. He died at his home in 1616.

In the more than four centuries since it was first played, few have regarded *Hamlet* as anything but one of the towering achievements of the Western stage. Its title character has several soliloquies; in the most famous, beginning "To be or not to be," Hamlet muses on life, action, sleep, death, suicide—and life after death. At the climax of the soliloquy, he notes wryly the consequences of the fear of divine judgment on present action:

there's the respect
That makes calamity of so long life;
For who would bear the whips and scorns of time,
The oppressor's wrong, the proud man's contumely,
The pangs of despised love, the law's delay,
The insolence of office and the spurns
That patient merit of the unworthy takes,
When he himself might his quietus make
With a bare bodkin? Who would fardels bear,
To grunt and sweat under a weary life,
But that the dread of something after death,

The undiscovered country from whose bourn
No traveler returns, puzzles the will
And makes us rather bear those ills we have
Than fly to others that we know not of?
Thus conscience does make cowards of us all;
And thus the native hue of resolution
Is sicklied o'er with the pale cast of thought,
And enterprises of great pith and moment
With this regard their currents turn awry
And lose the name of action.

Hamlet, act 3, scene 1

Because of the limited number of records about Shakespeare, especially his early life, some scholars have questioned whether the playwright existed. Others accept the existence of Shakespeare but assert that he was merely an actor. They contend that the actual author of the works was an aristocrat who used Shakespeare's name as a cover to avoid potential retribution because of the content of some of the plays and sonnets and the fact that playwriting was considered ungentlemanly. Collectively, these two groups are commonly referred to as the anti-Stratfordians.

Doubts that Shakespeare actually wrote the work attributed to him began to emerge in the eighteenth century. The lack of concrete information on Shakespeare's education and his status as a commoner led many to assert that he did not have the knowledge of foreign locales, the law, or classical tongues to fill his plays with the wide range of references they contained. A few scholars even believe that the historical figure named William Shakespeare may well have been semiliterate. This notion came in part from the fact that Shakespeare spelled his name several dozen ways; there were, in addition, no formal records of his school attendance.

In the nineteenth century, some argued that Francis Bacon was the real author of Shakespeare's works. Adherents of this theory contend that there are cryptograms (ciphers or codes) within the plays and sonnets. They argue that, when these cryptograms are decoded, they prove that the English philosopher and mathematician was the author. However, by the twentieth century, most anti-Stratfordian scholars had abandoned the Bacon theory in favor of one that Edward de Vere, the earl of Oxford, wrote the works attributed to Shakespeare. Supporters of Oxford became known as Oxfordians. At the century's end they had become the most formidable anti-Stratfordian group.

The Oxfordians argue that there are many parallels between the earl's life and events in Shakespeare's plays. In addition, Oxford wrote letters that contain many similarities to passages in Shakespeare's sonnets. Finally, a number of contemporary accounts speak highly of Oxford's skill as a writer and playwright, although few examples of plays or other publications by the earl have survived.

A further group does not deny that Shakespeare was involved in the writing of the works, but this collection of scholars contends that the plays and sonnets were the result of collaborations between several authors and not the work of a single person. This group has few members.

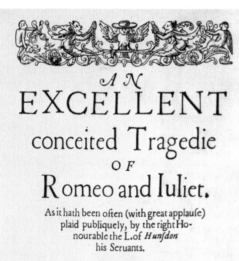

► *An engraving used to produce playbills for* Romeo and Juliet *in 1597. To help them follow the play, audiences were handed playbills, which contained an outline or some of the text of the story. They also served as a means to publicize the play among friends and family of patrons.*

FURTHER READING

Chambers, E. K. *William Shakespeare: A Study of Facts and Problems.* New York, 1988. Reprint.

Fraser, Russell. *Shakespeare: The Later Years.* New York, 1992.

Greenblatt, Stephen. *Will in the World: How Shakespeare Became Shakespeare.* New York, 2004.

O'Connor, Garry. *William Shakespeare: A Popular Life.* New York, 2000.

Ogburn, Charlton. *The Mysterious William Shakespeare: The Myth and the Reality.* New York, 1984.

Speaight, Robert. *Shakespeare: The Man and His Achievement.* New York, 2000.

Thomson, Peter. *Shakespeare's Professional Career.* New York, 1992.

Tom Lansford

SEE ALSO
• Bacon, Francis • Chivalry • Education
• Elizabeth I • England • Humanism and Learning
• Literature • Marlowe, Christopher

Spain

LATE IN THE RENAISSANCE A UNITED SPAIN EMERGED AS A GREAT POWER. IT WAS A DOMINANT FORCE IN EUROPE AND ON THE WORLD STAGE BETWEEN 1476 AND 1598.

Before the sixteenth century the area of the Iberian Peninsula that would later become Spain was made up of several independent kingdoms. The kingdoms of Aragon, Catalonia, and Valencia formed a confederation that was under Christian rule, while to the south Granada was ruled by Arabic-speaking Muslims. Christian Castile was the most powerful kingdom in Iberia; however, during most of the fifteenth century, its influence was hampered by internal struggles over political power.

On the eve of the Spanish Renaissance, a variety of cultures—Christian, Muslim, and Jewish—coexisted uncomfortably on the Iberian Peninsula. With the repeated invasions from North Africa and the continuing presence of Muslims in the south came a steady influx of ideas from the east. These influences were most evident in architecture, the arts, dress, diet, and social customs. The kingdom of Granada provided a haven for a large community of Jewish immigrants who had been expelled from other European nations. Jewish communities were also present in other areas of Iberia, including Castile and Aragon. While excluded from some areas of society, Jewish people excelled as financiers, scholars, and physicians. Despite the frequent outbreaks of war, each kingdom in Iberia relied on the cooperation of the others. In areas that had been reconquered by Christian forces, non-Christians were often allowed to continue their own religious and cultural practices. However, as the sixteenth century dawned, this period of *convivencia* (mutual understanding) was dismantled by the husband-and-wife monarchs Isabella I of Castile and Ferdinand II of Aragon.

The Catholic Monarchs

Isabella (1451–1504) was the daughter of John II of Castile and León (reigned 1406–1454) by his second wife, Isabella of Portugal. Her marriage to Ferdinand of Aragon, in 1469, was designed to strengthen her position as heir to Castile. The marriage was conducted in secret owing to the opposition of Louis XI, king of France, who hoped to marry his brother, the duke of Guienne, to Isabella. Isabella's marriage also angered her half brother, Henry IV, the king of Castile (reigned 1454–1474), who had long hoped to use Isabella's marriage as an instrument for his own political strategy. As a result, Henry IV disowned Isabella and named his infant daughter, Joan, as heir. Nevertheless, upon Henry IV's death in 1474, Isabella was crowned queen of Castile. Her accession to the throne did not immediately end all political strife in Castile. Alfonso V of Portugal invaded Castile, with the intention of marrying Henry's daughter and placing her on the throne of Castile. Alfonso's defeat at the Battle of Toro in March 1476 signaled the end of the insurrection; by the end of that year, most of Castile's nobles supported Isabella.

▼ The facade of the Mesquita (mosque), in Córdoba, Andalusia, is an example of the Moorish style that exerted an important influence on Spanish Renaissance architecture. This graceful style is characterized by intricate decorative carving, horseshoe arches, geometric patterns, and the use of tiles and mosaics.

Ferdinand was the son of John II of Aragon (1397–1479) and a noblewoman of Aragon, Joan Enriquez. John II ruled a confederation of kingdoms that included Navarre, Aragon, Catalonia, and Sicily. During his reign there was widespread unrest and revolt that resulted in the loss of Navarre. John's decision to marry Ferdinand to Isabella was part of a strategy to secure peace in Aragon through an alliance with the more powerful Castile. John also formed alliances with Naples and Burgundy to help safeguard Aragon. These strategies had the desired

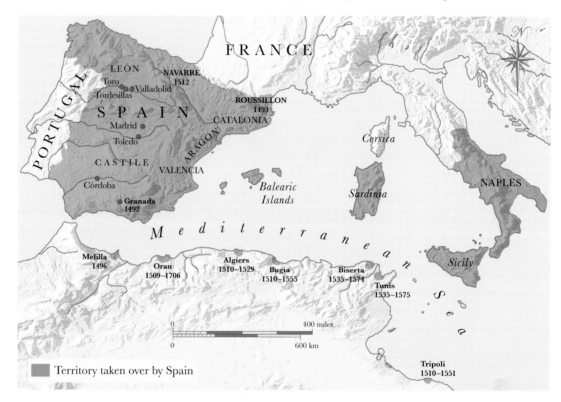

► This map shows Spain and the territories it had conquered by 1560. The Spanish empire also included the Netherlands in northern Europe.

Territory taken over by Spain

THE INQUISITION

Ferdinand and Isabella aimed to create a unified Christian society in the Spanish kingdoms, and for this purpose a strong regulatory instrument was required. The Inquisition was set up in 1478 with the permission of Pope Sixtus IV. The ostensible reason for the creation of the Inquisition was the perceived danger to the Catholic faith from converted Jews (conversos) and Muslims (Moriscos) who had not genuinely adopted Christianity and were instead propagating their former faith.

In 1483 Tomás de Torquemada was chosen as the inquisitor general for the lands held by Isabella and Ferdinand. He established procedures and a network of local inquisitors in key cities throughout Spain. For fifteen years Torquemada oversaw the imprisonment and execution of over two thousand conversos and others accused of heresy; this was the bloodiest period of the Inquisition. In later years, when execution of heretics tended to be the exception, torture, seizure of goods, and public humiliation were still common punishments.

The Inquisition operated according to a standard procedure that began with a sworn denunciation of the suspect. The accused was given a period of between thirty and forty days either to recant or to prepare a defense. The accused was provided an advocate or lawyer and could be examined by the officers of the court only in the presence of two disinterested priests. The accused did not find out the identity of the accuser and was presumed guilty until proven innocent. Convicted heretics were subject to an auto-da-fé (act of faith), a religious ceremony for the punishment of convicted heretics and the reconciliation and readmission into society of those who recanted. This process entailed the carrying out of public penance, which could include wearing penitential garments, public renunciations, and even a term of imprisonment.

The Inquisition quelled the practice of other religions and brought new discipline to Christian religious practice in Spain. Mysticism, sudden conversions, and other unorthodox or extremist religious experiences were discouraged through the machinery of the Inquisition, as was the intellectual exploration of unorthodox religious notions. Thus, the Inquisition functioned as a form of religious and indeed political censorship, although present-day scholars consider its effectiveness far more limited than earlier accounts had long led many to believe. The Inquisition continued to formally exist in Spain until 1834.

effect; the revolts and power struggles that had plagued the kingdoms were finally brought under control. Upon John II's death in 1479, Ferdinand inherited a relatively stable political situation in Aragon, Catalonia, and Sicily. Isabella and Ferdinand's positions in their respective kingdoms were finally secured.

This basis of security enabled the two monarchs to begin an aggressive policy of expansion that ended the centuries-old *convivencia* in Iberia. Isabella and Ferdinand launched a sustained military campaign to reconquer the last of the Moorish kingdoms in Spain. In 1492 Granada was the final kingdom to succumb to Christian forces. (In acknowledgement of Isabella and Ferdinand's success, Pope Alexander VI bestowed the title Catholic Monarchs upon the pair.) Isabella and Ferdinand initiated a religious and cultural transformation of the Spanish kingdoms. On March 31, 1492, the Jews were expelled from Spain, while nearly 200,000 Muslims—over half of the Spanish Muslim population—emigrated to North Africa. Many Jews and Muslims were forced to convert to Christianity, while others converted voluntarily to avoid expulsion. However, suspicions over the genuine nature of the conversions became a source of religious and political concern throughout the period and a principal reason for the creation of the Inquisition.

The Flowering of the Spanish Renaissance
Following the reconquest of Granada, Ferdinand overcame Roussillon and Navarre, areas on the border with France. By adding this territory to the kingdom of Aragon, he redrew the northern border of Spain. From this time the country experienced a period of relative stability that allowed for the flourishing of Renaissance ideas. The revival of ancient Greek and Roman literature that was to fuel the Renaissance had first occurred in earnest during the reigns of Isabella's father, John II of Castile, and Ferdinand's grandfather Alfonso V of Aragon (reigned 1416–1458). Alfonso V (known as the Magnanimous) spent much of his reign in Italy, amassed an impressive library of manuscripts, and hosted a humanist academy. During this time Spanish scholars at the University of Bologna established

contacts with Italian humanists and thus had access to many of the emergent humanist ideas of the day. In Aragon, Iñigo López de Mendoza, the marquis of Santillana (1398–1458), created a large library of manuscripts and commissioned several treatises and classical translations; he was also the first poet to experiment with the Italian sonnet form in Castilian. Iñigo López's descendants, the powerful Mendoza family, became the most important patrons of Spanish literature and art during the first part of the Spanish Renaissance. The archbishop of Toledo Pedro González de Mendoza, an important adviser to Ferdinand and Isabella, supported the early printing of humanist texts as well as providing patronage to leading scholars. He founded the College

▼ A fine example of Spanish Renaissance painting, this detail from the altarpiece of the Church of the Holy Cross in Blesa, Spain, by Martin Bernat and Miguel Jimenez (1485–1487), celebrates Saint Helena as the finder of Christ's cross. During Isabella's reign parallels were frequently drawn between the queen and the saint.

of Vera Cruz in Valladolid, the building itself an example of early Spanish Renaissance architecture.

Isabella and Ferdinand also supported classical scholarship. The Andalusian scholar Antonio de Nebrija (1444–1522) wrote a Latin grammar book intended to replace medieval Latin manuals. He dedicated this book to Isabella, who supported and promoted the humanist move-ment by taking up the learning of Latin at the age of thirty-one. She also founded a grammar school for the young noblemen of her court and provided a classical education for her son and daughters. Thus, the stage was set for the greatest period of classical learning in the Spanish Renaissance, during the reign of Charles V.

Ferdinand and Isabella's Heirs

Isabella and Ferdinand had five children. A son named John and a daughter, Isabella, died in 1497 and 1498, respectively. Their daughter Joan (1479–1555) was the mother of the future monarch of Spain and Holy Roman emperor Charles V. Another daughter, Maria, became queen of Portugal, while their youngest daughter, Catherine of Aragon, married Henry VIII of England. Joan assumed the role of heiress to her parents' thrones in 1500, after the death of her older siblings. Upon her mother's death Joan assumed the throne of Castile. However, Ferdinand acted as regent owing to Joan's reported mental instability, described at the time as a profound melancholia. Joan's husband, Philip, gained control of Castile in 1506 and became Philip I of Castile, but he died within a month of gaining the crown. Ferdinand again became regent, and upon his death in 1516, Joan's son Charles became king of a united Spain—although Joan, imprisoned at Tordesillas, remained legally the queen of Castile until her death in 1555.

Charles V

Raised in the Burgundian court at Brussels, Charles received the education of a Renaissance prince, which included training in the arts and Latin and Greek as well as military history and strategies. In 1519 he was elected as Holy Roman emperor. In 1526 he married Isabella of Portugal.

Despite the responsibilities of running a large empire, Charles determined to make Spain the center of his administration and took personal

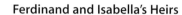
◄ *This illustration from a 1486 edition of Antonio de Nebrija's Latin grammar book,* Introductiones Latinae, *depicts the great Spanish humanist scholar imparting a grammar lesson.*

Queen Joan I of Castile   1479–1555

Generally known as Joan the Mad, Joan, the second daughter of Isabella and Ferdinand, may not have been as insane as has been suggested. Joan may have been imprisoned to facilitate the political ambitions of her father, her husband, and her son.

Joan was educated by the Italian humanists Antonio and Alessandro Gerardino. She proved a capable student and avid reader, fluent in Latin as well as modern European languages. At sixteen Joan was betrothed to Philip (known as the Handsome), duke of Burgundy (1478–1506). She traveled to the Netherlands in 1496 and married him almost immediately upon her arrival. Although the marriage was successful initially, owing to Philip's numerous love affairs, Joan's affection for her attractive husband turned to jealousy, and contemporaries accused her of lacking the ability to govern her emotions. Joan gave birth first to a daughter, Eleanor, in 1498 and two years later to a son and heir, the future Holy Roman emperor Charles V (Charles I of Spain).

In 1500 Joan became heir apparent to the realm of Castile. She returned to Spain with her husband and gave birth to another son, Ferdinand, in 1503. At this point her mental illness began to manifest itself more clearly in bouts of bad temper and depression. Philip returned to the Netherlands in 1502, and the separation appears to have exacerbated his wife's problems. Joan was finally allowed to rejoin her husband in 1504, but upon discovering yet another mistress, she reacted violently.

Following Isabella's death in November 1504, Joan was proclaimed queen of Castile. However, Ferdinand convinced the Castilian government of Joan's mental instability and was named regent in her place. In 1506 Philip managed to wrest control of the government from Ferdinand and assumed the throne on Joan's behalf. Soon after, Philip became ill and died. In some quarters it was believed that Ferdinand had had Philip poisoned. Joan, obsessed with her husband even after his death, refused to be parted from the corpse. The grieving widow, retreating to the fortress of Tordesillas, gave birth to a daughter, Catalina, en route. It was reported that during the journey she continually had the coffin of her husband opened, ostensibly to ensure the body had not been stolen.

Joan was never to proceed farther than Tordesillas, where she was imprisoned for the rest of her long life. Her children Charles, Eleanor, and Ferdinand remained in the Netherlands and were raised by Philip's sister, Margaret of Austria. The infant Catalina remained with Joan. Upon her father Ferdinand's death, Joan's son Charles took the throne of Spain; he decided that his mother should remain in prison, although he left his ten-year-old sister in her care. Joan lived to the age of seventy-five in captivity.

▶ *A painting by Juan de Flandes (c. 1465–1519) of Joan I of Castile. Her son Holy Roman Emperor Charles V kept her in captivity, but she remained legally the queen of Spain for most of his reign.*

charge of the country. He gave his Austrian possessions to his brother, Ferdinand (later Emperor Ferdinand I), in 1522 and in the following years bestowed him with further responsibilities in order to remove the popular prince from the center of Spanish politics and prevent any threat to Charles's authority. In the Netherlands, Charles established a permanent regency; he first named his aunt Margaret and subsequently his sister Maria of Hungary the regent. Despite his successful delegation of responsibility within the empire, Charles was often absent from Spain, a fact much lamented by his nobles. After 1529 Charles appointed his wife, the empress Isabella, as regent of Spain and embarked on a peripatetic life in an attempt to maintain control over his vast empire during a period of intense civic and religious unrest.

In his 1522 book on Augustine's *City of God,* Juan Luis Vives writes of a mythical Spanish age from which the best Spanish qualities descended:

In Spain, before silver and gold were found, there were many Philosophers, and the people lived wonderfully and religiously: every society ...had chosen [its rulers] out of the most learned and judicious rank of men [to give] justice then, without laws.... Few or no controversies were there: and those that were did either concern virtuous emulation, the reasons of gods, of good manners, or of some such themes, which the learned disputed of and called the women to be auditors.

Saint Augustine, *Of the City of God: With the Learned Comments of Juan Luis Vives*

▲ *This unattributed sixteenth-century oil of Juan Luis Vives reveals a thoughtful scholar surrounded by the tools of scholarship; his gesture prompts the viewer to focus not on the man but on his works.*

The religious unrest was sparked by the Protestant Reformation. While Protestantism never took hold in Spain itself, the political implications of the Reformation embroiled the country for nearly a century. In an attempt to mediate the growing unrest caused by Martin Luther's efforts to reform the Catholic Church, Charles called for a diet in the city of Worms in 1521. The diet rejected Luther's spirited defense of his religious position, and Charles issued an edict condemning Luther, an act that caused conflict between Charles and many of his northern European princes.

Charles's engagement with wider European affairs ensured that Spain participated fully in European intellectual and artistic life. Renaissance ideas flourished. Towns and cities opened grammar schools teaching Latin and Greek for the sons of caballeros (Spanish gentlemen) and leading citizens, and twenty new universities were founded. The expansion of education was propelled by Christian humanism, as expounded by its greatest scholar, Desiderius Erasmus (c. 1466–1536). Christian humanists encouraged speculation about human nature and the cosmos. They promoted the acquisition of knowledge through an educational process that included the study of grammar, rhetoric, history, poetry, and moral philosophy based on Latin and Greek classical texts.

Many members of Charles V's court had been educated in the humanist tradition and embraced Erasmus's ideas. Erasmus's works were translated into Castilian, and he himself was invited to the university in Acalá by Charles's Castilian regent, Francisco Jiménez de Cisneros. Erasmus turned down the invitation, although he took especial pains to praise the scholarship produced in Acalá. Another notable humanist scholar, Juan Luis Vives (1492–1540), was sent away from Spain at the age of sixteen and lived most of his life in the Netherlands. In 1522 he declined an invitation to take up a chair at Alcalá University, undoubtedly because he perceived that the political and religious movements in Spain would soon prevent further Spanish involvement in European humanism and would signal a retreat into a position of relative intellectual isolation.

Vives's life itself demonstrates the changes in the political and religious climate in Spain. In 1520 Vives's father, a converso, was burned at the stake for privately practicing the Jewish religion. His father's death and political developments in general drew Vives to remark to Erasmus in 1534 that "we are going through times when we can neither speak nor be silent without danger." Vives would have been aware of a number of movements in Spain that ultimately brought an end to the Christian humanism espoused by Erasmus and others. These movements included the rise and subsequent persecution of the *alumbrados,* a group of mystics that eschewed traditional Catholic dogma. The *alumbrados* embraced humanist beliefs about the importance of the individual; they grounded their religious practice in the belief that one should enter into a personal relationship with God. The popularity of this movement convinced the Catholic authorities that humanist philosophy threatened the power of the Catholic Church in Spain. Protestantism, which was gaining both religious and political strength in northern Europe, also led many Spaniards to question whether Erasmus's ideas were essentially different from those of Martin Luther; both believed in the desirability of an individual relationship with God rather than a relationship that was mediated through the priests of the Catholic Church. By the end of the 1530s, most of the great Spanish humanists were dead or had left the country. For the remaining years of Charles V's reign, as well as the entire reign of his son, Philip II, Spanish society, rejecting influences from Protestant countries, returned to Italian culture as well as to its own indigenous culture for artistic, religious, and intellectual inspiration.

Philip II and the Spanish Empire

Philip II (1527–1598) became king in 1556 upon his father's abdication. He inherited a vast and growing empire that included Spanish acquisitions in the Americas. Charles V had carefully guided his son's political beliefs and practices from a young age; his *Instruction* of 1543 was essentially a manual of government for

▲ In this oil painting from around 1580, Philip II appears a confident monarch in severe and unostentatious dress. The rosary he holds is emblematic of his piety.

Philip, in which he enjoined him to uphold the Inquisition, suppress heresy, and maintain control over his councillors and advisers. Under Philip religion and politics did indeed remain deeply entwined. His reign was marked by a foreign policy driven by religious concerns—the long-running conflict with England under Elizabeth I and the struggle to maintain Spanish control of the Netherlands. The Spanish church was brought under the direct control of Philip II in order to defend it against heresy and to reform the clergy. Philip's religious policies continued to be enforced by the Inquisition. Among these policies was censorship, which may have acted as a check upon countervailing religious and cultural forces in Spain.

These restrictions notwithstanding, the sixteenth century was a notable epoch in Spain's history. Scientific developments included significant achievements in the fields of mechanics, engineering, navigation, and shipbuilding, which

In The Burial of the Count of Orgaz *(1586–1588)*, an oil executed for the Church of Santo Tomé, in Toledo, El Greco illustrates the miraculous appearance of Saint Stephen and Saint Augustine at the burial in 1323 of the devout count of Orgaz. One of the remarkable elements of the painting is the dichotomy between the abstract depiction of heaven above and the realistic appearance of the burial scene below.

furnished the requirements of Spain's burgeoning empire. Spanish engagement with the Americas also stimulated progress in cartography, natural science, and metallurgy.

During the same period Castilian became the language of Spain. There was a great flowering of Castilian literature, including the plays of Lope de Vega and Pedro Calderón de la Barca, the poetry of Juan Boscán Almogáver, and many picaresque and chivalric novels; one example is *Don Quixote,* the well-known satirical portrait of Spanish culture by Miguel Cervantes (1547–1616). Spanish painting was infused with Italian mannerist influences and culminated in the work of El Greco (Doménikos Theotokópoulos [1541–1614]). Thus, the sixteenth century saw a celebration of Spanish identity in much of its art and literature; Spaniards themselves call it the "golden century."

Despite the steady influx of gold and silver from the Americas, the many foreign wars in which Spain was involved in this period proved to be an almost intolerable drain on the country's resources. Although the Americas were a great source of wealth, their conquest, settlement, and administration were also expensive. In addition, at the beginning of the sixteenth century, only Portugal was a serious competitor in the New World. By its end the English, Dutch, and French had also become important colonial powers. Finally, Philip II's policy of isolation in the later years of his reign tended to put him out of touch with governmental and religious institutions.

Decline and End of Empire

The lack of focus that dominated Spanish political activity throughout the seventeenth century is ultimately traceable to Philip II's autocratic approach to government. This situation was exacerbated by the style of governance adopted by his son, Philip III (reigned 1598–1621). Unlike his father, Philip III had no desire to rule directly; instead, he left administrative duties to political councils and relied on his favorite, the duke of Lerma, to take on many of the onerous chores of rule. This approach characterizes the entirety of the reign of Philip III. When he died in 1621, his sixteen-year-old son, who became Philip IV, was left to run a country on the brink of economic collapse.

Philip IV (reigned 1621–1625) had as little ability to govern as his father. By 1637 Spain was at war with France, tax riots had broken out, and Catalan troops had refused to fight. Open rebellion in Catalonia and Portugal followed. In the final years of his reign, Philip IV allowed his chief minister, Luis Méndez de Haro, to run the country while he himself retired to Madrid. While not entirely successful, Haro's rule at least ensured the survival of the regime over the following several decades.

Upon Philip IV's death, Spain was essentially bankrupt, in the throes of a Portuguese rebellion, and with no clear heir to the throne; Philip's demise, for all practical purposes, marked the

SPAIN AND THE AMERICAS

Spanish involvement in the Americas was fundamental to the development of Spanish imperial power. The successful conquest of Mexico by Hernán Cortés by 1521 inspired the age of the conquistadores, who were motivated primarily by greed. The men who participated were not nobles but mainly impoverished adventurers in search of riches. The conquerors were soon followed by more permanent migrants for whom the New World presented an opportunity for rapid financial and social advance as well as an escape from their feudal lords in Spain. The initial wave of immigrants to the Americas consisted of men alone, but the number of women rose dramatically and reached over 28 percent after 1560. More than 200,000 Europeans moved to the Americas during the sixteenth century.

Missionaries perceived the potential to create a Christian land in the Americas, uncorrupted by the evils of the Old World; many saw the indigenous population as innocent of vice. The exploitation and enslavement of large numbers of native peoples by the settlers in order to found their communities was roundly condemned by many missionaries and even by the monarchs back in Spain, including Isabella of Castile and Charles V. The settlers were often in conflict with the humanist and Christian motivations of the missionaries.

Even more devastating to the indigenous population than exploitation and enslavement were the diseases the Spanish brought with them. It is estimated that in Peru the preconquest population of 9 million dwindled to 600,000 by 1620. This drastic reduction in population, along with the continual demand for labor, resulted in the massive importation of slaves from Africa by the European settlers. By 1600 there were more Africans than Spaniards in the Americas.

The Americas provided Spain with a major source of revenue to fuel its continuing military needs in Europe and the Mediterranean. By the 1590s more than two million ducats in gold and silver a year arrived from the New World.

◀ This illustration from a 1578 manuscript by Diego Duran, entitled Historia de las Indias, portrays a triumphant Hernán Cortés meeting the inhabitants of the Tlaxcala region of Mexico.

FURTHER READING

Barghahn, Barbara von. *Age of Gold, Age of Iron: Renaissance Spain and Symbols of Monarchy.* Lanham, MD, 1985.

Kamen, Henry. *Spain, 1469–1714: A Society of Conflict.* New York, 2005.

The Renaissance in Italy and Spain. Introduction by Frederick Hartt. New York, 1987.

Jessica L. Malay

end of the Spanish empire. Yet the significance of Renaissance Spain, or of any other society of the period, is far more than a matter of imperial success. The richness of the culture that flourished during Spain's golden century has already outlived all the empires of the period.

Spenser, Edmund

EDMUND SPENSER (1552/53–1599)
WAS A POET OF IMAGINATIVE FORCE
AND STYLISTIC INVENTION; MANY
THINK HIM THE GREATEST POET OF
THE ENGLISH RENAISSANCE.

▲ *This anonymous seventeenth-century portrait in oil shows a fashionably dressed Edmund Spenser. The high ruff was a popular feature of both sexes' garments at the court of Elizabeth I.*

Edmund Spenser was born in London to Elizabeth and John Spenser; his father was a free journeyman of the Merchant Taylors' Company. In 1561 Spenser became one of the earliest pupils to attend the Merchant Taylors' School, along with Thomas Kyd and Thomas Lodge (who would later become dramatists). In his final year before going to Cambridge University, Spenser translated a series of twenty-one poems, six by the Italian Petrarch and fifteen by the Frenchman Joachim du Bellay. These poems were published in the introductory material to Jan van der Noot's *A Theatre Wherein Be Represented As Well the Miseries and Calamities That Follow the Voluptuous Worldlings,* a Dutch collection that was translated into English and published in 1569. Spenser's headmaster, Richard Mulcaster (who was acquainted with van der Noot's cousin, Emanuel van Meteren) may have recommended Spenser's work for this important publication.

In May 1569 Spenser entered Pembroke College, Cambridge, as a sizar (an impoverished entrant who had to work for his room and board). In 1570 and 1571 he received money from a fund set up by Robert Nowell for poor students. It appears Spenser did not mind his duties as sizar; he spoke fondly in later years of his time at Cambridge, calling it "my mother Cambridge" in the *Faerie Queene.* At university Spenser would have had the opportunity to deepen his study of classical literature and languages and to increase his knowledge of other subjects, including French, Italian, astronomy, mathematics, and philosophy. In 1570 Spenser met Gabriel Harvey, who had been elected to a fellowship at

---

THE MERCHANT TAYLORS' SCHOOL

The purpose of the Merchant Taylors' School was to bring up "children in good manners and literature, to the number of two hundred and fifty," of which as many as one hundred could be talented sons from poor families, who were permitted to attend the school for reduced fees. The headmaster was the humanist scholar Richard Mulcaster. In addition to providing the students with a firm grounding in classical languages, the school curriculum included physical training and fitness as well as music education. The only known record of Spenser's attendance at the school dates from 1569, shortly before he left for Cambridge. On February 26 of that year, Spenser was given one shilling and a gown to wear at the funeral of the wealthy lawyer Robert Nowell. The receipt of this gift, which was allocated to poor students, may indicate that Spenser's family was experiencing financial hardship.

Pembroke College. Harvey was to have a significant influence on Spenser over the next ten years. Spenser graduated with a bachelor's degree in 1573 and a master's degree three years later.

Early Adulthood

After Cambridge, Spenser may have visited Ireland. It is recorded that he delivered letters from William Drury, president of Munster (in Ireland), to Robert Dudley, the earl of Leicester, in July 1577. The following year Spenser became secretary to John Young, bishop of Rochester, and probably moved into the bishop's residence in Bromley, Kent. In addition to performing his secretarial duties, Spenser continued to write poetry. During this time he wrote a series of works now lost, including a verse work, "Dreames, Legendes, Courte of Cupide" and a treatise on poetry, "The Englishe Poete."

In 1579 Spenser wrote to Harvey to announce his new employment with the earl of Leicester, one of the most powerful noblemen in England and Queen Elizabeth's favorite. In this year Spenser also published *The Shepheardes Calender,* a work of pastoral poetry that covered a variety of topics, including politics and religion as well as more personal ones of love and other biographical subjects. The *Calender* proved popular and was reprinted regularly throughout the following decade. Now living in London, Spenser joined the literary circle headed by Philip Sidney that included the poets Edward Dyer and Daniel Rogers. This group, sometimes referred to as the Areopagus, in imitation of the French poetic coterie the Pléiade, may have participated in discussions that gave Sidney ideas for his treatise on poetry, *An Apologie for Poesie.* In 1579 Spenser married Maccabaeus Childe (they had two children, Sylvanus and Katherine).

Irish Sojourn

After just over a year in London, Spenser became the secretary to Arthur, Lord Grey of Wilton, lord deputy of Ireland. Spenser's new employment took him to the heart of the conflict raging in Ireland between the native Irish and the increasingly powerful English settlers. Some historians have suggested that Spenser was sent to Ireland with Lord Grey as a punishment for a satire he produced that was critical of William Cecil, Lord Burghley, Queen Elizabeth's most influential counselor. In Ireland, Spenser

CHRONOLOGY

1552/1553
Edmund Spenser is born in London.

1579
The Shepheardes Calender is published.

1580
Spenser becomes secretary to Lord Grey of Wilton, lord deputy of Ireland; goes to Ireland.

1583
Becomes deputy to Lodowick Bryskett, clerk of Munster, in Ireland.

1591
Completes *Colin Clouts Come Home Againe.* Is granted a life pension of fifty pounds per annum by Elizabeth I.

1595
Amoretti and *Epithalamion* are published.

1598
Spenser's extended essay *A View of the Present State of Ireland* is entered in the stationers' register but is not published until 1633.

1599
Spenser dies in London on January 13.

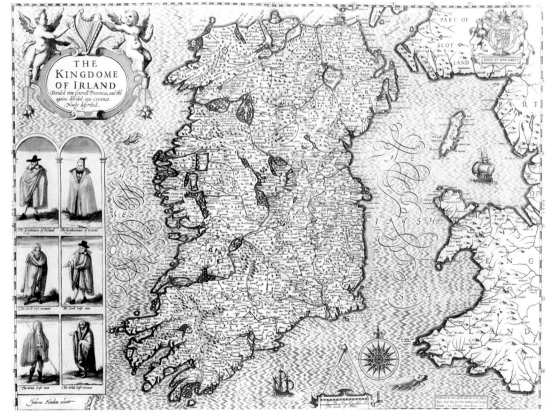

◄ John Speed's map "The Kingdom of Ireland," engraved by Jodocus Hondius (Joost de Hondt; 1563–1612), appeared as a part of Speed's Theatre of the Empire of Great Britain, *published by John Sudbury and George Humble in 1610. This engraving presents Ireland as a patchwork of counties. On the left typical Irish citizens are depicted in the traditional dress Spenser would have recognized.*

▶ This 1581 woodcut, which depicts the month of February and includes an image of the fishes of Pisces, was one of a series of vignettes that accompanied an early edition of Spenser's Shepheardes Calender.

probably witnessed the slaughter of six hundred Spanish and Italian soldiers who surrendered to Lord Grey in 1580. A letter to the queen in Spenser's hand vehemently defends this action.

In Ireland, Spenser was finally able to secure his position as a gentleman. While living in Dublin, it is likely that he became a member of the city's intellectual circle, which included Barnaby Googe, whose *Eglogs, Epytaphs,* and *Sonettes* (1563) may have had some influence on Spenser's *Shepheardes Calender.* In December 1581 Spenser was granted an official lease for the abbey and manor of Enniscorthy, in County Wexford. He also acquired other properties, mainly confiscated from Irish landowners, in an attempt to improve his financial situation. In 1582, with Lord Grey's departure from Ireland, Spenser's secretaryship ended. Spenser remained in Ireland, however, and was appointed a commissioner for the musters—the task of organizing local men for military service—in County Kildare. At this time Spenser resided in New Abbey, near Kilcullen, in County Kildare, twenty-five miles from Dublin. Over the following eight years Spenser held several administrative positions in Ireland and amassed a large amount of property, including 3,028 acres attached to Kilcolman, a ruined Norman castle in County Cork. Spenser probably lived in an adjoining house. This land acquisition was not without problems, however, and a lawsuit by Lord Roche, claiming that he owned the lands, including Kilcolman, remained troublesome for Spenser throughout the next decade.

Throughout this period Spenser worked on his epic poem, *The Faerie Queene.* He brought a copy of the first part (books 1–3) when he returned to England with Sir Walter Raleigh in 1589. The title was entered into the stationers' register (the record of texts approved for printing in England) on December 1, 1589, and published in early 1590. It is likely that Spenser read portions of the poem to the queen herself, for which she rewarded him with the grant of a pension of fifty pounds a year. In 1590 Spenser was also given the manor of Kilcolman by royal grant; his ownership was thus confirmed, as was his position as a landed gentleman.

Literary Production

The confirmation of Spenser's social status did not slow his literary production. In late 1590 *Complaints,* a collection of his shorter poetic works (including "The Ruins of Time") was published. William Ponsonby, the printer who set the *Complaints,* explained that it was to be "all complaints and meditations of the world's vanity, very grave and profitable." One poem, "Mother

*T*he Faerie Queene is indisputably a product of the Renaissance; classical writers such as Virgil and Homer influenced the scope and shape of the work. Also influential was the Italian poet Ludovico Ariosto, in whose work *Orlando furioso* (1516) Spenser found a model for his heroine, Britomart. Spenser derived his archaic poetic language and models for the allegorical depictions of moral values from Geoffrey Chaucer. Through the sophisticated allegorical framework of *The Faerie Queene*, Spenser explores the Protestant doctrine of grace. The poem is also a highly politicized work, ostensibly a celebration of Queen Elizabeth and her defense of Protestantism in defiance of powerful threats, especially from the Spanish. Yet it is not simply a moralistic allegory or a political tribute; it also contains a vibrancy that communicates anxiety over the transience of beauty and the almost overwhelming demands of the spirit.

Hubbard's Tale," is a very slightly veiled attack on William Cecil in the form of an allegory featuring the adventures of a fox and an ape at court. Spenser bitterly accuses Cecil in the lines "But his own treasure he increased more / And lifted up his lofty towers thereby." The towers Spenser refers to were both the magnificent Burghley House in Lincolnshire and the even grander Theobalds in Hertforshire. Cecil built both houses, the second supposedly as an alternative royal palace, which Queen Elizabeth visited regularly. The *Complaints* was quickly recalled after publication, probably because of the attacks on Cecil. Having once again incurred the wrath of Elizabeth's most powerful counselor, Spenser now returned to Ireland.

During the years 1591 to 1594, Spenser undertook a variety of administrative positions in Ireland, including the role of queen's justice (judge) for Cork. He continued his legal battle with Lord Roche over lands they both claimed and developed his estate, which had become home to several families of English settlers. The policy of settling the newly established plantations with English families and displacing the local Irish population proved very unpopular and contributed to frequent violent uprisings.

Spenser continued to write: he completed the autobiographical *Colin Clouts Come Home Againe* and a beautiful and moving sonnet sequence, the *Amoretti,* which depicts Spenser's courtship and marriage to Elizabeth Boyle—a relative of Richard Boyle, later earl of Cork—on June 11, 1594. (It is not known when Spenser's first wife died.)

In 1596 the second edition of *The Faerie Queene* was published with an additional three

THE FAERIE
QVEENE.

Diſpoſed into twelue books,
Faſhioning
X I I. Morall vertues.

LONDON
Printed for William Ponſonbie.
I 5 9 0.

In 1590 William Ponsonby published the first three books of The Faerie Queene; pictured is the engraved title page to the first London edition. The publication was greeted with general admiration.

books and a revision of the first three. The work was once again dedicated to Elizabeth I. While received warmly in general, Spenser's depiction of Mary, Queen of Scots, caused James VI of Scotland to protest the book's characterization of his mother and request that Spenser be punished. In 1596 *A View of the Present State of Ireland* was entered in the stationers' office but was not printed until 1633. In this work Spenser's deep distrust and abhorrence of the Irish people is apparent.

SPENSERIAN STANZA

The Spenserian stanza is a nine-line stanza that Spenser developed for his own poetic purposes. The stanza consists of eight lines in iambic pentameter (that is, lines of ten syllables) followed by a ninth line in iambic hexameter (twelve syllables). Even more unusual than the metric irregularity is the stanza's rhyme scheme: ababbcbcc. It is a difficult verse pattern, especially for a poet writing in English, because of the limited number of rhymes available. The example that follows is stanza 40 from canto 11 of book 1 of *The Faerie Queene;* the hero, the Red Cross Knight, who is fighting a dragon, has just chopped off his adversary's tail:

Hart cannot thinke, what outrage, and what cryes,	[a]
With foule enfouldred smoake and flashing fire,	[b]
The hell-bred beast threw forth unto the skyes,	[a]
That all was covered with darknesse dire:	[b]
Then fraught with rancour, and engorged ire,	[b]
He cast at once him to avenge for all	[c]
And gathering up himselfe out of the mire,	[b]
With his uneven wings did fiercely fall	[c]
Upon his sun-bright shield, and gript it fast withall.	[c]

The brilliant success with which Spenser used his stanza made the form, despite its inherent difficulties, attractive to poets in the following centuries. The Spenserian stanza achieved a second flowering through its frequent adoption by the greatest English romantic poets of the nineteenth century: John Keats, Percy Bysshe Shelley, and Lord Byron.

▶ *This decorative medallion from a George II commode (c. 1790), taken from a 1783 engraving by Thomas Burke, portrays Una and the Lion, featured characters in book 1 of* The Faerie Queene.

Exile from Ireland

In 1598 Spenser was promoted to sheriff of County Cork. However, at this time a conflict later known as the Nine Years War was raging in Ireland; Hugh O'Neill's Irish forces were rapidly approaching the area, and Spenser and his family were forced to flee their home in Kilcullen for the relative safety of Cork. His estate in ruins, Spenser returned to England in December 1598 with a letter from Thomas Norris, president of Munster, to the Privy Council, explaining the precarious position of the county. Spenser died on January 13, 1599. His funeral was paid for by the earl of Essex, the queen's favorite courtier at the time. The historian William Camden wrote of the funeral that Spenser's "hearse [was] attended by poets, and mournful elegies and poems, with the pens that wrote them, [were] thrown into the tomb." Spenser was buried near Geoffrey Chaucer in Westminster Abbey. Elizabeth I ordered a tomb to be erected but did not live to see her wishes fulfilled. A monument was finally erected for Spenser in 1620, paid for by Anne Clifford, countess of Dorset, herself a patron of writers.

FURTHER READING

Hadfield, Andrew. *Edmund Spenser's Irish Experience: Wilde Fruit and Savage Soyl.* New York, 1997.

Mohl, Ruth. *Edmund Spenser, His Life and Works.* New York, 1988.

Waller, Gary. *Edmund Spenser: A Literary Life.* New York, 1994.

Jessica L. Malay

SEE ALSO

• Chaucer, Geoffrey • Chivalry • Church of England
• Elizabeth I • England • Established Churches
• Humanism and Learning • Iconoclasm
• Literature

Spinoza, Baruch

BARUCH SPINOZA (1632–1677) IS KNOWN FOR THE PROFUNDITY OF HIS THOUGHT. HE WAS A MAJOR FIGURE IN THE RATIONALIST MOVEMENT OF THE SEVENTEENTH CENTURY, WHICH SOUGHT TRUTH OUTSIDE RELIGION.

Baruch Spinoza was born in Amsterdam, the son of a Jewish merchant. He received an excellent elementary education in preparation for further study, but for reasons unknown, Spinoza left school at the age of seventeen and embarked on a path that ultimately led to his excommunication from the Jewish community. Spinoza's later life

was devoted to developing the philosophical concepts that earned him the enmity of his former coreligionists. When he died, at the age of forty-five, his works were published posthumously but banned in his native country.

Amsterdam and Marrano Culture

Spinoza's parents had moved from Portugal to Amsterdam to escape the Inquisition, which in the early 1600s sought religious and cultural homogeneity by offering Jews and Muslims on the Iberian Peninsula the choice of leaving or converting to Christianity. In Amsterdam the Spinozas became a part of a small community of Marranos—Jews who had become Christians to avoid investigation by the Inquisition but who retained many of their Jewish practices in private. Relatively safe in Amsterdam, the Jewish community quietly resumed most elements of their lifestyle and religious practices. However, the necessity of leading a double life, embracing Christianity in public and Judaism in private, was to have a great effect on Spinoza's outlook and thought.

As a child Spinoza attended the Talmud Torah School, where he received a traditional Jewish education. At the age of seventeen, he left school and started work in his father's business along with his half brother Gabriel. Spinoza's education continued in a more informal environment. As a merchant he interacted with a broad variety of people, and during this period he began to attend meetings of small groups, called colleges, whose members discussed various philosophers and their theories. When Franciscus van den Enden, a former member of the Jesuits, a Catholic order of priests, started a school, Spinoza gladly attended. Under van den Enden's tutelage, Spinoza was first introduced to the works of René Descartes, a seventeenth-century French philosopher also known for his contributions to mathematics, particularly analytical

◀ *After he was excommunicated in 1656, Baruch Spinoza began using the forename Benedictus to mark his break with the Jewish community. This portrait was painted in 1670 by an unknown German artist.*

THEOLOGICAL-POLITICAL TREATISE

In the *Theological-Political Treatise*, Spinoza tackled the issue of the multitude and the power of the clergy. In his examination of society, Spinoza was struck by the constantly shifting opinion of the people around him. He was alarmed at the capacity of the multitude (as he labeled the majority of people) for violence. Spinoza believed that the power of the multitude, coupled with the power the clergy exercised over society, inhibited philosophers from free thought. Ruled by superstition and emotion, the multitude posed a danger to the stability of society and inhibited the freedom of others, particularly philosophers, from pursuing higher thought. In turn, the clergy capitalized on the irrationality of the multitude and utilized it as a foundation for its own power.

To remedy these problems in society, Spinoza proposed a dual approach. He held that the multitude could never achieve rationality, that they were controlled by their emotions rather than their minds and therefore were irrational. He felt that they could be coerced into exhibiting a semblance of rationality only through religion. A religion that was universal, that drew its authority from revelation as found in the Bible, would attract the loyalty of the multitude. The role of prophets should not be emphasized. Religion should promote societal values such as justice and solidarity. According to Spinoza, the state would hold the ultimate authority to interpret religion and administer punishment for infractions. It would act as a civilizing agent for the multitude while at the same time diminishing the power of the clergy. Spinoza hails democracy in this work as the best form of government to achieve his ends.

geometry. Descartes had an enormous influence on Spinoza.

When Spinoza began to voice his own opinions, the elders of the Jewish community indicated their disapproval. Although there are no records that describe the precise nature of

▶ *In 1663 Spinoza published his commentary on Descartes's major work, the* Principia. *While he was critical of many aspects of Descartes's theory, Spinoza was profoundly indebted to the Frenchman's philosophy, which provided the foundation for his own system. This was the only work Spinoza published under his own name and one of only two books that Spinoza published in his lifetime, along with the* Theological-Political Treatise.

Spinoza's views, his later works provide strong hints. His denial of Judaism and Christianity and his arguments against the power of the clergy threatened the foundation and stability of the Marrano community. In 1656 he was excommunicated. This act did not merely cut his connections with the religious community; Jews were no longer permitted to patronize his business or associate with him. Spinoza was forced to leave Amsterdam.

The chronology of the next years is unclear. Spinoza took up lens grinding and continued his studies. He spent time at the University of Leiden, where he probably received formal training in Cartesian philosophy.

Later Life and Works

In 1661 Spinoza relocated to Rijnsburg. He began the *Treatise on the Emendation of the Intellect,* which outlined themes that he would explore in his later works, including the nature of definition and types of knowledge. He also wrote *A Short Treatise on God, Man, and His Well-Being.* In this text Spinoza laid the foundation for part of his greatest work, the *Ethics,* which explores questions of the identification of God with nature.

In 1663 Spinoza moved again, this time to Voorburg, where he resided for the next seven years of his life. Encouraged by friends, he edited

and published his lecture notes on the teachings of Descartes: *René Descartes's Principles of Philosophy, Parts 1 and 2, Demonstrated according to the Geometric Method by Benedict de Spinoza of Amsterdam*. In this work he challenged Descartes's views by claiming that God and creation were not separate substances. Spinoza began the *Theological-Political Treatise* while living in Voorburg, though he did not complete it until 1670. When it was published in that year, the *Treatise* generated considerable controversy among both Christians and Jews. Critics claimed that Spinoza was an atheist and a heretic. This criticism had a profound effect on Spinoza, who refused to publish any more of his works lest they receive the same response.

▲ *René Descartes (c. 1595–1650) was a philosopher and mathematician whose numerous works had a profound impact on Spinoza. This 1645 oil-on-canvas portrait is by the French painter Sebastien Bourdon.*

Last Years

In 1670 Spinoza made his final move, to The Hague. There he completed a series of works, including the *Ethics* (1675), which proved to be his best-known work. Owing to the controversy that had ensued following the publication of the *Theological-Political Treatise,* Spinoza opted not to publish the *Ethics.* He turned instead to a new work, the *Political Treatise,* an attempt to improve governments. It remained unpublished at the time of his death.

Spinoza died in 1677 at the age of forty-five as a result of glass dust in his lungs, an occupational hazard from his job as a lens grinder. A year later his unpublished works were collected and published by friends. They were promptly banned in the Netherlands.

Philosophy

Spinoza wrote under the shadow of Descartes. As a young man Spinoza was intrigued by Descartes's teachings, though he did not agree with his theory of substance—the basic material that makes up both the physical and the spiritual realms. Descartes made a sharp distinction between mind and body, holding that the two existed in entirely different ways. In order for human beings to find truth, Descartes thought that they should focus not on material things, such as the body or its senses, but rather on the mind itself; his famous phase "I think, therefore I am" embodies his thought. For him the goal of philosophy was to help people turn away from the material and toward the intellectual or the spiritual.

Through his philosophy Spinoza provided an alternative to Descartes's theory of substance; he argued that mind and body were connected, rather than separate. By emphasizing this connection, Spinoza sought to show that mind and body were two attributes, or qualities, of one substance. He went farther by claiming that this substance was the basis for all things in the universe and therefore was God or nature.

THE *ETHICS*

In the *Ethics,* Spinoza addresses the problem of how man can find happiness. The first part discusses the relationship between God and nature, while the second develops Spinoza's contention that man is an extension of the attributes of God (for example, like God, man is able to think). The third and fourth sections address man's place within the universe and how man can find happiness.

The *Ethics* is structured according to the geometric method that was used by the Greek philosopher Euclid in the third century BCE. Though Spinoza was not the first to utilize this method, he is known for his modifications of it. The *Ethics* proceeds through a series of propositions or definitions, each built upon the previous one. Spinoza does not create new terminology but strives to clarify terms, mostly religious in nature. He creates a system of definitions that function as both philosophical and religious truths. For example, to say that God is omnipotent is both a philosophical and a theological truth according to Spinoza.

Spinoza's views on God derive from his definition of substance as the most basic unit of independent existence. Because substance does not depend on anything else for its existence, God is the *only* substance. Though God has infinite attributes and ways of expressing these attributes, man can grasp only two modes of expression. The physical world is the overflowing of God's infinite power. Thus, a flower is a mode of God. Thoughts are also modes of God. Man knows God through these extensions of attributes. Most people, however, are ignorant of the connection between God and the natural world and unable to comprehend that the world is a mode of God. They therefore possess an inadequate understanding of the world.

Within the *Ethics,* Spinoza outlines three types of knowledge. This first is opinion or imagination. This type of knowledge is faulty and controls the multitude. The second and third types of knowledge—reason and intuition—belong to the philosophers. In order to experience happiness, man must transform his false knowledge into true knowledge by altering his mind from passive to active. A passive mind generates inadequate ideas by failing to strive to understand God's relationship to creation. Spinoza gives forty-eight emotions that stem from passivity but emphasizes desire, pain, and pleasure as the dominant feelings man experiences. In contrast, a person with an active mind can move from opinion to reason and then to an intuitive knowledge of God, the highest form of knowledge. In this final stage man acquires an adequate conception of self and all things that are within his understanding. This knowledge brings happiness.

Spinoza's philosophy is marked by his criticisms of historical religions, Judaism in particular, which seemed to him to be arbitrary. To Spinoza the laws of the prophets were not the laws of God; rather, God's laws were manifest in nature. To be more precise, nature and God were one and the same. Spinoza was a monist—he did not believe that there was a difference between God and the universe. For Spinoza, God moved in the world and was present in creation.

Spinoza did not believe that human beings have free will. Because God is the only substance, God is free. All other things are connected in an intricate causal system that precludes freedom. For Spinoza all events are causally inevitable or caused by the events that precede them. Man deceives himself when he thinks his actions are not predetermined.

Though Spinoza wrote many treatises, the *Theological-Political Treatise* and the *Ethics* are the best known. The *Ethics,* which builds on the principles laid out in the *Theological-Political Treatise,* moves from Spinoza's initial questions about how to control the multitude to considerations of how to find happiness.

Influence

Spinoza's impact on later thought is significant, although it long got less attention than it merited. Whether they admired him or disliked him, Enlightenment philosophers had to address Spinoza's theories. For example, John Locke, a seventeenth-century English philosopher (1632–1704) who emphasized the need for observation in the formation of knowledge, incorporated many of Spinoza's ideas into his own writings. Gottfried Wilhelm Leibniz (1646–1716), the cocreator of calculus, a branch of mathematics that focuses on motion and change, was profoundly influenced by Spinoza's thoughts on freedom (Leibniz changed from an admirer to a critic of Spinoza). Nineteenth-century advances in science brought a brief revival of interest in Spinoza's work, especially his theories on continual motion and the absence of vacuums. Modern studies continue to discover traces of Spinoza's thought in unexpected places. In short, the picture of Spinoza's influence is a work in progress.

BENOÎT SPINOSA *né en 1632, mort en 1677.*

FURTHER READING

Allison, Henry. *Benedict de Spinoza: An Introduction.* New Haven, CT, 1987.

Curley, Edwin. *Behind the Geometrical Method.* Princeton, NJ, 1988.

Nadler, Steven. *Spinoza: A Life.* New York, 1999.

Wolfson, H. A. *The Philosophy of Spinoza: Unfolding the Latent Processes of His Reasoning.* 2 vols. New York, 1960.

Yovel, Yrmiyahu. *Spinoza and Other Heretics.* Vol. 1, *The Marrano of Reason;* vol. 2, *The Adventures of Immanence.* Princeton, NJ, 1989.

Lisa R. Holliday

SEE ALSO

• Descartes, René • Judaism • Philosophy

▲ *Following the unfavorable reception of the* Theological-Political Treatise, *Spinoza declined to publish any more of his works. He spent the remainder of his life writing the* Political Treatise, *which was published posthumously. In 1762 Jean-Charles François crafted this copper engraving of Spinoza after an earlier work by Delhay.*

Stuarts, The

THE STUARTS HELD THE SCOTTISH THRONE FROM THE FOURTEENTH CENTURY. WHEN KING JAMES VI BECAME JAMES I OF ENGLAND IN 1603, THE STUARTS RULED THE BRITISH ISLES.

The first Stuart (the Scottish spelling of the name is Stewart) to hold the throne of Scotland was Robert II (reigned 1371–1390), who was the son of Walter Stewart, a leading Scottish noble. The Stuart kings of the fourteenth and fifteenth centuries gradually consolidated their control of the crown, although they had to manage a class of powerful nobles who were willing to rebel against any king that displayed either political weakness or despotic tendencies. James I (reigned 1406–1437), a strong king whose aggressive moves enhanced the power of the monarchy, was murdered by a conspiracy of noblemen in February 1437. James III (reigned 1460–1488) was killed by another group of disaffected nobles at Sauchieburn in June 1488.

James IV (reigned 1488–1513) and his son James V (reigned 1513–1542) both extended the power of the Scottish crown. James IV gained the submission of most of the highland chiefs of the north and west of Scotland, improved royal finances, and expanded the scope of the central legal system. James V brought further order to Shetland, Orkney, and the Western Isles and continued his father's legal reforms. Both kings managed the noble factions capably, and both possessed the personal qualities and strength of character needed to impose direct rule on a country whose official institutions were underdeveloped in comparison with those of other European nations. James V, however, acquired a reputation for brutality; he ruthlessly pursued his political enemies to the death and benefited from the confiscation of their estates. Both kings presided over the development of a sophisticated Renaissance court culture; they patronized musicians and poets and sponsored extensive building works that reflected the Scottish aristocracy's admiration for French culture.

Despite their domestic success, both kings came to grief trying to maintain Scottish independence in the struggles with their neighbor and traditional enemy, England. James IV, forced by his alliance with France into a war against

▶ King James II acquired the MacDuff family castle in Falkland, in Fife, eastern Scotland, and made it a royal home. The castle was replaced by James IV and James V with the Renaissance-influenced Falkland Palace pictured here; James V added a royal tennis court that survives to this day.

▼ *This illustration, from a 1588 manuscript titled* The Arms of the Nobility of Scotland, *depicts James IV of Scotland and his wife, Margaret, the daughter of King Henry VII of England. Their marriage in 1503 gave their great-grandson, James VI, a strong claim to the throne of England one hundred years later.*

England, was killed in September 1513, together with a large number of Scottish nobles, by the forces of Henry VIII at the Battle of Flodden (the site of battle is sometimes called Branxton Moor). James V died at age thirty after a failed attempt to repel invading English forces at the Battle of Solway Moss (1542). A broken heart, brought on by his failure, was once thought responsible, but a swift, virulent disease was the more likely culprit. James V's heir was his infant daughter from his marriage to Mary of Guise, the daughter of the duke of Guise, a powerful French nobleman. That infant later became Mary, Queen of Scots.

Mary, Queen of Scots, and the Scottish Reformation

Mary Stuart was six days old when her father died. To protect Scotland from English aggression, the so-called Auld Alliance with France was yet again renewed, and the young Mary was sent to the French court on August 7, 1548, promised in marriage to the heir to the French throne, the dauphin Francis. Mary grew up as a Frenchwoman and was married to Francis on April 24, 1558. He became king the next year.

Meanwhile, on November 17 of the same year, Elizabeth Tudor inherited the English throne. Henry VIII, Elizabeth's father, had married her mother, Anne Boleyn, after divorcing Catherine of Aragon and breaking with the

Roman Catholic Church (the pope had refused to annul the marriage to Catherine). Many Catholics refused to accept the validity of the divorce; they were therefore hostile to Elizabeth not only because she was a Protestant but also because, viewing her as an illegitimate child, they considered her an illegitimate ruler.

▲ *This portrait, a copy of a work by the Frenchman Jean Clouet (c. 1485–c. 1540), depicts Mary Stuart (Mary, Queen of Scots) around age eighteen.*

support of the new Protestant English regime under Elizabeth allowed the lords of the congregation to take over the government of Scotland. The so-called Reformation Parliament that met on August 1, 1560, produced a new confession of faith, which abolished the Mass, denied the jurisdiction of the pope, and established the doctrine of the Church of Scotland (known as the Kirk) along Reformed, Calvinist lines. Although she was a Catholic, on her return Mary did little to slow the progress of the Reformation. Her main priority seems to have been to win recognition as the legitimate heir of Elizabeth of England, a very unlikely event given Elizabeth's reluctance to make firm statements on the matter.

Mary's subsequent marriages were disastrous errors of judgment. Her second husband was Henry, Lord Darnley, a brainless drunkard intent on gaining official recognition of his claim to equal power with his wife in government. He joined a faction of nobles who, dissatisfied with Mary's policies, murdered her Italian secretary, David Rizzio, when he was in the room adjacent to that of the pregnant queen. In a crisis-ridden atmosphere Mary gave birth to Prince James on June 19, 1566. Darnley, loathed by almost all the political elite, was strangled on February 10, 1567, probably by a coalition of nobles that included James Hepburn, earl of Bothwell. Bothwell was certainly considered the leading culprit, and Mary caused a scandal when she married him in May of the same year. Historians believe that Bothwell may have raped her and that Mary, who was politically isolated, saw no other choice than to consent to marriage.

In the following power struggle between Bothwell and Mary on one side and a coalition of hostile lords on the other, Mary was captured, imprisoned, and forced to abdicate. After an attempt to regain power failed, Mary escaped over the border to England in May 1568. Expecting succor and safe refuge, she was arrested and confined for the rest of her life. While imprisoned, she became the focus of Catholic plots to release her and place her on the throne. In 1586 she was tried for complicity in the Babington Plot, a conspiracy led by the Catholic nobleman Anthony Babington to overthrow or murder Elizabeth and replace her with Mary. Mary's guilt

Through her grandmother Margaret, Mary, Queen of Scots, was the nearest Catholic heir to the throne of England. The English royal arms were used in pageantry and iconography associated with Mary. This appropriation infuriated English Protestants, who saw it as an attempt to stake Mary's claim to the English throne.

Mary's mother, Mary of Guise, acted as regent of Scotland on the queen's behalf from 1554 to 1560, a critical period for religion and religious politics in Scotland. Protestantism in Scotland was not widespread, but an influential—albeit small—faction of Protestant nobles, known as the lords of the congregation, began to agitate for religious change. Mary of Guise's death in January 1560, the failure of Mary Stuart to return to Scotland until August 1561 (despite her husband's death the previous December), and the

having been established by her correspondence with Babington, she was executed in 1587.

James VI, King of Scotland

Born in 1566, James VI, like his mother, became monarch in his infancy (1567); he later described himself as a cradle king. Unlike his mother, however, James was destined to become one of the most successful Scottish monarchs. After Mary's flight to England in 1568, the Scottish nobility fought a civil war until 1573, when the remains of Mary's party were finally defeated. For the rest of James's minority, the government was more stable, and his majority was declared in 1585. The young king was educated by the pre-eminent Scottish humanist George Buchanan, who subjected his young charge to an intellectually rigorous and physically harsh education that included regular beatings. Thanks to his education, James became perhaps the most scholarly of all British kings.

Following the example of James V, James VI attempted to strengthen royal control as soon as his minority ended. James VI combined authority with accommodation in his political approach to the Scottish nobility and parliament. This approach has won him praise from historians of Scotland, but their high opinion contrasts notably with his less stellar reputation as occupant of the English throne.

◄ A drawing by an unknown Dutch artist of the execution in 1587 of Mary, Queen of Scots. When her cousin Elizabeth died sixteen years later, Mary's son, James, came into possession of both their crowns.

THE POLITICAL THOUGHT OF JAMES VI

James VI (also James I of England) wrote prolifically on many different subjects. His best-known works are *The Trew Laws of Free Monarchies* and *Basilikon doron* (Royal Gift), both written in 1598 and 1599, before his accession to the English throne. The *Trew Law of Free Monarchies* was James's attempt to enter into a political debate about the nature of kingship. He sought to counter the so-called resistance theory—of which George Buchanan was a prominent exponent—which argued for the rights of a prince's subjects to depose a ruler who governed badly. James argued that, since the power of kings was ordained by God, only God could take that power away. *Basilikon doron* was a practical manual on how to govern a kingdom, written to advise James's young son and heir, Prince Henry, whose death in 1613 prevented him from implementing his father's advice. James also wrote theology, poetry, and tracts on witchcraft and tobacco.

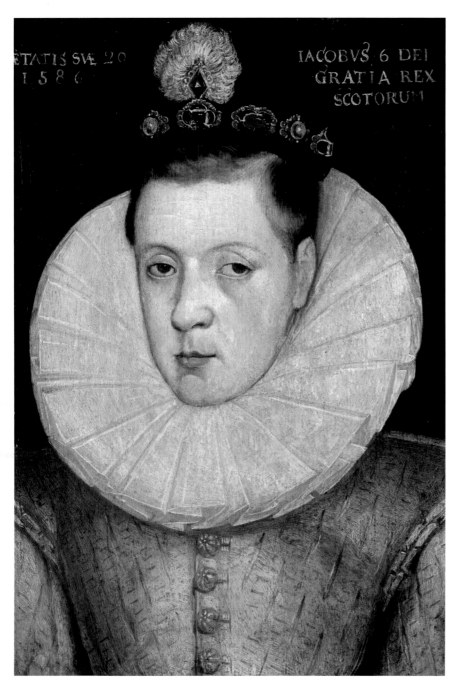

ETATIS SVÆ 20
1586

IACOBVS 6 DEI
GRATIA REX
SCOTORUM

▲ *This unattributed oil-on-panel portrait of James VI was painted in 1586, when the Scottish monarch (and future king of England) was twenty.*

James's most memorable achievement was his management of the Scottish Kirk. With great care and a considerable degree of conflict with the more radical Scottish clerics, James revived the office of bishop and the authority of the monarch in the Scottish church. He thus developed a church that appeased a wide range of Scottish Protestant sensibilities and proved immensely popular in the parishes.

James I, King of England

James VI of Scotland succeeded Elizabeth I to the thrones of England and Ireland on March 24, 1603. Although his accession was greeted with relief by Protestants thankful that the specter of a Catholic successor had failed to materialize, most English men and women had no love of the Scottish nation, which they perceived to be inferior in every way to their own. James's first priority—the union of his realms into one kingdom—was thus doomed from the start. The English Parliament, resenting the presence of Scots at court and fearing that English wealth would drain into Scotland, utterly rejected this project. The Scots, just as reluctant, preferred instead to retain their institutional independence from the English. James returned to Scotland only once, in 1617, but the effective Scottish government he had developed continued to function much as it had done before 1603.

The frustration of James's cherished plans for more than a personal union soured his relations with the English Parliament, and relations were damaged yet further by his terrible financial management. The debts James inherited from Elizabeth were increased by his need to provide suitable households for his wife and children and to reward his Scottish and English followers. Many members of Parliament regarded the king as wantonly extravagant. His debts mounting, James tried to exploit sources of revenue in ways that provoked dislike and resistance. He claimed the right to use the natural authority of the crown to levy certain commercial duties without parliamentary consent. This perceived overreaching prompted questions as to the nature and extent of the royal prerogative, and quarrels over financial matters developed into arguments over constitutional principles. These arguments were aired with increasing bitterness in the parliamentary debates of James's reign.

If the king's extravagance was seen as one aspect of an endemic corruption in his court, his tendency to raise up favorites was seen as another. One of those favorites, Robert Carr, became embroiled in a murder scandal that shocked the whole nation. The most notorious, however, was George Villiers, who became duke of Buckingham in 1623. Buckingham's rapacious ambition and control over most patronage networks engendered bitter resentment and envy among those outside the duke's favor.

As had been the case in Scotland, James proved extremely adept in his management of the complex and sensitive issue of religious politics in England. An extremely tolerant policy allowed Catholics in the English church to coexist peacefully if they took an oath of loyalty to the crown. James was no Catholic himself, but while he insisted that the doctrine of the Church of England and of Scotland remain fundamentally Calvinist, he refrained from heavily restrictive government of the church. Under James the English church was a more inclusive and harmonious body than it had been at any time since the Reformation.

James's efficacy as a monarch of England deteriorated with the outbreak of the Thirty Years War, a pan-European conflict, in 1618. James was opposed to war on ideological grounds. He took pride in his diplomatic skills and had renewed relations with Catholic Spain, much to the chagrin of many of his Protestant subjects. However, his son-in-law, Frederick V, the elector palatine, was at the heart of a conflict that polarized Europe along confessional lines. Frederick lost the Bohemian crown and his lands in the Palatinate. Horrified, James tried to remedy the situation by arbitration. His scheme for reconciliation included the marriage of his son Charles to a Spanish princess, a proposal that met with widespread public hostility in England. When the marriage negotiations failed, Charles and Buckingham turned in favor of war. In James's final months, England finally entered a conflict that the old king had done all he could to avoid.

▲ A contemporary engraving by Franz Hogenberg of the coronation of James VI of Scotland as James I of England on July 25, 1603. James was the first Scottish monarch in three hundred years to be crowned on the sacred Stone of Scone, which Edward I had taken from Scotland in 1296 and placed in Westminster Abbey.

Charles I

When James's son Charles came to the throne in 1625, the country was in the midst of a diplomatic crisis. Disillusioned by his failed attempt at a Spanish marriage, Charles determined to enter into the war against the Hapsburgs, but parliamentary support did not extend as far as adequate funding. A new alliance with France and a French bride could not support Charles's dreams of restoring his sister and brother-in-law to the Palatinate, and the underfunded military expeditions that did take place were disastrous failures. Debaters in the Parliament of 1629 began to criticize Charles's financial and religious politics. The king dissolved Parliament and ruled without it for the next eleven years.

Charles's rule in the 1630s appeared to be peaceful. His court, in contrast with his father's, was chaste and decorous. He managed to decrease the royal debt by ending English involvement in the Thirty Years War and by exploiting older sources of revenue. However, the reactionary religious policies of Charles and his archbishop of Canterbury, William Laud, became increasingly unpopular, and the combination of Charles's openly Catholic wife, Henrietta Maria, and the presence of Catholics at court convinced many English men and women that a conspiracy was under way to subvert the Church of England. Charles had a particularly elevated view of kingship that clashed with the vision of those lawyers and

▲ *Included in this family portrait, a copy of an oil by the court painter Anthony Van Dyck (1599–1641), are King Charles I, his wife, Henrietta Maria, and two of their children. For Charles, who recognized the propagandistic value of art, Van Dyck's paintings were a way of trumpeting the glory and prestige of the house of Stuart.*

THE LATER STUARTS

When the Stuarts were restored to all three of their kingdoms in 1660, many of the problems that they had faced throughout their earlier rule of Scotland, England, and Ireland still existed. Suspicions in England especially that the Stuarts were inclined to a belief in their divine right to rule and a royal prerogative that impinged upon the privileges and liberties of their subjects were not wholly appeased by the Restoration settlement, although Parliament had assured itself a permanent place in the English constitution. Nor had the Restoration settlement provided adequately for the king's finances. The licentious and scandalous court of Charles II did nothing to subdue widespread anxieties about corruption. The difficulties of governing three administrations and three different Protestant churches—as well as a significant Catholic population—remained. Continuing Protestants fears of a "popish" plot to gain the throne produced several episodes of panic under Charles II. The culmination of these fears was the forced abdication and flight into exile of Charles's brother and successor, the openly Catholic James II, in 1688, after which James's daughter Mary and her Dutch Protestant husband, William of Orange, were invited by Parliament to take the throne. The Stuarts' interrelated problems of financial strain, corruption at court, the constant need to answer accusations of papal influence, and difficulty holding together a tripartite monarchy had been solved neither by the civil wars nor by the Restoration.

members of Parliament who held that royal authority was circumscribed by the laws of the land. He was also shy and aloof and lacked his father's capability of engaging in debate and understanding the point of view of others.

The financial security of the monarchy under Charles lasted only as long as the king was not forced to fight a war. The peace was finally shattered in 1637. The introduction of a new prayer book in Scotland, in conjunction with other high-handed policies of Charles toward the Scottish political classes, sparked a Scottish resistance focused in a movement bound by a covenant (hence, its adherents were called Covenanters). Charles moved to suppress the Covenanters by force; to do so, he required funding that only Parliament could provide. In the Parliaments of 1640, Charles was faced with an array of grievances concerning his religious and financial policies. The situation was exacerbated when the Irish Catholics rebelled in the autumn of 1641.

Charles declared war on Parliament in 1642, and a bloody conflict ensued. Civil conflict dominated all three kingdoms, and although an uneasy peace was reached in 1646, Charles's continued intrigues and attempts to play the different parts of his realms off against one another led to a renewed outbreak of conflict in the summer of 1648. After a second parliamentary victory, a minority of the army's leaders became convinced that Charles should not be allowed to live. The king was tried and executed on January 30, 1649. The regicide provoked expressions of horror and amazement in England, Scotland, and all of Europe. Uncharacteristically, Charles behaved with great dignity and thereby won back much of the respect that he had forfeited. England, Scotland, and Ireland were governed without a king for the next eleven years, but in 1660 Charles's oldest son, Charles II, was restored to his father's throne.

FURTHER READING

Croft, Pauline. *King James*. New York, 2003

Goodare, Julian. *State and Society in Early Modern Scotland*. New York, 1999.

Guy, J. A. *My Heart Is My Own: The Life of Mary, Queen of Scots*. New York, 2004.

MacQueen, John, ed. *Humanism in Renaissance Scotland*. Edinburgh, 1990.

Mason, Roger A. *Kingship and the Commonweal: Political Thought in Renaissance and Reformation Scotland*. East Lothian, Scotland, 1998.

Sharpe, Kevin. *The Personal Rule of Charles I*. New Haven, CT, 1992.

Wormald, Jenny. *Court, Kirk and Community: Scotland, 1470–1625*. Edinburgh, 1991.

————. *Mary, Queen of Scots: Politics, Passion, and a Kingdom Lost*. Rev. ed. New York, 2001.

Anna Bayman

SEE ALSO

• Church of England • England • English Civil Wars
• Henry VIII • Scotland • Thirty Years War

▲ This oil portrait of Charles II, attributed to the studio of Godfrey Kneller, was painted around 1680. Charles attempted to win back the crown by force but was routed by Oliver Cromwell at Worcester in 1651 and escaped to France. After Cromwell's death, he regained the throne legitimately in 1660 with promises of a general amnesty, liberty of conscience, an equitable settlement of land disputes, and the restoration of parliamentary government.

Sweden

AFTER WINNING A LONG STRUGGLE FOR INDEPENDENCE FROM DENMARK, SWEDEN PROSPERED AND EMERGED AS A MAJOR NORTHERN EUROPEAN POWER IN THE EARLY SEVENTEENTH CENTURY.

▲ The Union of Kalmar (1397), which brought Sweden under Danish rule, was signed at Kalmar Castle, built in the twelfth century. In this anonymous seventeenth-century watercolor, the castle is depicted as it appeared after its extensive remodeling by Gustav I Vasa in the 1520s.

The kingdom of Sweden, dating from Viking times, lost its independence in 1397, when the Union of Kalmar brought the country under Danish rule. Denmark imposed high taxes to pay for its wars with the German Hanseatic League and the Teutonic Knights; so Danish rule was unpopular from the very beginning. Denmark's wars also damaged Sweden's trade, especially its exports of iron and copper. In 1432 and 1434 a wealthy mine owner by the name of Engelbrekt Engelbrektsson led popular rebellions with the aim not of breaking the union but of forcing the Danish king, Erik VII (reigned 1396–1439), to end the wars and the suffering that went with them. Engelbrekt's rebellion collapsed after he was murdered in 1436. The murderers were not Danes but Swedish nobles who feared that the rebellions threatened their own status and influ-

ence. However, Engelbrekt was regarded as a hero by the common people, who became increasingly hostile to the union with Denmark.

The first breach in the union came in 1448 after the death of King Christopher III (reigned 1440–1448). Christian I was chosen as king of Denmark (from 1448) and Norway (from 1450), but the Swedes chose Karl Knutsson (who reigned as Charles VIII). In 1457 the powerful Oxenstierna family, who supported the union with Denmark, forced Charles to flee Sweden. He made a brief comeback in 1464 but was again forced out by the Oxenstiernas. A civil war broke out between the unionists, led by the Oxenstiernas, and supporters of independence. The unionists were defeated, and in 1467 Charles VIII once again returned to the throne, where he remained until his death in 1470.

After Charles's death power was seized by his nephew, Sten Sture, who took the title guardian of the realm. Sture had strong support among the burghers of Stockholm (the Swedish capital) and among the peasantry, but the Oxenstiernas and most of the nobility supported Christian I. Christian invaded Sweden but was defeated by Sture in 1471 at the Battle of Brunkeberg. However, the nobility, who still supported the union, forced Sture into long negotiations with Christian. A settlement was reached, but Christian died in 1481 without ever having returned to Sweden.

The Swedish royal council offered the crown to Christian's son, John I of Denmark and Norway (reigned 1483–1513). This move was successfully opposed by Sture for many years, but when Sture was overthrown in 1497, John finally became John II of Sweden (reigned 1497–1501). Despite the generous treatment he received, Sture continued to oppose John. When John suffered a disastrous defeat while campaigning in Germany in 1501, Sture again seized power in Sweden, but at the moment of victory, he died. Even with Sture dead, however, John was unable to regain Sweden. Power passed to Svante Sture (who, despite the shared surname, was no relation of Sten Sture) and, after Svante Sture's death in an accident in 1512, to his son Sten Sture the

Younger. John II died in 1513 and was succeeded by his son Christian II. Christian invaded Sweden in 1520, killed Sten Sture the Younger in battle, and was crowned king in Stockholm. Eighty-two of Sture's leading supporters were executed, and his widow, Christina Gyllenstierna, was jailed.

The Vasa Dynasty

Christian's brutal treatment of Sture's supporters caused outrage and sparked a massive peasant rebellion, led by Christina Gyllenstierna's nephew, Gustav Eriksson Vasa. By 1523 the Danes had been expelled from Sweden, and Vasa was crowned king as Gustav I (reigned 1523–1560). A peace agreement that recognized Swedish independence was negotiated with Denmark the following year.

The borders of Gustav's kingdom differed considerably from those of modern Sweden. The country had only one narrow outlet to the North Sea, at Göteborg. All other routes between the Baltic Sea and the North Sea were under Danish control. On the other hand, Finland, which had been conquered in the Middle Ages, was firmly under Swedish control. Although it was a large kingdom, Sweden had little good farmland and was therefore sparsely populated. The rugged, forested terrain made overland travel slow and difficult. Sweden's main exports were iron and copper and the so-called naval stores—timber, flax and hemp (for ropes and cables), and pitch and tar (for waterproofing and preserving timber). As Europe's maritime expansion gathered pace in the sixteenth and seventeenth centuries, these products would give Sweden considerable strategic importance, but at the time of Gustav's accession, the country was still poor and politically marginal.

▲ King Gustav I Vasa, the leader of Sweden's successful struggle for independence from Denmark, is the subject of this anonymous portrait, which was painted in 1542, when Gustav was forty-six.

Angered by the Catholic Church's refusal to contribute to the crown's finances, in June 1524 King Gustav I Vasa retaliated by refusing the bishops' demand that he outlaw the Protestant teachings of Martin Luther:

Regarding your request that we forbid the sale of Luther's writings, we do not know by what right it could be done, for we are told his teachings have not yet been found by impartial judges to be false. Moreover, since writings hostile to Luther have been circulated throughout the land, it seems but right that his too should be kept public, that you and other scholars may detect their fallacies and show them to the people. Then the books of Luther may be condemned.

Letter to Bishop Hans Brask of Linköping

▲ *A contemporary portrait, by Steven van der Meulen, of Erik XIV (reigned 1560–1568), who suffered from mental illness. Deposed by his brother John in 1568, Erik died in 1569, probably poisoned on John's orders.*

Sweden's territory. The Roman Catholic Church, the largest landowner, owned one-fifth of the kingdom. After the church refused his demands for financial support, Gustav gradually came under the influence of Lutheran Reformers who were critical of the church's wealth. Gustav was not a natural Protestant; his interest in Lutheranism was purely pragmatic. In 1527 he confiscated the church's lands and transformed the crown's finances at a stroke. Although there was no formal breach with Rome, over the next few years, Lutheran doctrine was gradually imposed on the Swedish church.

In addition to church lands, Gustav confiscated the lands of the defeated unionists. Steadily increasing revenues from mining also added significantly to the wealth of the crown. Gustav built a strong royal government, reformed the treasury, and encouraged overseas trade (which provided tax revenues) and foreign investment. The Dutch in particular invested heavily in Swedish mining and metalworking. Gustav spent large sums on fortifications, artillery, warships, and recruitment of professional soldiers and was still able to reduce his subjects' tax burden. By the time of his death in 1560, Sweden's economy was flourishing, and its army was strong. During the Middle Ages a major weakness of the Swedish monarchy had been its elective system, which prevented members of a single family from establishing themselves as a ruling dynasty. In 1542 Gustav took advantage of his popularity to persuade the Riksdag (parliament) to make the succession hereditary.

Mastery of the Baltic

During the Middle Ages the southern and eastern Baltic regions had been dominated by the Hanseatic League, an alliance of German cities that had achieved a virtual monopoly on trade in the area, and the Teutonic Knights, a German crusading order. The decline of these organizations in the early sixteenth century created a power vacuum that Denmark, Poland, Russia, and Sweden all sought to fill. The result was a complex four-cornered struggle for mastery of the Baltic that lasted 150 years.

The struggle began in 1558, when the Russian czar, Ivan IV (Ivan the Terrible), cap-

Gustav had built up large debts during the war against the Danes, and so his most pressing need was to increase royal revenue. Lands owned by the crown constituted only one-twelfth of

tured the Estonian port of Narva and thus won Russia its first outlet to the Baltic. Fear of further Russian expansion in Estonia led the city of Reval (present-day Tallinn) to appeal for Swedish help. Gustav, now old and ailing, refused, but his son and successor, Erik XIV (reigned 1560–1568), offered Estonia protection in return for Estonian recognition of Swedish sovereignty. The Swedes blockaded Narva, but the port held out until 1581, and a definitive peace treaty with Russia was not signed until 1595. Sweden had in the meantime successfully fought off an opportunistic attack by Denmark, Poland, and Lübeck, launched to take advantage of Sweden's preoccupation with the war against Russia.

An almost paranoid ruler, Erik XIV was deposed in 1568 in favor of his brother John (Johan) III (reigned 1568–1592). John's religious policy was controversial. Married to a Polish Catholic princess, he had strong Catholic sympathies and allowed his son Sigismund to be brought up a Catholic. He imposed on the Swedish church a new service book, known from the color of its cover as the Red Book, which reintroduced many Catholic practices. He also conducted halfhearted negotiations with the pope about reestablishing a link with Rome and allowed Jesuits (priests of the Society of Jesus, a Catholic order) to teach in the royal college at Stockholm. Opposition to John's religious policy was led by his brother, Duke Charles (Karl). Through Charles's influence, the church assembly officially endorsed Lutheranism in 1593, the year after John's death. The Red Book was condemned, and Catholic worship was banned.

The Polish Connection

In 1587 John III's son Sigismund had been elected to the Polish throne. The Poles hoped that his election would pave the way to a union between Poland and Sweden, a union that would gain Poland an ally against Russia. Sigismund returned to Sweden in 1593 to claim the throne, but he found the ban on Catholic worship intolerable and soon returned to Poland.

▶ *This unattributed portrait on lacquered metal, probably made to commission by a Chinese artist copying a drawing, depicts Count Axel Oxenstierna, a statesman who had great influence over Sweden's affairs.*

Axel Oxenstierna   1583–1654

Axel Gustafsson Oxenstierna was the leading Swedish aristocrat of the first half of the seventeenth century. Born into a powerful and influential family, Oxenstierna was educated in Germany and worked for the treasury before joining the royal council, which he soon came to dominate. He was appointed chancellor in 1612 by King Gustavus II Adolphus (reigned 1611–1632), who left Oxenstierna in charge of reforming the government while the king was on military campaigns. Oxenstierna's diplomacy was central to the favorable peace settlement with Poland in 1629. Though he disagreed with the king about his intervention in the Thirty Years War in 1630, the relationship between the two men was a close one.

After Gustavus was killed in 1632, Oxenstierna ruled Sweden as regent for Gustavus's daughter, Christina. Oxenstierna kept Sweden in the Thirty Years War until it ended in 1648, though the war's heavy costs made him unpopular. As one of the victorious powers, Sweden gained extensive new territories with the signing of the Treaty of Westphalia. Oxenstierna's relationship with Queen Christina was a difficult one. She regarded him, with some justification, as a champion of aristocratic privilege and a threat to royal authority. Nevertheless, she could not afford to dismiss him, and he was still firmly established in office when he died in 1654.

Sigismund's uncle, Duke Charles, then persuaded the Riksdag to declare him regent in the king's absence. In 1598 Sigismund invaded Sweden, but after he was easily defeated at the Battle of Stångebro in September, he returned to Poland, this time for good. In 1604 Sigismund was formally deposed, and Duke Charles was crowned king as Charles IX (reigned 1604–1611). Sigismund nevertheless maintained his claim to the Swedish throne, and years of hostility between Poland and Sweden ensued.

The desire of both countries to take advantage of Russia's so-called Time of Troubles (a period of political anarchy that lasted from 1598 to 1612) brought Sweden and Poland to war in 1605. The Swedes supported one candidate for the Russian throne, the Poles another. In 1610 the Poles occupied Moscow, and it seemed possible that Sigismund's son, Wladyslaw, might become czar of Russia. When the ambitious Danish king, Christian IV, declared war the following year, Sweden found itself completely surrounded by hostile powers. At this moment of crisis, Charles IX died.

Sweden and the Renaissance

Remote and poor, Sweden was completely untouched by the early stirrings of Italian Renaissance culture in the fourteenth and fifteenth centuries. During Sweden's independence struggle, the country's only university, at Uppsala, was closed at the end of the fifteenth century and did not reopen until 1566. The Reformation further set back the introduction of Renaissance thought because Swedish scholars and churchmen were less likely to visit or study in Catholic Italy. The confiscation of the church's wealth also had an impact, since the medieval church had given artists financial support. Gustav I, not a cultured man, had little interest in the arts. Only during the reigns of Erik XIV and John III did the crown emerge as a major patron of the arts. Erik was a talented musician and composer in his own right. John, an able draftsman, introduced Renaissance architecture to Sweden and rebuilt the royal palaces and castles in the latest Italian styles. Outside the royal court, Renaissance architecture was slow to catch on. The medieval Gothic style continued to be used for church buildings, and even the nobility remained in traditional simple wooden houses. Only in the seventeenth century, as Sweden's military and economic power reached its zenith, did the country truly enter Europe's cultural mainstream.

Sweden Becomes a Great Power

Charles IX's successor was his seventeen-year-old son, Gustavus II Adolphus. Charles had provided for a regency council to rule until Gustavus was

◀ A contemporary portrait of Christian IV of Denmark and Norway by the Dutch artist Karel van Mander III. Christian strove to restore Denmark's former preeminence in the Baltic, but his failure to capture Stockholm in 1612 was the first of many military setbacks. By the time Christian died, Denmark was a declining power with a ruined economy.

eighteen, but because of the young king's strong character and experience of government, he began his personal rule immediately. Gustavus's most pressing problem was Denmark, but after repulsing a Danish attack on Stockholm in 1612, he negotiated a peace settlement. Though its terms were poor, the treaty secured Gustavus's homeland and allowed him to turn his attention to Russia. The Poles had been expelled from Moscow in 1613, but the new czar, Michael Romanov, was not yet secure on the throne and was therefore willing to make concessions in return for peace. The Treaty of Stolbova (1617) gave Sweden Ingria and Karelia and cut Russia off completely from the Baltic Sea. During the war with Poland, which continued until 1629, Sweden gained control of Livonia and the key port of Riga.

In these military campaigns, Gustavus showed himself to be an outstanding general; his tactical innovations were eventually adopted across Europe. He equipped the Swedish army with the best muskets and field artillery of the day and enforced a rigorous system of conscription that made effective use of Sweden's scant manpower. The Swedish military was supported by an equally efficient government. In the sixteenth century most government activities had been performed by secretaries who worked under the close supervision of the king. Gustavus's frequent absences on campaign necessitated a complete overhaul of this system. The reforms were carried out largely under the direction of the chancellor, Axel Oxenstierna.

Although it was a small and thinly populated country in 1560, within a century Sweden became the leading Baltic power. Under the leadership of Gustavus II Adolphus, the national standing army that had been set up by his grandfather Gustav I enjoyed military success in the Thirty Years War.

MILITARY INNOVATIONS

Gustavus II Adolphus's military genius raised Sweden from obscurity and earned him the nickname Lion of the North. With the help of Sweden's advanced metalworking industry, Gustavus revolutionized the use of firearms and artillery on the battlefield by reducing their size and weight. He produced the first modern field guns that were light enough to be moved quickly and easily around the battlefield and thus could provide artillery support to infantry and cavalry wherever it was needed. He also halved the weight of muskets and, by adopting the cartridge (a charge of gunpowder with a ball attached), doubled their rate of fire.

These innovations allowed Gustavus to adopt new military tactics. In the sixteenth century musketeers had fought in relatively immobile squares surrounded by pikemen to protect them from cavalry while they reloaded their clumsy weapons. Given their weapons' higher rate of fire, Gustavus's musketeers were better able to protect themselves. As a result, Gustavus could reduce the number of pikemen and create smaller, more maneuverable formations. Instead of deploying his musketeers in squares, Gustavus organized them in lines, no more than six deep, with only a screen of pikemen. These linear formations, by giving the musketeers a clearer field of fire, maximized their fire power. The effect on close-packed enemy formations was devastating. Gustavus's tactics were eventually copied by all western European armies.

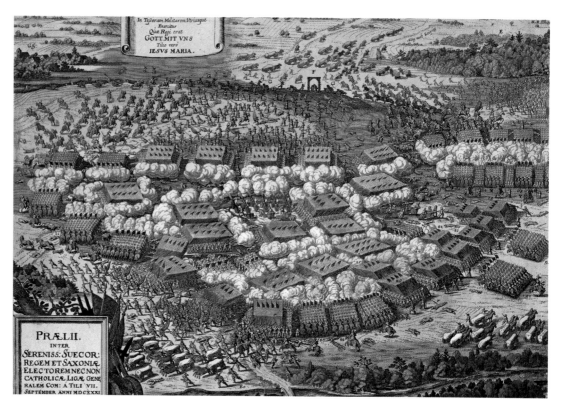

In Tesseram Militarem Utriusque
Exercitus
Quæ Regi erat
GOTT MIT VNS
Tilio vero
IESVS MARIA.

PRÆLII.
INTER
SERENISS: SUECOR:
REGEM ET SAXONIÆ
ELECTOREM NEC NON
CATHOLICÆ LIGÆ GENE
RALEM COM: A TILI VII.
SEPTEMBER ANNI MDCXXXI

▶ At the Battle of Breitenfeld, fought near the German town of Leipzig on September 7, 1631, the Swedes, under Gustavus II Adolphus, won the first major Protestant victory of the Thirty Years War when they routed the imperial Hapsburg army under Johann Tserclaes, the count of Tilly. This colored copper engraving of the battle was made by Matthäus Merian the Elder and published in 1637.

The new government was based on five great offices of state: the chancellor, responsible for local government and foreign affairs; the treasurer, responsible for finance; the marshall, responsible for the army; the admiral, responsible for the navy; and the steward, responsible for justice. Each officer headed a college, a committee that was responsible for policy in his particular sphere of administration. Each college fell under the overall supervision of the royal council.

The political situation in the Baltic region was greatly complicated when the Thirty Years War broke out in 1618. The possibility that the Protestant states of northern Germany might be crushed by the Catholic Hapsburgs caused alarm in Sweden. If victorious, the Hapsburgs might ally with Poland and impose the Catholic Sigismund on the Swedish throne. The year following his victory over Poland, Gustavus took an army to Germany and joined the war against the Hapsburgs. Gustavus's aim was not simply to defend Protestantism; he also hoped, by gaining control of the Baltic river ports through which grain and naval stores passed on their way to western Europe, to win Swedish economic and political dominance of the Baltic. He was aided by huge subsidies from France, whose leaders, though Catholic, saw the Hapsburgs as rivals.

Gustavus's intervention did not last long. He defeated the Hapsburgs in 1631 at Breitenfeld and in 1632 at Lützen, where he was shot and killed. Since his successor, his daughter Christina (reigned 1632–1654), was only five, the government was controlled by a regency under Axel Oxenstierna. Though a good administrator and a competent soldier, Oxenstierna was not the general that Gustavus had been, and Sweden's fortunes in the war took a downward turn. After the Swedish army was annihilated at Nördlingen in 1634, France was forced to support Sweden and the German Protestants by declaring war on the Hapsburgs. So heavy were Swedish losses that for the remainder of the war Sweden was forced to rely on expensive foreign mercenaries.

The French intervention proved decisive, and at the Treaty of Westphalia, which ended the war in 1648, Sweden gained the strategic ports for which Gustavus had gone to war. In the war's closing years, Sweden had also fought successfully against Denmark. In the process Sweden had gained Halland and the Baltic islands of Gotland and Oesel (present-day Saaremaa) and, from Norway, Jämtland and Härjedalen. Sweden had achieved a dominant position in the Baltic, but the question remained: could a country with such limited manpower hold on to that position?

The decline of Swedish power in the late seventeenth century was due largely to the withdrawal of support by other European powers. The position was described by an Englishman who visited Scandinavia in 1692:

The Swedes have still their eye upon Denmark, and long to be sole Monarchs of the North and Masters of the Baltic Sea. The interest of almost all the other princes of Europe concurs in preservation of the Danes by obstructing any further accession of power and territories to the Swedes.

Robert Molesworth, *An Account of Denmark As It Was in the Year 1692*

End of the Vasa Dynasty

A leading supporter of the Treaty of Westphalia was Queen Christina, who had come of age and been crowned in 1644. Owing to her refusal to marry, Christina's reign was characterized by profound political uncertainty. Although Sweden was gripped by insecurity during her reign, Christina nevertheless caused great consternation when in 1654 she abdicated, converted to Catholicism, and went to live in exile in Rome (where she became an influential patron of the arts). Christina was the last ruler of the Vasa dynasty: her successor was her cousin Charles X Gustav (Karl X Gustav; reigned 1654–1660). Eager to extend Sweden's Baltic territories, in 1655 Charles invaded and occupied Poland. His oppressive rule there led to a revival of Polish resistance in 1656, and the following year Denmark and Russia declared war on Sweden. When Charles occupied most of Denmark and laid siege to the capital, Copenhagen, in 1658, the Dutch and English decided that Swedish power now threatened their trading interests in the Baltic and intervened to save the Danes. The war ended with Charles's death in 1660. Sweden gained only the provinces of Skåne and Blekinge from Denmark.

The western European powers had been happy to allow Sweden to break Denmark's control of access to the Baltic and had given the Swedes various degrees of diplomatic, financial, and military support. What they were not happy to allow was the replacement of one monopoly (the Danish) by another (the Swedish). With a population of only 750,000, Sweden lacked the manpower to defend its Baltic empire. Once Russia had emerged as a great power under Czar Peter the Great (reigned 1682–1725), Sweden's Baltic dominance was quickly ended.

FURTHER READING

Derry, T. K. *A History of Scandinavia: Norway, Sweden, Denmark, Finland, and Iceland.* Minneapolis, 1979.

Kirby, D. G. *Northern Europe in the Early Modern Period: The Baltic World, 1492–1772.* New York, 1990.

John Haywood

SEE ALSO
• Christina • Muscovy • Poland • Reformation
• Thirty Years War • Warfare

▲ *This portrait of Charles X Gustav, whose reign marked the high point of Swedish power during the Renaissance, was painted by the Dutchman Abraham Wuchters (1608–1682).*

Switzerland

SWITZERLAND, AS HOME TO THE REFORMERS HULDRYCH ZWINGLI AND JOHN CALVIN, ROSE TO PLAY A MAJOR PART IN THE EVENTS OF SIXTEENTH-CENTURY EUROPE.

A poor and mountainous country without any great princes to act as patrons of the arts,

▲ This woodcut of around 1500 depicts William Tell and his confederates gathered by the Rütli River in 1307 in order to swear an oath to resist the Hapsburgs. Traditionally seen as the foundational moment of the Swiss Confederation, the oath is almost certainly legendary, as is William Tell himself.

Switzerland played no role in the flowering of Renaissance culture. At the onset of the Renaissance, Switzerland was still an emerging state whose independence had yet to be recognized internationally. The origins of the Swiss state are to be traced to 1291, when the three German-speaking cantons of Schwyz (from which the country gets its name), Uri, and Unterwalden declared independence from their Austrian Hapsburg rulers and formed a confederation for mutual defense. In the fourteenth century four more German-speaking cantons—Lausanne, Zurich, Bern, and Glarus—joined the confederation. The rough mountainous terrain, which was easy to defend against Hapsburg attacks, provided the confederation with a secure base from which it expanded further in the fifteenth and early sixteenth centuries to include French- and Italian-speaking cantons.

The growth of the confederation was not without its internal stresses and strains. The cantons valued their independence and would grant the diet (assembly) only limited powers. The idea of a shared citizenship was slow to spread, and it was almost impossible to forge a common foreign policy. Indeed, it was to avoid divisive disputes over foreign policy that the Swiss adopted their long-standing position of neutrality in the sixteenth century.

THE LEGEND OF WILLIAM TELL

The hero of the Swiss struggle for independence is William Tell. According to popular legend, Tell was a peasant from Bürglen who was forced to shoot an apple from his son's head with a crossbow as a punishment for defying the authority of an Austrian bailiff named Gessler. Tell later killed the bailiff in an ambush, and his deed inspired the Swiss to rise up against their Austrian oppressors and win their freedom. According to the eighteenth-century *Chronicon Helveticum* (Swiss Chronicle) by Aegidius Tschudi, these events took place in 1307 and 1308.

The story of William Tell's heroism has inspired many works of art, and Tell is the subject of many traditional Swiss songs and dramas. The legend gained international fame through the play *Wilhelm Tell* (1804), by the German dramatist Friedrich von Schiller, and through the opera *Guillaume Tell* (1829), by the Italian composer Gioacchino Rossini. During World War II, William Tell was an important symbol of the Swiss determination to resist any attempt by Adolf Hitler to invade and conquer their country.

Few modern historians now believe that William Tell really existed. No person called William Tell is mentioned in contemporary documents, and there is no record of a bailiff named Gessler. The earliest record of the story dates to 1470, more than 160 years after the events it describes. Similar stories that involve a test of marksmanship are scattered throughout folklore: it may be that William Tell was originally a folkloric figure who became associated with the independence struggle in Renaissance times.

The Swiss victory over Charles the Bold, duke of Burgundy, at the Battle of Granson (1476) is the subject of this illustration from Diebold Schilling's Berner Chronik (1483). Lacking artillery of their own, the Swiss pikemen advanced rapidly and thereby denied the Burgundians the time they needed to deploy their artillery against the Swiss. Burgundian losses in the battle numbered around one thousand, Swiss losses only two hundred.

The Hapsburgs gave up trying to reconquer Switzerland after concluding the Peace of Basel in 1499 but did not formally recognize Swiss independence until 1648. This continuing external threat proved crucial to the consolidation of Swiss national identity through the turbulent years of the Reformation, when religious tensions and civil war between Protestant and Catholic cantons threatened to tear the confederation apart.

Swiss Pikemen

Switzerland's main importance in the Renaissance lay in its military organization. For most of the Middle Ages, the armored knight dominated the battlefield, while infantrymen were used in a purely defensive role. In the fourteenth and fifteenth centuries the importance of the knight declined as new weapons and tactics increased the effectiveness of the infantry. The Swiss were at the forefront of these changes. Swiss territory is far from ideal for cavalry, and in any case, few Swiss were rich enough to afford warhorses and armor. Forced to innovate, the Swiss developed infantry tactics that allowed them to take the offensive and fight and defeat armored cavalry in open battle.

The main Swiss weapon was the twenty-one-foot pike. Since the Swiss pike was much longer than the lances carried by knights, it did not matter that Swiss infantrymen had little or no armor: in fact, the lack of armor was an advantage. With greater mobility on the battlefield, the Swiss were able to develop complex and highly disciplined battlefield maneuvers. Especially when running downhill, the charge of a formation of Swiss pikemen could be equally as devastating as a charge by armored cavalry. In the Battle of Sankt Jakob an der Birs (1444), an army of only 1,500 Swiss took on an invading French army of 30,000. Not surprisingly, perhaps, most of the Swiss were killed, but they caused such devastating casualties among the French that the French immediately withdrew.

Having repulsed armies from Austria, France, and Milan, by the middle of the fifteenth century, the Swiss had earned a reputation as the finest infantry force in Europe. The most impressive Swiss victories were against Charles the Bold, duke of Burgundy (reigned 1467–1477). Charles was attempting to turn his duchy, which stretched from eastern France to the Netherlands, into an independent kingdom, but his aggression in all directions made him many enemies, including the Swiss. In alliance with the southern German princes, the Swiss occupied Burgundian outposts on their borders in 1474.

In retaliation Charles invaded Switzerland in 1476. He was defeated twice, at Granson in

March and at Morat in June. In January 1477 the Swiss invaded Burgundian territory and defeated and killed Charles at Nancy. Charles had no male heirs, and France and the Hapsburgs spent much of the next seventy years fighting for control of his former territories. Switzerland itself gained another two cantons from the war, Solothurn and French-speaking Fribourg.

Because of their fearsome reputation, the Swiss were in great demand abroad as mercenaries: the Swiss Guards, who still protect the pope, are a surviving remnant of that tradition. Swiss infantry tactics were also widely imitated, especially by the Hapsburgs. Swiss military preeminence was undermined during the sixteenth century by the development of effective field artillery, to which tightly packed formations of pikemen were very vulnerable. In 1515 the Swiss were defeated by France in a struggle over control of the upper Po River valley. The Swiss made few territorial gains after this setback, and by 1536 Switzerland had reached more or less its present borders.

The Swiss Reformation

Soon after the end of the war with France, the influence of the Protestant Reformation came to Switzerland. Protestantism first became established at Zurich, where the Reformer Huldrych Zwingli persuaded the city council to abolish Catholic worship in 1525. Although Zwingli's form of Protestantism was more radical than Martin Luther's, some in Zurich who thought that Zwingli had not gone far enough formed the Swiss Brethren, an Anabaptist group that rejected the practice of infant baptism because it believed that becoming a true Christian required an adult decision. Anabaptists also believed that Christians should not swear oaths, should avoid all violence, including self-defense, and should hold all property in common, as had the apostles. To the Zurich authorities these ideas seemed a recipe for anarchy, and so the Anabaptists were savagely repressed. Many were executed by drowning for carrying out adult baptisms.

From Zurich, the influence of the Reformation spread to other Swiss cities, such as Basel, Bern, Glarus, Lausanne, Neuchâtel, and Schaffhausen. The more conservative rural

▼ *Switzerland, an important arena of religious conflict during the Reformation, remained deeply divided for more than a century thereafter. Nevertheless, the shared fear of Hapsburg intervention trumped the bitter division between Protestants and Catholics, and the cantons kept a lid on their disputes in order to prevent the Hapsburgs from becoming involved.*

1. Bern	10. Graubünden	19. Chablais
2. Lucerne	11. Veltlin	20. Fribourg
3. Zug	12. Chiavenna	21. Vaud
4. Zurich	13. Ticino	22. Orbe
5. Schaffhausen	14. Leventina	23. Neuchâtel
6. Thurgau	15. Uri	24. Bishopric of Basel
7. Appenzell	16. Schwyz	25. Solothurn
8. Toggenburg	17. Unterwalden	26. Basel
9. Glarus	18. Valais	27. Aargau

Protestantism established, 1500s
Catholic cantons and territories
Both Protestantism and Catholicism practiced
✕ Key battle, with date

100 miles

200 km

Huldrych Zwingli   1484–1531

The most important personality of the Swiss Reformation, Huldrych Zwingli was the only major Protestant Reformer whose movement did not develop into a church. The son of a prosperous peasant farmer, Zwingli received a good university education before he became a priest in 1506. On several occasions he was employed as a chaplain to units of Swiss mercenaries serving in papal armies in the Italian wars. The experience convinced him that it was morally wrong for any Christian to serve as a mercenary, even for the pope. After becoming priest to the people of Zurich in 1519, he preached controversial sermons against mercenary service and ecclesiastical corruption. He based his teaching solely on his readings of the Gospels and rejected church practices for which there was no biblical authority. Although their beliefs were similar in many ways, Zwingli went farther in his Protestantism than the German Reformer Martin Luther (1483–1546): for example, he ordered the removal of all religious images and organs from churches and rejected the Catholic doctrine of transubstantiation, which asserted that during the Eucharist the substance of bread and wine becomes the body and blood of Christ. In 1523 Zwingli published his Sixty-seven Articles, which defined his religious beliefs, and in 1525 he persuaded the council of Zurich to abolish Catholic worship. In 1524 Zwingli broke his vow of clerical celibacy and married Anna Reinhard. Between 1524 and 1529, he oversaw the first translation of the Bible into German.

Zwingli's work was hampered by his poor relations with Luther. Because of Zwingli's stance on transubstantiation, Luther refused to recognize his movement as a true evangelical reformation. A face-to-face meeting between the two men at Marburg in 1529 ended in acrimony. The failure to make common cause with the German Protestant movement left the Swiss Reformers feeling isolated, and so Zwingli urged a preemptive attack on the Catholic cantons. When civil war broke out in 1531, Zwingli accompanied Zurich's troops as a chaplain and was killed by Catholics at the Battle of Kappel. The Catholics burned Zwingli's body, but after the battle his supporters claimed to have found his heart, miraculously preserved among his ashes. After his death Zwingli's movement merged with the Calvinist church once an agreement had been reached on the issue of transubstantiation.

cantons remained committed to Catholicism. As tension between Protestant and Catholic cantons increased, Zurich, Basel, and Bern formed the Christian Civic Alliance for mutual defense. The Catholic cantons responded with their own Christian Alliance. Attempts by Protestants to force their beliefs on the Catholic cantons led to brief civil wars in 1529, 1531, and 1556.

Owing to a fear of Hapsburg intervention, the opposing parties prevented these conflicts from escalating and eventually reached an agreement that no canton would interfere in the religious affairs of another. This agreement did not bring religious toleration (it simply institutionalized the religious divisions between cantons), but it saved the confederation. The national policy of neutrality also helped to preserve Swiss unity by stopping the country from being drawn into the sixteenth-century wars of religion and the even more destructive Thirty Years War (1618–1648). Despite its neutrality, Switzerland benefited from the Thirty Years War, since its independence was officially recognized as part of the overall peace settlement.

Calvin and Geneva

After Zwingli's death Swiss Protestants came under the influence of the radical French Reformer John Calvin (1509–1564). In 1536

Calvin took up residence at Geneva on the invitation of Guillaume Farel (1489–1565), who had spread Protestantism to the French-speaking areas of western Switzerland. Two years earlier the citizens of Geneva had expelled their bishop and declared independence from Savoy. Needing an

▲ *Huldrych Zwingli (1484–1531), the most important figure of the Swiss Reformation, is the subject of this 1549 portrait by Hans Asper.*

An anonymous citizen of Zurich describes how the Reformation came to his city:

On Wednesday in Holy Week [April 12, 1525] the last Mass was celebrated in Zurich, and all altars which were still in the churches were stripped bare, and all the week there was no more singing nor reading, but all the books were taken out of the choir and destroyed. Yet what pleased one man well did not please his neighbor.

Quoted in B. J. Kidd, *Documents Illustrative of the Continental Reformation*

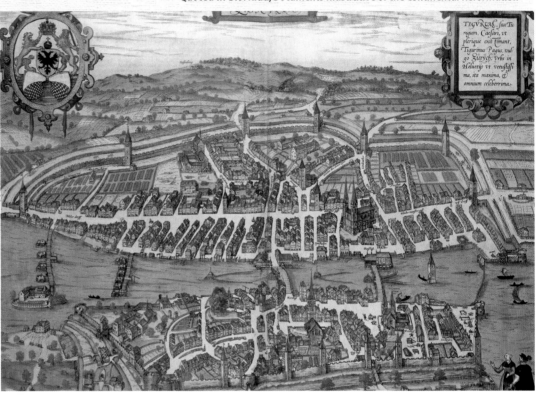

▲ *This panoramic map of Zurich, the center of the Swiss Reformation, is taken from Braun and Hogenberg's seminal atlas* Civitates orbis terrarum (Cities of the World), *published in Cologne, in Germany, in the late sixteenth century.*

ally against the Savoyards, the leading citizens declared themselves Protestant and asked Bern for protection. As a French speaker, Calvin had more popular appeal than Luther, Zwingli, and other German-speaking Reformers. With the help of a Bernese garrison, within five years Calvin had established his austere brand of Protestantism as the official religion of Geneva. Through a doctrinal agreement reached in 1549 with Heinrich Bullinger (1504–1575), Zwingli's successor at Zurich, Calvin's teachings later spread to Protestant cantons in Switzerland. (There are roughly equal numbers of Calvinists and Catholics in present-day Switzerland.)

Although Geneva became a refuge for persecuted Protestants from other countries, especially France, the city was no more religiously tolerant than the Catholic states were. Calvin enforced his beliefs ruthlessly and insisted on the death penalty for heresy. Church elders supervised the moral conduct of every citizen and even visited

every home once a year. Personal freedom was curtailed by strict laws that forbade usury (lending money for profit), all luxuries, and games, dancing, and other amusements. Many of the Protestant immigrants brought craft and commercial skills with them and helped turn Geneva into a thriving industrial center. As its prosperity increased, Geneva gradually relaxed its strict Calvinist laws, but its application to join the Swiss Confederation was blocked by the Catholic cantons for generations to come (it was admitted only in 1814).

FURTHER READING

Gordon, Bruce. *The Swiss Reformation.* New York, 2002.

John Haywood

SEE ALSO

- Burgundy • Calvinism • Erasmus, Desiderius
- Hapsburg Empire • Italian Wars • Nationalism
- Reformation • Warfare

Theater

IN 1350 DRAMA WAS PREDOMINANTLY ASSOCIATED WITH RELIGIOUS FEASTS AND OBSERVANCES. DURING THE RENAISSANCE A SECULAR THEATER EMERGED THROUGHOUT EUROPE. BY 1650 THE THEATER HAD REACHED FULL BLOSSOM IN THE REMARKABLE WORK OF MARLOWE, SHAKESPEARE, MOLIÈRE, AND OTHERS.

The culture of late-medieval Europe (from 1350 into the sixteenth century) was quite literally a culture of playing. The calendar was organized around often interchangeable civic and religious events. These events included a cycle of seasonal festivals as well as such major religious feasts as Christmas, Easter, and the Assumption (celebrating the bodily taking up of the Virgin Mary into heaven), each of which had its distinct character. The church calendar was further organized so that every day was a celebration of a particular saint (many days were dedicated to several saints). Each area had its own local traditions for giving honor to the saint or saints it held in high regard (Saint Patrick in Ireland, for example). Throughout this system of commemorative timekeeping, there were many opportunities for festive celebration that involved role-playing, processions, and often elaborate costumes and stage sets. Many of these festive occasions, such as the reenactments of Christ's Passion that occurred across Spain, were characterized by local traditions while at the same time being part of broader celebrations across Europe that shared similar features.

Religious festivals, however, were only one part of this playful culture. Also common were grand processions, often triumphal in nature, such as the annual *Ommegang,* which commemorated the entry of the Holy Roman emperor Charles V into Brussels on June 2, 1549. These parades often involved costumed performers who played allegorical roles, offered welcome or advice, and stood upon elaborate rolling platforms as the procession followed a lavishly festooned route. Some of these parades, such as those celebrating a royal visit, were one-time events, while others, such as those that were sponsored by civic groups and guilds (associations of traders and craft workers), were regular occurrences in the calendar.

Theatrical performance as a distinct and discrete activity took place within the context of this larger culture of pageantry and play. From Poland to Italy to Ireland, the seeds of theater lay in the bits of Latin dialogue, spoken in character and known as tropes, that had embellished religious liturgy since the tenth century. These embellishments grew into fuller dramatic events that were organized and paid for by lay people and civic groups rather than by the clergy.

▶ *A 1547 illustration by Hubert Cailleau (1547) of the scenery for* The Passion and the Resurrection of Our Saviour and Redeemer Jesus Christ, *a mystery play staged in Valenciennes, in northern France. Depicted are the fixed stage platform with its series of mini stages, or houses, between which the actors would move to act out different scenes.*

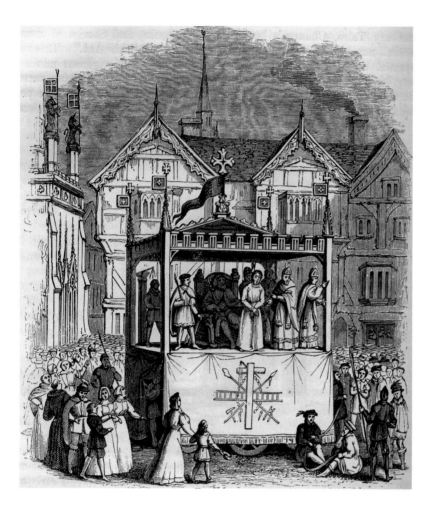

▲ This unattributed sixteenth-century illustration depicts the performance of a mystery play on a temporary stage in a public square in Coventry, in central England.

which became known as mystery plays in England, were merely part of a larger trend of religious theatrical performance throughout Europe. By the early fifteenth century a troupe known as the Brethren of the Passion had even built the first indoor theater in Paris for the purpose of performing religious drama.

A mystery cycle tended to be a sequence of performances that emphasized different aspects of Christian belief. York's Pater Noster guild, for example, regularly presented a series that illustrated "to the ignorant" each part of the Lord's Prayer (the first words of the prayer, "Our Father," are *pater noster* in Latin). A play depicting the woman accused of adultery before Jesus, for example, would be performed in order to illuminate the lines on forgiveness of sins. Trade guilds and merchant groups often took on the planning and performing of specific plays that were relevant to their occupation. Shipbuilders, for example, would perform the story of Noah and the flood. In some places these cycles of plays were performed on stages set up in the round, with the audience watching from the center. Other localities staged performances from moving platforms that processed through the town. Gradually, as the staging became more elaborate, only relatively few cities could undertake the big festivals. A cycle required huge involvement from the laity of the town or city and no doubt attracted the attention of many from surrounding areas. However, smaller-scale productions of miracle plays and saints' plays served the same function in towns and villages well into the latter half of the sixteenth century.

In its rudimentary form liturgical drama was performed to illustrate a biblical precept or a matter of church doctrine for the people of a local parish or simply to teach the stories of the Bible or the life of Jesus by enacting them. During the fourteenth and fifteenth centuries the plays grew in size and scope; they gradually moved out of the churches and were increasingly performed in open spaces and in the vernacular language of the community rather than in Latin. A few such public religious dramas, such as the *Festa,* which commemorates the Assumption and is performed in Elche, in southeastern Spain, and the Passion play at Oberammergau, in southern Germany, continue even to this day.

Mystery, Miracle, and Morality

By the fifteenth century many of these religious plays came to be organized into large festivals, known as cycles, that lasted for two or three days. The most famous cycles in England were held at York, Chester, and Wakefield for the feast of Corpus Christi. These religious performances,

Similar in nature to the mystery play, a miracle play was based on episodes in a saint's life and offered an example of the rewards of holy living and heroic faith. The morality play, however, gave expression to a somewhat starker view of the human condition. For example, the most famous morality play, *Everyman,* depicts the conflict between virtue and vice, forces that are vividly personified in allegorical characters whose names indicate what they stand for. In these plays distinctions between stage and audience were usually minimal. In contrast with modern theatrical conventions, performances of moralities included a high degree of audience

THE FOOL

The fool—who might also take the form of jester, jongleur, buffoon, or clown—features throughout medieval drama. Related to the traveling entertainers (especially jugglers and minstrels) whose traditions stretched back to ancient Rome, the fool eventually became associated with royal and noble houses. In the sixteenth century distinctions could be made between natural fools—those who had some form of mental disability—and artificial fools, who were witty. Their roles were diverse: they were political and social commentators as well as entertainers and comedians. In the following lines from act 1, scene 4, of *King Lear*, Shakespeare indicates the peculiar position of the fool within the court: at once privileged and precarious.

> KING LEAR. An you lie, sirrah, we'll have you whipped.
> FOOL. I marvel what kin thou and thy daughters are: they'll have me whipped for speaking true, thou'lt have me whipped for lying; and sometimes I am whipped for holding my peace. I had rather be any kind o' thing than a fool.

Alongside this tradition of foolery is a philosophical conceit of the fool as a source of wisdom. The Dutch humanist Desiderius Erasmus made much of this tradition in his *Praise of Folly* (1509), which he dedicated to his friend Thomas More. The work's Latin name is *Encomium moriae*, the word for "folly" providing a pun on More's name. Shakespeare utilizes this tradition when he presents Lear's fool, speaking in act 2, scene 4, as an example of "foolish" human tenderness and social concern:

> That sir which serves and seeks for gain,
> And follows but for form,
> Will pack when it begins to rain,
> And leave thee in the storm;
> But I will tarry; the fool will stay,
> And let the wise man fly:
> The knave turns fool that runs away;
> The fool no knave, perdy.

response and participation. Part of the thrill of watching a character such as Vice in a morality play must have been his direct taunting of the audience; for instance, he might tell spectators that while they watched the play, others from his troupe were busy robbing their houses.

These mystery, morality, and miracle traditions were surprisingly tenacious. On a large scale they came to an end toward the latter part of the sixteenth century in England, France, and other parts of Europe (although they survived for a longer period in Spain). The insecurity and violence engendered by the wars of religion in France and the intolerance shown by English Protestants toward a form of entertainment that, in their view, debauched religion and distracted people from the true business of salvation seem to have proved too much in those countries, though in England there is evidence of secret performances by traveling bands of actors even into the early seventeenth century.

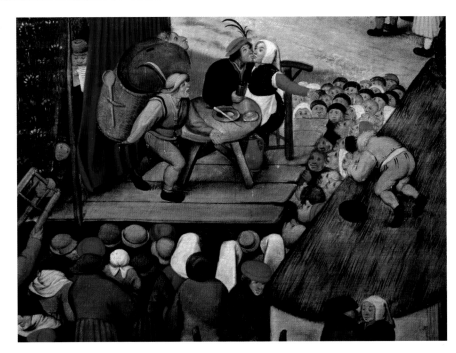

▲ In this detail from Village Fair, one of several similar oils painted by Pieter Brueghel the Younger between 1624 and 1635, little separates the action on stage—a familiar domestic confrontation—from the closely huddled audience.

The dramatic form commedia dell'arte, which originated in Italy in the mid-sixteenth century, came to be highly influential in other parts of Europe, especially France and Spain. Essentially a form of improvisation, commedia dell'arte developed into a kind of stockpile of set gestures, phrases, speeches, and exclamations that, in particular combinations, characterized particular roles. Each actor specialized in playing a certain part, and actors therefore developed a high degree of professional polish when performing their respective roles. The actors usually traveled as organized troupes. Some troupes traveled widely and developed significant reputations performing for royalty and nobility across the continent, while local theatrical troupes in Spain, France, and England began to adopt their techniques. Though commedia dell'arte survives in a greatly reduced form, as Punch and Judy puppet shows, many of its stock roles became the forerunners of character types that would dominate the theater for the next two centuries.

COLISEVS SI   VE THEATRVM

A parallel development in Russia was the *vertep*, a kind of triple-tier puppet show. The top and bottom tiers were spaces where paper figures performed the action; a middle tier housed the mechanism that made them move. Often a central feature at large city festivals, particularly around Christmas, *vertep* performances were stagings of such biblical stories as Christ's Nativity and the Massacre of the Innocents. Like the mystery plays, these stagings began with the purpose of providing religious lessons for the audience and gradually became more secular and comical—at times bawdily so. Unsurprisingly, they were banned owing to concern among the clergy, but notwithstanding this religious censure, their popularity continued well into the seventeenth century.

The Classical Revival

From the fifteenth century many Italians sought to overturn medieval approaches to scholarship, religion, and art. By reviving the writings and thoughts of the classical world, preserved in texts that were returning to light after many centuries of neglect, many scholars hoped to restore something of the manifold glories of the ancient Roman Empire. This trend affected drama no less than it did art, architecture, and literature; the works of the Roman playwrights Plautus (c. 254–184 BCE), Terence (c. 186–c. 159 BCE), and Seneca (c. 4 BCE–65 CE) were eventually brought to the Italian stage in the late fifteenth century. Considerable innovations in theater

◀ *This woodcut from a 1497 edition of Plautus illustrates the Roman design that influenced early Renaissance theatrical architecture.*

construction were developed over the fifteenth and sixteenth centuries as patrons looked back to the example of the ancients. Theater builders and designers drew especially heavily on Vitruvius's seminal first-century-BCE work *De architectura (On Architecture),* which gave vivid descriptions of the typical Roman theater, including the configuration and dimensions of stage, auditorium, and orchestra.

Another extremely influential work was Aristotle's *Poetics.* Italian playwrights generally paid close attention to Aristotle's principle of the three unities of time, place, and action; according to the fifteenth-century interpretation, a successful dramatic plot should focus on an action that could occur in a single place on a single day. On the other hand, proof of the strength and independence of the English and Spanish theater lies in the fact that, while aware of these trends, playwrights in those countries were not constrained by them. To give an extreme example, William Shakespeare ably jumped a span of sixteen years and leaped between two widely separated geographical settings between the third and fourth acts of *The Winter's Tale* (c. 1610)

Although the Aristotelian standard spread far beyond Italy to other parts of Europe, many of the dramas that conformed to the principle of the unities are bound to strike a modern audience as less than interesting. Perhaps in response to these lackluster plots, minidramas called intermezzi were introduced between acts. These light entertainments often involved mythological stories, sometimes accompanied by music. They utilized spectacular effects and ingenious machinery and in fact became more popular than the "serious" dramas they were intended to enliven.

Opera

Toward the end of the sixteenth century, the remarkable success visual and literary artists had enjoyed in the early part of the century seemed to be waning. In addition, in some places artists were being more careful in their choice of subjects, as they wanted to avoid the attention of the Inquisition (the religious tribunal responsible for rooting out and punishing heresy). In Florence a group of poets and musicians known as the Camerata came to believe that Greek tragedy had originally been performed to musical accompaniment. In 1598 Ottavio Rinuccini, a poet from Florence, organized a performance of the mythological story of the nymph Daphne, from Ovid's *Metamorphoses* (written early in the first century CE), with a musical accompaniment composed by Jacopo Peri and played by three of Rinuccini's musician friends. Rinuccini and the musicians of the Camerata thus gave birth to opera, a genre that has endured fundamentally unchanged since the Renaissance. Soon the spectacle of opulent sets and complex stage machinery made opera a passionate theater of the senses that would spread across the continent—and eventually the world.

▼ *In this sixteenth-century illustration of a commedia dell'arte scene, from* Il carnevale italiano mascherato *by Francesco Bertelli, an infatuated Cochalino sings to his beloved.*

The Spanish Golden Age

In 1492, after centuries of military efforts to reconquer the Iberian Peninsula, Spain's Christian rulers finally drove the Muslim Moors out of their last stronghold, Granada. Although Spain at the start of the sixteenth century had no culture of discrete dramatic performance, it had a well-developed tradition of performing what in later times would be labeled tales of romance. Perhaps as a result of the newly unified Catholic culture, which was boosted by a strong state consolidated under the rule of Isabella and Ferdinand, the theater in Spain was largely unaffected by the Reformation. Therefore, religious drama continued uninterrupted in Spain in a form similar to the mystery tradition in other parts of Europe. In fact, by the end of the sixteenth century, at the same time that Queen Elizabeth I was outlawing the performance of religious drama in England, in Spain, Philip II was outlawing secular drama. As a result, religious plays known as *autos sacramentales* developed into a serious dramatic form that found no parallel in other parts of Europe.

As traveling players from France and Italy toured Spain, they brought with them the renewed interest in classical Greek and Roman drama that had first flourished in Italy. However, the appeal of classicism had its limits in Spain. Nonreligious theatrical performances, though widespread, lacked money and permanent stages. By the time Lope Félix de Vega Carpio (1562–1635) began producing plays in the late sixteenth century, Madrid had only two unpromising playhouses. Traveling troupes of actors often performed in squares to an audience looking down from windows and balconies.

By the time Lope de Vega died, however, the theater had become a national institution in Spain. Vega's influence was unsurpassed. During his life, by some accounts, he wrote over two thousand plays, not to mention a vast body of poetry. Vega's work encompassed the whole range of genres that were popular in his day: farces, historical tales, tales of adventure, tales of love, and of course the religious *autos*. Vega's tendency to include representations of common folk (some of his characters are extremely rude)

▶ A portrait of Lope de Vega, attributed to Eugenio Caxes (1577–1642) and probably painted around five years before Vega's death in 1635.

Lope de Rueda   1510–c. 1565

Although the dates of his birth and death are uncertain and records indicate that his acting career was relatively short, Lope de Rueda is credited by both Miguel de Cervantes and Lope de Vega with being the father of Spanish theater. Born in Seville, in southwestern Spain, Rueda is first recorded as an actor at Benavente, in the northwest, in 1554. Later he led a troupe of actors that traveled across Spain and performed before a wide variety of audiences, from the common people of rural villages to King Philip II himsef. Rueda is thought to have become ill and died at Córdoba, and he may have been buried in the cathedral there.

Rueda's plays were published in 1567, after his death. Many of them are adaptations of earlier Italian works; included in this category are his comedies *Medora, Armelina,* and *Los engañados* and the dialogues *Camila* and *Prendas de amor.* Rueda's reputation, however, rests principally on his *pasos,* pieces of comic relief written in prose and performed between the acts of longer plays. These interludes made extensive use of the language of everyday life; the humor of some was so ribald that it had to be toned down when they were published.

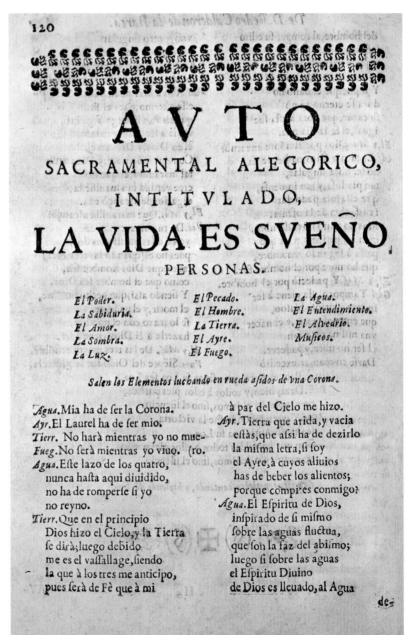

▼ *The opening page of* La vida es sueño, *from a 1690 book of Pedro Calderón's autos sacramentales edited by Juan Garcia Infanzon.*

places him in stark contrast with his Italian contemporaries.

In a similar vein, Pedro Calderón de la Barca (1600–1681) seemed to disregard classical examples. Calderón wrote comedy and tragedy with equal dexterity. Like the dramas of Vega, Calderón's plays stand in stark contrast to the often severe rationality of Reformation drama. They frequently involved supernatural plots or chivalric adventures and required spectacular staging. Together, Calderón and Vega embodied a tenacious medievalism of mind that remained thoroughly Catholic in its perspective.

The Jesuits and School Plays

The Jesuits made a significant contribution to European drama during the Renaissance not through writing any plays of note but through using drama as a teaching method in schools. Molière, for example, like many other playwrights of the period, was greatly influenced by his Jesuit education. Some scholars controversially suggest that Shakespeare, too, experienced something of a Jesuit education under the guidance of the outlawed Edmund Campion (1540–1581). Jesuit plays, often similar to the miracle plays of earlier times, were in fact one aspect of a wider tradition; drama was frequently used for educational purposes, particularly in grammar schools in England. At some schools—Saint Paul's (in London) and Eton (west of London), for example—the boys formed theatrical companies that performed in competition with the adult companies in London.

Anthony Munday   c. 1560–1633

Baptized on October 13, 1560, in Saint Gregory by Paul's, in London, Anthony Munday grew up to be a playwright who, whatever his intentions were, came to embody many of the religious and political contradictions of his age.

Orphaned by age eleven, Munday became an apprentice to the printer John Allde in 1576. Though bound to Allde for a period of eight years, he broke off his apprenticeship and set out for Rome, ostensibly to study languages. In February 1579 Munday entered the English College in Rome but left after a few months and was back in London by July. Some scholars have suggested that Munday went to Rome as a government spy. Others, pointing to apparent Catholic sympathies in his early writings, suggest that he went as a Catholic convert but later turned against Catholicism as a result of government threats. Whatever his real intentions, upon his return Munday's opposition to Roman Catholicism was pronounced. In 1582 he published an account of his stay in the English College in an anti-Catholic publication, *The English Roman Life*. Munday was involved in the capture and interrogation of members of a secret Jesuit mission, led by Edmund Campion, to reconvert England to Catholicism. He even claimed (falsely) to have interrogated Campion himself. As a spy for the Elizabethan intelligence system, Munday also helped to uncover Catholic priests working secretly, as well as recusant Catholics (those who, by refusing to attend Anglican services, were in breach of the law).

By the 1580s Munday had become an actor, but his relationship with the stage was no less contradictory than was his relationship with Roman Catholicism. His *Second and Third Blast of Retrait from Plaies and Theaters* (1580) is a vehement rant against the evils of theatergoing. According to one contemporary account, Munday was hissed from the stage by an audience that had wearied of his performance. Nevertheless, he appears to have recovered from this disappointment. By the 1590s he was writing plays for the theater manager Philip Henslowe, mostly in collaboration with other playwrights, to be performed at Henslowe's Rose Theatre. Among these works are *The Book of Sir Thomas More* and a number that were written with Thomas Middleton. Although he won praise from the theater critics of the day as "our best plotter," Munday quit writing plays in 1602. From that time until his death in 1633, he redirected his skills toward the scripting of civic street pageants.

▼ *This map of London (c. 1588) includes the Globe Theatre, the Bear Garden, and London Bridge. The Thames River, marking a cultural as well as a physical boundary, divided the ordered, largely Puritan society north of the river from the more licentious entertainment district to the south.*

Elizabeth and James: Theater and Religion

Along with the blossoming of Spanish drama, one of the most important developments in European theater was the theatrical culture that developed in England during the reigns of Elizabeth I (1558–1603) and James I (1603–1625). During William Shakespeare's lifetime (1564–1616), the English theater was the benefi-

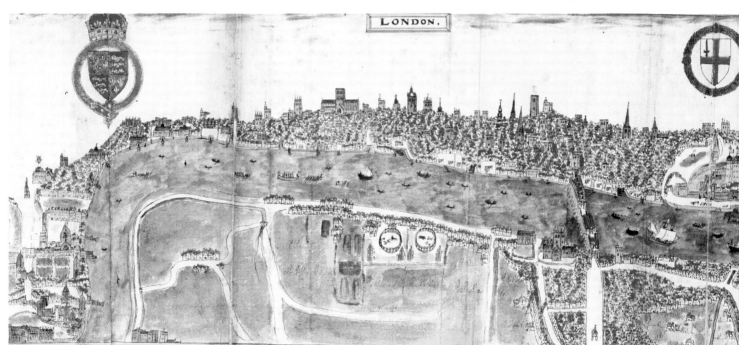

LONDON.

ciary of an explosion of talent that remains unparalleled to this day. Among the prominent playwrights working around the time of Shakespeare were Robert Greene, Thomas Kyd, Thomas Heywood, Christopher Marlowe, Ben Jonson, Francis Beaumont, John Fletcher, Thomas Middleton, and John Webster.

England had become a Protestant nation under Henry VIII, and a more vigorous Protestantism was enforced under Henry's son, Edward VI, who took the throne when he was only a boy and died at age sixteen. After Edward's short reign, the nation reverted to Catholicism under Queen Mary but upon her death returned once again to Protestantism under Elizabeth. These rapid changes to official church doctrine and practice were enforced by the authorities, and offenders could be severely punished (often with death). Amid this atmosphere of considerable religious uncertainty, Elizabeth introduced new laws forbidding the representation of any overtly religious theme on the stage. Therefore, it is hardly surprising that the English theater became more secular in character.

Whereas the late-medieval Catholic Church had embraced dramatic performance as a useful means of inspiring people with a sense of religious wonder, by the late sixteenth century many staunch Protestants rejected the theater as a place of idle debauchery where rebellion was liable to be stirred up. This position was a relatively new one. Even the early English Reformer John Foxe in 1560 had described "players, printers, [and] preachers" as "set up of God, as a triple bulwark against the triple crown of the Pope." Toward the end of the sixteenth century, a vocal minority began to oppose the theater for what they saw as its encouragement of moral laxity. For many of these dissenters, the theaters seemed to be perpetuating a form of shallow entertainment that was strikingly inauthentic and idle and provided a deadly distraction from the business of salvation. Protestant Reformers labeled Catholic worship "the pope's theater" in an attempt to strip it of its validity as a way of expressing Christian faith. For their part Catholics accused Protestants of creating religious services that were equivalent to an empty and evacuated theater. This conflict over what was and was not mere spectacle eventually

The Spanish Tragedy:

Or,

HIERONIMO is mad againe.

Containing the lamentable end of *Don Horatio*, and *Belimperia*; With the pitifull Death of HIERONIMO.

Newly Corrected, Amended, and Enlarged with new Additions, as it hath of late beene divers times Acted.

LONDON

Printed by *Augustine Mathewes*, for *Francis Grove*, and are to

▲ *This title page to a 1633 edition of Thomas Kyd's* Spanish Tragedy, *printed by one Augustine Mathewes, includes a woodcut depicting a key scene of the play.*

fueled the forces that pushed England toward a state of civil war and resulted in the closure of the theaters and the execution of King Charles I and Archbishop William Laud. Among the aspects of Charles's reign resented by the Puritans who opposed him in 1640 was his promotion of the High Church movement, which they claimed cultivated a renewed interest in a Christian liturgy, costume, and architecture that smacked all too much of "popish theater."

▲ *This depiction of London's Swan Theatre, built between 1594 and 1596 by Francis Langley, is a copy of a drawing made by Johannes de Witt of Utrecht shortly after the building's completion.*

The London Theaters

In 1576 the first permanent theater, called the Theatre, was built by James Burbage on the southern bank of the Thames River. Since the London city government, which was largely Puritan in character, discouraged the performance of plays and condemned theatergoing as a lewd pastime, the Theatre's position just outside city limits—and therefore beyond the authorities' jurisdiction—was significant. Soon other permanent playhouses were erected; the Curtain in 1577 was followed by the Rose (1587), the Swan (1594–1596), and eventually the Globe

(1599). Built to designs based loosely on the ancient Roman Coliseum, these theaters were generally circular buildings with stages that projected out into a yard. Penny-paying customers, known as groundlings, would stand in this yard, while customers paying a higher price sat on benches in one of the surrounding balconies. A typical audience was therefore socially diverse; it might include law students, craftsmen, laborers, and petty thieves.

Performers usually wore quite elaborate costumes (often purchased from a dissolved Catholic clergy), but plays tended to have minimal stage sets. Thus, the emphasis lay on the play's language and particularly on the actors' ability to give that language emotional power. Indoor theaters charged higher prices and attracted wealthier (often courtly) customers. Nevertheless, the same plays were performed for the court as for the audiences at the cheaper public theaters in the suburbs. The theatrical companies competed intensely with one another not only for box office sales but also for the patronage of a wealthy royal or noble who could give the company greater status and financial security. Playwrights often took cues from one another in their choice of subject matter—and also, on occasion, in the very lines they wrote. With the new century came a resurgence of boys' companies, which from 1599 (in the words of *Hamlet's* Rosencrantz) "berattle[d] the common stages" with sharp satire punctuated by interludes of dance and music.

Although the plays written during this time were largely secular, it is impossible to separate them from the religious controversies of their day. Despite the explicit restrictions on performing material of a religious nature on stage, most playwrights had religious opinions and leanings, however veiled their expression might have been. Thomas Dekker, for example, could be overtly anti-Catholic, especially when referring to the Jesuits. Thomas Middleton also made much of his Puritan leanings. At least some of the plays of Ben Jonson, on the other hand, have a distinctly Catholic odor; this failing eventually brought Jonson to the attention of the authorities. Shakespeare's religious leanings (as with so many other details of his life) are difficult to infer from

This illustration of traveling players arriving at an aristocratic manor house to present their performance is taken from Moyses Walens's Album amicorum (1605–1615). This German image harmonizes with the depiction of the life of traveling players found in Shakespeare's Hamlet.

his plays, since he included elements of both Protestant and Catholic culture in his plots and characterization. Taken together, the English plays of the period provide an interesting picture of contemporary political and religious life. The Puritans' condemnation of rebellion finds echoes in the anonymous *Life and Death of Jack Straw,* George Chapman's *Charles, Duke of Byron,* John Ford's *Perkin Warbeck,* and Shakespeare's history cycles. Religious language and allegory, although common, was oblique in its expression—as may be seen in *Hamlet* and *Othello.* One uncanny fact certainly did not go unnoticed, even at the time: the new theaters, including the Theatre and the Curtain, had risen up in the very places that had previously been occupied by the suppressed religious houses. The name of one indoor theater, the Blackfriars, clearly identifed the Dominican monastery that had formerly occupied the land on which the theater stood.

Playwrights sometimes trumpeted their political beliefs, particularly if those beliefs were in line with government policy. The following passage was written in the charged atmosphere following the attempt by Catholic extremists to blow up king and Parliament in 1605:

The Generall scope of this Drammaticall Poem, is to set forth (in Tropicall and shadowed collours) the Greatnes, Magnanimity, Constancy, Clemency, and other the incomparable Heroical vertues of our late Queene And (on the contrary part) the inveterate malice, Treasons, Machinations, Underminings, & continual bloody stratagems, of that Purple whore of Rome, to the taking away of our Princes lives, and utter extirpation of their Kingdomes. Wherein if according to the dignity of the Subiect, I have not given it Lustre, and (to use the Painters rhethorick) doe so faile in my Depthes & Heightnings, that it is not to the life, let this excuse me; that the Pyramid upon whose top the glorious Raigne of our deceased Sovereign was mounted, stands yet so high, and so sharply pointed into the clouds, that the Art of no pen is able to reach it. The streame of her Vertues is so immeasurable, that the farther they are waded into, the farther is it to the bottom.

Thomas Dekker, introduction to the printed edition of *The Whore of Babylon*

S. PAULES CHURCH

THAMESIS

Eell Schipes

The Gally fuste

The Bear Gardne

The Globe

▲ *In 1616 the Dutchman Claes Jansz Visscher made a panoramic engraving of London. This portion depicts the old Saint Paul's Cathedral (which burned down in the great fire of 1666) and opposite it, on the southern bank of the Thames, the Globe Theatre and the Bear Garden.*

Outside London

Theater thrived outside London, too. Numerous touring troupes, legal and illegal, went from village to village, often playing in the great halls of aristocratic houses. Even the best-known companies of players occasionally toured outside the city, especially during an outbreak of plague (such as the one in 1592), which might close theaters for a year or more. The Queen's Men became so accustomed to their touring lifestyle that they were able to maintain the queen's patronage even though they did not return to London until 1602. Some troupes, pursuing a sectarian agenda, performed a repertoire of miracle plays for select recusant audiences. One performance at Gowthwaite Hall in Yorkshire in the winter of 1610 prompted an official inquiry by the Court of Star Chamber. London's vibrant theatrical scene in the late sixteenth century was enriched by a dramatic culture that predated and in many senses gave birth to it. The Inns of Court, where the sons of the nobility—as well as those of a growing middle class—went to receive legal training, shared with Oxford and Cambridge universities long-established traditions of producing original and classical dramas. Annual festivities at the Inns of Court, particularly those held during Christmastime, always included theatrical entertainment. As it was not uncommon for the queen to attend these performances, they were often a subtle means for the lawyers-in-waiting to give advice or comment on royal policy without attracting royal disapproval. Many of these plays have not survived, and still others are preserved only in obscure manuscripts. Yet as virtually all the period's major playwrights had affiliations with one or another of the universities or Inns of Court (Shakespeare was an exception), the influence of these plays on the public theater cannot be underestimated.

Charles I, Closet Drama, and Civil War

Charles I and his Catholic wife, Henrietta Maria, had a great love of the theater, but their preferences are suggestive of the religious and political gulf that increasingly separated them from the nation. The monarchs' chosen forms of entertainment were court comedies, light and allegorical pieces that often greatly flattered the queen, and masques, more stylized and elaborate spectacles with gorgeous costume and sumptuous sets, as well as music and ballet, in which the aristocratic audience often took part. These choices, though quite innocent in many respects, reveal a preference for a closed theatrical performance removed from the bustle of common life and the common people. Masques in particular were about the conspicuous display of wealth (and therefore of royal status). The financial commitment required for their elaborate staging made them unprofitable for the public stage.

It is not difficult to find a connection between these artistic preferences and the values that

Thomas Middleton   c. 1580–1627

The son of a bricklayer who had acquired a coat of arms, Thomas Middleton was able to describe himself as a gentleman born. His father died on January 20, 1586, and left an estate worth approximately £335. Later the same year Thomas's mother, Anne, married Thomas Harvey, who had little in the way of property or financial security. The young Middleton's early life was shaped by the protracted series of lawsuits brought by his stepfather in a bid to gain control over the trust Anne had set up to protect the children's inheritance. Harvey eventually succeeded, and the children were left with nothing. These early experiences undoubtedly inspired Middleton's bitingly satirical representations of the legal profession in such plays as *The Phoenix* and *A Game at Chess*.

An ambitious but unsuccessful poet in his youth, Middleton attended Oxford but took no degree. He continued to write poetry but by 1602 was also writing plays in collaboration with Thomas Dekker, Michael Drayton, Anthony Munday, and John Webster—all staunch Protestants and all competing with William Shakespeare for recognition. Though sometimes labeled a Puritan for his strong Calvinist beliefs—the expression of which forms an undercurrent throughout his work—Middleton often poked fun at Puritans. However, as the Calvinism of the Church of England was increasingly challenged by Arminianism under James I, Middleton's work became critical of the dominant religious culture, especially after 1620.

Throughout his career Middleton crossed genre boundaries. He wrote for adult as well as boys' companies, for indoor and outdoor theaters, and for the court. The highlight of his collaboration with Shakespeare was what is often considered the most successful (or humorous) part of *Timon of Athens*. As Middleton's career progressed, he showed remarkable skill in his sympathetic characterizations of independent women; the notorious Moll Cutpurse in *The Roaring Girl* is the finest example of this aptitude. His last play, *A Game at Chess*, was his most successful; it ran for nine consecutive days at the Globe Theatre.

▲ *The title page of the 1611 edition of* The Roaring Girle; or, Moll Cut-Purse, *by Thomas Middleton and Thomas Dekker.*

Charles I encouraged in (and, through Archbishop Laud, imposed on) the Church of England. The theology of Arminianism, which values a person's good works, certainly alienated Calvinists, who believed that works had nothing to do with salvation. However, the new emphasis on ornate church architecture and the return of what Puritans saw as a Catholic "staging" of worship caused most offense. Charles and Laud wanted to restore majesty, mystery, and spectacle to English churches. Many in Parliament interpreted this wish as a desire for the decadent "popish" theater of old. In the end other factors, such as Charles's raising of new taxes, tipped the balance, but when civil war broke out, the new controllers in Parliament wasted no time in closing the theaters and, with escalating penalties, ensuring that they remained closed. They would not open again until the Restoration of monarchy in 1660 under Charles II.

FURTHER READING

Brubaker, David. *Court and Commedia: The Italian Renaissance Stage.* New York, 1975.

Duffy, Eamon. *The Stripping of the Altars: Traditional Religion in England, c.1400–c.1580.* New Haven, CT, 1992.

Heinemann, Margot. *Puritanism and Theatre.* New York, 1980.

Nicoll, Allardyce. *Masks, Mimes and Miracles: Studies in the Popular Theatre.* New York, 1963.

Twycross, Meg, ed. *Festive Drama.* Rochester, NY, 1996.

Wilson, Richard. *Secret Shakespeare: Studies in Theatre, Religion and Resistance.* New York, 2004.

Joseph Sterrett

SEE ALSO

• Church of England • Elizabeth I • Jones, Inigo
• Literature • Marlowe, Christopher • Molière
• Shakespeare, William

Thirty Years War

PARTLY THE RESULT OF PROTRACTED HOSTILITY BETWEEN CATHOLICS AND PROTESTANTS, THE THIRTY YEARS WAR (1618–1648) WAS FUELED BY ANTAGONISM BETWEEN THE BOURBON KINGS OF FRANCE AND THE HAPSBURG HOLY ROMAN EMPERORS AND, IN ITS LATER PHASES, BY SWEDEN'S ABILITY TO INFLUENCE EVENTS IN GERMANY.

The Thirty Years War was not a single war but at least ten separate conflicts that sometimes ran sequentially and sometimes overlapped with one another. The roots of the conflict lay in events and circumstances that originated before 1618, and its consequences extended beyond its formal ending with the Peace of Westphalia in 1648.

When the war began in 1618, Europe was a patchwork of kingdoms, principalities, duke-doms, bishoprics, and free cities held together by feudal loyalty to their rulers and ruling dynasties. The largest and most loosely organized of these political entities was the Holy Roman Empire. During the Thirty Years War the empire was governed by the Austrian Hapsburgs Ferdinand II (reigned 1619–1637) and Ferdinand III (reigned 1637–1657). Its territory encompassed not only the German imperial possessions and the hereditary Hapsburg lands, which were centered around Austria, but also territory in northern Italy. The somewhat smaller kingdoms that surrounded the empire—France, England, Scotland, Denmark, Sweden, and Poland—were just emerging as national states. (In the eighteenth and nineteenth centuries many of the kingdoms and principalities that made up the empire in 1618 would also be consolidated into nation-states.) To the southeast, extending up the Danube Valley, lay the Ottoman Empire, which

▼ *The key conflicts and campaigns of the Thirty Years War.*

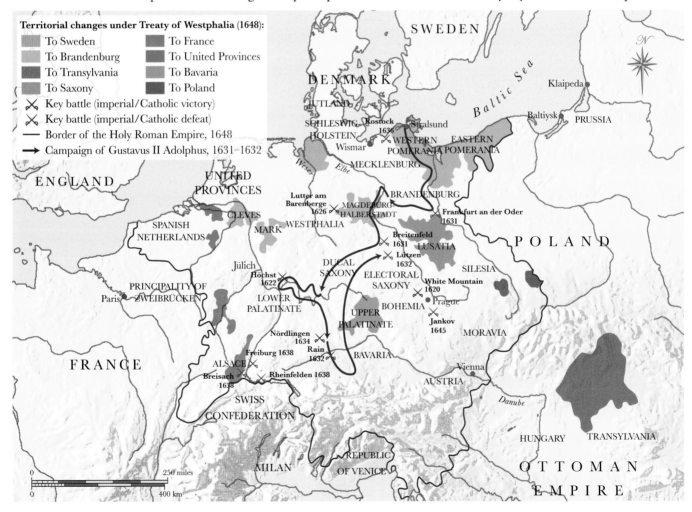

The center from which rebellion against the Holy Roman emperor spread across Europe, igniting the continent-wide conflict called the Thirty Years War, was the Bohemian capital, Prague. The first agents of rebellion were the Bohemian nobles, who were sympathetic to Protestantism and who, when Emperor Matthias died in May 1620, demanded that his successor, Frederick II, respect the privileges previously granted to Protestants. Frederick II refused, and when he had finally subdued Bohemia in 1627, he used the old presumption of the Diet of Augsburg, that the religion of the kingdom should be the religion of its ruler, to rescind certain privileges his predecessors had granted Bohemia and to make Roman Catholicism the only religion there.

We therefore enact, ordain, and will that not only shall all orders graciously enacted by Us in matters of religion ... be continuously and strictly observed, but that also all other ordinances and institutions, however entitled, contrary to the same and damaging, detrimental, and prejudicial to Our Holy Catholic Religion, shall now and forever be and remain cancelled; and further, any person deemed attempting to raise and promote the same shall be deemed ipso facto to have offended against the public order and to have forfeited his life, honor, and goods.

Revised Constitution of the Kingdom of Bohemia (1627), article 13

still posed a serious military threat to Christian Europe. Even smaller dukedoms and counties and bishoprics within the empire at times played an important part in the Thirty Years War.

Divided Loyalties

In the early seventeenth century religion was a major factor in everyday life. The Diet of Augsburg (1555) had applied the principle that the religion of the king should be the religion of the kingdom (formulated in the Latin phrase *cuius regio, eius religio*, which literally means "whose the region, his the religion"). Because religion together with loyalty to the ruling individual or dynasty provided society with its strongest bonds, princes were convinced that those who did not share the religion of the kingdom were politically unreliable. Therefore, the princes sought to achieve religious conformity even if in order to do so they were forced to persecute heretics and suffer mass outward migrations.

The Thirty Years War is often presented as a war between Catholic countries and Protestant countries, but in fact, European kingdoms were often fighting internal religious wars as they maneuvered for foreign alliances. In France tension between the Huguenot (Calvinist) minority and the Catholic majority caused a war of religion that lasted from 1562 to 1594 and included the infamous massacre of Huguenots on Saint Bartholomew's Day, August 24, 1572. The ultimate cost of Catholic victory was the emigra-

tion of thousands of French Protestants to Prussia, Holland, England, and British North America. Germany was a hub of religious controversy, with princes often striving to purge their territories of those holding opposing religious views even as they maneuvered for advantage against neighboring states whose rulers were of a different religious persuasion.

The Catholic and Protestant powers were never perfectly united under their respective religious banners (the Protestant Union was founded in 1608 and the Catholic League in 1609). Furthermore, the cause of religion, although never overtly abandoned, could on occasion be trumped by political interests. Although France

▲ *The Thirty Years War erupted against a background of violent religious conflict throughout Europe. This contemporary engraving depicts an event during the French wars of religion: on March 1, 1562, Huguenots (French Calvinists) were massacred as they prayed in a barn at Wassy. France, though a Catholic power, opposed the Catholic Hapsburg emperors in the Thirty Years War for reasons of dynastic rivalry.*

► *The French engraver Jacques Callot (1592/3–1635) was employed from around 1612 by the duke of Lorraine (who was loyal to the Hapsburgs). Callot made a series of etchings,* Miseries of War, *in response to the invasion of his hometown of Nancy in 1633 by German Protestant troops on behalf of Louis XIII. This plate documents the devastation of a monastery.*

was a Catholic power, French fear of the Hapsburgs—whose territory lay in Spain, the Spanish Netherlands, Milan, and the empire proper—led to France's alliance with Hapsburg enemies, the German Protestant powers and especially Sweden, during most of the Thirty Years War. However, when Swedish victory seemed inevitable, the Protestant rulers John George of Saxony and Frederick William of Brandenburg allied with the Catholic Hapsburg emperor.

Ferdinand II's primary concerns—to contain France and dominate the German princes—differed from those of his Spanish cousins, whose energies were devoted primarily to subduing the rebellious Calvinists of the Spanish Netherlands. Maximilian I, duke of Bavaria (reigned 1597–1651) and hence a vassal of the emperor, was given to vacillation; in the end he betrayed both sides. The pope throughout much of the war was Urban VIII (reigned 1623–1644), who sided with France against the emperor. Nevertheless, as part of its Counter-Reformation efforts, the church provided spiritual counsel to both sides in the struggle; the Capuchins, an order of Franciscan friars, were active in France, and Jesuit priests were influential in Hapsburg lands.

War for Principle or Property?

Historians will continue to debate whether King Gustavus II Adolphus, who ruled Sweden from 1611 to 1632, was a Lutheran champion or an opportunist who saw that the unsettled situation in central Europe offered a chance to increase Swedish influence and territory under a pretext of fighting for the Protestant cause. Similarly, Ferdinand II's imperial policies were inspired at once by his undoubted piety and by his desire to enlarge his territory.

Overlaid upon this general confusion of loyalties and territories was the disputed ownership of church property. In numerous regions Protestant princes had seized lands belonging to the

Catholic Church and appropriated the churches and monasteries on those lands. The Peace of Augsburg (1555) had decreed that lands held by Protestants in 1552 were theirs to keep. However, the 1629 Edict of Restitution, drawn up at a time when Catholics were in the ascendancy, required that Catholic property acquired by Protestant princes after 1555 be returned to the church. Yet this demand was deemed too revolutionary, and the cutoff date was moved to 1627. In 1648, as part of the Peace of Westphalia, that date was changed again, to 1624.

Great Men at War

The Thirty Years War was dominated by powerful personalities. One was the first Bourbon king of France, Henry IV (reigned 1589–1610). Henry, who had converted to Catholicism in order to become king, was famous for saying that Paris was worth a mass. He had conducted a spirited defense of French interests before the war began in earnest; this approach was interrupted by a decade of pro-Spanish policy under Catherine de Médicis but enthusiastically continued by Cardinal Richelieu, who became president of the council of ministers in 1624 and held that position until his death in 1642.

During the crucial years from 1623 to 1644, Urban VIII (born Maffeo Barberini) occupied the Chair of Peter. Urban pursued tirelessly the interests of both the church and the Barberinis; he founded new orders, pursued heretics, sponsored artists—most notably Gian Lorenzo Bernini—and encouraged French resistance to Hapsburg dominance.

Ferdinand II, undeterred by lukewarm papal support and the hostility of the other great Catholic power, France, persisted in his attempts to maintain his sprawling imperial government and to restore Catholic unity. Philip IV of Spain (reigned 1621–1665) lost Portugal in 1640 and pursued intermittent war against Calvinists in the Netherlands until the peace of 1648.

Two great generals fought for the empire. Albrecht Eusebius von Wallenstein (1583–1634), duke of Friedland and Mecklenburg, repeatedly saved the imperial cause, although the jealousy of Ferdinand II finally resulted in Wallenstein's murder at the hands of the sover-

eign he had served so faithfully. Johann Tserclaes (1559–1632), count of Tilly, more cautious but no less able than Wallenstein, fought for the imperial cause in the Netherlands and Hungary and, when Wallenstein fell from imperial favor, succeeded him. Tilly's zeal for the Catholic religion was his inspiration.

Only in the first half of the sixteenth century was Sweden able to influence decisively the politics of northern Europe. King Gustavus II Adolphus, a great general, made his Baltic kingdom the dominant power in northern Europe, and his intervention in the Thirty Years War in 1630 rescued the Protestant cause.

Wars within the War

The phenomenon called the Thirty Years War in fact includes at least ten distinguishable wars. If there was a winning side, it was the one that included the Protestant princes within the empire together with Sweden, Denmark, and their ally France. Time favored these powers, and they successfully prevented the Holy Roman Empire from becoming an absolutist state in which Catholicism was universally established.

▼ *This marble sculpture of Urban VIII was made between 1635 and 1640 by Gian Lorenzo Bernini, whom the pope patronized.*

▶ A contemporary portrait by an unknown German artist of Johann Tserclaes, count of Tilly, one of the key military protagonists of the Thirty Years War. Tilly, who was made commander in chief of the field forces of the Catholic League on the outbreak of war, scored a number of crucial victories against Protestant forces before he was routed by Gustavus II Adolphus in 1631 and 1632.

The War of the Jülich Succession (1609–1614)

When John William, ruler of the small duchy of Jülich, died on March 25, 1609, war broke out over the designation of his successor. The Hapsburgs wished to install an Austrian prince and thereby strengthen the position of the Catholic governors of the Spanish Netherlands, Jülich's neighbor just west of the Meuse River, who were struggling to control their rebellious subjects. The Protestant United Provinces (that is, Protestant Holland), seconded by England and France, opposed this succession. War was averted when the pro-Spanish Catherine de Médicis succeeded Henry IV of France on May 14, 1610. By the Treaty of Xanten (November 12, 1614), the disputed territory was partitioned between Brandenburg and Neuberg. However, for Catholics and Protestants, Hapsburgs and anti-Hapsburgs, the resort to arms now had a precedent.

The Bohemian and Palatine War (1618–1629)

The desire for reform of the church in Bohemia had roots in the fifteenth-century Czech nationalist movement led by Jan Hus (c. 1372–1415). Thus, when the Reformation became a popular movement in the 1520s, Reformed religion found a ready audience among the nobles of Bohemia, and in 1609 Emperor Rudolf granted an imperial charter securing the rights of Protestants in Bohemia. In May 1618 the nobility, rebelling against the future emperor Ferdinand II, signaled their dissent by throwing the emperor's regent and royal counselors from a window of the Hradčany Castle in Prague. This event is known as the second Defenestration of Prague (the first had occurred during a nationalist uprising in 1419). In 1619 the Bohemian nobles elected as king Frederick V, the elector of the Palatinate. Frederick's allies, the Protestant Union and Great Britain, failed him, and after his defeat by the count of Tilly at the Battle of White Mountain on November 8, 1620, the Bohemian rebellion was effectively ended, and Frederick deposed.

The Struggle for the Graubünden (1620–1639)

The most direct means of communication between northwestern Italy and Austria traversed a series of small states, called the Grisons by the French and the Graubünden by the Germans. To the east of Milan and north of Venice, the Adda River flowed through a mountainous region called the Valtellina that controlled the eastern end of this line of communication. The struggle for possession of this tiny region, which was contested from 1620 to 1639, ended with the Peace of Milan (September 3, 1639), which made the pope the area's nominal sovereign but gave control of it to the Holy Roman Empire.

The Swedish-Polish War (1621–1629)

The Swedish army entered the Thirty Years War in 1621, when, under the terms of the Peace of Stolbova (1617), it occupied the Russian regions of Karelia and Ingria, on the eastern shore of the Baltic Sea (and thereby cut Russia off from the Baltic). Sweden next launched the Swedish-Polish War, during which it occupied Riga, in Livonia, and the Prussian Baltic ports of Klaipeda (in German, Memel) and Baltiysk (Pillau). Responding to this threat, Wallenstein moved west and conquered Mecklenburg, a territory that included the western Baltic ports of Wismar and Rostock. Swedish troops rushed to defend the port of Stralsund, and with the Truce of

◀ A contemporary German engraving of the Battle of White Mountain, fought on November 8, 1620, outside Prague. The defeat of Frederick V, the elector of the Palatinate and chosen leader of the Bohemian Protestants, by the forces of the Holy Roman Empire and the Catholic League effectively ended the Bohemian uprising against the Hapsburg emperors.

Altmark (September 25, 1629), Sweden gained Livonia and the Prussian ports.

The Danish War (1625–1629)

In 1625 Christian IV of Denmark, unhappy about the Swedish domination of the Baltic coast and anxious to secure Danish supremacy in the estuaries of the Elbe and Weser rivers, entered into the Treaty of the Hague, under whose terms the Dutch and English were to subsidize the military efforts on behalf of Frederick V, the elector of the Palatinate, to reclaim his throne.

The restoration of Frederick was a kind of rallying point for the Protestant cause. As part of a widening conflict, Christian IV conquered lower Saxony; Christian of Brunswick (also known as Mad Christian) occupied Bavaria; Peter Ernst von Mansfeld moved east into Bohemia, Silesia, and Moravia; and the Transylvanian prince Gábor von Bethlen conquered Hungary and joined with von Mansfeld. In 1626 Christian was routed by Tilly's forces at Lutter am Barenberge and, as Tilly and Wallenstein entered Jutland, the Danish king was forced to enter a Protestant alliance with his old enemy the Swedes.

Ultimately, the Danish War, intended to bring hostilities to an end through a Protestant victory, instead brought the power and prestige of

ENGLAND IN THE THIRTY YEARS WAR

England became involved in the war as a consequence of the marriage of Elizabeth, the only daughter of James I of England, to Frederick, the elector of the Palatinate and, from 1619, king of Bohemia. Defeated at the Battle of White Mountain the following year, Frederick lost Bohemia to a Spanish Hapsburg army and earned the title the Winter King. English sentiment was of course strongly anti-Spanish and anti-Catholic. James I, who was as interested in the dynastic rights of his son-in-law, Frederick, as he was in the defense of the Protestant religion, permitted the raising of a volunteer army to embark for the Netherlands and drive out the Spanish. In 1625 the new king, Charles I, promised subsidies of money and troops to Frederick and encouraged George Villiers, duke of Buckingham, to undertake an ill-considered invasion of France in 1627 in defense of the besieged Protestant Huguenots of La Rochelle. The subsidies were never paid. Charles I, only able to raise money for his own household and government through forced loans and other unpopular measures, could not fulfill his promises, and Buckingham was defeated. From 1630 to 1649 English energies were devoted to an internal war between Puritans and Royalists that in some ways mirrored the Continental struggle.

the Holy Roman emperor to its highest point since the victory of Charles V at Schmalkalden in 1547 and ended the Danish bid for supremacy in the Baltic. From this position of power,

▶ *A contemporary portrait of King Gustavus II Adolphus of Sweden (reigned 1611–1632), an outstanding military leader known as the Lion of the North by Protestants.*

Ferdinand II was able to promulgate and partly enforce the Edict of Restitution, which returned all ecclesiastical property taken from the Catholic Church by Protestant princes after 1627.

The War of the Mantuan Succession (1628–1631)

Given the tensions gripping the European continent, no territory was too insignificant to be contested. Situated on the Po River just south of the republic of Venice, the small principality of Mantua controlled Hapsburg communications across northern Italy. When Vincenzo II Gonzaga, the duke of Mantua and Montferrat, died on December 26, 1627, France and the Hapsburgs both put forward candidates to succeed him. The legitimate heir, Charles, duke of Nevers, was supported by the French, but Ferdinand II, who wished to keep the French from controlling the eastern approach to Milan, rejected him.

Having cleared France of Huguenot opposition and secured peace with England, Cardinal Richelieu was free to oppose the Hapsburgs, who by the Treaty of Cherasco (June 19, 1631) agreed to the installation of the French candidate. Pope Urban VIII, whose hostility to Hapsburg power never faded, took this opportunity to annex Urbino; the Hapsburg monopoly over Italy, thus broken, was never reestablished.

The Swedish War (1630–1635)

Having defeated the Poles, Gustavus II Adolphus was ready in 1630 to invade the southern shore of the Baltic. He landed an army in Germany and presented himself as the champion of the liberties of the German princes against an oppressive Hapsburg emperor. Subsidized by France through the Treaty of Barwalde (January 23, 1631), Gustavus first attempted to stop the enforcement of the 1629 Edict of Restitution. He was opposed by the Protestant princes George William of Brandenburg and John George I of Saxony, who, though not fervent supporters of the emperor, objected to the Swedish invasion.

Until 1634 Gustavus Adolphus was successful; his overrunning of Brandenburg and Saxony and storming of the citadel of Frankfurt an der Oder forced his two opponents into a Swedish alliance. Tilly managed to save Magdeburg but was then defeated by Gustavus at the Battle of Breitenfield (September 18, 1631), a victory that won the allegiance of the lesser German princes. Gustavus then went on to capture Prague. These Swedish victories were interrupted only when, shortly after Wallenstein was recalled to lead the imperial armies, Gustavus was killed at the Battle of Lützen (1632).

Gustavus's chancellor, Axel Oxenstierna, took over the direction of affairs and consolidated the alliance with the German princes (except Saxony and Brandenburg) under the Treaty of Heilbronn. The Swedish army under Duke Bernhard of Saxe-Weimar captured the Catholic town of Regensburg, while Wallenstein captured Steinau, in Silesia. Because Wallenstein had attempted to make himself the arbiter of European affairs by treating with Gustavus Adolphus secretly, Ferdinand II turned a blind eye to Wallenstein's murder (by poisoning) on

February 24, 1634. The Swedes were defeated at Nördlingen, and the League of Heilbronn melted away. Through the Peace of Prague (May 30, 1635), emperor and princes were reconciled, and 1627, a date more favorable to the Protestants, was chosen as the year that determined rightful possession of ecclesiastical property.

The War of Smolensk (1632–1634)

While Gustavus Adolphus had been pursing the war in central Europe, he had used his diplomatic skills to create a second front against the emperor by enlisting Russia, Turkey, Transylvania, the Crimean Tatars, and the Ukranian Cossacks to attack the imperial territories in Germany from the east. It proved difficult to coordinate the various campaigns, but in 1632 the Russians finally invaded Poland and besieged Smolensk. Gustavus Adolphus's plan to deploy troops against Prussia in concert with the Russian attack was abandoned with his death in 1632. The Russians were soon occupied with a peasant revolt, and the Crimean Tatars decided to attack Moscow instead of Poland.

The French and Swedish War (1635–1645)

When the Swedes were no longer able to pursue the war against the empire, Richelieu took on an active role. In 1635 he concluded treaties with the Protestant United Provinces and with Sweden, declared war on Spain, sent a French army to Valtellina, and recruited Bernhard of Saxe-Weimar, the best of the German generals in Swedish service, into the French army.

◀ A painting by Jacques Courtois (known as Le Bourguignon; 1621–1676) of the Battle of Lützen (1632). After Gustavus Adolphus was mortally wounded, Bernhard of Saxe-Weimar assumed command, rallied the Swedish forces, and captured the entire imperial artillery. Wallenstein was forced to concede and retreat.

A contemporary oil portrait of Octavio Piccolomini (1600–1656), duke of Amalfi, by Jan Gerritsz van Bronckhorst. After serving the Holy Roman Empire and the Spanish, Piccolomini was promoted to field marshal in 1648 and was made a prince of the empire in 1649.

In 1636 imperial forces under Octavio Piccolomini, moving south from the Spanish Netherlands, took Corbie in northern France and thereby endangered Paris. However, this victory was neutralized by the defeat of Melchior von Hatzfeldt by Johan Banér, a Swedish general, at Rostock on October 4. Meanwhile, in the north, Swedish supremacy was reestablished in 1638 by Bernhard's victories at Rheinfelden (March 23), Freiburg (April 6), and Breisach (December 17), but the imperial armies under Piccolomini balanced these defeats with a victory at Thionville, on the Moselle River in Upper Lorraine, on June 7, 1639, the last great success of the Hapsburg armies. Thenceforth the war degenerated into freebooting: French, Swedish, and imperial commanders made war on their own initiative.

The Swedish-Danish War

The war that had begun with a Catholic-Protestant quarrel about the religion of the ruler of the tiny duchy of Jülich in 1607 ended with warfare between Protestant Denmark and Sweden; the imperial forces sided with Denmark. Sweden had become alarmed when, after the Battle of Breitenfeld, it seemed likely that Ferdinand III and Christian IV of Denmark would make peace. Imperial interference was ineffective. Sweden quickly conquered Schleswig-Holstein and Jutland in December 1644 and January 1645, destroyed the imperial army at Jüterbog (November 23, 1644), and proceeding to invade Bohemia, wiped out another imperial army at Jankov (August 23, 1645). Under the terms of the Peace of Brömsebro, Denmark ceded to Sweden the Baltic islands of Gotland and Oesel; Jamtland and Härjedalen, on the Norwegian frontier; and Halland, on the Kattegat Strait between Denmark and Sweden.

The End of the War

In 1648 a congress of 150 members met at Münster and Osnabrück in Westphalia and brought hostilities in central Europe to an end (France and Spain would remain at war until 1659). The Peace of Westphalia concluded the long war between Catholic Spain and the Protestant United Provinces of the Netherlands (January 30, 1648) and the war between the Protestant powers (and their ally France) and the Hapsburg emperor, Ferdinand III, and the Catholic princes (October 24, 1648). France gained territory in Lorraine, and Sweden exacted payment for its army, as well as territory in Pomerania. The cutoff year for ownership of church lands was moved yet again, to 1624, and religious toleration of Catholics, Lutherans, and Calvinists was recognized, except in hereditary Hapsburg lands. Religious disputes were to be solved amicably.

The long negotiations established diplomatic strategies and principles from which modern diplomacy would develop. The Peace of Westphalia recognized certain hard facts: that the emperor could not impose Catholicism and that the religious pluralism resulting from the Reformation could not be managed successfully through the sorting out of the continent into confessional states, each permitting only one lawful religion.

The intensity that fed the Protestant cause is apparent in this proclamation of 1623, in which the author, probably Gustavus II Adolphus of Sweden himself, warned of "a general persecution and an open war of religion." Noticing the success of the imperial armies Gustavus continued.

We learn also of places where the holy word of God has for many years been preached in purity, plainness, and honesty, that popish idolatry is brought in there again, and the abomination of desolation set up again in God's temple, to the accompaniment of fearful harryings and destruction. [In Germany,] where but now the light of God's word was freely preached, are abominations and image worship. Where once man was free to serve the Lord and keep his ceremonies, there is now persecution, oppression, and slavery.

Quoted in Nils Ahnlund, *Gustav Adolf the Great*

▼ *The Treaty of Westphalia, including the seals of the imperial electors. Negotiations began in 1644; the war continued until the Spanish-Dutch treaty was signed on January 30, 1648, and the treaty comprehending the Holy Roman Empire, the German princes, Sweden, and France, on October 24.*

yeomen and peasants. Ferdinand II had attempted to govern without the diet, the long-standing consultative body of the Holy Roman Empire, and without the advice of the electors. Westphalia restored the authority of the diet and the princes' right to make treaties among themselves and to raise and command their own armies.

The Thirty Years War also had a bleak legacy. It set the precedent for the ideological warfare of the nineteenth and twentieth centuries, in which the object was as much the defeat of ideas as the defeat of the opposing army and in which civilians would be seen as combatants. None of the participants in the Thirty Years War could achieve a decisive victory, partly because the contending powers were too evenly matched, partly because ideas cannot be dispatched with the sword.

FURTHER READING

Asch, Ronald G. *The Thirty Years War: The Holy Roman Empire and Europe, 1618–48.* New York, 1997.

Bonney, Richard. *The Thirty Years' War, 1618–1648.* Oxford, 2002.

Fletcher, Charles R. L. *Gustavus Adolphus and the Thirty Years War.* New York, 1963.

Mitchell, John. *Life of Wallenstein, Duke of Friedland.* New York, 1968.

Wedgwood, C. V. *The Thirty Years War.* New York, 2005.

James A. Patrick

Although royal absolutism, the theory that princes were accountable only to God, would persist into the nineteenth century, the negotiations established the principle that government should rest upon some degree of consent. This principle, the foundation of modern democratic theory, had been foreshadowed by the English Magna Carta (1215), although the freedom envisioned at Westphalia, like that enshrined in Magna Carta, was the freedom of the nobility from royal absolutism, not the freedom of

Trade

FROM THE 1300S ON, TECHNOLOGICAL ADVANCES IN NAVIGATION COUPLED WITH DEVELOPMENTS IN BANKING AND ACCOUNTANCY USHERED IN A REVOLUTIONARY ERA OF TRADE. AS THEY EXPANDED OVERSEAS, EUROPEAN POWERS BEGAN TO LAY DOWN THE FIRST TRULY GLOBAL TRADING NETWORKS.

Following the fall of the Roman Empire in the fifth century CE, western Europe entered a long period of political instability and economic stagnation. This period was marked by urban decline, a reduction in long-distance trade, and a reversion to barter rather than cash as the means of exchanging goods. Such long-distance trade as continued was mainly in low-bulk, high-value commodities, such as spices, silks, furs, ivory, and slaves, all of which could be transported easily in the small, undecked sailing ships of the time.

The recovery in trade that began around 800 was possible thanks to the emergence of stable kingdoms and to such agricultural innovations as crop rotation, which greatly improved productivity. Higher yields in turn led to growing populations, prosperity for peasants and landowners alike, greater demand and increased opportunities for trade and manufacturing, larger towns, more markets and fairs, and the re-establishment of cash as a means of everyday exchange.

By the beginning of the Renaissance, few Europeans lived more than a day's journey from a market town where they could trade farm surpluses for manufactured goods. Trade and manufacturing activities in towns were controlled by guilds, associations of merchants and craftsmen that set quality standards and sought to exclude external competition. Towns generally saw one another as competitors—Venice and Genoa, for example, fought several wars over control of the Mediterranean trade routes—but they also cooperated when they had common interests. The most notable example of such cooperation was the Hanseatic League, an association of thirty-seven northern German and Baltic cities; the league dominated trade in northern Europe in the fourteenth and fifteenth centuries. It negotiated trading privileges for its members, prepared navigation charts, and organized convoys for protection against piracy.

The emergence of towns as centers of demand, coupled with the development of larger merchant ships, made the long-distance trade in

◀ *The subject of this painting of around 1530 is the lively and extensive regional cloth market in 's Hertogenbosch, in the Netherlands.*

bulk products, such as grain, more economical. Long-distance trade was also stimulated by increased European contacts with the Middle East, a consequence of the Crusades in the twelfth century. These contacts continued even after the Muslims reconquered the Holy Land in 1291. Long-distance trade was further boosted by the development, beginning in Italy around 1300, of modern banking and accountancy systems and of the practice of insuring against marine risk. As a result, it became easier and less of a gamble to finance maritime trading ventures. Merchants increasingly assumed the role of capitalist by using credit to finance trading voyages overseas.

At the same time as these trends were developing, Europeans' geographical horizons were widening. One landmark in this process was the Venetian Marco Polo's journey (1271–1275) to China along the Silk Road, an ancient network of trade routes that crossed the entire breadth of Asia. Polo's accounts of the exotic and rich civilizations of the East stirred European interest in long-distance trade. However, direct European access to the Far East was blocked by the hostile Muslim states of western and central Asia. In the fifteenth century Portuguese navigators began exploring the coast of Africa with a view to finding a direct sea route to the Far East. Soon after Bartolomeu Dias rounded the Cape of Good Hope (Africa's southern tip) in 1487, new trade routes east to India and Southeast Asia began to open up. In the 1400s advances in navigation, shipbuilding, and weapons manufacture (including the invention of portable cannon) allowed European powers to gain monopolies on products they were gathering in distant lands. The period of remarkable oceanic exploration that started in the fifteenth century led directly to a great expansion of European trade.

▲ *Marco Polo's record of his travels altered the European worldview and won him international fame. This miniature of around 1400, from the Venetian manuscript* Li livres du Graunt Caam, *depicts Polo's departure from Venice. The illustration was made in England by an artist known simply as Johannes.*

COMMODITIES OF TRADE

Exotic luxuries from the Far East—notably spices—fetched such a high price in Renaissance Europe that states were prepared to go to war in order to win control of the trade in them. Yet most everyday trade in Renaissance Europe was in less glamorous necessities: grain, wine, salt, fish, wool, cloth, and metals.

Grain was grown mainly in southern Italy, northern France, and Poland and exported from there to the cities of northern Italy, Flanders, and the Rhineland, areas where the population had grown too large to subsist on the produce of the local countryside alone. The main wine-exporting regions were those that were well connected to northern Europe, where the climate was too cool for growing grapevines. The most prominent wine regions were Bordeaux, whose wine producers shipped their product to England, and the Rhineland, whence wine was sent downriver to Flanders for distribution around the North Sea.

In the days before canning and refrigeration, salt was an essential preservative for meat and fish. Though some salt was produced at inland brine springs or salt mines—those in England and the Alps, for example—most salt came from coastal salt pans in the Mediterranean Sea and the Bay of Biscay. Demand for fish in Renaissance Europe was kept high by the church's prohibition on eating meat on Fridays. Norwegian dried cod and salt herrings from the Baltic Sea were exported to southern Europe in vast quantities.

Most everyday clothing was made of wool. The best-quality wool was produced in England and Spain and exported to the major weaving centers in Flanders and northern Italy. From these places in turn textile workers exported finished cloth all over Europe. English wool exports declined as England developed its own textile industry in competition with that of Flanders. Sweden and Spain were important exporters of iron, and England was Europe's only source of tin, which was required to make useful alloys such as pewter and bronze.

Barter and Exchange

In medieval feudal societies goods were produced in very limited numbers and distributed and sold over only a small area. Most products needed to be used immediately and therefore could not be sent far away. By the late fourteenth century and the early fifteenth, however, the private production and sale of goods had begun to liberate individuals from the limits of feudal society, in which wealth was concentrated in the hands of the nobility and royalty. Markets and fairs provided the spur for such changes in Europe. Although in many early markets people traded by bartering, it was in markets that the use of currency for exchange began to take root.

Barter systems significantly limited the distances across which traders could disperse their goods. The gradual introduction of currency throughout Europe was a necessary precursor for the expansion of trade. The use of money or gold rid traders of the need to barter with specific materials and thus made it easier for them to venture outside their familiar market area. As a result, the exchange of goods between regions and eventually cultures became possible.

▶ *Advances in sail and hull design powered the Age of Discovery. These drawings of Portuguese oceangoing ships bound for India are taken from the* Livro das armadas *(Book of Fleets; after 1566).*

The Impact of Money

Money changed the lives of all people, whatever their class. As recognizably modern economies emerged, peasant families required money to pay rent and buy farming tools. The nobility and the monarchy required money on a grand scale. In the fifteenth century long-distance trade was bringing into Europe exotic and expensive luxuries. The consumer culture that began to appear as a result further stimulated the use of currency and accelerated the penetration of trade networks deeper into Europe.

The combination of trade and money led to a situation new to Europe: wealth could now be based on gold and currency rather than land. Interest in acquiring land showed no sign of disappearing, however. Some of Europe's rulers used their currency-based wealth to outfit not only merchant fleets but also fleets and armies of conquest. Of course, even those less interested in territorial expansion went increasingly to sea to acquire trade routes free from the dangers and constraints of overland travel.

The Voyages of Cheng Ho

Although Portuguese and Spanish sailors are usually thought of as the first explorers of the Renaissance, the Chinese uncharacteristically began exploring the world several decades in advance of Europe. In the early fifteenth century the Ming emperor Chu Ti (also referred to as Yung-lo; reigned 1402–1424) sent out the greatest navy the world had ever seen under the leadership of Admiral Cheng Ho. In all, during seven epic voyages between 1405 and 1433, the so-called treasure fleet explored the vast periphery of the Indian Ocean. Hundreds of Chinese junks had explored India, Arabia, and East Africa over fifty years before the first Portuguese explorers arrived. However, the emperor's aims were exclusively political and geographical, and the Chinese created no trade links. Chu Ti's successors, returning to China's traditional foreign policy, saw maritime expeditions as a waste of resources that would be better employed defending China's borders against the Mongols. The fleet was left to decay. China's retreat from the sea left the way open for the Portuguese to win control of the East Asian trade routes.

◄ This engraving of a Chinese junk, similar to the ones that would have been used in Cheng Ho's lifetime, is taken from Jan Huyghen van Linschoten's Discourse of Voyages into the East and West Indies (1579–1592). The key features of the junk, a large, flat-botttomed vessel, are a high stern, a square bow, and sails divided by battens.

SEAFARING TECHNOLOGY IN THE EAST AND WEST

In the mid-fifteenth century the oceangoing technology of China was superior to that of Europe in most respects, with the possible exception of navigation. The largest Chinese ships were around 500 feet (150 m) long and weighed around 1,500 tons (1.3 million kg). In contrast, oceangoing European ships were typically around 100 feet (30 m) long and weighed approximately 300 tons (272,000 kg).

The Chinese had been using multimasted ships for several centuries. In Europe only Portugal had developed this innovation with the caravel, a lightweight vessel rigged with lateen (triangular) sails that was generally used for the exploration of coastal waters. Most European oceangoing ships were rigged with a single square sail; although well suited to running across open distances, square rigs did not have the flexibility for moving against the wind and steering in close quarters. The Chinese had been using fore-and-aft lugsails, which were more efficient at beating a route upwind, since the ninth century. (Lugsails, which are often in the shape of a parallelogram, are distinguished by smaller supporting masts that run through the sail—usually one along the top and another along the bottom.) Nevertheless, by the fifteenth century Western and Eastern sail technology was comparable.

The mariner's compass originated in China, where navigators as early as 250 BCE rubbed a needle on naturally magnetic rock and hung it from a thread or placed it in a bowl of water (the Chinese called this simple device, which came to rest on a north-south axis, the point-south needle). Compass technology traveled along land routes to the Mediterranean and was adopted by Europeans during the twelfth century. By the fifteenth century sailors of both the East and the West had the mariner's compass.

As Portuguese and Dutch explorers rounded Africa and crossed the Indian Ocean, Europeans gained an upper hand in their knowledge of wind patterns and sea currents. Thanks largely to their contacts with Arab astrologers, Europeans were also more advanced in the field of celestial navigation, the technique of locating oneself by observing and measuring the positions of the sun or stars in the sky. In the fourteenth century the Arabs and the Portuguese developed the cross-staff (known in Portuguese as the *balestilha*), an instrument for establishing the height of the sun or a star. By the sixteenth century European mariners were clearly the best in the world, and the oceans had become the primary arena for European economic development.

ANTWERP: EUROPE'S TRADE METROPOLIS

One of the most important economic developments in medieval Europe was a gradual relocation of the main area of trade away from the Mediterranean region, the center of commercial activity since ancient times, and toward the countries around the southern rim of the North Sea, where it remains to this day. One sign of this shift was the rise of the Flemish city of Antwerp, which by the early sixteenth century had become Europe's most important trade center.

Situated close to the Rhine estuary and the English Channel, Antwerp's geography gave it the natural advantage of being at a crossroads of trade routes. By 1500 Antwerp was the major continental marketplace for English woolen cloth, and a large colony of German merchants traded Rhine wines and copper and silver there. However, the city owed its commercial dominance to Portuguese traders, who in 1501 decided that Antwerp would be their principal market for selling spices from the East Indies to northern Europeans. Because the Portuguese enjoyed a virtual monopoly on the spice trade, Antwerp boomed. By 1508 over 60,000 marks (around 17 tons [15,500 kg]) of silver were passing through Antwerp on the way to Lisbon. Venice, previously Europe's main spice market, suffered a severe decline in income. The booming trade made Antwerp a major base of operations for the leading German bankers, the Fuggers and the Welsers.

Because the Portuguese failed to maintain their monopoly on the spice trade, Antwerp's preeminence was waning by 1530. However, Spain, whose king had become ruler of the Netherlands in 1519, came to the rescue. In the 1530s huge amounts of silver from the Americas began flooding into Spain. Much of it was sent to Antwerp, where it was used to buy products that were needed to equip and supply Spain's fleets and armies. These products included naval stores (timber and tar) from Scandinavia, grain from eastern Europe, and linen and woolen textiles from England, Germany, and France.

Other products from the Americas, such as dyes and sugar, were also marketed at Antwerp. The Spanish government's declaration of bankruptcy in 1557 was a serious blow to Antwerp's prosperity, and the city suffered severely during the Dutch wars of independence (1566–1609). By 1600 Antwerp's place had been taken by Amsterdam.

▼ The Allegory of Commerce, a 1585 woodcut by the Swiss artist Jost Amman, includes detailed depictions of merchants, clerks, bookkeepers, and workmen engaged in commercial activity on the Scheldt River, near the important trading city of Antwerp.

Navigation Expands Networks

Although navigation was still a relatively imprecise science in the fifteenth century, sailors could make longer and more regular journeys than ever before. As Europe's economy developed, so too did the demand for imported goods and for new places to which to export local products.

At first, the sailors of the Renaissance took to the sea in order to become involved in the lucrative trade in Asian spices, precious gems, and fine silk that fetched such a high price in Europe. These exotic products were brought to Europe by a network of foreign traders who oversaw the transportation of the goods from source to market across the vast swath of Islamic territory that separated the two. The sea offered a great economic opportunity—by finding a route that directly connected Europe to the source of the Asian luxuries, the Europeans would control a profitable maritime trade network that bypassed the Islamic merchants. The sea route was also faster, safer, and cheaper.

The vessels that European traders typically used carried some of the world's first portable

This sumptuous sixteenth-century Flemish tapestry depicts the Portuguese explorer Vasco da Gama disembarking at Calicut, in southern India, on May 20, 1498. By sailing from Europe to India by way of the Cape of Good Hope (at the southern tip of Africa), Gama pioneered a new trade route that would bring South Asia's spices directly to Europe and greatly enlarge Portugal's role in world affairs.

cannon. These ships allowed Europeans to initiate a phase of trade in which coercion was used to open or enhance trade networks.

European explorations in Africa were spearheaded by the Portuguese voyages sent out by Prince Henry (1394–1460), known as Henry the Navigator. In 1418 Henry started the first school for oceanic navigation. Located at Sagres, in southwestern Portugal, Henry's school trained sailors in astronomy, navigation, mapmaking, and science.

From the 1420s on, Henry's sailors pressed farther south every year into uncharted regions. Between 1434 and 1460 they rounded, first, Cape Bojador and then Cape Blanc and Cape Vert, and finally they sailed as far as the Gambia River and Cape Palmas (on the coast of present-day Liberia). By the time Henry died in 1460, the Portuguese had established a trading post on Arguin, an island a little to the south of Cape Blanc, off the coast of present-day Mauritania. As part of the effort to defeat the Muslims who dominated northern Africa, the Portuguese worked to spread Christianity; they also opened up trade in gold, ivory, and eventually, slaves. As they pressed farther south, Portuguese sailors finally (in 1487) discovered the route around the southern tip of Africa that would take them to India entirely by sea.

The Age of Exploration

It seemed that by the late fifteenth century the boundaries of the known world were expanding with each passing year. In 1492 Christopher Columbus, aiming for the spice-rich islands of the East Indies, sailed west across the Atlantic and happened upon the Americas. Spanish conquistadores followed Columbus to the Americas throughout the 1500s. These soldier-explorers sought to spread Christianity and to find resources of value, specifically gold and silver. In 1519 in present-day Mexico, Hernán Cortés discovered plentiful gold among the Aztecs. Stories of fabulous cities of gold propelled the Spanish conquest of most of Mexico and South America.

The discovery of silver led to the beginning of silver mining in Mexico and South America. Much of this silver ultimately finished up in Asia. There being little demand for European goods in China and India, European merchants could obtain the oriental luxuries they desired only by paying for them with hard cash. In this way,

China and India were greatly enriched by the European discovery of the Americas. Explorers in the New World also found new products to cultivate and trade, including corn, tomatoes, tobacco, and chocolate. In some areas these and other crops were grown on plantations, large farms that were run and owned by Europeans but worked by native peoples or imported labor. Owners of such plantations took advantage of the non-European climates to grow exotic products, such as sugar, that could be sold for a high price in European markets.

Colonial Expansion

Numerous wars at home did not prevent European nations from exploring and conquering wide portions of the world, particularly in Asia and in the newly discovered Americas. In the fifteenth century Portugal led the way in geographical exploration, and in the sixteenth century Spain was predominant. These nations were the first to set up colonies in South America and trading stations on the shores of Africa and Asia. They were soon followed by France, England, and the Netherlands.

A colony was a fairly permanent base for trade and the harvesting of resources. Most European colonies had a climate different from that of the mother country. Typically, residents of the colonizing country furnished the colony with a civilian and military population. Each colonial enterprise was founded with capital from its mother country, provided by either private investors or government departments.

Each European nation employed different methods of colonial settlement and development. The trailblazing Spanish explorers eventually gave way to military and agricultural settlements, including communal pueblos and Christian missions. French explorers established trading posts. English mariners tended to set up colonies with a view to their becoming permanent settlements. Often these efforts were supported by joint-stock companies that, with the support of private

PIRACY AND THE LAW OF THE SEA

From the 1500s piracy functioned as a kind of evil twin of the accepted respectable norms of overseas exploration and trade during the age of sail. Piracy was based on a moral and ethical code that, since it involved stealing and killing, was unacceptable to the mainstream of European society. Nevertheless, the world of pirates grew into a stable and complex society based upon the use of the sea as an open and unrestricted public space.

Typically, pirates were tied to no specific nation. Owing to improvements in sailing technology, by the 1500s bigger and faster ships were transporting cargoes of goods ever greater distances from home. Once on the open ocean, ships became vulnerable to attack and capture. It became increasingly difficult for nations to protect their cargoes, which often included gold and other precious goods, while they were in transit on the high seas. Indeed, although the Spanish armada is still a byword for naval might, the plain truth is that individual Spanish ships were raided, almost with impunity, by English privateers (privateers were licensed pirates whose ships were paid to attack those of another country). Francis Drake (c. 1540–1596) was knighted, and other privateers were treated not as criminals but as heroes by the nation that sponsored them.

Mariner societies based around piracy took shape throughout the world. For instance, North African pirates found English ships easy prey. During the 1700s Madagascar pirates were supported by France. The most notorious pirates were those of the Barbary Coast (the coast of North Africa from the western border of Egypt to the Atlantic Ocean). From the 1500s to the 1800s, the Barbary Coast was occupied by independent Islamic states that were only nominal dependencies of the Ottoman Empire. In the early 1500s these states became centers for pirates. The careful organization of Barbary piracy is typical of many pirating societies. Captains, who formed a class in Algiers and Tunis, commanded vessels outfitted by wealthy backers, who then received 10 percent of the value of any loot.

A similar social stratification characterized the pirate societies that took shape in the Caribbean Sea. Primarily, these pirates sought to take advantage of the European ships that frequented the area. After capturing the ship's cargo, the pirates then often killed the crew or impressed the surviving members into service aboard the pirate ship.

◀ *While in transit, ships laden with precious cargo were extremely vulnerable to piracy. In this oil on canvas made in the studio of Willem van Velde II (1633–1707), Spanish ships are depicted being attacked by pirates off the notorious Barbary Coast of North Africa.*

investors as well as the colonizing government, harvested or developed the resources of the colony.

As overseas holdings increased and navigational capabilities grew, many European countries saw the need to create or enlarge an existing national or royal navy. Control of the seas correlated directly to a country's economic development and stability.

As more and more goods were transported by ship throughout evolving networks of maritime trade routes, armed naval fleets became critical factors in a country's commercial success. Navies patrolled important shipping channels and protected specific vessels from a number of dangers, including piracy, the inveterate menace to commerce on the high seas.

The Atlantic Trade Network

According to the logic of economic growth that was one of the factors driving European overseas expansion, New World resources became important elements in the acquiring and enhancing of military and political power at home. As part of the effort to optimize production of the subtropical and tropical crops that were the most important New World commodities, many governments and merchants resorted to the use of slaves—specifically, African tribespeople who, being losers in local wars, were gathered up and sold for transportation to the Americas.

People from sub-Saharan Africa had been traded as slaves for centuries. They were brought into Europe via the trans-Saharan trade routes that were run by North African Muslims. Between 1450 and the end of the nineteenth century, slaves were obtained from along the western coast of Africa with the full and active cooperation of African kings and merchants. In return, the African kings and merchants received various trade goods, including beads, cowrie shells (used as a form of currency), textiles, brandy, horses, and guns.

By the mid-1400s, Portugal had a monopoly on the export of slaves from Africa. It is estimated that during the 450 years of the transatlantic slave trade, Portugal was responsible for trans-porting more than 4.5 million Africans (roughly 40 percent of the total transported). During the eighteenth century, when over 6 million Africans were traded, it is estimated that Britain, then the most active slave-trading nation, was responsible for trading almost 2.5 million Africans.

The system of trade that took shape in the Atlantic Ocean is widely referred to as the triangle trade. This term describes the basic path trade goods followed—a path that was determined by prevailing ocean currents and wind systems, by which sailing ships were highly constrained. In this self-contained system, the westward winds that blow in the subtropical zones north and south of the equator came to be known as the trade winds. The trade winds enabled ships to sail west across the Atlantic from Africa to the Americas with a cargo of slaves. The northeastward winds that blew the ships from the Americas back to Europe came to be known as the westerlies, after the direction from which they blew. The Canary Current, which carried ships from Europe south to Africa, formed the third side of the triangle.

Manufactured commodities were exported from Europe to the African colonial centers and the American colonies. Slaves left Africa bound primarily for Central and South American colonies (especially Brazil and the West Indies). Tropical commodities (sugar and molasses for example) flowed from these colonies to the North American colonies and to Europe. North America exported tobacco, furs, indigo, and lumber to Europe.

Mercantilism

According to the rationale of the new European trading system, resources overseas translated into commodities at home. From the fourteenth century on, those who attended European markets and fairs began to develop an interest in traded goods. This interest at ground level fueled wider developments in the philosophical attitude toward trade, commodities, and money, particularly regarding individual profit. Eventually, such thinkers as the English philosopher John Locke (1632–1704) and the Scottish economist Adam Smith (1723–1790) would provide an intellectual underpinning for the economic "system" its

► *This engraving is taken from François Froger's* Relation of a Voyage Made in the Years 1695, 1696, 1697, on the Coasts of Africa, Streights of Magellan, Brazil, Cayenna and the Antilles, by a Squadron of French Men of War, under the Command of M. de Gennes. *Among the scenes recorded by Froger, a nineteen-year-old volunteer engineer who served aboard the* Falcon, *is this interchange between an African slave trader and a potential French buyer who has rowed ashore in a boat.*

Cape Coast Castle, on Africa's Gold Coast (in present-day Ghana), was built by the Swedish Africa Company in 1653. In 1664 the British seized the castle and transformed it into a base for their transatlantic slave trading. This engraving of the fort was made by Henry Greenhill in 1682.

MIDDLE PASSAGE

The leg of the trade system that carried Africans into slavery in the Americas was often referred to as the middle passage. European ships were loaded with groups of six people chained together with neck and foot shackles. On board, the Africans were put below the decks and placed head to foot, still chained in long rows. Most Africans suffered from seasickness and became dehydrated from vomiting. Poor food and fearful conditions contributed to diarrhea, and as a result, there were frequent outbreaks of disease below deck. Particularly common were typhoid fever, measles, yellow fever, and smallpox.

The unhealthy conditions were exacerbated by the common practice of overcrowding a ship in order to maximize profit. The longer the ship was at sea, the higher the number of slaves who died in transit. Shorter voyages were expected to result in a mortality rate of between 5 and 10 percent. On longer voyages traders expected between 30 and 50 percent of the slaves to perish.

Those Africans who suffered the extreme degradation of the middle passage were severely traumatized by the experience. The damage was compounded by a common fear among the Africans that they had been taken by the Europeans to be eaten, to be made into oil or gunpowder, or to have their blood drawn and used to dye the red flags of Spanish ships. In fact, traders sought to capitalize on the African slaves' abilities as agricultural laborers and on their adaptability to tropical climates.

opponents later called capitalism. The lynchpin of capitalism was the freedom of the individual to seek private economic benefit and profit (hence, the absence of truly systematic structures).

The combination of this nascent consumerism and advances in ocean navigation produced a European worldview that was shaped by profits and commodities. This worldview gave rise to an economic system that was later given the name mercantilism, which may be described as economic nationalism directed at building a wealthy and powerful state. Adam Smith, in his 1776 *Inquiry into the Nature and Causes of the Wealth of Nations,* coined the term *mercantile* to describe a system of political economy whose ultimate goal was to enrich a country by restraining imports and encouraging exports.

The mercantilist system dominated western European economic thought and policies from the sixteenth century through the late eighteenth. The goal of these policies was to achieve a balance of trade that would bring gold and silver into a country. In contrast to the previous agriculturally based economy, the mercantile system served the

John Smythe   died 1556

After London, England's most important port in the sixteenth century was Bristol, in the southwest of the country. Owing to its location, Bristol was ideally placed to trade with Ireland, western France, Spain, and Portugal and to take advantage of the emerging transatlantic trade routes. Bristol was dominated by a dozen or so of its wealthiest merchants, who used their political influence to advance their own interests and even to flout the law. Among this mercantile elite was John Smythe, who twice served as the city's mayor (in 1547 and 1554).

Smythe used his own ship, the *Trinity,* to carry his cargoes, and he also hired out space in the *Trinity's* hold to other merchants. Smythe's main business was importing wine from Bordeaux and iron from San Sebastián and Rentería (both in northern Spain). From Bordeaux he also imported woad (a plant from which a blue dye was produced), mordants (chemicals for fixing dyes), and oil, all for use in the local textile industry. In return Smythe exported woolen cloth, leather, and grain. Smythe was not engaged directly in selling to the general public; he did most of his business—buying and selling from other merchants—at fairs in small textile-producing towns in Somerset and Wiltshire.

Smythe kept meticulous accounts so that he could easily calculate the profit and loss on all of his trading ventures; his accounts have survived to the present day. They provide evidence that he often traded illegally. Customs dues, usually charged at 5 percent, were an important source of revenue for the crown, and it was obligatory to declare all imports and exports at the customs house. In addition, some goods, including grain and leather, could be exported only on purchase of an expensive license from the crown. Sometimes Smythe recovered these extra costs by selling shares in his export licenses to other merchants. More often, Smythe met up with small boats at sea and loaded unlicensed cargoes of grain and leather out of sight of customs officers. Smythe and other leading merchants were able to carry on this smuggling with virtual impunity because they used their local power and influence to intimidate any would-be informers.

Smythe was upwardly mobile, and in common with other wealthy merchants of the period, he aspired to social equality with the landed gentry. To this end he invested his profits in buying land, much of which had formerly belonged to monasteries dissolved by Henry VIII. In 1546 he bought the impressive manor of Ashton Court, outside Bristol, which remained the family seat until 1946.

▶ *This bird's-eye-view of John Smythe's Bristol is from* Civitates orbis terrarum, *a book of maps made in the late sixteenth century by Franz Hogenberg and Georg Braun. Bristol is situated near the mouth of the Avon River, which bisects the city; it was from here that the Italian explorer John Cabot in 1497 made the first European voyage to reach the North American continent since that of Leif Eriksson in the eleventh century. Cabot's discovery that the waters off the coast of Newfoundland were teeming with cod enticed numerous European traders and settlers to North America.*

In this oil painting on copper, *The Return to Amsterdam of the Fleet of the Dutch East India Company in 1599*, *Andries van Eertvelt captures the bustle and excitement that would have greeted the spice-laden ships.*

interests of merchants and producers, such as the British East India Company, whose activities were protected and encouraged by the state.

During the mercantilist period military conflict between nation-states was both more frequent and more extensive than at any earlier time in history. The armies and navies of the main protagonists were no longer temporary musters raised to address a specific threat or objective but instead were full-time professional forces. Their job—at least in the opinion of certain historians—was to assist and protect economic interests. According to this view, each government's primary economic objective was to command a sufficient quantity of hard currency to support a military that would deter attacks by other countries and aid its own territorial expansion. The extent to which there is substance to this speculation is a matter of ongoing dispute.

The evolution of new economic ideas had blossomed as a result of interaction among nations and trade in a variety of new resources. The mercantilistic system may have knitted together participating nations in a way never before seen, but its eventual and utter collapse in the face of genuinely free trade is also noteworthy.

FURTHER READING

Braudel, Fernand. *Civilization and Capitalism, Fifteenth to Eighteenth Century.* 3 vols. New York: 1982–1984.

Cipolla, Carlo M., ed. *The Fontana Economic History of Europe.* Vol. 2, *The Sixteenth and Seventeenth Centuries.* New York, 1977.

Keay, John. *The Spice Route: A History.* Berkeley, CA, 2006.

Milton, Giles. *Nathaniel's Nutmeg; or, The True and Incredible Adventure of the Spice Trader Who Changed the Course of History.* New York, 1999.

Spufford, Peter. *Power and Profit: The Merchant in Medieval Europe.* New York, 2003.

Thomas, Hugh. *The Slave Trade: The Story of the Atlantic Slave Trade, 1440–1870.* New York, 1997.

Voet, Léon. *Antwerp: The Golden Age.* Antwerp, Belgium, 1973.

Brian Black
John Haywood

SEE ALSO
....
• Agriculture • Banking • Columbus, Christopher
• Disease • Exploration • Feudalism
• Guilds and Companies • Machines
• Markets and Fairs • Science and Technology

Trent, Council of

THE COUNCIL OF TRENT MET IN SEVERAL SESSIONS BETWEEN 1545 AND 1563. IT FORMULATED THE RESPONSE OF THE ROMAN CATHOLIC CHURCH TO THE REFORMATION AND SHAPED CATHOLIC THOUGHT FOR THE NEXT FOUR HUNDRED YEARS.

Martin Luther set in motion the Reformation in 1517 when, according to the traditional account, he nailed his Ninety-five Theses to the door of the church in the castle of Wittenberg, Germany. When the changes he advocated ran into opposi-

tion from the pope and other Catholic authorities, Luther called for a meeting of representatives of the whole church—a general, or ecumenical, council—to resolve the controversies. Soon, however, he moved away from the idea of a council and concentrated on the Bible as the sole source of authority for his proposals.

Most Catholics agreed that only the pope could summon a general council. A long succession of popes, however, was unwilling to do so because of the memory of two councils in the previous century that challenged papal authority: the Council of Constance (1414–1418), held in southern Germany, and the Council of Basel (1431–1449), held in Switzerland. The popes and their supporters feared that if another council was called, it might revive these challenges instead of focusing on a reply to Luther and other leaders of the Reformation. They thought the necessary reforms in the Catholic Church could be introduced by the papacy without the need of a council.

When Pope Paul III (reigned 1534–1549) finally came round to favoring a council, there remained the delicate question of where to hold it. Paul wanted it to be in Rome or close by so that he could control it and thus avoid any repetition of the earlier events at Constance and Basel. However, the Holy Roman emperor, Charles V (reigned 1519–1556)—who was the most powerful ruler in Europe and the overlord of Germany, where the Reformation was achieving its greatest success—urged that the council meet in Germany so that it might have credibility with the Lutherans and thus make possible the healing of the divisions resulting from the Reformation.

Eventually the city of Trent was chosen as a compromise that was acceptable to both emperor and pope. Trent now lies in the German-speaking

◀ Titian's painting, dated 1543, of the city of Trent, shows the city as it was on the eve of the council (despite the date of its creation, the picture was painted not for the occasion of the council but rather to celebrate other positive contributions made by Pope Paul III to life in Trent). This image forms a single canvas with a portrait of Paul III; the better-known half of the canvas is shown on the facing page.

▲ In Titian's portrait of 1543, Pope Paul III is depicted without his skullcap. Though seventy-five, the pontiff clearly was still vigorous (frequent excursions in Rome and to the countryside kept him in good health).

part of northeastern Italy close to the border with Austria. Then, although it lay within the borders of the Holy Roman Empire, it was one of several papacy-owned territories outside of the Papal States and so fell under papal jurisdiction.

The Council

The assembly lasted eighteen years in all. Meetings fell into three periods: 1545 to 1547, 1551 and 1552, and 1562 and 1563. Following the practice of previous general councils, the core delegates, or council fathers, were the bishops of the Catholic Church. Some other leading clerics, such as abbots and cardinals who were not bishops, were also delegates. In addition, Emperor Charles V and other Catholic rulers sent officials who lobbied the council fathers and reported back on what went on, but these observers did not have voting rights.

Fewer than fifty bishops and other churchmen, mostly from Italy, attended the early sessions, but in the final two years over two hundred bishops and other delegates were present, mainly from the countries of Catholic Europe. There were five popes during the time, Paul III (reigned 1534–1549), Julius III (reigned 1550–1555), Marcellus II (reigned 1555), Paul IV (reigned 1555–1559), and Pius IV (reigned 1559–1565). The pope never came to the council in person, but he was represented by two or three legates who presided over the discussions and ensured a measure of papal control. Most of the important meetings were held in the Cathedral of Trent, while the less formal gatherings were held in other buildings in the city.

First Period: 1545–1547

The council quickly faced a key issue in the Reformation debate: the source of doctrinal authority for Christians. Luther and most Protestants emphasized almost exclusively the authority of the Bible. Trent, on the other hand, argued that the Bible must be complemented by "traditions." The council was not very precise as to what exactly these traditions were, and the term was modified to the singular, *tradition*. Trent was unambiguous, however, in its insistence that the Bible alone was not enough, for since its meaning was not always obvious, it needed to be interpreted and supplemented by the teaching of the church. Some scholars have argued that Trent proposed a two-source theory, as if the Bible and tradition were in effect independent authorities. Others point out that the council stated that there was only one source, "the gospel [that] Christ proclaimed," and that it thus saw the Bible and tradition not as two distinct sources but as two channels through which the single original source, the gospel message, was communicated.

During this first period the council discussed a second key issue in the Reformation controversies: the question of whether Christians were saved, or justified, in God's eyes by faith alone or whether good works also played a part. All the early Protestants placed almost exclusive emphasis upon faith, which they said was a free gift from God, given to some people without their merit-

▲ *The Last Judgment, painted by Michelangelo Buonarroti between 1536 and 1541, dominates the Sistine Chapel in Rome. In this central section of the painting, Jesus Christ, represented as sovereign judge, draws the figures on his right, some of whom carry the instruments of their martyrdom (a cross and a gridiron, for example), to salvation while condemning those on his left to damnation. Beneath him are angelic trumpeters whose book contains records of good and evil deeds.*

The Council of Trent made the following statements about scripture and tradition in a decree that was dated April 4, 1546:

Our Lord Jesus Christ, the Son of God, first proclaimed with his own lips the gospel, which had in the past been promised by the prophets [of the Old Testament] in the sacred scriptures. Then he commanded it be preached to every creature through his apostles as the source of the whole truth of salvation and rule of conduct. The council clearly perceives that this truth and rule are contained in written books and in unwritten traditions which were received by the apostles from the mouth of Christ himself, or else have come down to us, handed on as it were from the apostles themselves at the inspiration of the Holy Spirit.

The council further decrees, in order to control those of unbalanced character, that no one relying on his personal judgment … shall dare to interpret the sacred scriptures by twisting its text to his individual meaning in opposition to that which has been and is held by holy mother church, whose function is to pass judgment on the true meaning and interpretation of the sacred scriptures.

Canons and Decrees of the Sacred and Ecumenical Council of Trent

ing it in any way and withheld from others according to the mysterious wisdom of God. Some people, therefore, were predestined by God to heaven and others to hell. Trent accepted that salvation came to people as a free gift from God but insisted that Christians could accept or reject the gift. It also taught that those who were saved could grow further in grace and friendship with God and with one another.

Common Ground and Differences

Usually seen as a reply to the Protestant Reformation, the Council of Trent was equally important for its recognition of the common ground that Catholics and Protestants shared on a number of issues. There was a good deal of agreement in the first period and particularly in the council's treatment of the topics of authority (scripture versus tradition) and justification (faith versus good works). In later years the council became more hostile toward Protestant doctrines and more markedly Counter-Reformation in spirit. In the first period particularly, several of the leading figures at the council might be described as moderates or liberals who wanted to favorably consider the good insights of the Reformation. The Augustinian friar Girolamo Seripando, the Italian cardinals Marcello Cervini (later Pope Marcellus II) and Giovanni Morone, and the English cardinal Reginald Pole were among these influential figures.

The decree on justification indicates the common ground between Catholics and Protestants on the issue of God's freely given gift of faith. The council chose its words carefully in discussing good works. The decree is careful to avoid suggesting that a Christian may accumulate good works in the manner of a bank balance and thereby put God in his or her debt—a loathsome notion to the Reformers. It speaks rather of cooperation and friendship with God, ideas that were closer to Protestant thought.

Regarding authority, the importance of the Bible was accepted by both Catholics and Protestants even while Trent also emphasized the importance of tradition. In its decree on scripture and tradition, the council made a list of the books of the Old and the New Testament. In the Old Testament list Trent included a number of books

and passages that were accepted by Catholics but excluded by most Protestants on the grounds that they existed only in the Greek language—either they had originally been written in Greek or they had survived only in Greek translations—and therefore did not form part of the original Hebrew Bible. The books in question included Wisdom, Ecclesiasticus, Judith, Tobit, Baruch, and 1 and 2 Maccabees, as well as additions to the book of Daniel: the stories of Susanna and of Daniel in the lion's den.

▼ A seventeenth-century oil portrait by an unknown French artist of Cardinal Reginald Pole (1500–1558). Pole, the archbishop of Canterbury, was an influential figure in the first period of the council.

The Council of Trent made the following statements about faith and good works in its decree on justification, dated January 13, 1547. The language is theological, yet the ideas are expressed in clear and comprehensible terms.

The council declares that justification in adults takes its origin from a predisposing grace of God through Jesus Christ, that is, from his invitation which calls them, with no existing merits on their side. Thus, those who had been turned away from God by sins are disposed by God's grace inciting and helping them, to turn towards their own justification by giving free assent to and cooperating with this same grace. Consequently, though God touches a person's heart through the light of the Holy Spirit, the person does something in receiving the movement of grace, for he can reject it.

… So those justified in this way and made friends and members of the household of God, going from strength to strength, are, as the apostle Paul says [2 Corinthians 4:16], renewed from day to day by putting to death what is earthly in themselves and yielding themselves as instruments of righteousness for sanctification by observance of the commandments of God and of the church. They grow and increase in that very justness they have received through the grace of Christ, by faith united to good works.

Canons and Decrees of the Sacred and Ecumenical Council of Trent

▶ *This eighteenth-century engraving by Pio Panfili shows part of the central square of Bologna, in northern Italy. Some sessions of the council's second period (1551–1552) were held in the building on the right, now the city hall.*

Catholics and Protestants agreed on the list of books that made up the New Testament but gave them different emphasis. Protestants focused more than Catholics on the letters of Paul, especially his letter to the Romans, where the role of faith above good works is highlighted. Luther, moreover, while he accepted the letter of James as part of the New Testament, regarded it as lightweight—he called it a "letter of straw"—because its stress on good works conflicted with his teaching on justification by faith alone: "What does it profit if a person says he has faith but has not good works? . . . So faith by itself, if it has no works, is dead" (James 2, 14–17).

There were also differences regarding the church's role in interpreting the Bible, both the Old Testament and the New. Protestants tended to regard the Bible's meaning as clear and accessible to those who read it carefully and in prayer. Trent taught that the church was needed to interpret the Bible and that it was dangerous for a person to rely too much on personal judgment.

Trent was cautious on two issues stressed by most leaders of the Protestant Reformation: the importance of the original texts—Hebrew for the Old Testament and Greek for the New—and the need for translations into the vernacular languages. The best edition of the New Testament in its Greek original had been produced shortly before the council by Desiderius Erasmus (c. 1466–1536), a Catholic who refused to join the Reformation movement and remained what might be called a liberal Christian. In its decree of April 4, 1546, Trent gave preference to the Vulgate Bible, the Latin translation that had been made by Saint Jerome (c. 347–419 or 420) at a time when Latin was the common, or vulgar, language. In the century after the beginning of the Reformation, the best and most widely available vernacular translations of the Bible were made by Protestants: they included Martin Luther's translation into German and the English King James (or Authorized) Version.

The Second Period: 1551–1552

Pope Paul III was uneasy that the council was being conducted so far from Rome. An epidemic of typhus in the city of Trent during the winter of 1546/1547 provided an excuse for him to transfer the council to Bologna in March 1547. Since Bologna, which lay within the Papal States, was much closer than Trent to Rome, papal intervention in the council would be easier. Several sessions of the council were held there during that year in what is now the city hall. Charles V greatly resented the move to Bologna, and bishops loyal to him remained at Trent. As a result, the pope was soon obliged to suspend the council. He died two years later; his successor, who took the name Julius III, heeded the emperor's wishes and reconvened the council in Trent in 1551.

Discussion of the seven sacraments had already begun during the first period of the council, and the issue dominated the second period. In the Middle Ages the church had slowly reached the conclusion that there were seven special rites that were central to the practice of Christianity: baptism, confession (sometimes called penance), the Eucharist (also called the Mass), confirmation, marriage, orders (ordination as deacon, priest, or bishop), and last anointing (sometimes called extreme unction). All

▶ The seven sacraments are a common subject of altarpieces. In this fine example, made between 1445 and 1450 by the Flemish artist Rogier van der Weyden, the action is placed in a basilica with three aisles. The most important sacrament, the Eucharist, is depicted in the central section at the rood screen altar, underneath the Crucifixion—the event to which the Eucharist is directly related. The side aisles contain depictions of the other six sacraments—baptism, confirmation, and confession appear on the left, and orders, extreme unction, and matrimony on the right.

seven had been authoritatively declared sacraments at the Second Council of Lyons in 1274. Much fuller statements about them were made by the Council of Florence (1439–1443). Disagreeing with this medieval teaching, most leaders and theologians of the Reformation, including Luther and Calvin, declared there were only two sacraments—baptism and the Eucharist—because only these two had been introduced by Jesus Christ; the other five had been added to the list of sacraments by the medieval church. For the most part Reformers accepted the other five as rites but not sacraments, and even as rites they were rewritten in forms and phrases that differed from what had been customary in the Catholic Church.

The differences, therefore, were partly about language—how to define *rite* and *sacrament*—and partly about the nature of the rites *as* sacraments. Trent taught that sacraments were channels of divine grace, whereas for Protestants they were more akin to signs of God's grace,

which had already been given through justification by faith alone, and were therefore less crucial in terms of their effectiveness.

Regarding the Eucharist, there were important differences about Christ's presence in the sacrament: Protestants were divided on whether it was real or symbolic. Trent insisted upon the true and physical presence of Christ, though it was the risen and glorified Christ, not Christ in his earthly life. The council also insisted upon the doctrine of transubstantiation, developed during the Middle Ages and rejected by all Protestants as unfaithful to the Bible and to the teaching of the early church. Transubstantiation (from the Latin, *transubstantiatio*) means a "change in substance." The belief was that Christ was not merely present in the eucharistic bread and wine but that the bread and wine actually changed into the body and blood of Christ.

There was basic agreement between Catholics and Protestants on the sacrament of baptism. As a result, the Catholic Church recognized the

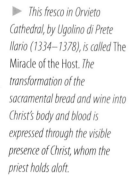

▶ *This fresco in Orvieto Cathedral, by Ugolino di Prete Ilario (1334–1378), is called* The Miracle of the Host. *The transformation of the sacramental bread and wine into Christ's body and blood is expressed through the visible presence of Christ, whom the priest holds aloft.*

◀ *This painting by the Flemish artist Peter Paul Rubens (1577–1640) expresses the confidence that the Council of Trent inspired in Catholics. The female figure at the left represents the Catholic Church overcoming the defeated Protestants; holding aloft the Eucharist, she moves forward triumphantly.*

validity of baptisms performed by members of Protestant churches, and vice versa. Trent implicitly recognized this consensus from the Catholic side, even though it did not say so explicitly. The agreement was an important area of common ground between Catholics and Protestants, since it was primarily through baptism that people could become Christians and thus benefit from Christ's redemptive sacrifice. Catholics and Protestants therefore recognized each other as Christians, whatever their other differences.

Trent's teaching on the seven sacraments had a huge influence on the practice of Catholicism. In reaffirming developments that had taken place during the Middle Ages and trying to do away

with abuses and superstitions, it did much to shape the devotional life of Catholics for centuries. Especially significant was the emphasis upon Christ's presence in the Eucharist, which formed the subject of a wide range of new devotions and prayers.

Trouble in the Holy Roman Empire—a rebellion of German princes—caused a second interruption of the council, in April 1552. As Charles V's support was vital for its success, the council was temporarily suspended while he suppressed the uprising. Pope Julius III, who had supported the council during the second period, died in 1555 and was succeeded by Marcellus II, who reigned for less than a month.

Marcellus's successor, Paul IV, was opposed to Trent because he believed the matters it was discussing should be dealt with by the papacy. However, he never went so far as to dissolve the council altogether. The result was a long gap of ten years. It was only in 1562, during the reign of Paul IV's successor, Pius IV, that the council was reconvened for the third time.

Third Period: 1562–1563

In its third and final period the council concluded its treatment of the seven sacraments and issued decrees on several other doctrinal topics that were disputed between Catholics and Protestants. These topics included indulgences (which had been the original cause of Martin Luther's protest and the main subject of his Ninety-five Theses in 1517), purgatory, and devotion to the saints. The council sought to maintain the teachings of the church on the three issues while at the same time removing any abuses. Thus, it warned against any suggestion that an indulgence (a reduction in the time the soul of a dead sinner spent suffering in purgatory before entering heaven) could be bought with money, either for oneself in anticipation of what lay ahead or for others already in purgatory. While the council strongly approved of prayers and devotions to the saints, it insisted upon the centrality of Jesus Christ.

During this third period the council's main concern was the moral reform of the church. Leaders of the Reformation frequently criticized the Catholic clergy for their low moral standards and lack of education. Trent replied with a very important decree on seminaries (a seminary is an institution set up for training priests). Religious orders had programs for training their priests, but for prospective parish priests, education and formation were far from well organized. During the Middle Ages fewer than 10 percent of those training to be parish priests studied at a university. For the large majority training was more like an apprenticeship under one or more priests that might include some studies within the parish or in the house of a religious order. Trent regularized the situation through its decree on seminaries, a decree that proved enormously influential; it provided for the Catholic Church an institution that remains the normal means of training parish priests. The council's characteristic attention to detail and zeal for reform were conspicuous in the decree.

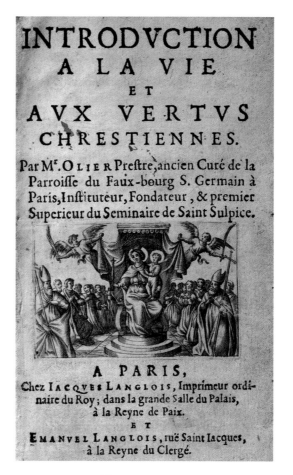

► *Pictured here is the title page of* Introduction to Christian Life and Virtues, *published in 1657. Its writer, the Parisian curate Jean-Jacques Olier, founded the Sulpician Order for training priests in 1641 and the Seminary of Saint Sulpice in 1642.*

In July 1563 the Council of Trent issued the following decree on the subject of priestly training:

If they are not rightly brought up, those of adolescent years tend to make for the world's pleasures. Unless trained to religious practice from an early age before habits of vice take firm hold, they never keep to an orderly church life in an exemplary way without very great and almost extraordinary help from almighty God. Hence the council decrees that every cathedral and greater church is obliged to provide for, to educate in religion, and to train in ecclesiastical studies a set number of boys, according to its resources and the size of the diocese. The boys are to be drawn from the city and diocese … and educated in a college chosen for the purpose by the bishop.

Those admitted to the college should be at least twelve years old, of legitimate birth, who know how to read and write competently, and whose character and disposition offers hope that they will serve in church ministries throughout life. The council wishes the sons of poor people particularly to be chosen, but does not exclude those of more wealthy parents provided they pay for their own maintenance and show an ambition to serve God and the church.

The bishop will divide the boys into the number of classes he thinks fit, according to their number, age, and progress in ecclesiastical learning. The college will be a perpetual seminary of ministers of God. The seminarians should always have the tonsure and wear clerical dress from the outset. They should study grammar, singing, keeping church accounts, and other useful skills; and they should be versed in holy scripture, church writers, homilies of the saints, and the practice of rites and ceremonies, and of administering the sacraments, particularly all that seems appropriate to hearing confessions.

The bishop should ensure that they attend Mass every day, confess their sins at least every month, receive the body of our lord Jesus Christ as often as their confessor judges, and serve in the cathedral and other churches of the area on feast days. He will punish with severity the difficult and incorrigible and those who spread bad habits, and expel them if need be. He will take the utmost care to remove all obstacles from such a worthy and holy foundation and promote all that preserves and strengthens it.

Canons and Decrees of the Sacred and Ecumenical Council of Trent

Trent's so-called *Tametsi* decree of July 1563, on the subject of marriage, contained the following statement:

The council orders that henceforth, before a marriage is contracted, an announcement of those intending to marry shall be made publicly during Mass by the parish priest of the couple on three successive feast days.

After these announcements have been made, and if no legitimate impediment is raised in objection, the celebration of the marriage must then take place in open church, during which the parish priest will, by questioning the man and woman, make sure of their consent. Then he shall say, "I join you together in marriage, in the name of the Father and the Son and the Holy Spirit," or use other words according to the accepted rite of each province.

Canons and Decrees of the Sacred and Ecumenical Council of Trent

▶ *This fresco by Taddeo Zuccari (1529–1566), in the Palazzo Farnese in Caprarola, in central Italy, shows the marriage in 1538 of Ottavio Farnese, duke of Parma and Piacenza and Paul III's grandson, to Margaret of Austria, Charles V's daughter.*

Marriage was another area of Catholic life that Trent sought to reform. The decree issued by the council, usually referred to as *Tametsi* because the decree begins with this Latin word, provided the basic framework for Catholic weddings ever since. It called for proclamation of the banns—public announcement of the marriage—well beforehand and required that marriage be celebrated in the parish church before a priest.

Trent also issued a long decree on religious orders. They had been severely criticized by Martin Luther—who had been an Augustinian friar until his break with the Catholic Church—and other leaders of the Reformation on the grounds that they were an invention of the medieval Church. They were abolished in all countries that accepted the Reformation.

The council defended religious orders of both men and women as legitimate and praiseworthy developments in the Christian tradition because they offered people the opportunity to respond to the Gospels' invitation to serve God fully and wholeheartedly. The council did seek, however, to uproot some glaring abuses: entry into a religious order at an excessively young age or without proper consent was one, and allowing one person to head several monasteries or convents at the same time was another.

The decrees of Trent held sway within the Catholic Church until revisions to some of them were approved by the Second Vatican Council (1962–1965), which is pictured here in session in Saint Peter's Basilica in Rome.

Postponed Issues

At its final session, in December 1563, the council left four matters to the pope on the grounds that it did not have time to treat them properly.

The first matter was revision of the list of books that Catholics were forbidden to read. The *Index librorum prohibitorum* (Index of Forbidden Books) had been first published in 1557 under Pope Paul IV. After Trent the list of books in the index grew to include many works of Protestants, "unreliable" Catholics, and others. The list exercised much influence over the thought patterns of Catholics, even if some of them did not always obey its strictures. The index was abolished only in 1966 by Pope Paul VI.

The second task left to the pope was to oversee a new catechism (a summary of Catholic doctrine). The Catechism of the Council of Trent was duly published in 1566. It contained the basics of Catholic teaching and was primarily for the use of priests. Numerous other, more popular catechisms followed, mainly for the use of the laity—most notably several by the Dutch Jesuit Peter Canisius (1521–1597).

The third matter was the revision of the Breviary, the prayer book based on the Psalms and other scriptural passages that priests and some lay people used for their daily prayer.

The fourth and final matter left to the pope was to revise and standardize the missal, the book containing the prayers of the Mass. The results were the Roman Missal and the Tridentine Mass (*Tridentine* means "of Trent"); after the missal's adoption the mostly Latin words of the Mass were the same for Catholics the world over for four centuries. Only after the Second Vatican Council was a new order of Mass devised, with texts translated into modern languages.

One major topic never formally treated by the council was the authority of the pope. Given that the rejection of papal authority was a crux of Protestantism, the council might have been expected to confront the issue. The complicating factor was that while all Catholics viewed the pope as the head of the church, there were strong differences of opinion as to how absolute or exclusive his authority was, especially in terms of the relationship between popes and councils. Because of these divisions within the Catholic community and reluctance to allow the pope's authority to be challenged as it had been at the Councils of Constance and Basel, the council avoided discussion of this sensitive topic. It was not until the First Vatican Council (1869–1870) and Second Vatican Council (1962–1965) that the topic was addressed by the Catholic Church.

The absence of a significant Protestant presence at the Council of Trent has raised the question in latter-day theological circles of the status of the council. Should Trent be regarded as an ecumenical council—that is, one representing the whole church (*ecumenical* derives from a Greek word that means "of the whole world")? If it *is* an ecumenical council, Trent's decrees must carry for Catholics the same binding authority carried by the decrees of the seven ecumenical councils of the early church from the First Council of Nicaea (325) to the Second Council of Nicaea (787). Some theologians have argued that Trent should be placed on a lower level, that of a general council of the Western rite of the Roman Catholic Church. In its decrees, however, Trent did not acknowledge any difference between the two grades of authority and called itself both an ecumenical and a general council. Shortly afterward, the Catholic Church placed the council firmly in the list of ecumenical councils, and there has never been a formal definitive or authoritative pronouncement on the issue of whether the general/ecumenical distinction is valid.

Because their churches were not represented at the council, Protestants never regarded it as having authority over them, nor did members of the Orthodox Church. Mainly as a result of the Second Vatican Council (1962–1965) and the Catholic Church's renewed overtures to other Christian churches, certain Catholic scholars have revisited the question of Trent's status. In an official letter written in 1974, Pope Paul VI referred to medieval councils as general councils of the Western church rather than ecumenical councils, a description that might also apply to Trent. The issue, an important one, still has to be worked through; upon it hangs the question of whether Catholics may regard the council's decisions as open to revision.

▶ *The ninth-century painting, on the iconostasis (partition screen) of Saint Catherine's Monastery in the Sinai Peninsula, Egypt, depicts the First Council of Nicaea, held in 325. The church saw Trent in a direct line of continuity with this first ecumenical council.*

A Critical Event

The Council of Trent counts as a major event in world history. It came to the rescue of the Catholic Church at a crucial moment and gave the church renewed confidence for a long time afterward. The council was a cornerstone of the Counter-Reformation, and its decrees crystallized the Catholic position on almost every topic in the Reformation debates. The council's range and success was a principal reason why more than three centuries passed before the summoning of the next ecumenical council of the Catholic Church, the First Vatican Council—there seemed no need for another council.

Arguably Trent deepened and prolonged the Reformation divisions, but such a view does less than justice to the subtlety and sophistication of many of its decrees. The council made points that needed to be made, and it may be seen as having done the best that the Catholic Church could have done in the circumstances: preserve important points in the Christian tradition.

FURTHER READING

Kelly, J. N. D., ed. *The Oxford Dictionary of Popes.* Oxford, 1986.

Tanner, Norman P. *Councils of the Church: A Short History.* New York, 2001.

———, ed. *Decrees of the Ecumenical Councils.* Vol. 2. Washington, DC, 1990.

Norman Tanner

SEE ALSO

• Calvinism • Erasmus, Desiderius
• Florence, Council of • Lutheranism
• Michelangelo • Painting and Sculpture • Papacy
• Religious Orders

Universities

DURING THE RENAISSANCE AND THE REFORMATION, UNIVERSITIES SERVED AS CENTERS OF SCHOLARSHIP FROM WHICH THE REDISCOVERED WORKS OF THE CLASSICAL WORLD WERE DISSEMINATED.

Despite the occasional application of the term *university* to centers of learning in the ancient world—Plato's Academy and Aristotle's Lyceum are the two most prominent examples—universities in the proper sense of the word did not come into being until the Middle Ages. During the Renaissance universities were distinguished from colleges much as they are in the modern age—by their size, their scholarly focus, the greater width and depth of their curricula, and their capacity to grant advanced degrees. Universities played a pivotal role during the Renaissance and the Reformation. Not merely an advanced educational establishment and training institute for future scholars and political figures, the university also served as a key intellectual battleground on at least two fronts.

First, those humanists who championed the rediscovered works of classical antiquity (in a number of cases, classical texts had been overlooked during the early Middle Ages rather than actually lost) encountered significant opposition among the educationalists and scholars who dominated most European universities. These figures had a vested interest in sustaining the status quo at their institutions and thus set themselves against the new learning of the Renaissance. The conflict between the old guard of Scholasticism and the new guard of humanism is a significant theme in the history of both the Renaissance and the Reformation.

Second, universities functioned as centers of political power. Protestant princes opposed to the rule of the Holy Roman emperor and the considerable secular and spiritual power still exercised by the pope set up universities during the Reformation in order to showcase their own power and create the next generation of scholars and political leaders, whose manner of education would, it was hoped, incline them to the ruler's point of view. Similarly, Catholic rulers used existing universities as part of their effort to resist the Reformers in the arena of ideas. Catholic-dominated universities also played a significant role in the Counter-Reformation.

▶ *A courtyard at the University of Bologna, one of Europe's oldest and most prestigious universities.*

Organization and Structure: *Studium Generale*

The first universities consisted of scholars who banded together to devise a curriculum and a core of instruction. The word from which *university* is derived—the Latin *universitas*—is sometimes translated as "corporation." The root of the word *universitas* is *universi*, which means "all together."

In the Middle Ages, *universitas* was originally a legal term derived from the Corpus Juris Civilis (Body of Civil Law). It denoted a group of individuals taken as a whole, that is, corporately. Thus, a university in this original sense consisted of what was called the *universitas magistrorum et scholarium*—"all of the masters and students gathered together."

Therefore, a university might exist even where no buildings had been set aside for the purpose of instruction. By the fourteenth century, however, this distinction had become considerably eroded, and *universitas* came to have the meaning of a specific institution of higher learning rather than merely the assembly of students and scholars residing in a given city or region.

Legal recognition—either by the church or by a secular ruler—entitled the assembly of scholars and students to designate itself a *studium* or, in the case of a more powerful or extensive *universitas,* as a *studium generale.* It was thus a fairly common phenomenon for a university to develop into a robust and active assemblage prior to gaining acceptance as a *studium* or *studium generale.*

In the Middle Ages and the Renaissance and well into the era of the Reformation, students were admitted to a university once they had mastered the seven elements of a classical education. These seven elements were broken down into the quadrivium (arithmetic, geometry, music, and astronomy) and the trivium (grammar, rhetoric, and logic; sometimes called the trivial arts). Generally speaking, university instruction aimed at completing the student's education by unifying and synthesizing the elements of the quadrivium and trivium. The more specialized universities, however, tended to direct the curriculum away from the more general liberal arts and toward the area in which the particular university excelled.

The gradual emergence of the *studium generale* is directly linked to the regulation of teaching and the licensing of teachers. In northern Europe the *chancellor scholasticus* or some other officer of a cathedral was responsible for issuing licenses to teach. In southern Europe this privilege most likely fell to the guilds representing teachers, although it came under increasing regulation and oversight by civil as well as ecclesiastical authorities.

▶ *This early-fourteenth-century relief, made by Agostino di Giovanni, is found in the cathedral in Pistoia, in western Italy, on the tomb of Cino dei Sighibuldi (known as Cino da Pistoia; c. 1270–1336 or 1337). Cino, a lawyer and poet whom Petrarch called his master, is depicted lecturing a group of scholars.*

EARLY UNIVERSITIES

The first institutions of higher learning that can properly be called universities were established in Europe during a period ranging from the ninth century to the thirteenth. The reasons for founding a university were largely particular to the individual institution. In general, universities provided some combination of legal, medical, and theological training; many were also centers of scholarship and teaching on classical texts (especially those of Aristotle) as well as commentaries on them, notably by such Muslim scholars as Ibn Sina and Ibn Rushd (known in the West as Avicenna and Averroës, respectively).

Among the more prominent early universities, Salerno, in Italy (founded in the ninth century), and Montpellier, in France (thirteenth century), specialized in medicine, while Paris (twelfth century) was a center for theological scholarship and teaching, and Bologna (eleventh century) focused on law. Other significant universities included Salamanca, in Spain (thirteenth century); Prague, in Bohemia, and Uppsala, in Sweden (fourteenth century); and Leiden, in the Netherlands (sixteenth century).

Most students and professors imitated their countrymen in the trades and commerce by organizing themselves into groups that resembled guilds. While students at first had considerable power in determining the curricula of their institution, this influence diminished fairly quickly, and the faculty was left in charge of matters of instruction.

During the Middle Ages universities were typically founded either by ecclesiastical authority or by royal fiat. However, a number of major universities were founded by migrating students and faculty. In the twelfth century students of English origin left the University of Paris in favor of what would become Oxford University owing to political differences between their mother country and France. To cite only one further example of many, in the fifteenth century the increasing prominence of Jan Hus's Czech nationalist movement led to the founding of the University of Leipzig by disaffected scholars of German extraction.

As the reputation and prominence of the universities increased, however, a number of them began to claim superior status and make assertions of universal (rather than merely regional) importance. These claims led to the new notion of a general rather than local curriculum that would permit students and scholars to study and teach broadly rather than remain limited to the region or locality of their birth. This development made the curricula, the students, and the teachers a great deal more cosmopolitan. A scholar who was recognized as a doctor of theology, law, medicine, or philosophy by one of the great universities was similarly recognized throughout Europe. In consequence, that scholar could teach at any university that would have him.

Students, too, were free to take advantage of the similarities that existed in various universities' curricula and transfer at will from one institution to another. Indeed, students from wealthy families were often expected to make the rounds of the continent's best universities, since doing so would increase both the breadth and quality of their academic learning and general experience. Since the language of instruction remained for the most part Latin, the rise of the *studium generale* eliminated, at least for those who could afford it, the last remaining barrier to a truly universal education.

The prestige and ability to wield influence that came with a university's recognition as a *studium generale* naturally led to a certain degree of contention over that privilege. Although an established university, such as Oxford, for instance, was not generally thought to require any further legal recognition in order to be considered a *studium generale,* the prevailing view among legal scholars by the middle of the thirteenth century was that future *studia generalia* could be established only by imperial decree or papal bull.

This view had numerous significant effects. Most obviously, it consolidated power in the Holy Roman emperor and the pope, both Catholic rulers. A local prince could establish his own university, but unless he sought and obtained its recognition as a *studium generale,* the institution would remain of no more than local importance and could not expect to attract the best scholars. Although such a concession by the Holy Roman emperor or the pope was not unheard of, it was a rare event. The extent to which a university, in order to obtain recognition as a *studium generale,* was beholden to the Catholic Church in one form or another also helps explain Martin Luther's invective against universities, which in turn was one of many contributing factors to the division of Christendom into Protestant and Catholic factions during the Reformation and the Counter-Reformation.

Triumph of the "New" Humanism

With the growing interest in the learning of the classical world came an increasing focus on the innate dignity and importance of humankind and the worthiness of studying and celebrating human achievement. In the fifth century BCE, the Greek philosopher Protagoras had proposed, "Man is the measure of all things." Plato (428–348/7 BCE), who is widely considered the founder of the Western philosophical tradition, is famously said to have brought philosophy down from the heavens in order to ask fundamental questions about the nature of human beings and especially about the attributes—rationality, for example—with which humans are by nature imbued.

With the resurgence in the study of ancient authors in the universities of the late Middle Ages, the focus gradually shifted away from the Scholastic interest in abstract theological questions and toward classically inspired inquiries into human nature. This anthropocentric focus

▼ *This anonymous illustration, from a fifteenth-century Italian manuscript, depicts a law lecture in progress at Bologna University.*

DIALECTIC VERSUS RHETORIC

The academic struggles between Roman Catholics and Protestants frequently involved the relative emphasis on two classical tools of rational inquiry: dialectic and rhetoric. Although the difference between the two is difficult to define with absolute precision, in general terms *dialectic* refers to learned exchanges between two or more persons who are considered to be expert in the topic under discussion, while *rhetoric* describes any attempt—written or spoken—to persuade an audience. A debate between two scholars is an example of public rhetoric, while a discussion among a panel of scholars about a literary work or a historical figure would more likely be considered a dialectical exchange.

The Scholasticism of the Roman Catholic Church and its universities was deeply reliant on dialectical argument as an integral part of its pedagogy. Dialectic is a useful tool for dissecting arguments and analyzing definitions, two of the more common activities engaged in by Scholastic thinkers and teachers. Unfortunately, over the course of time the overreliance on dialectic began to circumscribe and even dictate the terms of discussion. The result was a rather dull and unproductive "life of the mind" at Catholic universities.

Into this void sprang the humanists. Some were Roman Catholic; many were Protestant. Using a classical Latin that was far more robust and descriptive than the stripped-down dialectical version employed for theological study at universities, these scholars made effective use of a more colorful and persuasive rhetorical approach—an approach that in many cases was derived from the same classical sources favored by the Scholastics.

In the end, although rhetoric became more important than it had been for nearly a millennium, both dialectic and rhetoric remained integral parts of the curricula of most universities, both Catholic and Protestant, during the Renaissance and the Reformation.

◀ *This unattributed illumination of around 1490 depicts a theological lecture at the Sorbonne. Founded as a college for poor students by the French theologian Robert de Sorbon around 1257, the Maison de Sorbonne received official sanction from the pope in 1259 and rapidly became the core of the University of Paris. Sorbon (1201–1274) was a keen promoter of widespread access to higher education.*

placed advocates of the rebirth of the values of antiquity at odds with the custodians of the Scholastic tradition, whose practitioners used applied dialectics to draw the meaning out of (often poor) Latin translations of Aristotle and other classical figures, as well as out of the Christian scriptures of the Old Testament and the New Testament. Humanism appealed to a younger generation that had tired of the seemingly endless disputations of Scholastic philosophy. To the new generation of scholars, Scholasticism seemed more concerned with pointless controversy and circular arguments than with constructive engagement with the question at hand. The humanists generally favored a more lively rhetorical approach rather than the often dry and tedious dialectics typical of most medieval curricula.

▲ *The inner court of the University of Padua (Italy), built between 1546 and 1587, probably to a design by Andrea Moroni. In the foreground are a medical book and student garments of the kind that would have been used by the Polish astronomer Nicolaus Copernicus, a medical student at Padua from 1501 to 1503.*

of the ecclesiastically supported Scholastics was greatly facilitated by the fact that the majority of the educated public was already supportive of the humanists' views and goals. The luxuriant and often exquisite beauty of the poetry and philosophy of the ancient Greeks was far more in keeping with the spirit of material comfort and ease enjoyed by the ruling classes of Europe than was the austere and humorless learning that was passed, largely by rote, from master to student in the typical university curriculum. Since the humanistic naturalism of the Greeks was by no means entirely compatible with the outlook of the Roman Catholic Church, whose ecclesiastical authority was at least in the background at most universities, the triumph of humanism facilitated the challenge mounted by the Protestant Reformers against the power and influence of the church.

Yet it does not follow that humanism and Catholicism could not exist in harmony; they could and frequently did. Particularly in Renaissance Italy and France, there was relatively little civil or ecclesiastical strife associated with the rise of humanism, either in the universities or in society at large. Indeed, in those areas the universities, heavily influenced or even run by the church as they were, became prime instruments of research into the classical past.

It is also true that many humanists in northern Europe did not allow their love of classical learning to detract from their piety and their devotion to the church. Among the greatest humanists of the northern Renaissance were Desiderius Erasmus (c. 1446–1536) and Thomas More (1478–1535), both of whom were not only brilliant scholars but also devout Roman Catholics. Indeed, Erasmus was a Catholic priest, and More was a principled layman (and future saint) who chose to die rather than renounce his allegiance to Rome.

Renaissance Universities

Universities founded during the Middle Ages continued to play an active part during the Renaissance. Major early centers of learning in southern Europe include the Italian universities of Reggio nell'Emilia and Modena, both of which are known to have been active during the

Although initially the humanists worked reasonably well alongside their more traditional-minded colleagues, in time serious disputes broke out within the faculties of many leading universities and even between the universities themselves and the towns that hosted them. Oddly enough, these disputes had the effect of consolidating the power of the humanist upstarts. Under the pretext of instituting academic and personnel reforms, local leaders and princes alike handed power to the humanists, largely to quell further dissension and to advance their own political interests.

The victory of a rediscovered and reinvigorated humanism over the entrenched authority

twelfth century and both of which focused, as did Bologna, on the study of law. Two further examples from Italy are Vicenza (1204) and Padua (1222), both of which were founded by students migrating from Bologna.

The prominent Lutheran scholar Philipp Melanchthon (1497–1560) was among the teachers at the University of Tübingen, which was founded in 1477 in Germany with the usual four faculties of law, theology, arts, and medicine. The University of Aix-en-Provence, in southern France, was reorganized into a *studium generale*, with the University of Paris as its model, in 1409.

In 1431 Charles VII of France established the University of Poitiers as a counterbalance to the University of Paris, which he perceived as overly hospitable to students from England. In an unusual and controversial move, he granted Poitiers all of the rights possessed by the long-established universities at Paris, Toulouse, Montpellier, Angers, and Orléans. Moreover, he promised Poitiers the personal protection and support of the French crown. Other universities founded in France during the fifteenth century include Bordeaux (1441), Valentes (1452), Nantes (1463), and Bourges (1465). An interesting addition to this list is the University of Caen (1437), which was founded by the English during their brief ascendancy in Normandy. After the departure of the English, control of Caen's university was assumed by the French, and the institution was granted a new charter.

In northern Europe, Martin Luther inveighed against universities as "the devil's workshops." Luther's view was that universities should be abolished in favor of the teaching of the pure Gospel, newly translated and unadulter-

ated by what he saw as over a thousand years of papist obfuscation. Melanchthon, while sharing Luther's distaste for both Scholasticism and humanism, realized that continued antagonism toward higher learning would hinder rather than help the Reformers in their campaign to overhaul the religious status quo. Melanchthon also recognized that the nascent Reform movement would require institutions of higher learning for the appropriate training and education of its future leaders and clergy.

▲ *This portrait of Thomas More, painted in oil on a poplar panel, was executed by Hans Holbein the Younger (c. 1497–1543), who was then in More's employ.*

"THE KING'S GOOD SERVANT, BUT GOD'S FIRST"

Thomas More is reported to have described himself with the above words when he refused to swear allegiance to King Henry VIII (in place of the pope) as the head of the church. More repeatedly swore that he always had borne and always would bear allegiance to Henry as his lawful king but that his conscience and his deep Catholic faith required him to maintain his loyalty to the pope in all religious matters. More, a close friend of the Catholic humanist Desiderius Erasmus, shared with Erasmus both a powerful allegiance to the Catholic Church and a profound attachment to humanistic learning. Notwithstanding his loyalty to the pope, More died a loyal subject of the monarch who had him beheaded. According to one account, More, moving his beard off the chopping block before the executioner's ax fell, quipped, "it, at least, was not guilty of treason."

As deeply as Melanchthon shared Luther's view of the Bible as the only authoritative source of knowledge about God, methodologically Melanchthon had much in common with the humanists. Melanchthon is generally credited as the founder of the German secondary school, or gymnasium, which still retains both the name and much the same form that Melanchthon prescribed. He also received authority to make significant, Reform-based changes to the curricula and faculties of those universities already in place. Further, he established new Protestant universities at Marburg (1527), Königsberg (1544), and Helmstadt (1574). The study of classical works predominated, rhetoric drove out dialectic, and the last vestiges of Scholasticism were eliminated almost entirely in these universities. For all these efforts Melanchthon earned the title preceptor of Germany (a preceptor is a headmaster).

Melanchthon's universities were funded with endowments secured via property and lands that had been confiscated from the Catholic Church. Thus, the church's enemies were empowered to create rival institutions of higher learning literally at the church's own expense. Unfortunately for the Reformers and their intellectual heirs, since these new universities were set up and administered by secular rulers, over time the universities tended not to remain faithful to Protestant teachings but rather to be used for whatever ends best suited the political circumstances of the time.

Alliance of Convenience

At the time of the founding of the German universities, however, there was much to recommend the alliance of convenience that bound Reformers, Protestant princes, and humanists. All were united in their opposition to the Catholic hegemony and its intellectual underpinning, Scholasticism. A passionate adherent of the ancient, rhetoric-based approach to education—as embodied in the quadrivium and trivium—Melanchthon provided a classical pedagogy, while the humanists brought to the table their specific expertise in their chosen fields of study. Taken together, these intellectual contributions provided a complete curriculum, ostensibly Protestant but steeped in the classical tradition. For their part the princes provided patronage. Indeed, it was politically advantageous to them to do so; they gained political power and prestige by becoming patrons of higher-learning institutions that could often be bent to serve the princes' interests.

The long-term effect on higher learning of this temporary union of interests was not wholly salutary. In place of the *studium generale* of the older, mostly Catholic universities, there emerged in these new Reformed universities curricula that were tailored for a particular region or taste. In time, these institutions became universities in name only. The cosmopolitan character of the older universities was diluted and within a relatively short space of time was lost almost entirely. A kind of intellectual inbreeding prevailed within

▼ *The German humanist and Reformer Joachim Camerarius (1500–1574), the subject of this nineteenth-century woodcut portrait by Moritz Klinkicht, promoted Latin and Greek studies as a professor at the universities of Tübingen and Leipzig. Camerarius also gave important assistance to Philipp Melanchthon's wide-ranging work in the field of education.*

The Roman orator and schoolmaster Marcus Fabius Quintilianus made an indirect contribution to the Reformation through his influence on Phillip Melanchthon, who established numerous Protestant schools and universities in Germany during the sixteenth century. Born around 35 CE in Calagurris (modern-day Calahorra, in northern Spain), Quintilian traveled to Rome for advanced education at about age sixteen. Like Melanchthon, Quintilian was a pedagogue and educational pioneer. In the year 88 he was appointed head of the first public school in Rome and was later acknowledged as the foremost teacher of the imperial capital.

Quintilian's *Institutio oratoria,* from its publication in the first century, served as a primary text for those concerned with the education of the young. So pervasive was its influence that it continued to be taught for several centuries (over the course of this time, the last known original copy of the work was lost). Quintilian's approach—like that of the humanists and the Reformers—is based on rhetorical theory, not on dialectic. Fourteen hundred years after his death, Quintilian's rhetorical pedagogy profoundly influenced the Protestant universities founded during the Reformation.

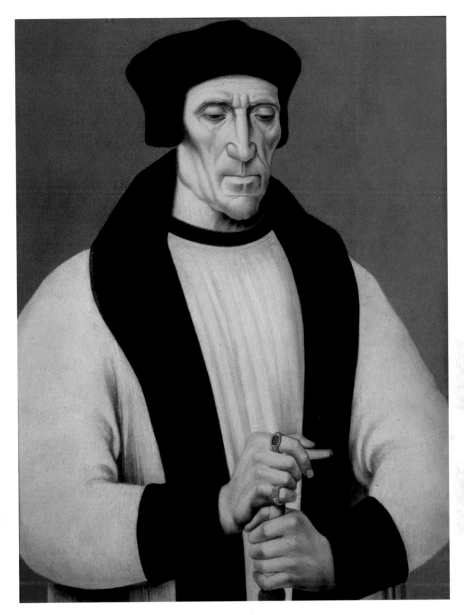

▲ *A contemporary oil portrait, by Hans Corvus, of the English prelate and politician Richard Foxe (c. 1448–1528), bishop of Winchester, lord privy seal to Henry VII and Henry VIII, and founder of Corpus Christi College, Oxford, in 1516.*

faculties, and local scholars, educated at what amounted to a regional university, returned to repeat the pieties of their masters for a new generation of students.

In an ironic twist, in the end these nominally Protestant universities came to resemble the old Scholastic universities at their worst, with tired formulas and bland platitudes spoken and unthinkingly absorbed. The spirit of inquiry that had characterized these pioneering institutions of higher learning early on quickly deteriorated, and they perpetuated a style of instruction that seemed to mock their founders' early ideals and aspirations.

Universities in the British Isles

It has been noted with some degree of irony that arguably the greatest single influence on Renaissance culture in England was the Dutchman Desiderius Erasmus. At the time of Erasmus's arrival in 1497, the study of classical philology had been imported from Italy by Thomas Linacre, William Grocyn, John Colet, and Erasmus's friend Thomas More. Nevertheless, Erasmus served as a catalyst for the furthering of classical studies in England. Other significant figures included Richard Foxe, the bishop of Winchester, and Cardinal Thomas Wolsey. Foxe founded Corpus Christi College, Oxford, in 1516 and provided for the endowment of a position dedicated to the teaching of the Greek language and classical culture; nine years later, Wolsey established the Cardinal's College in Oxford (it later became Christ Church).

The most significant universities in England in the early sixteenth century, Oxford and Cambridge, played an important role in the controversy regarding King Henry VIII's separation from the Catholic Church when, in 1534, they approved Henry's declaration that he was both the secular and religious ruler of his subjects. This declaration was followed in 1535 by royal injunctions that forbade the teaching of Catholic canon law and by the looting of Catholic monasteries, which had previously given shelter to scholars of limited means and those at odds with Henry's designs. In the years that followed, universities were required to remove every remaining vestige of "popery," and many religious artifacts and manuscripts were destroyed.

Although this attempt to banish Catholicism from the land was reversed during the short reign of Mary Tudor (1553–1558), under Elizabeth I the universities continued to support the consolidation of both secular and ecclesiastical authority under the monarchy. All students at Oxford, for example, were required to profess their acceptance of the Thirty-nine Articles, which claimed that the Roman Catholic authorities "hath erred, not only in their living and manner of Ceremonies, but also in matters of Faith." Students were also required to subscribe to the Act of Supremacy, which imbued the monarch with the full power of both church and state and styled the king or queen leader of the Church of England. Despite some temporary successes by English Catholics in their attempts to bring England back into their fold, England would remain a Protestant nation. Much of the religious opposition to the notion of combining in the person of the monarch both secular and religious authority came from the Puritans. Opponents of certain elements of university discipline, the Puritans gained control over Emmanuel College,

▼ Emmanuel College was founded in 1585 at Cambridge University by Walter Mildmay, a Puritan whose intention was that the college serve as an institution for the training of Protestant preachers. Soon after its founding, the college broadened its curriculum to encompass a variety of subjects. At the center of this photograph is the chapel designed by Christopher Wren.

UNIVERSITIES AND LIBRARIES

During the Middle Ages libraries were established in monasteries; members of royalty and certain wealthy commoners might also hold private manuscript collections. Although some libraries were associated more or less closely with universities, there is little to suggest that libraries played as integral a role in the academic life of either the Middle Ages or the Renaissance as they do in the present day.

Indeed, the idea of a modern university without a library or the idea of a library that did not permit scholars to use its resources seems absurd. Yet during the Renaissance and Reformation, libraries, some of them quite extensive, were held by monasteries, secular rulers, and ecclesiastical authorities; relatively few were directly affiliated with a university. Roman Catholic scholars could gain access to most church libraries, but access to private libraries was more restricted. As the power of secular rulers (particularly the Holy Roman emperor) grew, these rulers established libraries as instruments of power and often as somewhat pretentious badges of scholarliness.

As interest in the ancient pagan systems of thought intensified, so too did the size and extent of privately held libraries. Although in many cases a secular ruler might establish a *studium* or, in the case of the more powerful rulers, a *studium generale*, evidence that libraries and universities routinely functioned in tandem is meager and by no means convincing. It is not even clear that most libraries were centers of scholarship. Many, like France's Bibliothèque du Roi, offered only very limited access, and their resources do not seem to have been available at all to mere students.

When put into its proper context, this situation is not as odd as it may at first seem. The predominant method of teaching was the lecture, which involved relatively little student interaction. This style of teaching was in part born of necessity; although the master or professor might possibly have a copy of the texts under discussion, he was just as likely not to have one, given their relatively scarcity and the difficulty and expense of making copies of manuscripts. Students might learn all about Aristotle's *Metaphysics,* for example, without so much as seeing a copy of the book, much less actually reading it. They were expected to absorb the material through lecture.

Thus, while libraries—both private and religious—were absolutely vital to the preservation of ancient learning throughout the medieval period and into the Renaissance and the Reformation, in practical terms education relied heavily on the memory and expertise of the teacher, and classes were very often conducted without benefit of the very texts under discussion.

▼ *The library of Trinity College, Cambridge, was built between 1676 and 1695 to a design by Christopher Wren. Pictured on the lectern are some of Isaac Newton's papers. Newton studied at Trinity from 1661 and was appointed a fellow of the college in 1667 and a professor in 1669 (he remained in Cambridge until 1701).*

Cambridge. However, the Puritan resistance was eventually contained; their failure to bring about significant change in English religious practice was among the reasons that prompted many Puritans to leave England for North America in the seventeenth century.

Universities of the Reformation and Counter-Reformation

The Reformation was a period of great transition for universities, both the new Protestant institutions and the established Roman Catholic ones. The need for a Catholic response to the Protestant challenge was answered in the form of the Counter-Reformation, formulated at the Council of Trent (1545–1563). In Catholic regions Counter-Reformation efforts brought about significant changes in the teaching and promulgation of church doctrine at institutions of higher learning

In this 1847 engraving by Gustav König, Martin Luther is depicted lecturing at the University of Wittenberg. This scene took place in the autumn of 1508, when Luther was still an Augustinian monk.

Good, and the Beautiful were for Plato the most important ideas, and the raison d'être of humankind was to pursue these ideas and thereby gain knowledge of the One (centuries later, Christian Neoplatonists equated the One with God). After Plato the ancient Greeks continued to teach, in one form or another, that the quest for wisdom involved the pursuit of truth, goodness, and beauty. Some thinkers, including Plato himself, maintained that these three qualities were in fact merely differing representations of the same fundamental truth. Thus, one could not pursue truth without a concern for goodness and beauty any more than one could seek beauty in its purest form without also being in love with truth and goodness.

With the renewal of this attitude toward learning in Renaissance Italy, however, came a kind of intellectual frivolity, and in the end Italian universities turned their attention away from the deeper philosophical and theological questions in favor of a focus on literature and poetry. In Platonic terms that a humanist might repeat, they might stand accused of pursuing the beautiful without giving adequate attention to truth and goodness.

Initially, the outlook for the development of universities in northern Europe was bright, particularly in Germany. If northern Europeans were not as flamboyant in their professions of love for beauty, their devotion to it seemed real enough, and there could be no doubt that the spirit of the age in northern Europe included at least for a time a genuine concern with truth and goodness. While southern Europe produced some of the greatest artists the world has ever known, the north produced noteworthy philosophers and theologians at a remarkable rate. Unfortunately, the continued and increasingly acrimonious

For the ancient Greeks the pursuit of knowledge was an endeavor of the utmost metaphysical significance. Their understanding of the import of learning was renewed in the universities of Renaissance Italy. In Platonic philosophy the world of objects that people experience through their senses is in fact merely a shadow or imperfect copy of a higher realm of reality, the world of ideas. Just as there are many horses, for example, there is the idea of a horse. Just as there are many things that are beautiful, there is the idea of beauty, or the Beautiful. Indeed, the True, the

UNIVERSITAS VERSUS CONLEGIUM

The word *corporation,* which is one way of translating the Latin *universitas,* is also an appropriate translation of another classical-era Latin word, *conlegium.* Principally, *conlegium* designates a group of colleagues (academic or otherwise), and from it is derived the English word *college.* Colleges arose around the same times as universities—the first appeared in the twelfth century in Paris. The original purpose of a college was to provide lodgings for scholars. In time, though, colleges took on many of the historical responsibilities of universities, such as instruction and curriculum development, and universities were left with the duties of testing and establishing criteria for the conferral of degrees.

In this colored copper engraving by Jakob van der Heyden (1570–1637), students at the Collegium Musicum, a musical college in Strasbourg, in eastern France, are depicted giving a concert.

debates between Protestants and Catholics, as well as the internecine battles between Lutherans and Calvinists, poisoned this plentiful well before much water could be drawn from it. In consequence, the intellectual and theological gardens of the north remained largely unwatered, and academic life there developed into a series of more or less petty controversies.

As already noted, among the first Protestant universities were Marburg, Königsberg, and Helmstadt, all established as Lutheran institutions under the guiding hand of Phillip Melanchthon. Marburg's conversion to Calvinism in 1605 at the direction of Count Maurice represented a watershed moment in the development of Protestant universities and revealed their relative weakness when faced with the exertion of temporal power. The conversion also led to the founding of the Lutheran University of Giessen nearby two years later.

The Lutheran University of Jena, founded in 1558, was noteworthy for the very marked degree of its adherence to Luther's doctrines and for the equal contempt in which it held Catholicism and non-Lutheran Protestantism. The Universities of Altdorf (1526) and Strasbourg (1621) complete the list of northern Europe's major Reformation universities.

The first university founded with an explicitly Counter-Reformation curriculum was the University of Bamberg, which was established on September 1, 1648. During the early period of its operation, Bamberg had only faculties of arts and theology; it added law and medicine to the curriculum in the eighteenth century. The universities of Innsbruck (1672) and Breslau (1702) were also created as instruments of the Counter-Reformation.

FURTHER READING

Green, Lowell C. *How Melanchthon Helped Luther Discover the Gospel: The Doctrine of Justification in the Reformation.* Fallbrook, CA, 1980.

Grendler, Paul F. *The Universities of the Italian Renaissance.* Baltimore, 2002.

Ridder-Symoens, Hilde de, ed. *A History of the University in Europe.* 4 vols. New York, 2003.

Schmitt, Charles B. *The Aristotelian Tradition and Renaissance Universities.* London, 1984.

Summers, Claude J., and Ted-Larry Pebworth, eds. *Literary Circles and Cultural Communities in Renaissance England.* Columbia, MO, 2000.

Daniel Horace Fernald

SEE ALSO

- Aristotle • Erasmus, Desiderius
- Established Churches • Florence • France
- Guilds and Companies • Holy Roman Empire
- Humanism and Learning • Lutheranism
- Papacy • Paris • More, Thomas • Reformation
- Rome

Urbino

THE DUKES OF URBINO WERE ONE OF SEVERAL DYNASTIES OF MINOR PRINCES THAT FEATURED PROMINENTLY IN THE LIFE OF RENAISSANCE ITALY NOT ONLY FOR POLITICAL REASONS BUT ALSO BECAUSE THEIR COURTS WERE IMPORTANT CULTURAL CENTERS.

The dukes of Urbino governed a small state in a region of central Italy called the Marche, near the Adriatic coast. They were not sovereign rulers of this state; their lands were part of the Papal States, and, like other dynasties of signori (lords) of papal territories, such as the Malatestas and the Manfredis, they were papal vicars—they ruled on behalf of the pope. As with other Italian princes, revenues they earned from military contracts helped to support a small but cultivated court, which was a center of artistic patronage.

The Montefeltros

In the fourteenth and fifteenth centuries, Urbino was governed by the Montefeltro family, which had built up power in the area independent of the papacy. The Montefeltros had acquired lands and jurisdiction as warlords and as leaders of the Ghibelline faction. Ghibellines supported the Holy Roman emperor against the pope (whose supporters were known as Guelfs), and the first authority that the Montefeltros received to rule Urbino came from the emperor Frederick II (reigned 1212–1250); their title as counts came from an earlier imperial grant in 1155. When the papacy fought to establish effective rule in the Papal States in the fourteenth century, the counts of Montefeltro came under pressure, and in 1359 Antonio da Montefeltro was forced into exile by the papal legate Cardinal Albornoz. When misgovernment by papal officials caused the people of Urbino to join a general rebellion in the Papal States in 1375, they called Antonio to return as their lord. In 1384 he accepted the lordship of the town of Gubbio. Following an agreement with the papacy, he became papal vicar of these towns and other territories.

On his death in 1403, Antonio was succeeded by his son Guidantonio (1378–1443), who strengthened the position of his family by enjoying a successful career as a condottiere, a

▶ *The ducal palace of Urbino, designed largely by Luciano Laurana, an architect from Dalmatia, in the late fifteenth century. The palace's beauty is enhanced by Laurana's use of Dalmatian limestone, which can be polished to resemble marble.*

Federigo da Montefeltro   1422–1482

Born in 1422, Federigo da Montefeltro was the illegitimate son of Guidantonio da Montefeltro; his father had him legitimized by Pope Martin V in 1424. From 1432 to 1434, he was educated at Vittorino da Feltre's famous school in Mantua, which had been set up for the children of the marquess of Mantua and other noble and wealthy families. Federigo took great pleasure in reading books throughout his life and over the course of time amassed a fine library.

In 1438 Federigo assumed his first military command over a company of troops that had belonged to a friend of his father, Bernardino della Carda. Athletic, courageous, and physically tough, Federigo soon demonstrated that he could lead men and win their loyalty, as well as understand military tactics and strategy. In 1441, in a daring raid, he recaptured for his father the fortress of San Leo, which had been taken by the rival Malatestas. At the death of his father in 1443, Federigo's worthless but legitimate half brother, Oddantonio, succeeded to the dukedom of Urbino. Oddantonio was assassinated the following year—unfounded rumors that Federigo was involved in his murder dogged Federigo for the rest of his life—and the people of Urbino summoned Federigo and acclaimed him their lord. The pope soon sanctioned Federigo's rule, but he was not given the title of duke until 1474, when a match was arranged between one of his daughters, Giovanna, and a nephew of Pope Sixtus IV, Giovanni della Rovere—their son Francesco Maria would be the first della Rovere duke of Urbino.

As one of the most sought-after commanders in Italy, Federigo earned much-needed income; his military fame and political judgment made him a figure of much greater weight in Italian politics than his small state warranted. As a result of his involvement in Italy's military and political affairs, for most of his life, he was absent from Urbino. Nevertheless, from 1465 until his death, he spent much money rebuilding the city and especially the palace. He also employed one of the foremost architects of the day, the Sienese Francesco di Giorgio. Among the paintings he commissioned was the altarpiece *Madonna and Child with Saints and Angels* by Piero della Francesca, renowned for its use of perspective. The work portrays Federigo in armor kneeling at the feet of the Madonna.

◀ *In this contemporary portrait of Federigo da Montefeltro (thought to be by either Pedro Berruguete or Justus of Ghent), the duke is depicted as a soldier, his face scarred by battle, and as a lover of books. The boy at his knee is his son and heir, Guidobaldo.*

mercenary general. He served Pope Martin V (reigned 1417–1431) and was rewarded with the grant of the duchy of Spoleto for life and with the hand in marriage of Caterina Colonna, the pope's niece, in 1424. Guidantonio's heir, Oddantonio, who was only sixteen when he succeeded his father, was granted the title of duke by Pope Eugenius IV (reigned 1431–1447). Oddantonio's vicious conduct and extravagance provoked a conspiracy among the citizens of Urbino, and he was murdered in 1444. His illegitimate half brother Federigo, who succeeded him, became the model of a Renaissance soldier-prince. Federigo's son Guidobaldo was only ten when he succeeded his father in 1482, but when he grew older, he received *condotte* (military contracts). However, Guidobaldo suffered from a chronic illness that left him unable to beget children; consequently, there was no Montefeltro heir to succeed him. In 1502 Guidobaldo joined the ranks of papal vicars dispossessed by Cesare Borgia, the son of Pope Alexander VI (reigned 1492–1503), but his subjects remained loyal to him, and as soon as news arrived of the death of Alexander in August 1503, the people of Urbino rebelled, and Guidobaldo returned.

The Della Roveres

Four years before Guidobaldo died in 1508, he adopted as his heir one of his nephews, Francesco Maria della Rovere, whose father was Giovanni della Rovere, lord of Senigallia, and who was also the nephew of the pope, Julius II (reigned 1503–1513). Julius had persuaded Guidobaldo to choose Francesco Maria as his heir; so the fortunate young man was able to take possession of the duchy of Urbino with no difficulty in 1508 and naturally was granted the papal vicariate. In 1512 Julius gave him the vicariate of another city in the Marche, Pesaro.

However the next pope, Leo X (reigned 1513–1521), wanted the duchy of Urbino for his own nephew, Lorenzo de' Medici, and Francesco Maria had to fight for his lands. As a military commander, Francesco Maria was noted for his strategy of avoiding engagement with the enemy if at all possible. Nevertheless, as the commander of the Venetian army from 1523 until his death in 1538, he had the protection of Venice against the pope. By marrying his son Guidobaldo II to Giulia Varano, the young heiress of the duchy of Camerino in 1534, he hoped to extend his family's lands in the Marche

◄ *A portrait of Francesco Maria I, the first della Rovere duke, by Federico Barocci (c. 1535–1612). Francesco Maria's military skill and political connections helped him in his long battle to keep his duchy.*

THE DELLA ROVERES AND THE MEDICIS

Although Giovanni de' Medici, as Pope Leo X, confirmed Francesco Maria della Rovere in his papal vicariates, Leo set his sights on taking the duchy for his own family. Francesco Maria began to look to his defenses. In 1516 he was formally accused of having behaved treacherously toward his uncle, the late Pope Julius II, as well as toward Leo. All Francesco Maria's papal vicariates were taken from him, as was the title of duke. Leo's nephew, Lorenzo de' Medici, led the army that invaded the duchy of Urbino in May and June 1516. After a rapid conquest Lorenzo was made duke of Urbino. Although he fought to recover much of his territory in 1517, Francesco Maria was forced to come to terms.

The duchy did not remain under the Medicis for long. Lorenzo died in May 1519, and Urbino passed under the direct rule of the church. Within a few weeks of Leo's death in early December 1521, Francesco Maria was able to recover almost all of his former territories. He managed to gain the support of the college of cardinals, and the new pope, Adrian VI (reigned 1522–1523), restored Francesco Maria's title and vicariates in March 1523. In September, a week before the death of Adrian, Francesco Maria became commander of the Venetian army. In consequence, he had the protection of Venice and troops to support him against the renewed Medici threat that arose when Cardinal Giulio de' Medici was elected pope in November (he reigned as Clement VII from 1523 to 1534). Clement avoided renewing Francesco Maria's vicariates but did not attack him. Only when Clement wanted Venice to make a league with him and the Holy Roman emperor, Charles V, in December 1529 did he finally succumb to pressure from the Venetians and confirm Francesco Maria in his possession of the duchy.

If the Medicis never recovered the duchy of Urbino, they did at least in the end benefit from the inheritance of the della Rovere dukes. The infant granddaughter of the last duke, Vittoria, was betrothed to the young grand duke of Tuscany, Ferdinand II de' Medici in 1623. Francesco Maria agreed with Pope Urban VIII (reigned 1623–1644) that, while his state would devolve to the papacy on his death, his private property, including his art collections, would go to Vittoria—and hence they passed to the Medicis.

still farther, but in 1539, three months after his father's death, Guidobaldo was forced to relinquish Camerino to Pope Paul III (reigned 1534–1549), who wanted it for his own family.

Like his father, Guidobaldo II served as a Venetian commander, but in 1553 he had to give up this captaincy and take up the command of the papal troops. His military commands were not as lucrative as his father's, and the papacy was seeking to reduce the powers of the remaining papal vicars, and so Guidobaldo was less secure in his rule than earlier dukes. The only rebellion against a duke of Urbino by his subjects took place during Guidobaldo's reign, in 1572 and 1573. Guidobaldo's son Francesco Maria II, who succeeded him in 1574, failed to obtain a major military command but in 1582 did manage to arrange a lesser *condotta* with Spain and thereby gain Spanish protection. In 1570 Guidobaldo had forced his son to marry Lucrezia d'Este, the sister of the duke of Ferrara; her large dowry pleased Guidobaldo, but she was fourteen years older than Francesco Maria, and he did not disguise his dislike of her. Not until after her death in 1598 and his second marriage to his cousin, Livia della Rovere, did Francesco Maria finally father an heir, Federico Ubaldo. Born in 1605, Federico Ubaldo, an eccentric, difficult child who did not promise to make a good duke, died at age seventeen, a year after his marriage to Claudia de' Medici. Rumors circulated that he had been assassinated on the orders of the Medicis because he had mistreated Claudia. When Francesco Maria II died in 1631, his granddaughter Vittoria could not succeed him, and his state passed under the direct rule of the papacy.

◄ *Francesco Maria II, the last duke of Urbino, had a close rapport with Federico Barocci, who painted this oil portrait of the duke and many other commissions for him. Noting Barocci's death in his private diary in 1612, the duke expressed more emotion than he had expressed when noting the death of his first wife, Lucrezia d'Este, in 1598.*

▶ *The outstanding intarsia (inlaid wood) decoration of Federigo da Montefeltro's study creates the illusion of statues, open cupboards, and shelves holding books and other objects (including a pet squirrel).*

City and State

Like many signori in the Papal States, the counts and dukes of Urbino governed on the basis of authority delegated from below (from the people) and from above (from the pope). Each town within the vicariate granted them a salary, and they were supposed to make an annual census (payment) to the pope in recognition of his superiority. In order to maintain their rule peacefully, the dukes needed the approval of both people and pope. Oddantonio da Montefeltro failed to win over his people and was assassinated; less disastrously, Francesco Maria della Rovere's troubles arose in consequence of the hostility of Pope Leo X.

The city of Urbino itself was not large; it was dominated by the ducal palace, and the ducal court, where several hundred people worked, would have been the largest employer. During the fourteenth and fifteenth centuries, Urbino was the center of the state, and the administration for the vicariate was based in the palace (the civic council, elected by the citizens, administered the internal affairs of the city). Its period of greatest prosperity was the reign of Federigo da Montefeltro. It was at that time that the palace became known as one of the most beautiful in Italy; it was transformed by the Dalmatian architect Luciano da Laurana, who worked on it from 1465 to 1474 (the top story was completed around 1536). Its most celebrated room, Duke Federigo's study, is quite small. Its walls were panelled with intarsia (mosaic made of wood), and painted portraits of famous men were placed above the panels.

The city of Urbino declined under the della Rovere dukes, who each moved the capital to a different town of the expanded state; the palace of Urbino was used only as a summer residence and thus remained empty for much of the year. Francesco Maria chose Pesaro, where he built a new wing on the fifteenth-century villa of the former signori, the Sforzas; it has been argued that the whole complex was intended as a kind of theatrical setting for court entertainments. Guidobaldo II's preferred residence was

CASTIGLIONE AND THE COURT OF URBINO

Il cortegiano (The Courtier) by Baldassare Castiglione (1478–1529) is the most famous treatise on the ideal courtier of the Renaissance—or indeed of any age. From its first publication in Italy in 1528, the book was a great success, and it was soon translated into Spanish, French, English, and Latin. It served as the model and source for other treatises on the subject and as a guide to good conduct.

Castiglione was in the service of the dukes Guidobaldo and Francesco Maria from 1506 to 1516. *Il cortegiano* is set in the court of Urbino in 1506; Castiglione presented his book as a portrait of that court during times he looked back on nostalgically. It takes the form of a series of conversations between residents of the court and some distinguished visitors, such as Lodovico da Canossa, a Veronese nobleman and diplomat; Giuliano de' Medici, the brother of Leo X; and Pietro Bembo, a writer and later a cardinal. Duke Guidobaldo is not portrayed (he was said to retire to bed early because of his infirmities); his wife, Elisabetta Gonzaga, and the witty lady Emilia Pia presided over the court.

Castiglione analyzes the moral and physical qualities of the ideal courtier. He should be a nobleman, skilled in the use of weapons and in horsemanship, an athlete, physically graceful, eloquent, knowledgable about the arts and literature, and able to write and speak elegantly. There is much discussion of how the courtier might best display his skills and serve his prince. Ladies of the court should have many of the same cultural accomplishments, although it was more important for a lady to be beautiful than for a gentleman to be handsome, and a lady had to be discreet in her demeanor in order to preserve her reputation.

▼ *Elisabetta Gonzaga, the subject of this oil-on-wood portrait painted by Raphael around 1504, was the cultivated wife of Duke Guidobaldo da Montefeltro. Elisabetta corresponded frequently with her sister-in-law, Isabella d'Este, another woman celebrated for her learning and taste.*

Senigallia, while Francesco Maria II, the last duke, chose the small town of Castel Durante (now called Urbania), where he could indulge his love of study and of hunting. Castel Durante was also famous as a center for the production of painted ceramics known as majolica, for which the duchy was famous. Investing in this and other ventures—from the breeding of horses to the building of ships—brought Francesco Maria great wealth.

Francesco Maria's enterprises made up for his lack of a sizable military commission. *Condotte* had been an integral part of his predecessors' powers. The dukes did not use their troops to overawe their subjects; in fact, they raised many of them from among their subjects and so provided employment for many men. The income from *condotte* enabled the dukes to keep taxation down and thus contributed to the prosperity of the whole duchy.

FURTHER READING

Clough, Cecil H. *The Duchy of Urbino in the Renaissance.* London, 1981.

Osborne, June. *Urbino: The Story of a Renaissance City.* Chicago, 2003.

Christine Shaw

SEE ALSO

 Leo X • Medicis, The

Velázquez, Diego Rodríguez de Silva

THE SPANISH PAINTER DIEGO RODRÍGUEZ DE SILVA VELÁZQUEZ (1599–1660) IS ONE OF THE MOST IMPORTANT FIGURES IN EUROPEAN PAINTING. HIS ABILITY TO RE-CREATE THE WORLD ON CANVAS HAS SELDOM BEEN MATCHED.

Few documents concerning Velázquez or his works survive. What is known of his life and career has largely been reconstructed through scholarly studies in art history, including *Arte de la pintura* (The Art of Painting), published by Francisco Pacheco in 1649, and a biography from the early eighteenth century by the Spanish art historian Antonio Palomino de Castro y Velasco (1655–1726).

Diego Rodríguez de Silva Velázquez was born in Seville on or shortly before June 6, 1599. He was the eldest of seven children born to Juan Rodríguez de Silva and his wife, Jeronima Velázquez. Little is known about Velázquez's parents except that they were of noble Portuguese extraction and that his father was a lawyer. Velázquez may have served a brief apprenticeship with Francisco de Herrera the Elder (1576–c. 1656), though his only documented teacher was Francisco Pacheco. A mannerist painter spe-cializing in religious themes, Pacheco, clearly impressed by his pupil both as an artist and as a responsible young man, sanctioned the marriage of Velázquez to his daughter, Juana.

Velázquez studied with Pacheco for six years, though there is little evidence of the impact of Pacheco's academic style on his young student. In 1617 Velázquez became a member of the local guild of painters and was permitted to set up his own workshop. His early years as an independent painter were spent honing his skills. He carefully copied objects and people to create naturalistic still-life images; from this period date his earliest *bodegónes* (kitchen or tavern scenes), sometimes with religious overtones, in which he already demonstrated his uncanny ability to depict his subjects with a visual accuracy that belies their two-dimensional construction from paint on canvas. He also continued to develop his understanding of the medium of oil paint and his ability to manipulate paint to create the visual effects he desired.

Madrid and the Royal Court

In 1622 Velázquez left Seville for Madrid in search of commissions from the Spanish royal court. Though he did not meet with immediate success, he was recalled to Madrid early in 1623 by Gaspar de Guzmán, count of Olivares (1587–

► Christ in the House of Martha and Mary *(1618) is an early example of Velázquez's work. He combines a biblical scene, visible through the serving hatch, with a* bodegón *(a kitchen or tavern scene).*

BODEGÓNES

Bodegónes are a distinct subgroup within Spanish still-life painting particularly associated with Seville, Velázquez's native city. Focusing on food and cooking utensils, a bodegón often contains painstakingly detailed depictions against a very simple background. Velázquez set his bodegónes in rustic kitchens and taverns, wherein he executed the food and utensils at least as carefully as the human figures—sometimes more so: his aim was to accurately represent the visual world rather than to tell a particular story.

1599
On June 6, presumably shortly after his birth, Diego Velázquez is baptized in Seville.

1611
Is apprenticed to Francisco Pacheco, a mannerist painter, with whom he remains until 1617.

1618
Marries Pacheco's daughter, Juana.

1623
Now resident in Madrid, is appointed court painter to Philip IV of Spain.

1629–1631
Visits Italy for the first time.

1634
Paints *The Surrender of Breda*.

1649
Returns to Rome to buy artworks for the Spanish royal collections.

1656
Completes *Las meninas*, widely regarded as his most influential painting.

1660
Dies of a fever in Madrid on August 6; Juana dies eight days later.

1645), principal minister to King Philip IV (reigned 1621–1665). This time Velázquez's talents were brought to the king's attention; after he painted Philip's portrait, he was immediately appointed court painter and spent the rest of his career in the royal entourage. The artist-patron collaboration between Velázquez and Philip IV was long and in some ways mutually beneficial. Velázquez received tremendous respect and indulgence from Philip; it appears that the king was fond of Velázquez and intrigued by his artistic talent—he visited the painter frequently in his studio to observe him at work. Velázquez, in return, spent much of his career painting portraits for the king and his family and faithfully

▲ *Early in his career Velázquez painted a number of* bodegónes *featuring food and cooking utensils. In Old Woman Frying Eggs (1618), Velázquez treats the various pans, jugs, and foodstuffs with the same care that he gives his depictions of the human figures.*

serving the royal household as a courtier, counselor, diplomat, majordomo, and curator of the royal art collections. The advantages of Velázquez's position—notably financial security and artistic renown—were obviously highly sought after by artists of the time, including the young Velázquez, but may have come at a price: his duties at court probably curtailed his artistic development and contributed to the relatively small size of his oeuvre (around 150 paintings).

Bartolomé Esteban Murillo 1617–1682

Bartolomé Esteban Murillo spent his entire life in his native city of Seville. After studying briefly with the painter Juan del Castillo (1584–1640), by 1640 he had established himself as an independent artist. In 1660 Murillo helped to found the Sevillian Academy of Fine Arts and served as its first president. He is best known for his scenes of beggars and of children, executed in a style influenced by his contact with Velázquez (whom he probably met on a visit to Madrid around 1650) as well as his exposure to the works of Titian and Rubens. Murillo quickly became the most famous Spanish painter of his day, popular with patrons throughout Europe and the New World; his preeminent position lasted until the nineteenth century, when the works of Velázquez, Francisco de Zurbarán (1598–1664), and others became known outside of Spain

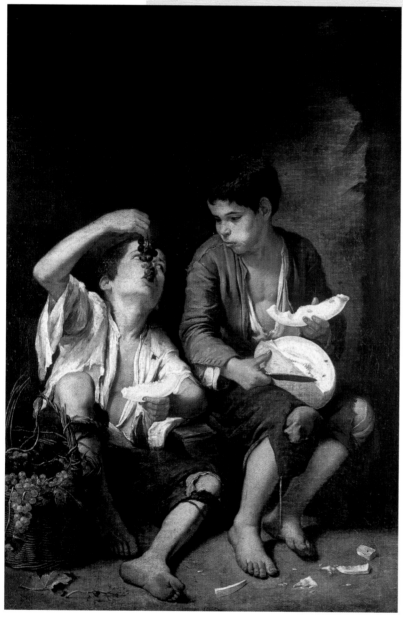

▲ *Bartolomé Esteban Murillo's Grape and Melon Eaters (c. 1650) is a good example of the kind of genre paintings that made Murillo the most famous Spanish artist of the 1600s and 1700s.*

Italy before settling in Spain; and by the famous Flemish painter Peter Paul Rubens (1577–1640). During his early years in Madrid, Velázquez modified aspects of his style and technique as a result of his exposure to the works of other important artists. His early penchant for dramatic lighting, based on the Spanish predilection for tenebrism—the use of stark contrast between light and shadow popularized by the Italian painter Caravaggio (Michelangelo Merisi; 1573–1610)—was refined into a subtler use of light and shade, often to indicate raking daylight. Exposure to paintings by Titian and others contributed to his understanding of color, but this understanding was generally expressed within a limited, cool palette, not the bold, flamboyant colors so beloved by Rubens. A similar point could be made about subject matter; Velázquez eschewed full-blown drama and sensuality in favor of a more reserved, at times ascetic approach.

Rubens had a profound albeit indirect impact on Velázquez. The two painters met in 1628 during Rubens's second visit to the royal court in Madrid. A generation older than Velázquez and by this time an established statesman and diplomat, Rubens befriended the younger painter and spent many hours in conversation with him. Certainly Rubens's free handling of the paintbrush and daring application of paint to canvas bear certain similarities to Velázquez's own technique. Though both artists exhibited masterful control over their medium, Velázquez's approach was the more virtuosic. The lifelike naturalism that he created can be appreciated only from a distance; up close the viewer instantly recognizes that Velázquez always preserved the inherent qualities of the paint. Rubens, in contrast,

In Madrid, Velázquez had access to the works in the royal art collections. He studied paintings by the Venetian masters Titian (Tiziano Vecelli; 1488/90–1576) and Tintoretto (Jacopo Robusti; c. 1518–1594); by El Greco (Doménikos Theotokópoulos; 1541–1614), who trained in

retained a firmer control over his paint, which was subordinate to the overall effect.

Rubens must have provided Velázquez with a model for the lifestyle and status that the young painter craved. Here was a Flemish painter, initially without courtly connections, who had risen to a position of international fame and respect. His work was sought after by secular and ecclesiastical leaders alike, and he had elevated the status of painter from that of skilled artisan to cultured artistic genius. Where other great painters, such as the Dutch master Rembrandt (1606–1669), achieved success within the social sphere to which artists were thought to naturally belong, Velázquez, emulating Rubens within a Spanish context, aspired to gain a loftier social and cultural standing. *The Feast of Bacchus,* or *Los borrachos* (The Drinkers), painted while Velázquez was befriending Rubens, displays an interesting mixture of high baroque subject matter and style (gleaned from the artist's study of Rubens and Titian), typically bold Spanish realism, and Velázquez's distinctively naturalistic rendering (particularly noticeable in the modern-looking faces of the drinkers).

Velázquez in Italy

Rubens may well have pushed Velázquez to further his knowledge of Italian painting. Velázquez undertook his first trip to Italy in 1629, shortly after he met Rubens. While in Venice he copied the works of Titian and Tintoretto, and in Rome, besides sketching classical sculpture, he familiarized himself with the works of the greatest masters of the Italian Renaissance, including Raphael (1483–1520) and Michelangelo (1475–1564). Little survives of the work executed by Velázquez during this initial visit to Italy. Two paintings that he is believed to have brought back for King Philip, *Joseph's Bloody Coat Brought to Jacob* and *Vulcan's Forge,* display a monumentality, a slightly bolder palette, and a new sense of dramatic narrative that mark a more mature phase in Velázquez's artistic development.

▲ The Feast of Bacchus *(also called* Los borrachos; *1628–1629) displays the influence of Italianate baroque painting on Velázquez (it was painted around the time he met Peter Paul Rubens). Note the contrast between the naturalistic figures of the drinking men and the smooth, glowing body of Bacchus, the god of revelry.*

▶ *In* The Surrender of Breda *(1634–1635), popularly known as* The Lances, *Velázquez adds vitality to the genre of history painting through the use of such naturalistic elements as true-to-life portraiture and unaffected poses. To a modern observer, the overall effect is akin to that of a photograph.*

Artistic Maturity

After a year in Rome, Velázquez returned to Madrid, where his duties at court required him to devote much of his time to portrait painting. Despite the frequency with which he painted Philip and his entourage, Velázquez's portraits exhibit an impressive array of settings, poses, and compositions, frequently inspired by those of Titian and Rubens but still individual. Several of his most impressive portraits of Philip IV date from this period, along with notable images of courtiers and dwarfs (whose diminutive size and abnormal proportions intrigued the court). Each portrait depicts the subject without sentimentality but with a truthfulness that seems to expose something of the inner person behind the flesh.

The Surrender of Breda, usually called *The Lances,* the only surviving history painting by Velázquez, was painted in 1634 and 1635 to decorate the throne room at the newly built Buen Retiro Palace. Recording the ceremonial capitulation of the Dutch city of Breda to the Spanish in June 1625, *The Lances* continued the northern European tradition of Dutch and Flemish historical composition and group portraiture, though Velázquez's bold use of naturalistic compositional motifs (the hindquarters of the horse in the foreground, for example) and startlingly lifelike portraits of the primary figures lend this work a quality that would now be called photographic.

In 1649 Velázquez departed a second time for Italy; this time, like Rubens when he first visited Spain (1603), Velázquez was sent on a diplomatic mission to deliver some paintings as a gift from Philip IV to Pope Innocent X (reigned 1644–1655). During his three-year stay he traveled to many places but again spent much of his time in Venice and Rome. Paintings by the Venetian masters such as Titian, Tintoretto, and Veronese (Paolo Caliari; 1528–1588) continued to draw his attention, and in Rome he became a member of the highest artistic circle, which included at that time the French classical painter Nicolas Poussin (1594–1665). Velázquez completed a number of works while resident in Italy, among them his famous portrait of his servant, Juan de Pareja (1649–1650), and his portrait of Pope Innocent X (1650), which quickly became his best-known painting outside of Spain. Two views of the Villa Medici in Rome, the only landscapes by Velázquez to survive, can also be dated to this period, possibly along with the nude figure of Venus (the *Rokeby Venus*). Italy obviously provided Velázquez with inspiration for subject matter (the reclining Venus and the Medici Villa) and compositions (the portrait of the enthroned pope): more important, during his time there the bold use of paint (both in thick passages of impasto and in sections so thinly applied that the bare canvas can be seen) and free brushwork already familiar in his works became even more uninhibited so that his final works have a sense of animation and a visual immediacy that even modern viewers find disconcerting.

THE *ROKEBY VENUS*

The *Rokeby Venus* is Velázquez's only painting of a female nude. Venus reclines on a bed as she gazes into a mirror held up by her winged son, Cupid, who is also naked, save for a sash. The innovative brushwork, especially noticeable in the frothy gauze in front of Venus and in her reflection in the mirror, is typical of Velázquez, but the subject, composition, and color scheme are all borrowed from the Venetian tradition. The strong connection with Venice has led to confusion over the date of this work, which, like most paintings by Velázquez, was never signed or dated. It may have been painted during the artist's second trip to Italy (1649–1651), when he spent time in Venice and would have encountered the reclining Venuses painted by Giorgione (c. 1477–1511) and Titian, among others.

There is no doubt that this image would have shocked contemporary viewers. Though it avoids the direct gaze and suggestive gestures of Titian's reclining *Venus of Urbino* (1538), the *Rokeby Venus*'s bared neck, sensuously curved hip, and apparent nonchalance about her nakedness were painted for private viewing. The painting was commissioned by the Marquess del Carpio, the son of the Spanish prime minister; its appearance on an inventory made in June 1651 provides a date by which the painting must have been completed.

Before the painting entered London's National Gallery in 1906, it hung in Rokeby Hall, Yorkshire, from which the painting received its popular name.

◀ Venus at her Toilette, *also called the* Rokeby Venus *(c. 1650) is one of the only examples of a reclining Venus by a Spanish painter of the baroque period; the church in Spain frowned upon depictions of the female nude in the visual arts.*

▶ Juan de Pareja (c. 1610–1670) was a mulatto slave in the service of Velázquez. This portrait, completed during Velázquez's second visit to Rome in 1649 and 1650, is said to have been painted to impress potential Roman patrons with Velázquez's uncanny ability to paint lifelike images on canvas.

Final Years at Court

Throughout Velázquez's career at court, he had regularly received honorary posts, many with additional (mostly ceremonial) duties and most without any accompanying rise in salary. In 1652, a year after his return to Madrid from Italy, Velázquez was appointed palace chamberlain, a position that involved overseeing the decoration of the royal apartments and arranging the various journeys undertaken by the royal entourage. Ultimately, however, these duties proved too demanding for the painter, now in his fifties. His obligations as official royal portraitist increased from 1649 with the arrival of a new queen, Mariana, archduchess of Austria (1634–1696), and the subsequent arrival of royal offspring. Aside from portraits of the royal

family and court, Velázquez, now head of a workshop employing numerous assistants and apprentices, found time to paint two great works: *Las meninas* (*The Maids of Honor;* 1656), an idiosyncratic group portrait that includes Velázquez himself, and *Las hilanderas* (*The Spinners;* c. 1657), which depicts the myth of Arachne, the needleworker whom the goddess Athena turned into a spider.

Despite having secured papal backing by 1650 for his induction into the Order of Santiago, an honor that the artist truly desired, Velázquez did not receive the knighthood until 1659. He died the following year while overseeing preparations for the wedding of Princess María Teresa (1638–1683) to Louis XIV of France (reigned 1643–1715).

Nothing is straightforward about *Las meninas*. Velazquez's huge canvas measures 10 feet, 5 inches by 9 feet, 1 inch (3.18 m x 2.77 m). It depicts identifiable members of the Spanish royal household—including Infanta (Princess) Margarita (1651–1673), her *meninas* (ladies-in-waiting), and Velázquez himself, who looks out from behind a similarly outsized canvas. However, beyond these figures' identities, the painting is enigmatic. Utilizing interlocking triangles, a central circle, and strong vertical and horizontal demarcations, the complex composition avoids giving any figure precedence. The prominence of the central figure, the infanta, is immediately challenged by the ghostly reflections of her parents, Philip IV and Queen Mariana, in the mirror on the back wall (which serves as the vanishing point). Other rivals for the viewer's attention include the courtier who looks in from the strongly lit doorway and the figures of Maribarbola the dwarf and Velázquez, both of whom gaze directly at the viewer.

By abandoning the traditional chiaroscuro (stark contrasts between highlight and shadow) in favor of subtle gradations from light to dark (with the occasional highlight) and limiting his palette to mid tones, Velázquez created a scene strikingly close to one a viewer might actually see. The precise nature of the scene, however, continues to elude students of the painting and seems at odds with the visual transparency of Velázquez's technique. On what work is the artist engaged? It is illogical to see the canvas before him as containing the image visible to the viewer. Is he painting a portrait of the king and queen (as their reflection in the mirror would suggest)? If such is the case, why is so much effort being made to keep the infanta in her formal pose? If Velázquez is painting the infanta, she is not in a helpful place. On the other hand, if all are posed before a mirror, how then to account for the reflection of the king and queen? Equally confusing abstract interpretations of *Las meninas* have ranged from its description as an allegory of ways of seeing—through painted images, reflections, and optical illusions—to Velázquez's visual expression of social hierarchies (from animals to dwarfs, servants, courtiers, and finally princesses, queens, and kings). Any thorough analysis must, however, assign Velázquez the rank that work of this caliber and complexity deserves. To have included himself so prominently in a portrait of the royal family, his doublet adorned with the emblem of a noble order to which he did not (yet) belong, suggests tantalizing secrets that the work may never divulge.

◄ Las Meninas *(1656), Velázquez's most celebrated work, is included on virtually every list of the world's greatest paintings. Its uncanny optical realism, complex iconography, and enigmatic content combine to create a thought-provoking experience.*

Velázquez's work was little known outside of Spain until the early nineteenth century, when his extraordinary talents caught the attention of artists and connoisseurs throughout Europe and America. Numerous later artists, including Francisco de Goya (1746–1828), Gustave Courbet (1819–1877), and James McNeill Whistler (1834–1903), acknowledged their debt to Velázquez.

FURTHER READING

Brown, Jonathan, and Carmen Garrido. *Velázquez: The Technique of Genius.* New Haven, CT, 1998.
Sérullaz, Maurice. *Velázquez.* Translated by I. Mark Paris. New York, 1981.
Stratton-Pruitt, Suzanne L., ed. *The Cambridge Companion to Velázquez.* New York, 2002.

Caroline S. Hull

SEE ALSO
* Caravaggio * Painting and Sculpture
* Rubens, Peter Paul * Spain

Venice

THE REPUBLIC OF VENICE, RULED BY A MERCHANT ARISTOCRACY, GREW TO BECOME A WEALTHY AND POWERFUL MEDITERRANEAN STATE. THE CITY WAS A MAJOR CULTURAL AND COMMERCIAL FORCE IN RENAISSANCE ITALY.

Renaissance Venice was famed for its unexampled beauty—its palaces and churches appeared to onlookers to be built on water—as well as for its wealth, the stability of its political system, the skill of its diplomats, and its proud tradition of independence.

The city's origin antedates the year 500 CE, when Gothic fishermen, who had settled on sandbanks and mudflats in the shelter of a lagoon on the coast of the Adriatic Sea, came together to form a community. Foundations were provided for Venice's earliest buildings by driving wooden piles into the mud and sand. With no land to farm, the Venetians had no alternative but to earn their living through fishing and trade. They became the major intermediaries between the markets of northern and western Europe and the lands of the eastern Mediterranean—both the Byzantine Empire and the Muslim territories. The Venetians' familiarity with these lands was manifested in the architecture and art of Venice, which showed the influence of Byzantine and Islamic styles.

A complex republican constitution was developed. Although only nobles could hold political office, Venice did not suffer from the frequent changes of government and outbreaks of civil dissension that troubled many other Italian cities—Venice became known as *la Serenissima* ("the most serene one"). Venetian nobles were proud of their republican system, their city's political stability and wealth, and the extensive colonies they acquired in the eastern Mediterranean.

Economy and Empire

Venetian wealth was based on trade with the eastern Mediterranean. At the beginning of the thirteenth century, Venice had a large part in organizing the Fourth Crusade, which was diverted from its goal of regaining the Holy Land

▼ *This painting by Michele Marieschi (1696–1743) depicts the entrance to the Grand Canal, Venice's main thoroughfare. The Church of Santa Maria della Salute, pictured in the foreground, was built in the mid-seventeenth century to mark the end of an epidemic of plague.*

Venetian diplomats were famous for their powers of observation, their ability to gather information, and the quality of their reports. Owing to the geographical range of Venice's commercial interests, Venetian ambassadors and representatives were present throughout Europe and the Mediterranean lands. Their reports were read out to the senate, and returning envoys also addressed that body. They gave a general description of the state to which they had been accredited—its geography, natural resources, economy, finances, and political and social system—and they analyzed the character, abilities, and interests of the leading figures with whom they had dealt. These reports (relazioni) kept the Venetians well informed about the world. They have become a valuable resource for historians.

to the capture and sack of Constantinople, the capital of the Greek Byzantine Empire. Venice took over many Greek harbors and islands, including Crete and, in the fifteenth century, Cyprus. Asserting a right to control navigation in the Adriatic Sea, Venice took other ports and harbors on the Balkan shore and tried to take over such Italian coastal towns as Ravenna, in the Papal States, and Brindisi, in the kingdom of Naples. Although they never succeeded in driving out all their Italian rivals for the lucrative trade with the eastern Mediterranean—the Genoese were particularly powerful competitors—the Venetians were the most successful.

In building up their empire, the Venetians were especially interested in acquiring harbors along the major trading routes, where their fleets could find shelter and take on supplies. The typical Venetian trading vessel was a galley powered by oarsmen; in the conditions of the Mediterranean, using man power rather than relying on the winds allowed faster, more predictable voyages. Most galleys had sails as well as oars; a wise captain used sails and wind power when he could to rest his men.

Most of the galleys were built and owned by the state; they were leased to individual noblemen, who sold places on the galleys to merchants who wanted to transport goods. Only Venetian noblemen, citizens, or others who had been granted the trading privileges of citizens could put their goods on these vessels. In the fourteenth and fifteenth centuries the galleys traveled in *mude*—state-run convoys that controlled the trade and provided protection for the fleet.

The most profitable commodity that the Venetians traded in was spices; other goods brought from the East included cotton, raw silk, sugar, gold, and slaves. Cloth, particularly from Germany, was the main commodity that the

Venetians took eastward. Travel over the Alps to the German lands was the major land route for Venetian merchants.

Competition and Adaptation

After their voyages of discovery opened up maritime routes between the Indian Ocean and western Europe in the late 1400s, the Portuguese tried to divert the spice trade to their own vessels. The Venetians certainly suffered from this competition, but in fact the Mediterranean spice routes flourished for much of the 1500s. Another challenge was the rise of the Ottoman Turks. Although the Turks gradually drove the Venetians out of their Aegean colonies and trading outposts, the rivals reached agreements that allowed the Venetians to go on trading.

Venice's strength as a trading power was seriously undermined only when Dutch and English ships began to move into the Mediterranean trade in the late sixteenth century. In addition,

▲ By 1500 Venice's territorial acquisitions and control of key Mediterranean trade routes made it the dominant state in northeastern Italy and a major European power.

piracy increasingly became a danger to all Mediterranean shipping, and even though the Venetians' convoy system declined, they continued to build galleys rather than the smaller vessels that were better suited to the new conditions of trade.

From the late sixteenth century on, manufacturing became ever more important to the Venetian economy. The vast complex of shipyards, the *arsenale,* where the Venetian galleys were built, was the largest state-run manufacturing center in Europe. Workers in the *arsenale* were well paid, proud of their status, and loyal to the state. Venice also became famous for its silk textiles, fine Murano glass, and printed books.

The Terra Firma

Apart from the town of Treviso, acquired in 1339, Venice held no territory on the mainland of Italy until the fifteenth century. From 1405, by taking over such major cities as Verona, Vicenza, and Padua, Venice became the dominant state in northeastern Italy. Its territories extended north toward the Alps, eastward to the frontiers of the duchy of Milan, and south to the Papal States. This expansion brought Venice into conflict with the Hapsburgs over the lands at the head of the Adriatic, with the Visconti and the Sforza dukes of Milan over Bergamo and other northern Italian cities, and with the papacy, as Venice acquired Ravenna in the Papal States. Venice's new role as an aggressive territorial power aroused jealousy and hostility in other Italian states; fears arose that the Venetians were trying to dominate Italy.

The ill will that the Venetians had roused brought down on them in 1509 the War of the League of Cambrai, a coalition whose main members were Pope Julius II, Louis XII of France (who ruled Milan), Ferdinand of Aragon (who ruled the kingdom of Naples), and the Holy Roman emperor, Maximilian. At one point during the war, which lasted until 1517, Venice had lost nearly all its mainland cities, and an enemy army was encamped near Venice. Most of the territory was recovered, but the war marked the end of Venetian expansion on the mainland. Some Venetian nobles still desired more territory, but others concluded after the Cambrai war that seeking possessions on the mainland had distracted Venice from its true destiny as a maritime trading power.

There was disapproval, too, of the increasing interest Venetian nobles showed in buying estates on the mainland, especially the land around Padua. This threat of losing land caused disquiet among the leading families of Venice's subject cities, for whom land was an important element in their wealth and status. Becoming landowners and building villas on the mainland gave Venetian nobles a different perspective, and some became more like the landed nobility of the mainland in their outlook and behavior.

The Venetians made pacts with towns under their rule. The towns generally kept their own councils and controlled some aspects of local administration, but Venetian nobles were sent as rectors (governors) and castellans (commanders of fortresses). Even nobles from subject towns were not allowed political rights in Venice or in Venetian colonies. Venetian clerics were appointed to the bishoprics of the terra firma and to many other of the most important ecclesiastical benefices. Merchants from the subject towns were allowed to trade with other states only through the city of Venice, although there was much smuggling. The Venetians boasted that they brought peace and good justice to their subject territories and that their subjects were content under Venetian rule. However, aware that many resented their subordinate role, the Venetians watched their subjects carefully, especially in their contacts with other powers.

The Nobility

All political offices in Venice and its subject territories and colonies were reserved for Venetian nobles. The nobles were descendants of the fam-

ilies represented in the great council in 1297, who had decided, in what became known as the *serrata* ("closing"), that only their families would be eligible to sit in that council from then on. A few other families were allowed to join this privileged group in the fourteenth century, notably thirty families that lent money to the state during the War of Chioggia against Genoa in the 1390s. Others were allowed to join for contributing money for the prolonged Siege of Candia in the mid-seventeenth century.

All adult male Venetian nobles, except clerics, had the right to sit in the great council, the source of political authority in the state, and to speak and vote there.

▲ Donatello's bronze statue of the Venetian commander Gattamelata (Erasmo da Narni), inspired by the equestrian statue of the emperor Marcus Aurelius in Rome, was erected in Padua in 1453.

THE VENETIAN ARMY

Until the Venetians began to expand into the mainland in the fifteenth century, they did not have an army. They built up an army using condottieri (mercenary troops) from all over Italy and from their subject territories. Venetians themselves rarely became soldiers—although Venetian nobles did command and fight on the galley fleets—instead, they worked with the commanders as civilian administrators.

Although their troops were mercenaries, the Venetians won their loyalty with long-term contracts, well-organized winter quarters, and pensions for long or outstanding service. While other states were inclined to distrust the condottieri, the Venetians built up an effective and reliable army by offering them good conditions and the prospect of lifetime employment.

▲ *The ceremonial dress of the doge, as seen in this portrait of Doge Francesco Foscari by Gentile Bellini (c. 1492–1507), included a distinctive cap. Foscari was forced to resign in 1457 after old age and illness kept him from attending council meetings. Such a forced resignation was a rarity in Venetian history.*

The balance between the number of nobles and the number of offices caused problems. In the early fifteenth century, when about four hundred men attended meetings of the great council, there was concern that there were not enough suitable nobles to fill the offices that fell vacant (generally, offices were held only for limited terms). In the late fifteenth century, when there were 1,500 or more nobles eligible to hold them, fears arose that competition for offices was encouraging corruption. The workings of the system allowed minor offices in the terra firma to be held by incompetent men. This source of discontent among Venetian subjects was counterbalanced by the high quality of those filling major offices.

There was an ethos among the nobility of service to and identification with the state. Great importance was attached to maintaining secrecy of state affairs; it could be very difficult for outsiders to find out what was said or decided in Venetian councils. Particular efforts were made to prevent awareness of any divisions among the nobles. Venetians were proud that there were no political factions in their city of the kind that disrupted the life of many Italian towns. There were, however, differences between, for example, the older families (the *lunghi,* or "long") and the newer families (the *curti,* or "short") and between those who disliked the resources of the state being diverted from the maritime empire to the mainland and those who wanted to protect their investments in lands on the terra firma. Such divisions surfaced in debates on policy.

Nobles took great interest in the elections for offices. A complicated system of nomination committees and secret ballots was in place to prevent lobbying for offices and vote rigging, and it was largely, if not entirely, successful. Frauds that were detected could be punished severely, sometimes by lifelong exile. As many nobles were poor, holding an office that brought a salary—most of the highest offices in the state did not—was important to them.

By the late sixteenth century the number of nobles was in decline. As economic circumstances became more difficult, families tried to conserve their wealth by restricting the number

THE MYTH OF VENICE

From the thirteenth century Venetians celebrated their city and their state. The myth of Venice encompassed the magnificence and beauty of the city, its role as the focus of the trade of the known world, the wealth and patriotism of its nobility, the stability of its political system, the justice of its government, and the benevolence of its rule over its colonies and subject territories.

Naturally, not everyone, even in Venice, subscribed to this myth. Venetians could be corrupt, unjust, treacherous, and divided over policy; to their subjects Venetians could seem repressive and selfish. In their relations with other states, Venetians were often perceived as devious, aggressive, and arrogant—not least because of the self-image enshrined in the myth of Venice and promoted by the Venetians themselves.

of marriages. Many men remained bachelors, while their sisters often were sent to convents. Nobles became less ready to accept an office that might involve them in expenditures.

System of Government

Venice was governed by a complicated set of interlocking and overlapping committees and councils. The most important were the *signoria* (the major executive committee), the *collegio* (which carried out day-to-day government), and the senate (the deliberative council that supervised the most important matters). An executive council, the Council of Ten, became increasingly important during the fifteenth century: building on its responsibility for state security, it took control of external policy and the conduct of wars, as well as the government of the terra firma. The doge (head of government) was elected for life. Holding an office of great dignity and honor, the doge was the focus of elaborate ceremonial as an embodiment of the majesty of the Venetian republic. However, the doge's powers of initiative were restricted so that at best he could influence but never direct policy; there was no possibility of the doge trying to make himself lord of the city.

By the late fifteenth century the great council, while still the forum where most elections were held, had lost much of its policy-making power to the senate, while the Council of Ten was encroaching on the senate's power. The Council of Ten (in which several dozen might in fact sit) became the focus for an elite group that emerged from within the nobility. Concern that the growing power of the Ten might distort the proper functioning of the government led to its reform in 1582 and 1583: the number that could attend was reduced, and it was stripped of the additional powers it had gradually accumulated.

Citizens

The various grades of Venetian citizenship brought corresponding privileges. No citizen could hold political office, but those from established Venetian families, who came to be known as *cittadini originari* ("original citizens") could hold certain important posts reserved for them within the government bureaucracy.

◀ *In a government famed for the secrecy of its proceedings, the Council of Ten, which was responsible for state security, acquired a sinister reputation for making arbitrary judgments. In this illustration of the council, which is taken from a fifteenth-century French manuscript describing the Venetian nobility, the doge is surrounded by nine prelates; below, clerks record the goings on.*

Citizens could serve as secretaries of embassies and might also be entrusted with confidential missions. Some citizens had the right to trade in Venice and its dominions, others only in the city itself. Such trading privileges might also be granted to non-Venetians. Only a full citizen could be chancellor of Venice.

▲ *A Venetian merchant sells imported ivory objects in this unattributed sixteenth-century painting. As a wealthy merchant city, Venice was a center for the sale of a wide range of luxury goods.*

Citizens also had the privilege of holding office in the religious and charitable confraternities known as the *scuole*; nobles could become members of a *scuola* but could not hold office in one. Some of the major *scuole* were very wealthy institutions that patronized important artists and played a prominent role in civic rituals.

That citizens could become wealthy and hold influential and prestigious offices is believed to be an important factor in their acceptance of being barred from political office. Indeed, there is no record of citizens rebelling to protest their exclusion.

An Open City

As a great merchant city, Venice attracted foreigners from the Mediterranean and throughout Europe. German merchants had their own major trading base, the Fondaco dei Tedeschi, on the Grand Canal, and Ottoman merchants had one too. Some national groups had their own confraternities, such as the Scuola dei Schiavoni for the Slav inhabitants of the city. Many immigrants came from Venice's own dominions: some specialized in certain occupations—for example, men from Bergamo often worked as porters. Seeking refuge in Venice, some political exiles were even given financial support by the state, in case they might prove useful. The Venetians prided themselves on keeping their city open to all, whatever their origin or religion.

Religion and the Church

Despite the religious tolerance within the borders of their city, the Venetians prided themselves on being champions of Christendom in their battles with the Ottomans. Although many of the nobles were sympathetic to ideals of church reform, Venetians were on the whole religiously orthodox, even conservative. The city's many fine churches exemplify local piety.

Venetians were, however, critical of Rome and repeatedly clashed with the popes, who naturally resented their efforts to take over parts of the Papal States in the fifteenth and early sixteenth centuries and their determination to keep important ecclesiastical benefices (appointments) in their territory under Venetian control.

THE ARTS IN VENICE

Venice was one of the major artistic centers of Renaissance Europe. The Basilica of Saint Mark, built in the eleventh century, shows most clearly the influence on Venice of Byzantine art and architecture, while the nearby Doges' Palace is an example of the graceful, highly decorated Venetian Gothic style of architecture and sculpture at its height, and its interior, the grandeur of the Renaissance style. Decorating the Doges' Palace are frescoes and sculpture that celebrate the triumphs of Venice and the virtues of Venetian government.

Owing to the site of the city, safe in a lagoon, Venetian palaces and public buildings did not have the somber air of fortification that characterized the buildings of many less peaceful Italian towns. Often Venetian facades were decorated with elaborate window openings and loggias. The epitome of the Venetian Gothic palace is the Ca' d'Oro (the Golden House), so called because the details of the sculpture on the facade were originally gilded. It is one of many sumptuous palaces on the main waterway of the city, the Grand Canal.

Renaissance architecture came to Venice in the second half of the fifteenth century. In the sixteenth century the Florentine Jacopo Sansovino (1486–1570), who had also worked in Rome, brought the developing High Renaissance style to Venice, as seen in the numerous palaces and churches he built, as well as the two major government buildings he designed opposite the Doges' Palace: the library and the mint. On the Venetian mainland the Paduan architect Andrea Palladio (1508–1580) built some of the finest classical villas of the Renaissance.

An astonishing series of great painters worked in Venice, their style characterized by opulence and luminous color. Building on the achievements of Gentile (c. 1429–1507) and Giovanni (c. 1430–1516) Bellini and Vittore Carpaccio (c. 1460–1525/26) in the late fifteenth century and the innovative work of Giorgione (c. 1477–1511) in the early sixteenth century, artists such as Titian (Tiziano Vecelli; 1488/90–1576), Tintoretto (Jacopo Robusti; c. 1518–1594), and Veronese (Paolo Caliari; 1528–1588) made the sixteenth century the golden age of Venetian painting.

Venice was never a major center of literary activity, but it did become an important locale for the printing and sale of books. Among the pioneers were the famed humanist Aldus Manutius (1449–1515), founder of the Aldine Press, and Ottaviano dei Petrucci (1466–1539), who produced the first printed music score in 1501.

In the later sixteenth century, Venice had an important role in the development of religious music, especially in the music for Saint Mark's Basilica, whose architecture provided a setting and an acoustic that enabled glorious effects, with divided choirs and resonant instrumental accompaniment, particularly from brass instruments.

Gasparo Contarini   1483–1542

Gasparo Contarini was a member of one of the oldest Venetian noble families. He studied philosophy and theology at the University of Padua from 1501 to 1509. He considered joining a religious order but decided to remain a layman. Despite sharing some of the religious views of the Lutherans, he remained loyal to the Catholic Church.

In the 1520s Contarini served as an ambassador to the Holy Roman emperor Charles V (reigned 1519–1556) and then to Pope Clement VII (reigned 1523–1534) until 1530. For the next five years he held offices in Venice, including the important position of head of the Council of Ten. In 1535, while still a layman, he was appointed cardinal by Pope Paul III (reigned 1534–1549). After his appointment he took holy orders and moved to Rome, where he was prominent among the cardinals who advocated reform of the church. In 1541 he acted as papal legate in the discussion between Catholic and Protestant theologians at Regensburg, in Germany, but the compromise he promoted was rejected by the pope and by Luther. Contarini died in 1542.

Contarini's writings included treatises on the power of the pope, of which he was a notable defender, and the duties of a bishop. His best-known work was a description of the government of Venice, *De magistratibus et republica Venetorum* (On the Magistracies and Government of Venice).

▶ The winged lion of Saint Mark, Venice's patron saint, became the symbol of Venetian government. Images of the lion in the form of statues, reliefs, and paintings—such as this one, from the Doges' Palace—were displayed in government buildings and public places in Venice and its subject towns.

It was not enough for the Venetians that Venetian nobles held these benefices; they wanted to choose which nobles were appointed. Nobles who accepted benefices from the pope without the sanction of the government could be effectively exiled in Rome. *Papalisti*—those who had relatives with connections to Rome—were regarded with suspicion and could be excluded from debates and votes on matters in which the papacy might have an interest. After the War of the League of Cambrai, the Venetians lost the right to nominate candidates for bishoprics and other benefices, but they continued to try to control religious institutions and clerics in the city and its territory and insisted on sharing with the Inquisition responsibility for controlling heresy. Under Pope Paul V (reigned 1605–1621) the conflict between Venice and the pope became so serious that Venice was placed under an interdict (a ban on holding religious services) that lasted for a year (1606/1607).

FURTHER READING

Brown, Patricia Fortini. *Private Lives in Renaissance Venice: Art, Architecture, and the Family.* New Haven, CT, 2004.

Chambers, David, and Brian Pullan, eds. *Venice: A Documentary History, 1450–1630.* Cambridge, MA, 1992.

Finlay, Robert. *Politics in Renaissance Venice.* New Brunswick, 1980.

Lane, Frederic C. *Venice: A Maritime Republic.* Baltimore, 1973.

Christine Shaw

SEE ALSO

• Lepanto, Battle of • Monteverdi, Claudio
• Palladio, Andrea • Paul V

Viscontis, The

During the Italian Renaissance, the city of Milan was economically and militarily powerful and politically and culturally significant. For approximately 150 years, from the beginning of the thirteenth century until midway through the fifteenth, the Visconti family played a predominant role in Milan's political, economic, military, and cultural life. The Viscontis won and maintained their prominence by converting the considerable wealth that grew out of their commercial interests and military strength into political influence in Milan and the surrounding region of Lombardy.

Agriculture and Commerce

From the eleventh through the thirteenth century, a period that included the High and late Middle Ages and the dawn of the Renaissance, a cluster of commercially powerful city-states sprang up in northern Italy between the Ligurian and Adriatic seas. Initially, coastal city-states such as Venice, Genoa, and Pisa proved the most economically prosperous owing to their capacity to act as hubs for the trade of raw materials and finished goods between Europe and the empires of the Middle East and Asia. Over the long term, however, two of their inland neighbors, Milan and Florence, proved equally adept at generating wealth by capitalizing on their central location, which served as a geographic bridge linking western Europe to the east and to the south.

As was true of their Florentine rivals, the Milanese lacked direct access to the sea lanes connecting Italy to Africa, the Middle East, and Asia. However, the Viscontis turned this apparent geographical shortcoming to their advantage by casting Milan as the administrative hub of the highly productive agricultural system that developed throughout the territory under Milan's control. From this basis the Viscontis generated the wealth necessary to exercise control over Milan's political system and to acquire the requisite military power to expand their holdings into the surrounding region.

▶ A sixteenth-century view of Milan, the Viscontis' center of power. This fresco was painted in a lunette above a door of the Palacio del Viso, in southern central Spain. The palace was built in 1568 for Don Álvaro de Bazán, the marquess of Santa Cruz and foremost naval commander of his day.

▲ *This 1522 fresco by Bernardino Lanzani offers a bird's-eye view of the city of Pavia, which lies around twenty-two miles (35 km) south of Milan. At the center of the fresco, which is in Pavia's Church of San Teodore, is the Castello Visconteo, begun in 1360 under Galeazzo II and completed in the fifteenth century.*

The Viscontis focused on the cultivation of agricultural goods for which there was a growing demand in the manufacturing centers of Italy and northern Europe—most notably woad (a plant whose leaves yield a blue dye), which was highly sought after by English and Italian textile mill owners. The heart of the Viscontis' dye plant operation lay in a 580-square-mile (1,500 km²) tract of fields between Milan and Genoa, with the latter city and seaport serving as an embarkation point for shipments to England. The operation was propelled in part by the con-

struction of a network of inland canals that provided the means for both irrigation and commercial transport in Lombardy.

Although the family generated a great deal of wealth through its agricultural system, it also struggled to maintain a surplus in the Milanese treasury, owing in part to the determination of Visconti rulers, such as Gian Galeazzo (1351–1402), to enlarge the territory under their control by way of costly military operations. In order to finance those operations, the Viscontis had to extract progressively larger proportions of the incomes of inhabitants of cities across northern Italy. These extractions left the Viscontis' subjects embittered and more prone to consider staging revolts.

The Politics of the Viscontis

While not nearly so enduring as the reign of the Medicis of Florence, the rule of the Viscontis over Milanese municipal affairs and the politics of the surrounding region lasted nearly two centuries. It commenced when Ottone Visconti (1207–1295), then the archbishop of Milan, was recognized as lord of the city after defeating the rival Della Torre family. Visconti rule ended with the death of Filippo Maria Visconti (1392–1447), who died without having produced a male heir.

As was typical in Italian city-states during the Renaissance, the Viscontis established and administered a political system that allowed limited autonomy to the citizens of Milan and those residing in towns across Lombardy but was, on balance, autocratic in nature (that is, a single ruler wielded absolute authority). Essentially, the head of the Visconti family at any given time presided over a hierarchical governmental structure whose most prominent officials he had appointed.

For example, although the Viscontis installed a nine-hundred-member governing council in Milan, most power rested in the hands of an intimate twelve-member Consiglio delle Provvisioni ("provisional council"), a body that served for just two months at a time. The family nominated the members of the Consiglio, who then decided on the composition of the formal nine-hundred-member council. In addition, while the Visconti lord was technically subject to the laws governing the council, his power to change its membership every few months effectively gave him the real authority.

The long list of Visconti lords who benefited from the autocratic nature of the Milanese governmental system includes Galeazzo II, Gian Galeazzo, and Filippo Maria, as well as Galeazzo I (1277–1328), Azzone (1302–1339), and Lucchino (1292–1349). Galeazzo I, Azzone, Lucchino, Galeazzo II, and Gian Galeazzo were all successful in maintaining control over

Milanese politics while expanding the Viscontis' sphere of influence within and beyond Lombardy.

Ultimately, though, the Viscontis' insistence on territorial expansion proved costly. In order to support its military initiatives, the family often had to resort to hiring mercenaries, known as condottieri. The most famous such mercenary was Francesco Sforza (1401–1466). As a reward for assisting the Viscontis, Sforza was granted the right to marry Filippo Maria's daughter, Bianca, in 1441. When Filippo Maria died in 1441 without a male heir, the family lost its hold on power, and Sforza soon stepped in to assume the title of duke of Milan.

Securing a Hold on Power

Among the principal concerns of the Viscontis—as is true for any ruling authority at any time—were the security and stability of the territory under their control. Milan was faced with both internal and external security threats between the fourteenth and mid-fifteenth centuries. As the most prominent and powerful Milanese family during that period, the Viscontis had two sets of security interests to manage: on the one hand, the maintenance of internal political stability and, on the other, the defense of the city and broader

▼ The castle pictured below was built in 1473 under Galeazzo Maria Visconti by Marco Civedati and Antonio Salvini according to a design by Bartolomeo Gadio. It is situated in Soncino, in the province of Cremona, and was used primarily as base for hunting expeditions.

duchy of Milan against threats posed by external powers across central and northern Italy—powers whose interests often conflicted with those of the Viscontis.

Ultimately, the internal and external threats faced by the Viscontis were very much interconnected, since both essentially stemmed from the family's determination to expand its territorial holdings. That expansion required financial resources, which the Viscontis obtained by taxing the citizens of Milan and the surrounding towns of Lombardy (and in the process fomented much resentment among those who perceived such taxation as excessive and unjust). In addition, the Viscontis had to work hard to maintain stability in a sphere of control that expanded as a result of aggressive conquests by Gian Galeazzo and other Visconti rulers. Internecine family squabbles also made the preservation of order difficult; Gian Galeazzo's plot against his uncle Bernabò, which resulted in Bernabò's imprisonment and possible murder, was perhaps the most conspicuously nefarious example of such a squabble.

▼ *This Milanese gold ducat, in use from 1412 to 1447, bears the image of Filippo Maria Visconti.*

With the continual enlargement of the territory over which the Viscontis presided between the early fourteenth and early fifteenth centuries, there came confrontations with other Italian city-states—most notably Florence to the south and Venice to the east. The Viscontis were able to avoid a broader struggle with the Holy Roman Empire thanks to adroit economic and political maneuvers, including Gian Galeazzo's payment to the Holy Roman emperor Wenceslas (reigned 1378–1400; also King Wenceslas IV of Bohemia, 1378–1419), in return for which Gian Galeazzo secured the title of duke of Milan.

Among the most militarily successful of the Visconti leaders were Galeazzo I, Azzone, Lucchino, and Gian Galeazzo. The first three established, expanded, and maintained the family's control over territory in Lombardy, Piedmont, and to a limited degree, Tuscany. For his part, Gian Galeazzo, moving farther south and then east, seized Pisa, Sienna, Perugia, and Bologna and advanced to the city limits of Florence before his own death brought the Visconti advance to an end in 1402.

Filippo Maria faced an early challenge to maintain internal stability as familial rivals sought to fill the power vacuum created by Gian Galeazzo's death. Once he had prevailed, Filippo Maria began to rebuild the Viscontis' military power base, albeit with Francesco Sforza's help. An alliance between the former rivals Florence and Venice against the duchy of Milan complicated matters and left the door to power virtually open for Sforza when Filippo Maria died in 1447.

Politics and Religion

As was the case in city-states across Italy (and, to a degree, throughout Europe), cultural, political, and religious developments were very much interconnected in Renaissance Milan.

Unlike that of the Medicis of Florence, the Viscontis' relationship with the papacy in Rome was frequently turbulent. Whereas two of the Medicis eventually became popes, the Viscontis' dealings with the papacy were ambivalent at best and confrontational at worst. The principal reason for the troubled state of relations between Milan and Rome was political. At Ottone

Gian Galeazzo Visconti   1351–1402

One of the most strategically and politically adept—and ruthless—of the Visconti rulers, Gian Galeazzo presided over and continually expanded the size of the family's territorial possessions from the time he seized power from his uncle Bernabò through treacherous means in 1385 to his own death in 1402.

Gian Galeazzo assumed control over Milan after convincing other family members to have Bernabò thrown in prison (where he died, possibly by foul means). Gian Galeazzo then enhanced his own prestige and bolstered the family's power and influence in northern Italy (and indeed in central Europe) by purchasing the title of duke of Milan from the Holy Roman emperor Wenceslas for 100,000 florins.

On numerous occasions Gian Galeazzo proved willing to use severe measures against his opponents, whether in Milan or in conquered territories across Lombardy. A forty-day period of torture known as the Lenten Treatment was one particularly brutal example of such severity. Nevertheless, Gian Galeazzo also allowed many towns a measure of financial and governmental autonomy.

Above all, Gian Galeazzo, who had served as lord of Pavia before ousting Bernabò from his position as lord of Milan, viewed Wenceslas's dictate as an opportunity to consolidate further the Viscontis' holdings in northern Italy. This expansion brought the family into conflict with the equally powerful Florentines to the south. Initially, the momentum was clearly in Gian Galeazzo's favor. After seizing Bologna in 1402, the Viscontis imposed a siege on Florence, which appeared destined to end in victory. However, fate intervened in the form of a plague-related fever that took Gian Galeazzo's life. The family then endured a period of decline as Gian Galeazzo's son Filippo Maria struggled unsuccessfully to regain past Visconti glory.

▼ *This colored lithograph, a copy of a manuscript illumination by the great French chronicler Jean Froissart (c. 1333–c. 1405), depicts Gian Galeazzo Visconti ambushing his uncle Bernabò and taking him prisoner (an event that took place in 1385).*

Visconti's behest, in the thirteenth century Milan had aligned itself with the anti-Vatican Ghibelline factions in their struggle against the pro-Rome Guelfs. Ottone and his successors Mateo I (1255–1322) and Galeazzo I focused much of their military and political attention on the battle against the papacy. On balance, all three were successful in expanding the Viscontis' territorial possessions in Lombardy, but they faced intermittent opposition from Guelf factions situated in cities across the region.

In a departure from the policy of Ottone, Mateo I, and Galeazzo, Azzone chose to make peace with the Vatican. However, the relations between the Viscontis and the papacy alternated between peace and conflict over the course of the family's time in power in Milan. The relationship at any given time often reflected that between the ruler of the Holy Roman Empire and the pope. The Viscontis tended to maintain better relations with the emperor than with the pope; Gian Galeazzo's financial dealings with Wenceslas testify to the family's warm relations with the empire.

Although the Viscontis were known primarily for political and religious intrigue and military expansion, some of their number also cast themselves as patrons of intellectual and artistic development. Galeazzo II, for example, was a patron of the great humanist Petrarch (1304–

▶ The university of Pavia, one of the oldest universities in Europe, grew out of an institution that had taught canon and civil law and theology since the ninth century. In 1361, at the request of Galeazzo II Visconti, it received official recognition as a studium generale (essentially, an accredited university) by the Holy Roman emperor, Charles IV.

The most serious threat to the security of the Viscontis' rule of Milan, a threat that ultimately proved decisive, was the dying out of the family's male line. With no male heir to replace Filippo Maria upon his death in 1447, the Viscontis quickly lost their place to the Sforzas as the leading family of Milan. The predictability of such a dynastic crisis had been correctly forecast by one Florentine writer at the start of the fifteenth century:

Always [the Florentines] comforted themselves with the hope, which in their eyes was a certainty on which they could count, that a Commonwealth ... cannot die, while the Duke was one single mortal man, whose end would mean the end of his empire. ... And consequently ... the Florentines never rested; when one remedy had worn thin or failed, they resorted immediately to some other.

Gregorio Dati, *History of Florence, 1380–1406*

1374), while he himself was founder of the University of Pavia. Petrarch spent time under Gian Galeazzo's protection during the Western Schism, which left a divided Catholic Church with popes sitting in both Rome and Avignon in 1378.

A Fleeting Legacy

While the Viscontis were clearly the predominant force in the politics of Milan and the surrounding region of Lombardy for nearly two centuries, their legacy is a limited one, particularly when their exploits are compared with those of their rivals, the Medicis of Florence. The Viscontis are remembered above all for the autocratic control they exercised over the duchy of Milan and the military power with which they threatened and confronted their neighbors. The Medicis, in contrast, despite their intrigues and vices, are remembered for their enduring cultural contributions to the Renaissance. The Viscontis' appetite for expansion led to their eventual fall and the subsequent rise of the Sforzas to the rule of Milan.

FURTHER READING

Chamberlin, E. R. *The Count of Virtue: Giangaleazzo Visconti, Duke of Milan.* New York, 1966.

Muir, D. Erskine. *A History of Milan under the Visconti.* London, 1924.

Robert J. Pauly Jr.

SEE ALSO

- Agriculture • Banking • Florence
- Holy Roman Empire • Italian City-States
- Italian Wars • Manufacturing
- Medicis, The • Papacy • Petrarch
- Renaissance • Rome • Venice • Warfare

Warfare

During the Renaissance and the Reformation there were dramatic advances in the tactics, weapons, and strategies of combat. These developments became the basis of modern ways of making war.

Although much of the art and literature of the early Renaissance celebrated traditional notions of chivalry and trumpeted the importance of the individual knight, by 1300 the armored, mounted soldier was increasingly less significant in combat. Over the next few centuries gunpowder revolutionized military affairs, and as firearms replaced sword, bow, and spear, there were equally important changes in strategy and tactics. Traditional castles ceased to be the major defensive fortifications; instead, earthworks and trenches became the principal means to defend cities and communities.

Gunpowder and Cannon

Gunpowder had been used in China for several centuries before Europeans began experimenting with it. As trade with China increased at the end of the Middle Ages, Europeans started to make cannon and firearms based on Chinese designs. By the 1320s Europeans were building crude cannon that used gunpowder to fire large iron arrows or stones. Cumbersome, inaccurate, and difficult to load and fire, these early European cannon often exploded and either killed or injured the firing crew rather than discharging their load.

For the next few hundred years, problems with the consistency of gunpowder and the design of cannon limited their utility. In any case, catapults and other contemporary weapons had become very efficient by the late Middle Ages. The counterweight catapult, known as the trebuchet, could lob a three-hundred-pound projectile a distance of three hundred yards with great accuracy. In contrast, early cannon could fire only small projectiles and had half the range of the trebuchet.

Gunpowder was expensive at first because saltpeter, one of its main ingredients, had to be imported from India and Asia. Its quality often degraded during the long journey, too. Gunpowder became cheaper and more consistent as manufacturers found alternative sources of saltpeter, such as lime and oyster shells. Europeans also succeeded in making gunpowder more powerful.

There were concurrent improvements in the design of shot and cannon. Cannoneers began using iron shot instead of stones. The iron cannonballs were harder and had more penetrating power than the stone shells and so were better able to damage castle walls. The use of molds to cast the balls also ensured that the projectiles had the same predictable weight and shape.

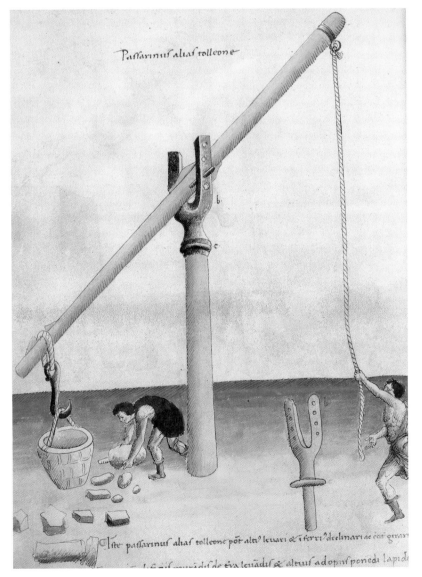

▼ This illustration of a catapult comes from De machinis bellicis (On War Machines), a 1449 manuscript by the renowned Sienese artist and engineer Mariano de Iacopo Taccola.

▶ This illustration of a cannon is from Roberto Valturio's handbook for soldiers, De re militari (On Military Affairs; 1455–1460). This early cannon bears little resemblance to later models. As its shape indicates, the gun was designed to be fired upward against castle walls, not straight at enemy foot soldiers or cavalry.

pults and other medieval weapons became obsolete. The last major use of catapults was during the siege of Rhodes in 1480, when the island was surrounded by the fleet of the Ottoman sultan, Mehmed II (reigned 1444–1446 and 1451–1481).

Some early cannon were made of hollowed-out tree trunks reinforced with straps. However, these wooden guns often proved as dangerous to the cannoneers as to the enemy; after repeated use, the barrels split and showered the cannon crew with deadly splinters. Wooden barrels were abandoned fairly early, although there were still some instances in which wood cannon were used to defend cities in the 1600s when no alternatives were available.

Little better than wooden ones, early iron cannon were prone to explode if they overheated or if they had been poorly cast. Cannon makers worked hard to improve metal weapons. Through the fifteenth and sixteenth centuries, they also experimented with bronze-made barrels. Lighter and less prone to explode than iron, bronze was also far more expensive as it was extremely scarce. During the Reformation, Protestant forces often melted down church bells from Catholic cathedrals and recast the metal into cannon. It was not until the sixteenth century that safe, reliable iron cannon began to

One early improvement to the cannon was a lengthened barrel that enabled it to fire greater distances. By the 1500s most cannon employed a ratio in which the length of the barrel was twelve to thirty times the width of the muzzle. In addition, there were improvements in the construction of cannon. By the middle of the fifteenth century, as gunpowder became more consistent and cannon design improved, cata-

CANNON STANDARDIZATION

The standardization of cannon and cannon shot greatly increased their efficiency. As armies utilized an ever-increasing number of cannon, they needed standardized weapons so that the same size shot could be used in different weapons.

Cannon began to be classified by a common method: on the basis of the weight of their projectile. A full cannon fired a 50-pound ball and weighed about 9,000 pounds; a half cannon fired a 25-pound shell and weighed 7,000 pounds; and a quarter cannon fired a 16-pound projectile and weighed 3,500 pounds. Smaller cannon had a range of nicknames: a falcon was a cannon that fired a 3-pound ball, for instance, while a falconet fired a 1-pound shot. Over time, cannon were simply named according to the weight of the shot they fired; a cannon that fired a 25-pound ball was a 25-pounder, and so on. The use of standard-sized cannonballs simplified the logistics and supply of artillery for armies.

The amount of gunpowder used, known as the charge, also became standardized by weight. Most cannon consistently used a charge that was two-thirds of the weight of the cannonball. Using a heavier charge was dangerous as it increased the likelihood that the barrel would explode during firing. In order to alter the range of the cannon, the barrel would be either elevated (to increase distance) or depressed (to shorten distance). Elevation also became regularized through the use of standard wooden wedges that were placed under the back of the barrel.

Just as the cannon barrels became standardized, the carriages for the weapons were also improved. Carriages with two very large wheels and a trail that rested on the ground increased the mobility and stability of the weapons so that they could be used in pitched battles, not just sieges.

Finally, cannoneers were highly specialized, trained troops. Thanks to standardization, commanders could deploy and transfer cannon crews to operate a range of weapons during a battle, with minimal additional training.

be produced in large quantities, initially in England. Over the next hundred years, iron gradually replaced bronze as the main material for cannon barrels.

Castles and Other Fortifications

The castles of the Middle Ages had evolved into elaborate defensive works with integrated moats, keeps, and extraordinarily thick walls. One result was that for most of the Middle Ages, the defender had the advantage during a siege. In spite of catapults and other siege weaponry, many attackers relied on prolonged sieges, treachery, or the threat of starvation to capture castles. The evolution of cannon quickly made the medieval castle obsolete. Expensive and heavy, early cannon were not much use in conventional battles; they were used primarily during sieges and, as a result, grew ever larger. By the 1500s siege cannon often weighed more than five tons and fired five-hundred-pound cannonballs a distance of more than half a mile.

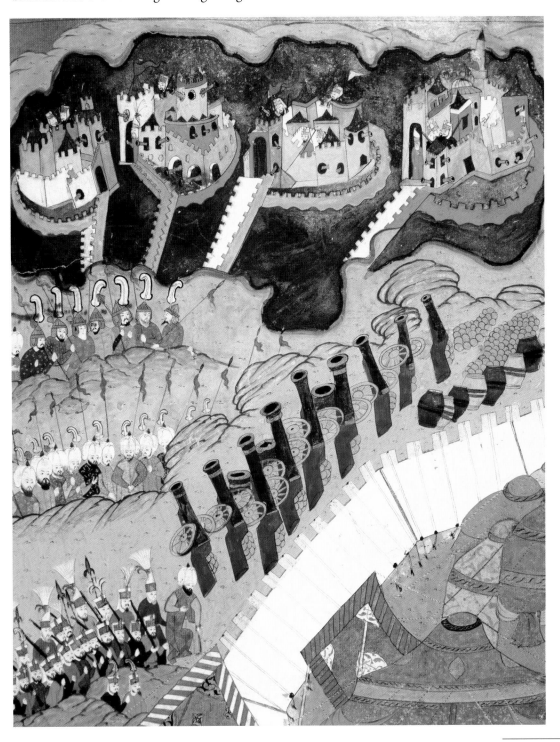

◄ *This mid-sixteenth-century illustration of a Christian fortress under siege is taken from* The Military Campaigns of Süleyman I, *by the Ottoman sultan's court-appointed chronicler, Seyyid Lokman. Artillery was used to knock holes in castle walls so that the infantry could invade the citadel.*

Large siege cannon eventually led to the demise of the traditional castles, as they could easily breach the stone walls. In 1453 the Ottoman Turks used large cannon to breach the heavy walls of Constantinople during their fifty-day siege. From the 1400s into the next century, attackers gained the advantage over defenders.

Defensive fortifications had to change dramatically to counter the effectiveness of the siege weapons. A range of innovations gradually restored the equilibrium between attacker and defender. First, cities began to build fortifications with sloping walls. The slopes helped to deflect the cannon shots and reduce their penetrating power. In addition, walls became lower and less rigid, and so they were less likely to shatter or collapse. Earthworks were built around walls or as defensive perimeters (the earth absorbed the impact of cannonballs instead of breaking or

shattering as stone did). Fortresses called angle bastions were multisided, a design that helped deflect cannonballs. Also, if a wall of an angle bastion was breached, attackers would not necessarily capture the entire fortress. Finally, defenders began using their cannon to destroy those of the besiegers. Since the siege guns of the day were heavy and difficult to move, they proved easy targets for the defenders' cannon, which often had the advantage of height and could therefore fire farther. New structures known as artillery towers were built to house the cannon of defenders. Shorter than the traditional medieval keeps or towers, dozens of the new towers ringed the walls of a well-designed Renaissance fortress.

Many existing castles had to be rebuilt or modified, an expensive and time-consuming process that only large and powerful entities, such as kingdoms or empires, could afford. A smaller political body such as a city-state or principality often lacked the funds to pay for the new fortifications and other technological advances and was therefore likely to fall to its larger neighbors and rivals. By the end of the sixteenth century, few traditional castles were being built in Europe, except in peripheral states such as Poland and Russia, and by the early years of the seventeenth century, most major European cities had revised their fortifications.

Decline of the Knight

Initially, cannon and other firearms had little impact on battlefield tactics. The early, large cannon were primarily used in sieges, while personal firearms were too slow and inefficient for widespread use. However, other military technologies began to change battlefield tactics. Through most of the Middle Ages, heavy cavalry were the most potent force on the battlefield. Mounted knights, in heavy armor that made them impervious to most weapons, smashed through infantry units. The cavalry was composed of members of the landed aristocracy. A feudal vassal was required to provide his liege, or overlord, with a specific number of knights and infantry during a military campaign.

▲ Mercenaries receive their pay in this detail from The Council Finances in Times of War and of Peace, by Benvenuto di Giovanni (1436–c. 1518). Wages for mercenaries were one of the main expenditures during European wars of the Renaissance.

MERCENARIES

The late Renaissance and the Reformation marked the height of the use of mercenaries (paid foreign soldiers) in Europe. Although mercenaries had been used during the Middle Ages, the feudal system had provided the bulk of troops for military service. With the demise of feudalism and the rise of the central state, sovereigns needed a new source of troops, especially as battles became increasingly larger in scope. They also needed forces that were familiar with the new weapons, such as cannon and firearms, and tactics, such as the Swiss phalanx formation (a phalanx was a group of armed infantry deployed so close together that they were very hard to attack).

As the variously sized and governed states of the period lacked the ability to forcibly conscript, to inspire, or otherwise to induce men to volunteer for military service, mercenaries filled a need for trained soldiers that could be retained in large numbers. Mercenaries could even be hired under long-term contracts. Beginning in 1474, France entered into a contract for 6,000 Swiss mercenaries who had to be available within a short period of time after notification from Paris. Mercenaries were also extensively used during the various civil wars and dynastic struggles of the period. In 1487, during the English Wars of the Roses, some 2,000 German mercenaries on the side of the Yorkists were killed by Lancastrian forces. After the death of Henry VIII in 1547, his nine-year-old son, Edward, assumed the throne (as King Edward VI) under the regency of Edward Seymour, the duke of Somerset. Somerset procured some 7,500 foreign troops to protect the young king.

There were a number of problems with mercenaries. Leaders often questioned their loyalty, especially in cases where large bodies of mercenaries from the same foreign country faced each other across a battlefield. At the Battle of Dreux (1572), waged between French Catholics and Huguenots, two groups of Swiss mercenaries refused to fight each other while two German contingents fired their weapons into the air instead of at each other. Mercenaries were often also involved in financial fraud: mercenary commanders pocketed their soldiers' pay and embezzled funds that were supposed to be spent on weapons or supplies. In addition, mercenary troops often committed crimes against civilians, such as property theft and rape. Despite all these problems, mercenaries remained an integral part of warfare until the rise of the professional army in the eighteenth century.

The early modern period saw significant innovations in naval warfare tactics. The development of larger ships, such as the caravel, made navigation on the open seas practical and marked the transition from galleys to sail. Caravels were later replaced by galleons, which were in turn superseded by frigates and later ships of the line. Initially, naval warfare involved ramming and then boarding enemy vessels. Small cannon and harquebuses were used in the battles. By the end of the Reformation, boarding was replaced by cannon exchanges.

Larger vessels allowed navies to conduct operations away from the coastal areas and set the stage for the expansion of European power during the Age of Exploration and for the rise of commercial naval powers such as Holland and England. Under Henry VIII, the English fleet increased to fifty-eight ships by 1547. English naval ships and privateers joined to defeat the Spanish armada in 1588 in the greatest naval encounter of the era. There were also three naval wars fought between the English and Dutch between 1652 and 1674, and throughout the era English and Dutch privateers attacked Spanish treasure convoys en route from colonies in the Western Hemisphere.

Larger vessels provided stable platforms for cannon, which they carried in ever larger numbers. For instance, at the Battle of Nevis in 1667, the ships were three to four hundred tons and equipped with up to forty cannon. Cannon allowed vessels to engage in naval combat at greater distances. The ships could also provide support for infantry on shore by bombarding towns or enemy formations.

▶ *Throughout the Renaissance cavalry was the dominant military arm. Depicted in this illustration from a fifteenth-century French manuscript is a force of English cavalry, led by King Edward III, attacking French forces at Blanchetaque as the English cross the Somme River. The event was a prelude to the Battle of Crécy, a key early conflict of the Hundred Years War.*

During the Renaissance heavy cavalry gradually lost some of its prominence owing to the use of two weapons, the longbow and the pike. The longbow, at least four feet in length, was extremely accurate and had an effective range of about two hundred yards. Simple and inexpensive, it could fire up to twelve arrows per minute. Its shot could penetrate most heavy armor, although longbows had their greatest impact killing a knight's horse and thereby taking away the main advantage of the mounted warrior. During the Hundred Years War (1337–1453), the English deployed large numbers of longbow-men, and they proved decisive at the Battle of Crécy (1346) and the Battle of Agincourt (1415). The longbow was also one of the main weapons used during the English civil wars (1642–1651).

The other major weapon that undermined the effectiveness of the cavalry was the twenty-one-foot (6.4 m) Swiss pike. The Swiss revived the pike-and-phalanx formation favored by the ancient Macedonians; by using this formation, the Swiss were able to stop cavalry charges. In 1422 Swiss pikemen repulsed the cavalry units of Milan at the Battle of Arbedo. In 1477 the pikes helped the Swiss win the Battle of Nancy, and afterward, many aristocrats hired Swiss pikemen as mercenaries. The Swiss were not the only units to use the pikes against cavalry. Shorter versions of the pike were effectively used by the Scots against English cavalry at the Battle of Bannockburn in 1314.

Firearms

The effectiveness of cavalry was further weakened by the introduction of the individual firearm. The first personal guns were inaccurate, slow loading, and also very heavy. One early gun, the harquebus, had to be fired from a supportive stand. Throughout the Renaissance, a bowman could fire faster than an opponent armed with a gun could.

Nonetheless, even the early guns had advantages. First, the weapons did not require the training necessary to use a longbow or the complicated techniques necessary to operate in a phalanx formation. A soldier could be trained to operate a firearm in a week and did not have to have the physical strength needed for the heavy pike or the longbow.

Firearms could penetrate heavy armor at increasingly long ranges. Another important advantage was the far greater efficiency with which guns could knock holes in the lines of opposing forces. Of course, firearms were much more expensive to produce in large numbers than either pikes or longbows.

The first widespread use of firearms occurred in northern Italy in the 1520s. Like cannon, firearms improved gradually. First it was necessary to develop standards so that ammunition and parts for weapons were interchangeable. The harquebus was heavy and relatively inaccurate; however, the emergence in the mid-sixteenth century of the smoothbore musket began to transform the role and importance of infantry. The musket was more powerful than the longbow and could penetrate even the heaviest armor at a distance of two hundred yards. Barrels that were rifled—that had long, spiral grooves inside to spin the bullet and so improve accuracy—were produced in the 1600s, but they were very expensive and used mainly by snipers.

▲ *Early firearms were large and cumbersome and required several people to operate them. This ink and watercolor depiction of different types of weapons from around 1512, by an unknown German artist, is a copy of a drawing by Jörg Kölderer, court painter to Emperor Maximilian I.*

By the late Renaissance battles were large and highly complex and involved a range of different types of troops and formations. This 1587 oil painting by Jan Snellick of the Battle of Moncontour (fought on October 30, 1569, during the French wars of religion) conveys something of the scale of military engagements in the sixteenth century.

By the 1540s a small firearm that could be fired with one hand began to appear: the pistol. Although it was far less accurate than the musket and had only a short range, the pistol nevertheless proved highly effective as a cavalry weapon. In Germany cavalrymen began carrying two or more pistols. When they engaged at close range with other cavalry or with infantry, the pistols were more effective than swords. A cavalryman using a pistol—unlike a swordsman, for example—did not need to be especially strong or skilled (the same was true of a musketeer). Moreover, the use of pistols coincided with and contributed to the emergence of the officer class, a development that further eroded the traditional role of the knight. The decline of aristocrats as military leaders occurred as professional military forces replaced peasant conscripts.

Tactics and Organization

With the new weapons came new tactics and organization. Previously, the cavalry had been dominated by noblemen, but the late Renaissance saw the rise of an officer class in which rank, though not always status, became equal throughout the branches of the military.

The basic military unit for both the cavalry and infantry was the company, led by a captain. Within companies, sergeants directed smaller units, or troops, of men. Several companies formed a battalion, and two or more battalions formed a regiment, led by a colonel. A general commanded a division, a group of regiments. Increasingly, senior officers were assisted by an organizational staff, and an army's support troops included a supply corps. Thenceforth, a mounted soldier was usually no longer a knight or aristocrat but simply a soldier on horseback. In addition, as a professional class of generals emerged, monarchs and princes became far less likely to personally lead troops in battle. For instance, Philip II of Spain (reigned 1556–1598) managed his numerous conflicts from his capital and relied on battlefield generals.

Formations and movement became far more rigid and professionalized. Soldiers were expected to master complicated maneuvers in formation and march in step. Commanders began using maps to plan and execute battles. As the professionalization of the military spread across Europe, armies of all nationalities used the same tactics, formations, and organization.

Albrecht von Wallenstein   1583–1634

One of the greatest military commanders of the Holy Roman Empire, Albrecht von Wallenstein epitomized the ambition and greed of many military commanders of the period. Born in Bohemia, he joined the army of Emperor Rudolf II (reigned 1576–1612) and won fame during the siege of Esztergom in 1604.

When the Thirty Years War commenced, Wallenstein rebuffed the advances of rebels and raised a loyalist cavalry regiment. He subsequently won a series of victories and was rewarded with titles and properties. Along with the Flemish general Johann Tserclaes, count of Tilly (1559–1632), Wallenstein forced Denmark to withdraw from the Thirty Years War in 1627.

Wallenstein then led imperial forces in Germany. His command became increasingly independent, and his army used plunder to support itself. In 1630 Emperor Ferdinand II (reigned 1619–1637) removed Wallenstein from his command, but two years later he recalled him after the Swedes invaded Germany.

Wallenstein won battles in Bohemia; defeated the Swedish king, Gustavus II Adolphus (reigned 1611–1632), at the Battle of Alte Veste in 1632; and then commanded imperial forces at the Battle of Lützen, where Gustavus was killed.

In 1633 Wallenstein began negotiations to switch sides and force a peace upon the emperor. His treachery was discovered in January 1634, and he was removed from command. Wallenstein attempted to join the Swedes but was killed by loyalist officers on February 25, 1634.

New weapons, such as firearms and cannon, were incorporated into battlefield tactics. At first, musketeers were often placed among pike or other infantry units as a way to give these formations offensive and defensive firepower. Later, musketeers began to be grouped together in formation. Cannon, which became lighter and more mobile, were used to support infantry and cavalry. They began to fire exploding shells or, much like a large version of a modern shotgun, shot that was composed of a number of small rounds. One innovation, the organ cannon, had four to six small cannon linked together that could be fired simultaneously against advancing infantry and cavalry. The integration of tactics and weapons continued beyond the seventeenth century as armies became increasingly professional.

FURTHER READING

Arnold, Thomas F. *The Renaissance at War.* New York, 2006.

Black, Jeremy. *A Military Revolution? Military Change and European Society, 1500–1800.* Atlantic Highlands, NJ, 1991.

Eltis, David. *The Military Revolution in Sixteenth-Century Europe.* New York, 1995.

Hale, J. R. *War and Society in Renaissance Europe, 1450–1620.* Baltimore, 1986.

Hall, Bert S. *Weapons and Warfare in Renaissance Europe: Gunpowder, Technology, and Tactics.* Baltimore, 1997

Keegan, John. *A History of Warfare.* New York, 1993.

Tom Lansford

SEE ALSO

- Agincourt, Battle of • Armada, Spanish
- English Civil Wars • Feudalism • French Civil Wars
- Hapsburg Empire • Hundred Years War
- Italian Wars • Lepanto, Battle of • Monarchy
- Nationalism • Peasants' Revolts
- Science and Technology • Thirty Years War

▲ *By the end of the 1500s, artillery technology had dramatically improved. Cannon were more mobile and so could be used against castles and ground forces alike. This pencil and watercolor drawing, which portrays a soldier loading a cannon from the breech (rather than the muzzle), is taken from Veit Wolff von Senftenberg's late-sixteenth-century book* L'art de l'artillerie *(The Art of Artillery).*

Women

WOMEN MADE AN INESTIMABLE CONTRIBUTION TO EVERY ASPECT OF RENAISSANCE LIFE, WHETHER AS RULERS OF LARGE TERRITORIES, FAMOUS (OR INFAMOUS) FIGURES IN LOCAL SOCIETY AND POLITICS, RELIGIOUS CONFORMERS OR REFORMERS, INTELLECTUALS, POETS, AND ARTISTS— OR AS LESS HERALDED BUT NO LESS VITAL MANAGERS OF THE FAMILY AND HOUSEHOLD.

The first part of a girl's life was taken up with education. A young woman was educated in a manner considered appropriate to the life she was likely to lead. Thus, all women were to some degree educated in the household arts, including food preparation, textile production (spinning, weaving, and needlework), household maintenance (especially cleaning and caring for household objects), domestic decoration and design, and any other skills necessary to maintain the condition and comfort of the home and to boost the prestige of the household in the eyes of visitors.

▼ This medallion by Antonio Pisanello (c. 1395–1455) bears the portrait of Cecilia Gonzaga, the famously learned daughter of Gianfrancesco Gonzaga, marquis of Mantua. Although portrait medallions were common during the Renaissance, they usually commemorated men; this medallion stands as a clear indication of Cecilia's high status at the court of Mantua.

For many girls this education at first took the form of instruction from the older female members of the household, including the girl's mother. Later in life, many young women would be sent out to gain further experience as apprentices in other households. In England and Wales, young women from well-to-do families were often sent to even wealthier households to be educated in a manner appropriate to their social status. By sending their daughters to such households, well-to-do or ambitious parents could be assured that their daughters would make advantageous marriages, as was certainly the case with the young Margaret Dakin (1571–1633). Margaret's relatively wealthy parents, who were members of the lower gentry class, sent her to live in the household of the earl of Huntingdon. There Margaret not only learned how to manage a large household but also met two of her future husbands; one, Walter Devereaux, was the son of the earl of Essex, and the other, Thomas Sidney, was the brother of the poet and courtier Philip Sidney. Huntingdon, who was guardian to both these young men, arranged both marriages. Even in later life, when widowed for the second time, Margaret looked to Huntingdon for marital advice.

During the Renaissance it was becoming more common to educate girls in various forms of literacy and numeracy, from simple reading, writing, and arithmetical skills to more advanced forms of learning, including contemporary European languages and classical Latin and Greek. However, this intellectual education was no less geared toward the preparation of a woman for the life she was likely to lead as a wife, mother, and head of a household. The development of a woman's intellect was calculated to enhance such desirable virtues as moral sense, charity, humility, and social self-awareness.

The Spanish humanist Juan Luis Vives (1492–1540) believed that the purpose of educating a woman was to save her from ignorance: "She ought to learn many things, but only such as are of use to her to know" (*Instruction of a Christian Woman*). What exactly was of use for a woman to know depended upon her social

In a work of 1509 dedicated to Margaret of Austria, a German theologian, physician, and humanist philosopher declared his belief in the full equality of the sexes.

In everything else they are the same. Woman does not have a soul of a different sex from that which animates man.... Women and men were equally endowed with gifts of spirit and reason and the use of words; they were created for the same end, and the sexual difference between them will not confer a different destiny.

Cornelius Agrippa von Nettesheim, *On the Nobility and Excellence of Women*

A contemporary portrait of Margaret of Austria (1480–1530) by Bernaert van Orley. After her first husband, the infante Juan of Spain, died, Margaret married Philibert II, duke of Savoy. She was twice regent of the Netherlands (1507–1515, 1519–1530).

status. Women of the merchant and working classes were thought to need very little formal education beyond the ability to read books on domestic issues and the possession of sufficient arithmetical skills to keep the household accounts. Many women in these classes could not write, although some rudimentary skill in writing was seen as an advantage. In the Protestant countries after the Reformation, reading and writing took on greater value for men and women of all classes, as an individual reading of the Bible became an important part of Protestant worship (and so, to an extent, did reflecting upon spiritual matters through confessional writing). The poorest members of society had little access to formal education, and so poor women rarely could read or write.

Most women from wealthy families throughout Europe could read and write at a reasonably sophisticated level. Indeed, the level of scholarship among women of high status reached an apogee that it would not reach again until modern times. Cecilia Gonzaga (1425–1451), for example, attended the prestigious academy of Vittorino da Feltre along with her brothers. She could speak Latin and Greek fluently from a very young age. Lucrezia Marinelli (1571–1653) was educated in philosophy, as well as in Latin, Greek, and Italian literature. She published several books, including *L'Enrico, ovvero Bisanzio acquistato (Henry; or, Byzantium Gained)*. The intellectual ability of Cassandra Fedele (1465–1568) was so impressive that Queen Isabella of Castile invited her to the Spanish court. In fact, in Spain there was no dearth of highly educated women. Isabella set up an academy to educate the young women and men of her court according to a humanist curriculum that included instruction in Latin, Greek, philosophy, literature, and religion. Isabella's daughter Catherine of Aragon (later married to King Henry VIII of England) was tutored by Juan Luis Vives and became renowned for her learning. Catherine also provided a humanist education for her daughter, Mary (1516–1558), later Mary I of England.

Ct commence le liuur au siuure au Pau

In this manuscript illumination from the workshop of the Master of the Cité des Dames, Christine de Pisan presents her poems to King Charles VI of France. Christine's work was prized by many royal courts, and several illuminated manuscripts of her writings are preserved throughout Europe.

Middle Ages and early Renaissance. Christine's talents were so prized that Henry IV of England, desiring her to come to his court, held her son prisoner for a short time in the hope of pressuring her to agree. Christine was also favored by Charles VI of France.

Still, it remains true that the primary purpose of educating women was not to spur them to great intellectual, artistic, or political achievements but to ensure that they were well suited to the considerable demands and duties of everyday life as wife and mother. Education of females was designed primarily to serve the well-being of the family rather than to maximize the individual woman's personal fulfillment. Indeed, the very subject of whether women should be educated beyond the basic skills required for household maintenance remained a highly controversial one during the period. By the beginning of the eighteenth century, the education of women was widely discouraged.

Work

Whatever a woman's education, the overwhelming likelihood was that she would marry and therefore take on as her primary responsibility the bearing and rearing of children in an atmosphere conducive to the children's survival, growth, and eventual prosperity. Women of all social classes and in all countries in Renaissance Europe shouldered this responsibility. Yet the means through which they fulfilled it was by no means uniform.

Arranging a marriage was generally the responsibility of the couple's parents. The father's influence was often the greatest in such matters. Arranging a marriage was a complicated business involving monetary negotiations, considerations of class and status, family allegiances, and in most cases (though not all), the question of the compatibility of the two partners. All these matters, of course, depended on the social status of the couple. Among couples from trade and working classes, the compatibility of the prospective bride and groom and the question of whether any children issuing from the marriage could be supported were generally the main concerns. Since it took a long time for a young man to complete his apprenticeship and establish

In England it was the norm for daughters of wealthy families to receive a humanist education. Mary's younger half sister, Elizabeth I (1533–1603), could write Latin and Greek by age nine. Margaret More, the daughter of the writer and statesman Thomas More (1478–1535), received an extensive humanist education, as did the renowned Cooke sisters.

Throughout Europe many women gained fame through their learning. Helene Kottannerin (c. 1400–after 1458), an Austrian, was so highly respected that her advice on legal issues regarding the crown of Hungary was sought by the Hungarian queen, while Kottannerin's memoir, *Denkwürdigkeiten* (literally, "things worth remembering"; 1450–1451), is believed to have been written partly to remind the young king of Hungary of his responsibilities. In France, Christine de Pisan (c. 1365–c. 1430) is the best known of several learned women of the late

THE COOKE SISTERS

Thanks in no small part to the education provided by their father, the five daughters of Anthony Cooke (c. 1505–1576), of Gidea Hall in England, were among the most learned women of their day. Cooke himself, who served as a tutor to King Edward VI (1537–1553), was a well-respected scholar in his own right. Another scholar, Walter Haddon, described the atmosphere of Gidea Hall in a speech at Cambridge University: "And what a house did I find there, yea, rather a small university." Cooke stated that his purpose in educating his daughters so thoroughly was that they "might have for their husbands complete and perfect men, and that their husbands might be happy in complete women." Cooke undoubtedly achieved this goal. All five daughters—Mildred, Anne, Margaret, Elizabeth, and Catherine—were acknowledged as fine, even extraordinarily gifted scholars. Their education centered on Greek rather than Latin and especially New Testament Greek and the writings of the Greek church fathers (theologians of the first centuries CE). Mildred's translation of Saint Basil's fourth-century sermon on Deuteronomy 15 still survives, as does Elizabeth's translation of the *Way of Reconciliation*, a work written in Latin by John Ponet (c. 1514–1556), a controversial bishop of Winchester.

Anthony Cooke was justified in believing that educating his daughters well would enable them to make good and successful marriages. Mildred Cooke married William Cecil, later Lord Burghley, Elizabeth I's secretary of state. Margaret married a London goldsmith, Ralph Rowlett, but died after only five weeks of marriage. Anne married Nicholas Bacon, the lord keeper of England, and bore him two sons, Anthony Bacon and the great philosopher, writer, and statesman Francis Bacon. Elizabeth married, first, Thomas Hoby, a translator and ambassador, and second, Lord John Russell, the son of the earl of Bedford. Catherine married Henry Killigrew, a diplomat. Each of the four Cooke sisters who survived took an active role in promoting their Protestant beliefs. All supported the controversial Puritan cleric Edward Dering. They continued to write in English, Latin, and Greek and composed a variety of books and texts. As patrons of other authors, they promoted not only religious but also literary writing.

The House of Saint-Cyr, in Paris, a school for the daughters of impoverished noble families, was founded in 1686 by King Louis XIV and his wife Françoise d'Aubigné (known as Madame de Maintenon). The school's curriculum reflected changing attitudes about what constituted a good education for girls. This oil painting, by an unknown contemporary artist, shows the students preparing for the dramatic productions for which the school was known.

himself in a trade, among people of the lower social classes, marriage occurred relatively late. In England the average marrying age for women from poorer families was around twenty-six, while for men it was twenty-eight. Late marriages also resulted in fewer children, and so it was more likely that these children could be profitably established in life.

▲ In this oil painting of 1523 by Lorenzo Lotto, Marsilio Cassotti, the son of a cloth merchant, and his young bride, Faustina, are portrayed in celebration of their marriage. The allegorical Cupid playfully garlands the couple with the yoke of their marital responsibilities.

In wealthier households marriages were often arranged when the prospective partners, especially the female, were young. Marriage was a way of forming allegiances between important families. A young marriageable daughter was an important asset for a family ambitious to improve its social position or to maneuver itself one way or another politically. Felice della Rovere (1483–1536), the daughter of Giuliano della Rovere (later Pope Julius II), was married at age fourteen in order that her father might secure local influence. Catherine Fieschi, the daughter of an aristocratic family in Genoa, was married at fourteen to the thirteen-year-old Giuliano Adorno, the son of a rival family. The marriage was arranged to promote the ambitions of Fieschi's brother. In England, Elizabeth Hardwick, as part of her highly advantageous

marriage to George Talbot, the sixth earl of Shrewsbury, stipulated that two of the earl's children, Gilbert (aged fourteen) and Grace (aged eight), would marry two of her children, Mary (twelve) and Henry (eighteen). This arrangement suited the political and financial goals of both families, though the complicated alliances created a great deal of family dissension in later years.

Once a woman entered into marriage, her first responsibility was to bear a child. Generally speaking, the first child was born relatively quickly, and a woman could expect several pregnancies throughout her years of fertility. Most poorer women breast-fed their own children, and since breast-feeding greatly reduces the chances of a woman becoming pregnant, poorer women usually gave birth every two to three years. Wealthy women, on the other hand, often sent their children to be fed by a wet nurse, and so such a woman might bear a child nearly every year. Some wealthy women bore an enormous number of children. The Florentine Antonia Masi (d. 1549) gave birth to thirty-six children, while Magdalucia Marcello bore twenty-six. Yet these are extreme examples; many women did not live long enough to bear large numbers of children. As many as 10 percent of all women died in childbirth. In the early 1400s the Italian Gregorio Dati wrote that three of his four wives had died of complications related to pregnancy and labor.

Once a successful birth was concluded, the duty of looking after the health and well-being of the child began. During the Renaissance many children died in infancy. In the French town of Argenteuil, for example, nearly 19 percent of children from wealthy families died in infancy, while up to 23 percent of middle-class infants and 26 percent from poorer families died. These

The pseudonymous Jane Anger, in a pamphlet published in 1589, contrasts the life and nature of men and women:

We are the grief of man, in that we take all the grief from man: we languish when they laugh; we lie sighing when they sit singing, and sit sobbing when they lie idle and sleeping.... We are contrary to men because they are contrary to that which is good. Because they are blind and cannot see into our natures and we see too well into theirs.

Her Protection for Women

rates mirror similar numbers throughout Europe. A mother's first duty was to ensure that her infant survived the odds. The numbers of books of advice, letters discussing the care of children, and tender epitaphs on the tombs of dead offspring attest to the attention mothers paid to their children's survival in early life. However, it was not enough merely to survive. Women were closely involved in bringing up their children in such a way that they thrived. It usually fell to the mother to provide her child's earliest education and generally to guide her child's life.

In addition to bearing and rearing children, women had charge of the running of the household. In poorer families a woman's core responsibilities were to ensure that the house was clean, to care for the health of the family, and to provide ample food and clothing for all the members of the household. Women of poorer families might maintain a few animals and some form of kitchen garden; many also contributed to family income by working as a servant in a more prosperous household. As the wealth of a family grew, so too did the complexity of the demands placed on the woman of the household. The wife of a tradesman or an artisan was often involved in the family business. She was expected to provide care for the young apprentices and to teach them the rudimentary skills of the trade.

As often as not, a woman was as capable as her husband in her husband's trade. When a tradesman died, his wife often carried on a business she had already been heavily involved in. Documents from fifteenth-century Strasbourg list women working as blacksmiths, goldsmiths, gardeners, tailors, and grain dealers, among other professions. In many German towns widows were found in such roles as jailer, tax collector, and gatekeeper. In England over 12 percent of households were headed by women. Up to 10 percent of printers in London in the sixteenth century were women, and similar numbers were involved in other professions. Many guilds and trade associations recognized the right of a widow to continue her husband's trade and to take on apprentices. However, these organizations might also stipulate that, if a widow's new husband did not belong to the same guild as her deceased husband, she would have to quit the trade.

◀ The Month of January, *a fresco in the Palazzo Pubblico, in Siena, by Cristofano Rustici (1560–1640), is a domestic scene in which members of the household engage in a number of daily tasks in a typical home of the period.*

The idea of remarriage was given careful consideration by women who found in widowhood a degree of social and legal independence that most married women did not enjoy. Moreover, remarriage often jeopardized the future of any children from a former marriage. Many women chose not to remarry at all. In Montpellier (in southern France), for example, between 1288 and 1348 only 7 of 132 widows remarried. In England the period between the death of a spouse and remarriage was substantially longer for women than for men. Most men remarried within a few months of losing a wife, while women frequently waited years.

In Italy a widow was often assigned a male guardian, who saw to the widow's material and personal well-being. An Italian widow might be returned to her family and thus separated from her children—who were seen as belonging to the husband's family.

Women of the upper classes participated fully in promoting and extending the influence and prestige of the family, often by running vast estates, especially when the man of the house was absent on government or personal business. (The resources of a large estate during the Renaissance were comparable with those of a modern medium to large corporation.) The third husband of Margaret Dakin was Thomas Posthumous Hoby, Elizabeth Cooke's son. Margaret Hoby ran the manor of Hackness, an estate that covered a huge area in northeastern Yorkshire and included several farms and a busy Tudor manor house. She managed the accounts, paid wages, hired and fired employees, and supervised the agricultural activities of the main manor farm and a nearby farm, Harwood Dale. Margaret's diary records her giving agricultural advice, maintaining important contacts with powerful local families, running the household, training daughters of the gentry, practicing medicine in the community, and providing for the religious well-being of the neighborhood—a task that included hiring clerics and inviting clerical visitors.

The range of Margaret Hoby's duties and responsibilities was not exceptional for aristocratic women. Indeed, one of the criticisms leveled against one Elizabeth Littleton before she married Francis Willoughby was that she was not likely to be interested in managing an estate. This accusation proved true when she elected to spend most of her time in London, despite her husband's repeated requests that she return home. On the other hand, Robert Sidney, lord de Lisle, had to reassure his wife, after he hired a steward, that he was not attempting to usurp her authority but rather to save her from tedious tasks so that she had more time to devote to more important activities, including supervising the building of a new wing to their manor house at Penshurst, in Kent. Thus, in the Renaissance, while a woman's work might be labeled domestic, it demanded mastery of a huge range of skills and knowledge—intellectual, practical, and emotional—as well as a great deal of energy.

▼ In Antonio Moro's oil on panel Widow and Her Son (1564), the young boy in his bright garments stands out against the black of the widow's clothing worn by his mother. He points to her as a mark of respect, while the small dog relieves the severity of the widow's stiff bearing.

1564

A Conversation Between Women, *an oil on panel attributed to Abraham Bosse (1602–1676), presents a scene of life among the privileged classes. The women, dressed in the fashionable attire of the period, sit together amid the opulent surroundings of a French palace of the seventeenth century. Note the waiting gentlewoman standing to the left. Women from families of the lower gentry or nobility often served in the houses of the higher nobility as a form of training and to put them in contact with desirable marriage partners.*

Women and Religion

The upheavals of the Reformation provided numerous opportunities for women dissatisfied with the status quo to take a more active role in matters of religion than was generally possible within the framework of Catholicism. Several prominent Protestant women made crucial contributions to the Reform movement. Many lent support in their capacity as household managers. For example, Wibrandis Rosenblatt, a Swiss woman, eventually became the widow of four prominent Protestant Reformers; the last was the influential German Martin Bucer (1491–1551). Rosenblatt was so famed that Bucer's first wife, Elisabeth, as she lay dying of plague, recommended Rosenblatt to Bucer. Rosenblatt welcomed numerous Protestant refugees into her household and provided them with the comfortable and ordered environment they needed to carry out their work.

Another Protestant, Anne Vaughan Locke (or Lok), also married three times. She formed a close spiritual friendship with the Scottish Reformer John Knox (1513–1572). Knox had such a high opinion of Locke that he encouraged her to leave her husband and go to Geneva, where she joined with other Protestant refugees fleeing England's return to Catholicism under Mary I. Also in Geneva, in 1560 Locke trans-

In a long narrative poem of 1610, Emilia Lanier rejects the argument, which enjoyed reasonable currency during the Renaissance, that women were more concupiscent—that is, they were more apt to sin. Some used this theological argument to support the conventional view that women needed to be subject to the authority of the men of their family. Lanier, however, contends that, whereas Eve erred only through the desire to do good, Adam ate from the apple simply because it was pleasing. Such being the case, she demands,

Then let us have our Liberty again,
And challenge to your selves no sovereignty
You came not in the world without our pain,
Make that a bar against your cruelty;
Your fault being greater, why should you disdain
Our being your equals, free from tyranny?
If one weak woman simply did offend,
This sin of yours, hath no excuse, nor end.

Salve Deus Rex Judaeorum

lated John Calvin's sermons and appended thereto a sonnet sequence. Called *A Meditation of a Penitent Sinner*, Locke's poem—the earliest sonnet sequence written in English—is based on Psalm 51, a favorite of the exiled Protestants because in it they found a justification for their theology. Locke's works were published in Geneva and imported back into England, where they were influential in promoting the radical

Protestantism supported by Knox and by Locke's second husband, Edward Dering.

Many other Protestant women drew on their learning to write spiritual texts, not only for the edification of their community but also for the benefit of a wider general readership. Women also participated in other forms of Reformist activism. Of the five Protestants burned in Canterbury, in southwestern England, on November 10, 1558, two were women. Indeed, many of the 287 Protestants martyred during Mary I's reign were women. In Italy the fervent desire of Catherine of Siena (1347–1380) to correct what she perceived as abusive Catholic practices brought her into conflict with many in the church, although her influence was so great that in 1378 Pope Urban VI called for Catherine to support him in his conflict with the antipope Clement VII.

Many women, both Catholic and Protestant, underwent personal experiences of God outside of the pattern of structured worship. An Englishwoman, Margery Kempe (1373–1439), had visions over a period of several years; her accounts of what she had experienced brought her into conflict with several clerics, including the archbishop of Canterbury. In Spain, Teresa of Ávila (1515–1582), also a visionary, set up houses for nuns and friars founded on a simple regimen of prayer, devotion, and aid to the poor. Maliciously accused of heresy, Teresa was repeatedly reported to the Spanish Inquisition, which dismissed the charges. She was canonized in 1622 and later declared a doctor of the church.

In Protestant England, Catholic women were instrumental in maintaining Catholic households, setting up safe havens for visiting priests, and funding the Catholic missionary movement. Anne, countess of Arundel (1557–1630), maintained a Catholic household and served as a patroness of Robert Southwell, a Jesuit missionary. She suffered greatly as a target of Elizabeth I's wrath but continued her religious work throughout her long life.

▶ *This anonymous seventeenth-century painting displays Saint Teresa of Ávila symbolically sheltering the nuns of her order, whose members became known as Discalced Carmelites. Saint Teresa began a reform movement in 1562 and founded several convents committed to absolute poverty in answer to what she perceived as the growing laxity of the convents of her time.*

Matthew Hopkins Witch Finder Generall

My Imps names are

Holt

1 Ilemauzar
2 Pyewackett

Jarmara

acke Sugar

3 Pecke in the Crowne
4 Griezzell Greediguтt

Newes

Vinegar tom

▲ This engraving was printed in London in 1647 as part of a book called (in full) The Discoverer of Witches in Answer to Severall Queries Lately Delivered to the Judges of the Assize for the County of Norfolk by Matthew Hopkins, Witchfinder for the Benefit of the Whole Kingdom. Hopkins rooted out what he believed was a diabolical rising of witches in 1645. However, as this title suggests, within a year of his campaign, during which several supposed witches were killed, his methods and findings were being questioned.

Women and Politics

Although the sphere of activity of the majority of women during the Renaissance (whether married or unmarried) was the home, some women occupied important positions in the political arena. Though they were few in number compared with dukes, princes, kings, and popes, those women who did exercise political power had a considerable and lasting impact on the territory they controlled, whether a locality, a region, or a country; in certain cases a woman's political influence extended across the breadth of Europe.

The most visible of these female authority figures were the monarchs. Among the most powerful was Isabella I of Castile (1451–1504) who, together with her husband, Ferdinand of

EUROPEAN WITCH HUNTS

Between 60,000 and 110,000 women accused of witchcraft were put to death during the Renaissance. The phenomenon of witch hunting indicates the tenacity of medieval supersition in an age when Europeans in other respects seem possessed of a modern sensibility. The witch hunts originated in Switzerland during the Middle Ages and lasted until the last frenzy of hangings in colonial New England at the beginning of the eighteenth century. During sporadic and devastating outbreaks of witch crazes, the village healer was often most at risk, as was any woman who exhibited any sort of eccentricity. Widows whose property was coveted by male relatives or by neighbors bearing some grudge could also become targets. The trial and execution of witches became an industry in and of itself, and the accused was held responsible for paying the court costs of prosecution, defense, and her own stay in jail.

Yet the roots of witch hunts lay at a deeper level than mere petty jealousies or desire for financial gain. According to a tradition that had persisted since early Christian times, women were suspected of some form of inherent evil owing to an interpretation of the Book of Genesis that cast Eve as the sinning temptress. King James I of England, using Eve as his example, argued that women were more susceptible to the enticements of Satan.

Many did not share James's view and condemned the practice of executing witches. John Scot, in his *Discoverie of Witchcraft* (1584), wrote that it was ridiculous to believe that Satan would choose impotent old women (those most frequently condemned as witches) as his handmaids and accused the judiciary of unprofessional practices. Yet Scot's repudiation of witch hunts was in turn repudiated by a number of writers—including James I—who insisted that witches represented a force of evil that was attacking Europe. In truth, Europe was suffering a period of political and religious upheaval. For those who had a prejudicial distrust of women, witches were a convenient scapegoat in profoundly uncertain times.

Aragon, ruled over a united Spain. Isabella and Ferdinand, by completing the centuries-long *Reconquista*, the campaign to oust the Moors from Spain, inaugurated a Spanish golden age.

In France, Catherine de Médicis (1519–1589), serving as regent during the minorities of her sons, exerted unparalled influence in the French court. Another Frenchwoman, Mary of Guise (1515–1560), became the regent of Scotland soon after the death of her husband, James V. Mary replaced James Hamilton, the earl of Arran, who was seen as ineffectual by the Scottish parliament. Unfortunately, her conformity to the Catholic faith at a time when Protestant fervor, whipped up by the preaching of John Knox, was sweeping Scotland, led to political unrest and civil war. Mary's daughter, Mary, Queen of Scots (1542–1587), was initially welcomed by the Scottish parliament when she returned to Scotland from France in 1561. Recognizing the religious situation in Scotland, Mary pursued a pragmatic policy of religious toleration. However, a series of mistakes and the hostility of the Scottish Protestants doomed her to ruin. In 1568 she was forced to flee to England, where her presence made her the rallying point for Catholics rebelling against Protestant rule. Accused of a series of intrigues against Elizabeth I, Mary was executed in 1587. Elizabeth was the most powerful of all the female monarchs of the Renaissance. Having survived the reign of her half sister, Mary I, Elizabeth ruled England as absolute monarch for over forty years. She chose never to marry and thus never had to share power, as other female monarchs did. Her reasonably tolerant religious policy as well as her reluctance to embroil herself in European conflicts served greatly to England's economic and cultural benefit.

These extremely powerful women were at the pinnacle of a political structure that provided numerous opportunities for women to occcupy influential positions in Renaissance society. Generally speaking, women would enjoy privileged access to a female ruler and a degree of

▲ *This portrait of Mary, Queen of Scots, painted more than two hundred years after her death by Calixte-Joseph Serrur (1794–1865), offers a romanticized portrayal of the queen, one that was popular in the nineteenth century. It bears little resemblance to paintings made during or directly after Mary's death. Serrur painted his subject in conformity with contemporary standards of beauty. The early-seventeenth-century clothing is also anachronistic.*

Mary of Burgundy (1457–1482), the only child of Duke Charles the Bold and Isabelle de Bourbon, ruled in the Netherlands after her father's death in 1477. Her daughter, Margaret of Austria (1480–1530), also served as regent in the Spanish Netherlands at the behest of Margaret's nephew the Holy Roman emperor Charles V (whom Margaret had raised). After Margaret's death Charles V chose his sister Maria of Hungary (1505–1558) to serve as regent.

In 1558 a leading Scottish Reformer wrote the following invective aimed at two female Catholic rulers: Mary of Guise, then regent of Scotland, and Mary I, Queen of England. The attack did little to endear Knox to Mary I's successor, the moderate Protestant Elizabeth I.

It is more than a monster in nature that a woman shall reign and have empire above man ... for their sight in civil regiment is but blindness, their counsel foolishism, and judgment frenzy.

John Knox, *The First Blast of the Trumpet against the Monstrous Regiment of Women*

familiarity that was denied to men; this factor counted for a great deal at a time when considerable political power was to be gained through proximity to the monarch or regent. Noblewomen served in the households of ruling women and were constantly in attendance, some even sleeping in the same room as their mistress. Male and female courtiers, well aware of the power of attendant noblewomen, vied for the support of the ruler's ladies. Elizabeth I was well known for rewarding her ladies with favors, interesting herself in their affairs, and promoting their interests. Lady Elizabeth Russell (a daughter of Anthony Cooke), for one, was able to nominate the queen as guardian to Russell's male children, secure the tenancy of Donington Castle, and place her two daughters in the court of the queen—all thanks to the special relationship she had with Elizabeth I. Female courtiers, like their male counterparts, worked to secure favors and promote their family's political agenda through their access to the queens and female regents of Europe.

There are numerous examples of a woman serving her father, brother, or husband as temporary ruler of a province, citiy, or territory and of women governing areas in their own right. Lucrezia Borgia, for example, won the affection of the people of Ferrara when she rallied the city's dwellers to hold out against their enemies during the conflicts that lasted from 1509 to 1512. In 1488 Caterina Sforza, after the death of her husband, Girolamo Riario, fiercely defended the cities of Imola and Forlì against those who held her children hostage. Ruling those cities during times of peace, Sforza administered justice and maintained control. Anne Clifford (1590–1676) owned sizable estates in Cumberland and Westmorland, in northwestern England. She administered justice as "lord" of the manor as well as in her capacity as sheriff of Westmorland. She also provided social care for the communities within her manors; her projects included the building of schools and almshouses. She stood up to both King James I and Oliver Cromwell (lord protector during the period of the Commonwealth, a time when England had no monarch) when each attempted to interfere with her rights regarding her estates.

There are many other similar accounts involving women of wealth and influence. However, women from relatively humble families also played key roles in the political sphere. One of the best known is Joan of Arc (1412–1431), who for a short time during the later stages of the Hundred Years War led the armies of Charles VII of France against the English invasion force. Other women used their pen to influence political affairs by writing entreaties to those who wielded power. Jane Seager, Anna Walker, Esther Inglis, and others used pens, embroidery needles, and inks to make gift books that promoted the Protestant cause they and their families supported.

▼ *This portrait of Mary I, by an artist of the period known only as Master John, depicts a demure and uncertain Mary (at age eighteen) during the last years of her father's reign, when her relationship with king and court was extremely fraught.*

Caterina Sforza   1463–1509

The illegitimate daughter of Galeazzo Maria Sforza and Lucrezia Landriano, Caterina Sforza was married at age fifteen to the twenty-year-old Girolamo Riario, a nephew of Pope Sixtus IV. As part of the marriage settlement, the pope gave the young couple the cities of Forlì and Imola. After the death of Sixtus in1584, Caterina, hoping to influence the choice of the next pope, seized control of the Castle of Sant'Angelo in Rome. When this bid for influence failed, Caterina and her husband withdrew to Forlì and Imola.

The Orsi family laid siege to these two cities in 1488 and murdered Girolamo and captured Caterina and her six children. Caterina escaped and recaptured the fortress that overlooked Forlì. From this vantage point, she threatened to raze the city with her cannon, and the Orsis fled. In 1490 Caterina secretly married Giacomo Feo, who was murdered by assassins on a Forlì street in 1495. In 1496 Caterina was again secretly married, this time to Giovanni de' Medici, with whom she had one child, also called Giovanni (later Giovanni delle Bande Nere). Giovanni de' Medici died in 1598. The following year, Caterina angered Pope Alexander VI (born Rodrigo Borgia) by refusing to agree to a marriage between her son Ottaviano and the pope's daughter Lucrezia Borgia.

Wanting to seize Caterina's lands for his son, Cesare Borgia, the pope besieged Imola. Caterina energetically defended the city and even donned armor. Finally forced to surrender on January 12, 1500, she was taken captive, raped by Cesare, and held prisoner in the Castle of Sant'Angelo. Upon her release, she took refuge in Florence. After the death of Alexander VI in 1503, Caterina attempted to regain her cities but was thwarted by her brothers-in-law Pierfrancesco and Lorenzo de' Medici. She retreated to the convent of Annalena with her son Giovanni de' Medici and died there on May 10, 1509.

► *Lorenzo di Credi painted this portrait of Caterina Sforza in 1487. The countess, famed for her beauty and courage, is seated in a contemporary pose and exudes confidence. The landscapes in the background represent her lands of Forlì and Imola.*

Renaissance Women in History

Athough women do not form a numerical majority among the leading writers, artists, philosophers, rulers, and agitators of the Renaissance, their contribution to the glories and the traumas of life between 1350 and 1650 is no less estimable than that made by men. Many women found fulfillment by applying their talents domestically as part of a system in which the promotion of the family benefited all members of that family. Others, by the accident of their birth, the gift of natural talent, sheer ambition, or a combination of all three factors, broke free from the domestic role in which tradition cast them and in one way or another ensured that their names would be writ large in the annals of history.

FURTHER READING

Henderson, Katherine U. *Half Humankind: Contexts and Texts of the Controversy about Women in England, 1540–1640.* Urbana, IL, 1985.

King, Margaret L. *Women of the Renaissance.* Chicago, 1991.

Mendelson, Sara, and Patricia Crawford. *Women in Early Modern England, 1550–1720.* New York 1998.

Panizza, Letizia, ed. *Women in Italian Renaissance Culture and Society.* Oakville, CT, 2000.

Jessica L. Malay

SEE ALSO

• Borgia, Lucrezia • Catherine de Médicis
• Christina • Education • Elizabeth I
• Ferdinand and Isabella • Gentileschi, Artemisia
• Households • Joan of Arc

Wren, Christopher

REGARDED AS THE GREATEST OF ALL ENGLISH ARCHITECTS, CHRISTOPHER WREN (1632–1723) WAS ALSO ONE OF THE MOST DISTINGUISHED INTELLECTUALS OF THE SEVENTEENTH CENTURY.

Although Christopher Wren is known as an architect and designer, his career did not begin with training in these disciplines. While still a teenager, Wren used his mechanical understanding and his problem-solving ability to invent an instrument that wrote in the dark, a pneumatic engine, and a new language for the deaf and dumb. Among his first contributions to society was the perfection of a working barometer.

▼ *Wren enjoyed a lofty status in English society; this 1713 mezzotint by J. C. Smith, after Godfrey Kneller, gives a sense of the esteem in which he was held.*

The breadth of Wren's interests and accomplishments owe much to Renaissance scholarship. In common with many of his contemporaries, the starting point for Wren's efforts was his readiness to question accepted knowledge and to trust in the alternative ideas that arose from his own sensibilities. It was only by chance that he became an accomplished architect.

Education

Born in Wiltshire, in southern England, in 1632, Wren grew up in a privileged environment. Physically rather frail and quite small in stature, he was well educated and began his pursuit of knowledge at a very young age. In 1635 Wren's father was appointed dean of Windsor, and from then until the outbreak of war in 1642, Wren spent time playing with Prince Charles (the future King Charles II) in Windsor Castle.

At this young age Wren was most fascinated by drawing and science. He was taught by a private tutor until he turned nine and was then sent to Westminster School in London. In 1646 Wren left Westminster but did not enter university immediately. During the next three years he acquired a broad knowledge of science. There are records of experiments he made with sundials, probably in 1646, and also a pasteboard model of the solar system that exhibited his artistic and astronomical skills.

Wren became an even more proficient scientist during his time at Wadham College, Oxford. Working in the field of anatomy, he made drawings of the human brain and devised a method for blood transfusion. He became a fellow of All Souls and was distinguished in mathematics and physics. His intellect was greatly admired by the time he finished his education.

An Intellectual in London

In his work as a scientist, Wren concentrated on astronomy, physics, and anatomy. However, his broad endeavors also encompassed experiments with submarine and telescope designs and road paving. When he was only twenty-five, Wren was offered the coveted chair of astronomy at Gresham College, London.

▲ *When designing Oxford's Sheldonian Theatre (1662–1663), Wren drew inspiration from the Theater of Marcellus in Rome. The Sheldonian, named for Gilbert Sheldon, chancellor of the university and the project's main financial backer, established Wren's reputation.*

Wren became Savilian professor of astronomy at Oxford in 1661—a post he held until 1673. During this time he gained an international reputation in mathematics. His accomplishments typify the capacity of the finest scholars of the Renaissance to excel, no matter how broadly they spread themselves. He applied his scientific and mathematical skills to the study of optics. He published a description of a machine to create perspective drawings and discussed the grinding of conical lenses and mirrors.

The greatest scientist of the era, Isaac Newton (1642–1727), rarely praised others. However, in his *Principia mathematica* (1687), Newton ranks Wren as one of the three leading mathematicians of his time. Yet the direction of Wren's career was about to change abruptly.

First Foray into Architecture

In the 1660s Wren began to pursue his interest in architecture. In 1661 he was invited to work on the fortifications of the harbor at Tangiers, a North African port then in the hands of the English. Although he did not accept the project, it is clear that he had become known as a potential designer.

Wren's first commission, the design of the chapel of Pembroke College at Cambridge University (1663), was quite likely the result of nepotism: his uncle was then bishop of Ely, near Cambridge.

Wren followed this design with one for the Sheldonian Theatre at Oxford University. In 1663 he visited Rome and made a thorough study of the ancient Theater of Marcellus; he examined both the ruins of the building and drawings that showed its original form. It was the Sheldonian Theatre, whose design Wren based on the Theater of Marcellus, that made his reputation as an architect.

In 1665 Wren visited Paris and recorded his impressions of the church of the Sorbonne—a college of the University of Paris—and other new buildings. After this influential trip, Wren's transformation into a designer of churches was complete. By August 27, 1666, his plan for the reconstruction of Saint Paul's Cathedral in London had been accepted. However, just six days later, tragedy struck London. The city of

In London, Wren's lectures became meeting places for intellectuals, and soon he became part of a scientific discussion group at Gresham College that, in 1660, initiated formal weekly meetings. Known at first as the Society of Experimental Philosophy, in 1662, under the patronage of Charles II, this group became the Royal Society of London. Wren was a major contributor to this esteemed group of thinkers in its early years. The remarkable range of his interests and his expertise in many different subjects aided the exchange of ideas among scientists of various disciplines.

predominantly wooden buildings clustered around narrow alleys was all but wiped out by a great fire.

The Rebuilding of London

In 1666 Wren submitted a proposal for the rebuilding of London, and in 1669 he was appointed surveyor general. Over the next forty-six years, he would design and supervise the building of fifty-one churches. Although each design differed, they all fell within a classical style. In his designs Wren developed a distinctive English "wedding cake" style, which included a steeple based on classical Roman temples. Part of Wren's success was due to his personal involvement in the work under his supervision. He insisted on the finest materials and a very high standard of workmanship.

Saint Paul's Cathedral

Despite his involvement in the monumental effort to rebuild London, Wren's work on his original commission at Saint Paul's Cathedral remains his masterpiece. A cathedral dedicated to Saint Paul had overlooked the city of London from the same location, just north of the Thames River, since 604 CE. Wren's replacement cathe-

dral was built between 1675 and 1710. Its architectural and artistic importance reflects the determination of the five monarchs who oversaw its building. They demanded that London's leading

▶ Saint Benet's Church, in the City of London (modern London's business and finance district), is the burial place of Wren's fellow architect Inigo Jones (1573–1652). This church, for which Wren did the design, was one of many built during the large-scale reconstruction of London after the 1666 fire.

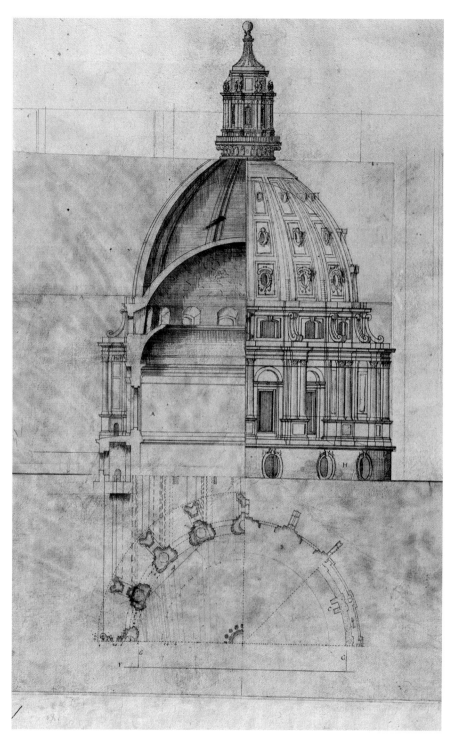

Wren's pencil sketch of the so-called Definitive Design incorporates a section, elevation, and half plan of the dome of Saint Paul's Cathedral. The design was radical, the plan for a centralized dome strikingly so.

tecture, this design and its revised version—called the Great Model—are remarkable for their use of the classicized style that typifies the Italian Renaissance and for their general planning. Wren created a central interior space set beneath a vast dome with subsidiary spaces located radially around the sides. However, the clergy, who were used to cathedrals shaped like Old Saint Paul's (long and thin) objected to the centralized plan. Frustrated, Wren was forced back to the drawing board.

The Warrant Design was worked out in 1675. In this new design Wren deliberately responded to the criticisms that had been leveled against the Greek Cross and Great Model designs. A longitudinal nave and choir area was flanked by lower aisles. The great towers and spire were designed to evoke the silhouettes of medieval England. The architectural style, however, remained classical.

The Warrant Design was approved by King Charles II, and work began in the summer of 1675. Wren's son recounts that the king "was pleas'd to allow [Wren] the liberty in the Prosecution of his work, to make some variations, rather ornamental, than essential, as from Time to Time he should see proper." Architectural historians agree that Wren exploited this opportunity to its full potential. In fact, the cathedral that rose in the summer of 1675 was substantially different from the approved Warrant Design. By the time Wren finally completed Saint Paul's, he was sixty-six years old.

Solidifying a Reputation as an Architect

With the completion of Saint Paul's and the ongoing reconstruction of London, Wren became well known throughout Europe. He designed many buildings in addition to churches, including Tom Tower at Christchurch, Oxford; the library at Trinity College, Cambridge; and the Royal Hospital at Chelsea. He also enlarged and remodeled Kensington Palace, Hampton Court Palace, and the naval hospital at Greenwich. Other buildings designed by Wren include the Royal Exchange, the College of Physicians, the Custom House, and the Drury Lane Theatre.

church be as beautiful and imposing as Saint Peter's in Rome.

Wren's earliest proposals for Saint Paul's called for rebuilding on the foundations of the old cathedral. In 1669 he created what is referred to as the First Model. Critics deemed it too simple, and the model was quickly abandoned.

Wren revised his design mightily. Between 1670 and 1672 he produced the Greek Cross Design. In the context of English cathedral archi-

Robert Hooke 1635–1703

For nearly fifty years the lives and careers of Christopher Wren and Robert Hooke were closely intertwined. Born in the 1630s, both were sons of Anglican clergymen (Wren's father enjoyed the more elevated position). Owing to frail health, each was educated at home before proceeding to Westminster School and then to Oxford, where, during the mid-1650s, they became lifelong friends.

Their first collaboration was the greatest project that either man ever undertook: rebuilding London after the great fire of 1666. Wren was a designer, whereas Hooke was one of three surveyors appointed to oversee the repairs and construction. In this capacity Hooke was responsible for issuing more than two thousand certificates on completed foundations. Many scholars believe that Hooke also drew a great number of designs. They argue that he often did not receive the credit he deserved and that some of his designs are wrongly credited to Wren. Whatever the truth may be, it is certain that Wren and Hooke together were instrumental in redesigning and rebuilding London.

Hooke, like Wren, was a man of considerable intellect. He is credited with many scientific breakthroughs related to microscopic investigation, including the use of the term *cell*. He is also credited with inventing the iris diaphragm used in cameras, the balance wheel used in watches, and the universal joint used in motor vehicles. He identified a law of physics that expresses the relationship between physical force and structural integrity. Overall, Wren was the better mathematician and more visionary architect, while Hooke was the more intuitive physicist and insightful cosmologist.

One of Hooke's greatest architectural accomplishments was the Monument, a column that commemmorates the 1666 fire. At 202 feet (62 m) in height, it remains the tallest free-standing Doric column in the world. Although Hooke appreciated the Monument's symbolic value, its design also had a scientific purpose: on May 16, 1668, Hooke scaled the Monument and carried out atmospheric pressure readings with his mercury barometer. He discovered that the mercury level at the top of the Monument differed from that at the bottom by one-third of an inch. This finding had significant implications for Hooke's research into atmospheric pressure. In addition, Hooke intended to use the column to test his theories concerning pendulums, specifically the ways in which they are affected by gravity.

Although scholars debate which buildings he should be credited with designing, Hooke, like Wren, achieved greatness and left an enduring legacy in the fields of science and mathematics, as well as architecture.

▲ The great Venetian painter Canaletto (1697–1768) spent the years from 1746 to 1755 living and working in England. This 1754 oil-on-canvas depiction of the completed Saint Paul's Cathedral evokes the scale and complexity of Wren's most celebrated building, which remains unchanged to this day.

When Christopher Wren died in 1723, he became the first person to be buried in the Saint Paul's Cathedral of his creation. Seen in the totality of his accomplishments, Wren emerges from the era of post-Renaissance England as a formidable transitional figure. Although his scientific prowess demonstrated the scope of his great intellect, his specific successes as an architect and planner anticipated the Enlightenment era that began within a generation of his death.

FURTHER READING

Bennett, J. A. *The Mathematical Science of Christopher Wren.* NY, 1982.

Hartley, Harold, ed. *The Royal Society: Its Origins and Founders.* London, 1960.

Inwood, Stephen. *The Man Who Knew Too Much: The Strange and Inventive Life of Robert Hooke, 1635–1703.* London, 2002.

Jardine, Lisa. *On a Grander Scale: The Outstanding Life of Sir Christopher Wren.* New York, 2002.

Brian Black

SEE ALSO

• Architecture • England • Jones, Inigo
• London

Index

Page numbers in **boldface** type refer to entire articles.
Page numbers in *italic* type refer to illustrations.

gunpowder *see* firearms
Gunpowder Plot 133
Gustav I Vasa *1304,*
   1305–1306, 1307,
   1308–1309
Gustavus II Adolphus 1307,
   1308–1309, 1332, 1333,
   1336–1337, 1339, 1415
Gutenberg, Johannes 1168,
   1169, 1193, 1218, 1220
Gutenberg Bible 1169, *1170*
Gyllenstierna, Christina 1305

H

Hamlet (Shakespeare) 1270,
   1271, 1275, *1326, 1327*
Hanseatic League 1340
Hapsburg Empire 1302, 1394
   Switzerland 1312, 1315
   see also Thirty Years War
Harvey, Gabriel 1286–1287
Harvey, William 1251, 1255
Hathaway, Anne 1268, 1269
Heidelberg Catechism 1174
heliocentric universe 1226,
   1249, 1250, 1252–1254
Henrietta Maria 1257, 1302,
   1328
Henry VII (England) 1261,
   1297
Henry VIII (England) 1175,
   1220, 1371, 1411, 1412
   monastery dissolution 1202,
      1203
   Reformation 1191,
      1196–1198, 1325, 1350,
      1374
   Scotland 1261, 1262, 1265,
      1297
   wives 1196, 1197, 1280,
      1297, 1417
Henry II (France) 1262, 1264,
   1265
Henry IV (France) 1240,
   1333, 1334
Henry the Navigator
   (Portugal) 1345
Hepburn, James, earl of
   Bothwell 1298
heresy 1251, 1278, 1283,
   1331, 1333, 1400

Calvinist penalty 1316
Scotland 1264, 1265
see also Inquisition
Hoby, Thomas 1419, 1422
Holy Roman Empire 1189,
   1200, 1221, 1232, 1317,
   1375, 1378, 1394, 1405
   Thirty Years War
      1330–1339, 1415
   Trent 1352, 1353, 1357,
      1359
   Viscontis 1403, 1404, 1405
Hooke, Robert 1258, 1433
households 1416–1424
Huguenots 1195, 1331, 1336
Huizinga, Johann 1160
humanism and learning 1189,
   1218–1221, 1224, 1240,
   1283, 1399
   Erasmus 1189
   James I 1299
   Luther 1371
   printing 1172–1173
   Rabelais 1176–1179
   Rome 1228, 1229, 1230,
      1231–1232, 1235
   Spain 1279–1283
   universities 1365, 1368–1370,
      1372, 1373, 1376
   women 1416, 1417–1418,
      1419
   Wren 1429–1430
   see also universities
Hus, Jan 1192, 1334, 1367

I

Ignatius of Loyola 1199,
   1205–1206
Index of Forbidden Books
   1178–1179, 1197, 1226,
   1234, 1363
indulgences 1169, 1189,
   1190–1191, 1192, 1231,
   1232, 1360
infant baptism 1314
Innocent III 1158
Innocent X 1388, 1389
Inquisition 1197, 1226, 1234,
   1251, 1254, 1278, 1279,
   1283, 1291, 1321, 1400,
   1424

Ireland 1265, 1300, 1302,
   1303, 1317, 1350
   Spenser 1287–1288, 1289,
      1290
irrigation 1402
Isabella (Castile) *see* Ferdinand
   and Isabella
Isabella of Portugal 1277
Islam 1250, 1277, 1278,
   1279, 1341, 1343, 1344,
   1348, 1367
Italian city-states
   Renaissance 1218–1226
   science 1249, 1250–1254,
      1256
   theater 1320–1321, 1322
   trade 1341, 1401
   universities *1365,* 1367,
      1368, 1370–1371
   Urbino 1378–1383
   Viscontis 1401–1406
   women 1420, 1422, 1424,
      1427, 1428
   see also Florence; Milan;
      Rome; Venice

J

James I (England) 1263,
   1289, 1296, 1298,
   1299–1301, 1324, 1329
   Scotland 1260, 1262, 1264,
      1265, 1299–1301
   Shakespeare 1269, 1272
   Thirty Years War 1336
   women linked with evil
      1425, 1427
James II (England) 1302
James I (Scotland) 1296
James III (Scotland) 1261,
   1264, 1296
James IV (Scotland)
   1296–1297
James V (Scotland) 1262,
   1263–1264, 1265, 1296,
   1297, 1299, 1426
James VI (Scotland) *see*
   James I (England)
Jesuits 1174, 1191, 1199,
   1204, 1205–1206, 1307,
   1324, 1332
   founding of 1353

suppression of 1209
theater 1323, 1326
Joan I (the Mad) 1277, 1280,
   1281
Joan of Arc 1427
John I (Denmark) *see* John II
   (Sweden)
John II (Aragon) 1278–1279
John II (Castile and León)
   1277, 1279
John II (Sweden) 1304, 1305
John III (Sweden) 1307,
   1308
John George I (Saxony) 1245,
   1246, 1247, 1332, 1337
John George II (Saxony)
   1247
John of the Cross 1207
John Paul II 1226
Jonson, Ben 1325, 1326
Judaism
   Spain 1277, 1278, 1279,
      1283
   Spinoza 1291, 1292, 1293,
      1295
Jülich Succession, War of the
   1334
Julius II 1186, 1187, 1230,
   1231–1232, 1380, 1394,
   1420
Julius III 1353, 1357, 1359

K

Kepler, Johannes 1250,
   1251–1252
King James Bible 1221, 1357
King's Men (London) 1270,
   1272, 1275
Kirk *see* Church of Scotland
knights 1313, 1314, 1411,
   1413
Knox, John 1265–1266,
   1267, 1423, 1424, 1426
Kottannerin, Helene 1418

L

languages, classical
   bibles 1159, 1160, 1355,
      1357
   humanism 1219, 1220,
      1280, 1282

Illustration Credits